Happy Birthday

Love Douglas.

Other books by Bernard Taper

Cellist in Exile: A Portrait of Pablo Casals
Gomillion Versus Lightfoot: The Tuskegee Gerrymander Case
Mark Twain's San Francisco (Edited)
The Arts in Boston

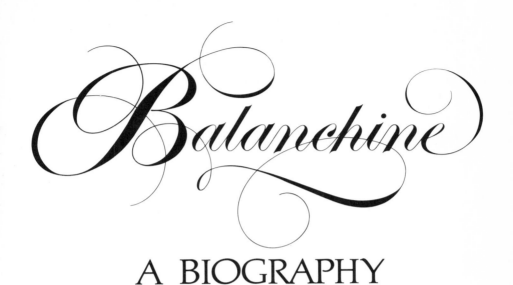

A BIOGRAPHY

BERNARD TAPER

Times
BOOKS

Published by TIMES BOOKS,
The New York Times Book Co., Inc.
130 Fifth Avenue, New York, N.Y. 10011

Published simultaneously in Canada by
Fitzhenry & Whiteside, Ltd., Toronto

Library of Congress Cataloging in Publication Data

Taper, Bernard.
　Balanchine, a biography.

　Includes index.
　1. Balanchine, George.　2. Choreographers—United
States—Biography.　I. Title.
GV1785.B32T3　1984　　792.8'2'0924 [B]　　84-40107
ISBN 0-8129-1136-9

Designed by Marjorie Anderson

Manufactured in the United States of America

84　85　86　87　88　5　4　3　2　1

CONTENTS

ACKNOWLEDGMENTS

The author expresses his appreciation to *The New Yorker*, where portions of this biography appeared in somewhat different form.

The author also wishes to express thanks and acknowledgments to the following sources of material quoted in this book: excerpt from "Diaghilev and his Period," in the August 1949 issue of *Dance News*, by permission of *Dance News*; excerpt from *Serge Diaghilev* by Serge Lifar, 1940, by permission of G. P. Putnam's Sons; excerpt from *Themes and Episodes* by Igor Stravinsky and Robert Craft, 1966, by permission of Alfred A. Knopf, Inc.; excerpts from *Striking a Balance* by Barbara Newman, 1982, by permission of Houghton Mifflin Company; excerpts from *Far from Denmark* by Peter Martins with Robert Cornfield, 1982, by permission of Little, Brown and Company; excerpts from *Baryshnikov: From Russia to the West* by Gennady Smakov, 1981, by permission of Farrar, Straus and Giroux; excerpt from *Erik Bruhn: Danseur Noble* by John Gruen, copyright © 1979 by John Gruen, by permission of Viking Penguin Inc.; excerpt from "An Olympian Apollo" by John Gruen, in the April 1981 issue of *Dance Magazine*, by permission of *Dance Magazine*; excerpt from "An American Genius" by Richard Poirier, in the October 11, 1980, issue of *The New Republic*, copyright © 1980 by The New Republic, Inc., by permission of *The New Republic*; excerpts from "George Balanchine (1904–1983)" by Arthur Gold and Robert Fizdale, in the June 2, 1983, issue of *The New York Review of Books*, reprinted with permission from *The New York Review of Books*, copyright © 1983 Nyrev, Inc.; excerpts from *Thirty Years: The New York City Ballet* by Lincoln Kirstein, copyright © 1973 by Alfred A. Knopf, Inc., copyright © 1978 by Lincoln Kirstein, by permission of Alfred A. Knopf, Inc.; excerpt from "Balanchine–Stravinsky: Facts and Problems" by Robert Garis, in the Fall 1982 issue of *Ballet Review*, by permission of *Ballet Review*; excerpt from "I Have Made You and You Are Beautiful" by Arlene Croce, in the August 5, 1974, issue of *The New Yorker*, by permission of The New Yorker Magazine, Inc., copyright © 1974; excerpts from "Balanchine: The Early Years" by Yuri Slonimsky, in *Ballet Review* 1975–1976, by permission of *Ballet Review*.

FOREWORD

I first met George Balanchine in the fall of 1957, when I set out to write a profile of him for *The New Yorker*. I had seen a lot of ballet, and much had given me pleasure, but I did not consider myself a balletomane then—nor do I now. What I did know then was that of the ballets I had seen, those that moved or delighted me most were by Balanchine. They affected me to a degree that was disproportionate to my expectations of what ballet could do. Among the strong incentives that made me want to undertake my project was the knowledge that he did not object to people watching him while he worked. To be able to see a new ballet being created before my eyes—this seemed to me a remarkable opportunity, and I took advantage of it. Over the years of my acquaintance with Balanchine, I was privileged to be present while he choreographed twenty-nine new ballets, as well as to see him rehearse and revise many others. Of all the research I did for this biography, this was the most rewarding.

My first meeting with Balanchine was arranged through Lincoln Kirstein. I went to the New York City Ballet's rehearsal studios, which in those days were on the second floor of a shabby building at the corner of Broadway and 83rd Street, and was introduced to Balanchine. He shook hands with me, bowed slightly, and suggested that I take a seat on the bench at the front of the room, for he was about to begin a rehearsal. The ballet he was choreographing was *Square Dance*, and he was working with Patricia Wilde and Nicholas Magallanes, as well as a number of corps de ballet dancers. I watched for two hours. At the end of the session, I thanked Balanchine. He bowed—a slight but definite inclination of head and shoulders, gravely courteous yet, it seemed to me, with a gleam of mockery in his eyes. I bowed in response (his elegance was catching), we shook hands, and I left. The next day I returned and went through the same procedure. I asked no questions. I was well aware, from what I had heard and read about him, that he distrusted words about important matters like ballet, though he loved words, as I found when I got to know him, for other, more whimsical, purposes—anagrams, double crostics, word games, nonsense rhymes, and puns, bilingual puns especially. So I didn't try to engage him in discussion about what he was doing or pose any of the thousands of questions biographers need to have answered. I just looked, and listened. The working world of the ballet studio was new to me. I had lots to learn, I was fascinated, and I was in no hurry.

On the days when *Square Dance* was being made, I sometimes found myself seated near Elisha Keeler, the square-dance caller who had been engaged to collaborate on this novelty ballet. To suites of court dances by Vivaldi and Corelli, Balanchine was making brilliant, exuberant classical choreography, and Keeler was supposed to take note of the steps and make up appropriate square-dance calls to go with them. That was to be the gimmick. But Keeler, who had never seen a ballet before, was nervous. He was afraid he was missing most of what was going on before his eyes. I heard Balanchine telling him one day not to worry. "You just do like you do. It will be all right." Reassured, Keeler settled down to produce his script. I remember him trying out some of the lines under his breath, as the corps did entrechats, "Now make your feet go wickety-whack!/Hurry up, girls, 'cause here comes Pat!"

On other days, when I arrived at the studio, different dancers would be present—Diana Adams, Arthur Mitchell, Todd Bolender, Melissa Hayden. The ballet Balanchine was working on with them was *Agon*. One day Stravinsky arrived to see a run-through of *Agon*. That was a high-energy day. I had the good fortune to be sitting next to Lucia Davidova, an old friend of Balanchine's and Stravinsky's. She was able to give me a running translation, like a U.N. interpreter, of the exchanges that went on that afternoon between the two men, for they communicated mostly in bursts of Russian. Even without an interpreter, there would have been no mistaking the rapport between them, the respect with which they treated each other, and the pleasure they took in their collaboration.

Also present in the studio that day was Martha Swope. This was her first day as a professional photographer. While a student at the School of American Ballet, she had taken some photographs that Lincoln Kirstein had found interesting. He told her the company could use her and suggested she go to rehearsal that day and shoot whatever caught her fancy. Nobody told her Stravinsky would be there or that the day would be in any way special. The consequence was the most memorable sequence of photographs that has ever been taken of a great composer and choreographer at work together. I am pleased to be able to include an array of them in this book.

Daily that fall I showed up at the studio, and daily Balanchine and I went through the same ritual of greeting and leave-taking. This went on for about six weeks. I still hadn't asked a single question. Then one day, after we had exchanged our farewell bows and handshakes, he suddenly said, "Do you want to talk? Let's go to the Russian Tea Room."

It was a gratifying moment for me. I had apparently won some measure of his confidence by being willing to look rather than talk. He was now willing to reciprocate—to be verbal, if that was what I as a writer needed, and to trust that I would be wise and discreet enough to recognize what could truly be put into words, and what couldn't.

After that we met frequently, for long conversations, for a period of about six years as I did the *New Yorker* profile and then the first edition of this book. We went to the Russian Tea Room, or to an Italian restaurant across from City Center, or, after the New York City Ballet had taken up residence at Lincoln Center, to the coffee shop of the nearby Empire Hotel. Sometimes we met at his apartment, sometimes at mine, and a few times we drove out to his country place in Connecticut. I continued to haunt the rehearsal studio, watching him choreograph, rehearse, or teach, and sometimes at the end of one of those sessions he would come over to where I was sitting and comment for me on what I had just observed—often just a playful or glancing remark, which nevertheless might prove trenchant or illuminating. Sometimes I went on errands with him, as he shopped for groceries or wine or the makings of one of his lavish Russian Easter feasts. Whatever he did, even if it was as minor a matter as picking out the right cucumber for a salad, he gave it always his complete attention. I never saw him be hasty, distracted, or inattentive. Truly, he lived in the present. He could make festive the most ordinary event. His friends, the pianists Arthur Gold and Robert Fizdale, have written about an occasion when they wanted to take a taxi to the theatre and he demurred. "'No, no,' he said, 'subway much better.' And like a mythical guide he made the dingy steps, the sinister train, the underground arrival at the State Theater a Tiepoloesque flight into heaven."

The conversation sessions we had for the purposes of this biography were not formal. I had blocked out the main areas to be covered—the epochs of his life and some of the main themes—and we went over those together. Sometimes he set the agenda. "Let's talk about critics, and what they don't know," he declared as soon as we met one day. What set him off on that tack, I no longer remember. Another day he surprised me by saying, as we were concluding our conversation, "Next time we must talk about the aesthetics of ballet." I had always assumed that would be something he would shy away from.

This book is not what is called an authorized biography. When I was in doubt about some point or other, I would question Balanchine closely and he responded patiently and graciously, but I was not expected to submit the manuscript to him for approval. It went to press without his seeing it. I was thankful to him for not interfering. He never once tried to suggest what I should say or how I should evaluate or present the facts of his life. "It's *your* biography, not mine," he said. Ultimately, I sought to treat the materials of his life in the same detached, objective, appreciative way he treated his dancers while choreographing a ballet. I think I learned some lessons from him in this respect.

Come to think of it, there was one time when he offered a suggestion as to how I should proceed. I was complaining to Balanchine one day about the scarcity of documentary materials pertaining to his life, particularly his inner life. I had been reading some biographies of literary figures—abounding in quotations from the subjects' diaries, letters, journals, and memoirs—and, as a biographer, I was feeling deprived. Balanchine had never journalized and in his lifetime had written perhaps fewer letters than the number of ballets he had choreographed. Balanchine listened to my complaint and then replied, "You should think of your task as if you were writing the biography of a racehorse. A racehorse doesn't keep a diary."

The first edition of this book appeared in 1963, the second eleven years later. For the second edition, I made only a few necessary corrections but added a long chapter, which was also published in *The New Yorker* as a second profile. For this third edition, I have welcomed the opportunity not merely to update the book but also to deal with it afresh. I have conducted new interviews, reviewed all my notes as well as new material that has been published in the intervening years, and have made numerous changes and additions throughout. I write this nine months after Balanchine's death. It is twenty-six years since I first met him and began, as a biographer, to think about him, his work, and his life. Much about him remains mysterious to me. This is inevitably the case with any biographical subject—with any human being—no matter how much one learns. Especially was it so with Balanchine. He guarded well his mystery.

Berkeley, California
January 28, 1984

Balanchine

CHAPTER ONE

Choreographer in His Element

The rehearsal studio of a ballet company is something of a cross between a convent and a prizefight gym. Before the dancers go into action, they paw a resin box in a corner, like fighters, and when they make their way about the room between classes or rehearsal sessions, they are apt—even the most petite of ballerinas—to walk with a pugilist's flat-footed but springy gait, shoulders swaying with a bit of swagger, arms hanging loosely. There is the acrid sweat smell of the gym, and the same formidable presence of lithe, steel-muscled, incredibly trim and capable bodies ruthlessly forcing themselves to become even trimmer and more capable. But there is also an aura of asceticism, of spirituality—a spirituality achieved, paradoxically, by means of single-minded concentration on the body. The mirror covering one whole wall from ceiling to floor would seem to speak of gross vanity, but the dancers, though they may have embarked on their careers for vain motives, have learned to rid themselves of conceit when they work. They use the mirror dispassionately, measuring their reflected selves with almost inhuman objectivity against the conception of an ideal to which they have dedicated their lives. The ideal is that of a particular kind of beauty, a centuries-old, thoroughly artificial way of moving, which, when shaped into ballets by a choreographer, becomes art of a special sort—an elusive, evanescent art, as fleeting as fireworks or soap bubbles, that nevertheless has the power not only to entrance beholders but even, in some mysterious manner, to convey an experience of lasting significance.

To see George Balanchine in such an environment, rehearsing his

☙ *Choreographing* Gounod Symphony, *with Maria Tallchief.*

3

New York City Ballet Company or, better yet, creating one of the new ballets he brought forth bountifully, season after season, was to have a rare pleasure—the pleasure of seeing someone who appeared completely attuned to his world. In his person, Balanchine suggested the quintessence of the ballet studio's paradoxical combination of qualities. A noble-looking man, with a proud, elegant bearing—"a *grand seigneur*," Cecil Beaton called him—Balanchine did not hesitate to throw himself on the studio floor in the course of demonstrating to his dancers some movement in one of his ballets, and he would often work himself into a dray-horse lather of perspiration during a rehearsal or choreographic session. In him, an intense, dedicated vision of a perfection of grace merged with an unquestioning willingness to submit to the arduous discipline, the specific physical efforts, required to attain—or at any rate, approach—this vision. "First comes the sweat," Balanchine used to say, speaking in a low, agreeable voice, tinged with the accents of his native Russia. "Then comes the beauty—if you're *vairy* lucky and have said your prayers." Someone once observed of ballet that it is "a science on top of which an art is precariously balanced." Balanchine would have agreed, although he would have preferred to substitute the word "craft" for the more resounding "science."

In the years that followed his introduction to this craft, at the age of nine, in the Imperial Theatre School in St. Petersburg, Balanchine knocked about in many parts of the world, but wherever, in the course of his wanderings, he was able to find a ballet studio, with a complement of dancers in need of something new to dance, there he was at home and in his element. The ballet studio—whether in Russia, France, Denmark, Monaco, England, or the United States—was his true native heath. It was much more to him than just the setting in which he worked; it provided the vital stimulus to his creativity—the rare and indefinable kind of creativity that made him the most esteemed and prolific inventor of ballets in our time. "I'm not one of those people who can create in the abstract, in some nice quiet room at home," he once said to me. "If I didn't have a studio to go to, with dancers waiting for me to give them something to do, I would forget I was a choreographer. I need to have real, living bodies to look at. I see how this one can stretch and that one can jump and another one can turn, and then I begin to get a few ideas."

As a man, aside from ballet, the impression Balanchine made was of someone who was pleasant, mercurial, authoritative, and fundamentally enigmatic. W. H. Auden characterized him, during a conversation we

⤳ Movements for Piano and Orchestra. *Jacques d'Amboise watches as Balanchine, working with Suzanne Farrell, shows him how his part should go.*

had one day, as the most intuitive person he had ever known. "Ideas come to him as images, not abstractions." Auden also said, "He's not an intellectual, he's something deeper, a man who understands everything." In tastes and interests, Balanchine fell into no category; he was highbrow, lowbrow, and middlebrow all mixed up together in a blend of his own. He liked Braque, Pushkin, Rockefeller, Stravinsky, Sousa, Jack Benny, Piero della Francesca, fast cars, science fiction, TV westerns, French sauces, and American ice cream. An adherent of the Russian Orthodox Church, he was deeply religious. He patronized only the best and costliest tailors, but the clothes he fancied were a sort of Russianized version of a wild West dude's garb—bright, pearl-buttoned shirts, black string tie, gambler's plaid vest, frontier pants. On him, these surprising outfits appeared natural and elegant. He lived for almost fifty years in America and remained enthusiastic about it the whole time. He said he loved the way it looked, sounded, and smelled; on occasion he would even remark what a pleasure it was to pay taxes to support a country it was such a pleasure to live in. Most of the time, he would rather talk about cooking or politics, or almost anything other than ballet—ballet, he felt, was something you do, not discuss. He relished luxury but not money. Witty and often playful, he was, however, fundamentally reserved about himself. Most people who had anything to do with him spoke of him with great devotion and affection, but they also said that while he was a very easy person to be with, he was not an easy person to know.

Admirers of Balanchine's work rank him very high among the creative artists of the age, using the word "genius" freely in referring to him. Balanchine himself would never speak in such terms. He could seldom even be trapped into speaking of ballet as an art and himself as an artist. He preferred to describe himself as an entertainer, an artisan, a professional maker of dances for a paying public. When he spoke of what he did, he often compared himself to a chef, whose job it was to prepare for an exacting clientele a variety of attractive dishes that would delight and surprise their palates, or to a carpenter, a good carpenter, with pride in his craft. Craftsmanship was what he respected most. I remember his once showing me a pair of Italian shoes he had bought and saying, "When I see shoes like that, I want to meet the man who made them and shake his hand."

Balanchine did not keep scrapbooks, programs, or reviews of his work; he claimed that he never bothered to read what critics and admirers wrote about him or his work. If someone happened to tell him about an article propounding a theory in regard to his ballets, he would listen politely. Then he would make his standard comment: "Too fancy!" He did not particularly blame writers for going on at length about ballet, if that was how they wanted to occupy themselves or make a living, but he thought that what they (including his most ardent admirers) wrote bore very little relation to what happened onstage while the music was playing. Though capable of expressing original and poetic insights himself in unguarded moments, he chose—out of deep-seated principle, it would seem, or perhaps out of a canny intuition that so elusive an art could not bear the burden of much theorizing or solemnity—to talk about his work as seldom as possible and then only casually, playfully, or in matter-of-fact technical terms. The numerous people who saw grave significance and profound portents in his ballets got no encouragement from him. "When you have a garden full of pretty flowers, you don't demand of them, 'What do you mean? What is your significance?'" he used to say.

Preparing a sequence for **The Goldwyn Follies** *in 1937, with Gisella Caccialanza and Daphne Vane.*

"You just enjoy them. So why not just enjoy ballet in the same way?" Of people who insist on seeing explicit meaning in ballet, he once said, "People never seem to understand unless they can put their finger into things. Like touching dough—when people see bread rising, they smell something and they say, 'Oh, is it going up?' And they poke their finger in it. 'Ah,' they say, 'now I see.' But of course the dough then goes down. They spoil everything by insisting on touching."

Despite his lack of solemnity, there was no mistaking his own or his company's dedication to ballet. "He doesn't do it by talking," a member of the company said, "but he implies at every moment that there is a great art of classical dancing that all of us, including him, are serving." Early in my acquaintance with Balanchine I had occasion to witness an instance of this concentrated dedication. It was an evening in 1958, when I attended a performance of the New York City Ballet at City Center. On the program that evening was *Apollo*, which had been revived for Jacques d'Amboise after being out of the repertory for some years. In the cast was Diana Adams as Terpsichore, Patricia Wilde as

Polyhymnia, and Jillana as Calliope. They gave a triumphant performance, received by the audience with enthusiastic applause and repeated bravos. I was there with another friend of Balanchine's, and we were both so moved by the ballet and the performance that we decided to go backstage and congratulate Balanchine and the dancers—to offer homage, as it were. When we got there, the scene that met our eyes surprised us. We had assumed that, on the heels of such success, we would find dancers and choreographer standing amid admirers, graciously acknowledging their praise. Instead we discovered them hard at work. They were, it seemed, going over aspects of *Apollo* that Balanchine wished to improve. They were grouped near the lowered curtain and must have begun this impromptu rehearsal the instant the last curtain call was over. Standing in the wings, we watched as Balanchine worked first with Patricia Wilde and then with d'Amboise. We heard no harsh words spoken, no reproofs; when Balanchine finished making his point to Miss Wilde, she smiled before departing to her dressing room and thanked Balanchine warmly for his help, as if she were a beginner rather than a distinguished ballerina who had just received an ovation. From her, Balanchine turned to d'Amboise, and we could see them going over various sequences together—facing each other, like one man looking in a mirror, while both danced. Occasionally they would stop for a few words of comment. "Your leaps are still too spectacular, you know," we heard Balanchine say. "Yes, I know," d'Amboise replied. "I'm working on that." Then they went into action again, face to face, about three feet apart. Time passed as they continued thus, and we watched them wonderingly. Dancers began to gather onstage for the next ballet. Bells could be heard ringing, announcing the imminent curtain. Stagehands hurried to their places. Totally preoccupied, Balanchine and d'Amboise ignored it all. When we finally left, without having had a chance to congratulate or pay homage, they were still at it. They were gone, though, when the curtain went up on the next ballet. At the very last instant, perhaps, the stage manager had taken each of them by an arm and led them off. Back in our seats, we could not help wondering if they might not be still working away in the wings.

Over the course of the years the hours I spent in the New York City Ballet studios watching Balanchine choreograph were a constant revelation. To watch him at work with his dancers, bringing into being little by little this new intangible entity called a ballet, was for me a continuing demonstration of the miraculous proposition that chaos could be mas-

∾ Agon—*with Diana Adams and Arthur Mitchell.*

tered, the world made capable of order, and that order and beauty could be one. I was not the only visitor who felt that way. There was an acquaintance of Balanchine's—a businessman—whom I saw in the studio from time to time. He told me that whenever he felt oppressed by the tangle of his own affairs or the confusion of the day's news, he liked to close up his office early and spend an hour or two watching Balanchine at work on a new ballet. He told me it was the best therapy he knew. In the world of ballet, the peaceful, assured, workmanlike way that Balanchine made his dances became legendary. Anecdotes concerning other famous figures of that world often revolve around some pyrotechnical display of temperament. The characteristic Balanchine story, on the other hand, has to do with some crisis or other in which Balanchine was to be found calmly and productively carrying on with his choreography, apparently unaffected by the chaos and hysteria around him. There are people who worked closely with Balanchine for ten years or more and never saw him lose his temper or heard him raise his voice in anger.

When Balanchine choreographed a new ballet, quite a number of spectators were usually present—seated on a bench that ran along the mirrored wall, leaning against the practice bars on the other walls, or standing around the piano off to one side. They observed Balanchine, they talked among themselves, they came and went. He paid no attention. His tolerance of visitors was exceptional among choreographers; many of them detest being watched and exclude from the room not only outsiders but also any members of the company who are not required at the moment. Even so, by the nature of his art, a choreographer can never fully enjoy the pleasure of creating in solitude; eventually he cannot escape the dancers who are the medium in which he works. If he gets stuck and runs out of ideas, there they are before him, waiting—"with patient, drawn faces," as Agnes de Mille has ruefully written—for him to find inspiration. As yet, none of the systems of notation that have been developed have gained such widespread acceptance as to permit the choreographer to do as a playwright or a composer does—that is, prepare his work at leisure on paper and give the script or score to his performers to study before rehearsal. Dance notation has been employed principally as a way of making a record of an occasional ballet after its creation. Before coming to the first rehearsal, the choreographer may work out in his mind a number of steps and patterns for his ballet and jot them down on paper in some shorthand of his own, or he may write out in words a detailed libretto of the action. But, ultimately, to create a new ballet, the choreographer must do what all the generations of ballet masters before him have done—get his dancers together in a large room and show them what he wants them to dance. The creation of a ballet has to be a public act. It is as if a composer had to assemble an orchestra and compose a symphony by standing in front of the musicians and making it up as he went along, first humming a snatch of music for the cellos to try, perhaps, and then turning to, say, the woodwinds and humming a theme they might play at the same time. For all its sophistication, ballet is really a prehistoric kind of art. Lacking a widely accepted written language, it has been able to preserve its masterpieces only by devoted, laborious effort, passing them on from one generation to the next by direct communication, like folk legends. And, like legends, few ballets survive this process unchanged.

These conditions of the craft, which some choreographers find extremely trying, did not disturb Balanchine; he took them for granted. In advance of the first rehearsal he would make no notes whatever. His way of creating a ballet was by extended improvisation under pressure. One of the most facile of all choreographers, he would usually take only about thirty rehearsal hours over a period of about three weeks to choreograph a major ballet, but under pressure he could work even faster. He choreographed the innovative *Symphony in Three Movements,* with its complex, formidable score, in one amazing week for the 1972 Stravinsky Festival. "He just tossed off steps without hesitation," Gordon Boelzner, the company pianist and associate conductor, told me. "He threw whole chunks of choreography at the dancers. I couldn't make head or tail of what was going on. Then Balanchine took one afternoon and cleaned it up, and all of a sudden it came absolutely clear. And I saw that it was a masterpiece."

The system under which he worked allowed no latitude for self-indulgence, dawdling, temperament, searching for inspiration, or getting in the mood. By the time he commenced choreographing a ballet, the ballet would have been announced in the press, the season's performances would have been scheduled, and the costumes and sets ordered. Balanchine's advance preparations for his choreographing would have consisted chiefly in studying the music he was to use until he had soaked it up completely. Sometimes, as part of this process, he made his own piano reduction of the orchestral score. The son of a composer and the product of several years of advanced conservatory training as a young man, Balanchine was unquestionably the most musical of all choreog-

raphers, and he analyzed an orchestral score the way a conductor does. At some point during his study of the music he had chosen for the ballet, he would decide what dance quality was best suited to it—what palette of movement it called for—settle on the size of the ensemble of dancers he would use, and determine who his principal soloists would be. That was likely to be the sum of his preparations. All the rest would have to be done at rehearsal, with the dancers assembled and waiting and the large clock on the wall ticking away the costly minutes of rehearsal time and moving inexorably toward the production hour. When Tchaikovsky was asked, on one occasion, what conditions he required in order to be inspired to compose, he replied, "My Muse comes to me when I tell her to come." Asked the same question about his choreographing, Balanchine gave a paraphrase of this and said, "My Muse must come to me on union time."

On the day rehearsals were to commence, Balanchine would arrive at the studio shortly before the scheduled hour and change into his working clothes—usually frontier-style slacks, a T-shirt or sport shirt, and soft-soled dancing shoes. Even in that garb, he did not lose his air of elegance. He had aplomb, in every sense of the word. ("Aplomb," as defined by the French ballet master Jean-Etienne Despréaux in 1806, is a specific kind of dynamic balance fundamental to every position and movement in classic ballet.) Promptly on the hour, he would come to the front of the rehearsal room and, standing with the mirrored wall at his back, clap his hands lightly. The dancers, who had been warming up or standing about in the spectacularly impossible attitudes ballet dancers naturally fall into in moments of repose, would gather before him. He would greet them with ceremonious courtesy. A minute or two of banter might follow, and then, rubbing his hands briskly, he would remark, like a journeyman carpenter about to knock together a toolshed, "All right. We begin."

Some choreographers, when beginning a new ballet, like to discuss their intentions at some length with the dancers, but Balanchine, who considered cerebration a deadly menace for dancers, preferred to engage in as little talk as possible. "You have to be *vairy* careful when you use your mind," he sometimes cautioned his dancers, "or you will get into trouble." In his cosmogony, dancers were like angels: celestial messengers who may communicate emotions but do not themselves experience the joys or griefs of which they bring tidings. The first thing he might do as he started to work was arrange the dancers in various poses, here and

Working on Don Quixote *in 1965, with two children from the school—Judith Fugate and Jean-Pierre Frohlich.*

there about the room, in the pictorial composition they would form when the curtain rose. As they held their places, he stood before them in silence, his hands clasped, head slightly bowed; he was listening to the first phrase of the music within him and summoning up in his mind's eye the dance phrase he would match to it—a phrase that might consist of five or six different movements by different soloists or groups at the same time. Standing there, he suggested a chess master planning a move. From the room next door, where other members of the company were rehearsing some other work, would come the sound of a piano thumping away, but it did not seem to penetrate Balanchine's concentration. As the dance ideas occurred to him, his hands would unclasp and his fingers come to life, as if they were dancing in the air. "All right," Balanchine would say, stepping over to one of his soloists—the principal ballerina, perhaps—"you do like this." And he would dance out for her the steps he had conceived, counting aloud each beat of the phrase as he did so. She would immediately reproduce his movements while echoing his count. "And you," Balanchine would say, turning next, perhaps, to the leading male dancer, "you do like *this*." In the same way, he would produce sequences for the other soloists and the ensembles of the corps de ballet. When he had communicated in this way all the movements of the dance phrase, he would have the pianist play the few bars of music for it while the dancers put it together for his scrutiny. He might have them run through it several times more, and he might tinker with it or even discard it and try a fresh approach, but often it would be just the way he wanted it from the start. With a nod, he would murmur, "Tha . . . at's right." The dancers would store their steps away in their remarkable muscle memories, and Balanchine, in the same manner as before, would take up the next phrase.

So the work proceeded through the session. Every once in a while Balanchine would make a quick foray to the piano to check something in the score—peering at the notes through a pair of glasses that he kept in his pants pocket—or to show the pianist how a troublesome passage should go. Occasionally, some dance movement or sequence he had devised would make the dancers gasp with laughter or astonishment. Now and then, a dancer might say that he doubted whether he could master some particularly intricate or difficult passage. If Balanchine assured him that he'd be able to work it out with practice, he questioned no more but said okay, he'd try it. The dancer knew that later on, if the passage remained awkward for him, Balanchine would devise a variation to take its place—one probably no less intricate but in some way or other more congenial to that dancer's body conformation and dance style. Though Balanchine put a continual challenge to even the most brilliant of the New York City Ballet's dancers, the choreography he ultimately provided was what each could dance best and most naturally. This was one of the things that Balanchine was noted for in the ballet world and that his dancers appreciated about him.

At the end of an hour of rehearsal, there would be a five-minute break, which Balanchine spent either at the piano with the score or chatting with some of the dancers. As soon as the five minutes were up, he would clap his hands and everybody would be ready to continue. Once more, all went forward with a kind of simple, serious unself-conscious concentration on the task at hand, as Balanchine spun his web of dance, producing his delights and surprises as promised and on schedule. By the conclusion of the session, which might last two hours, a measurable amount of progress would have been made—perhaps two minutes of ballet. The visitor who had sat in the studio while this was taking place would often find that a curious thing had happened to him. Whether or not he was familiar with the music before he arrived, he would discover that the steps and arrangements of movement that Balanchine had worked out already seemed to him absolutely inevitable—as if the music itself had asserted a demand to be linked with just this pattern of dance and no other. Martha Graham told me that she felt something of this sort when she visited Balanchine's studio one evening in 1959. It was the first time in her long career that she had ever watched another choreographer at work.

This visit was at a time when they had embarked on their unusual joint project, the ballet *Episodes*, set to the complete orchestral works of Anton Webern, that master of compression, whose entire lifetime orchestral output amounted to but an hour of music. Miss Graham was to choreograph the opening part of the ballet, using her own company but with the addition of one Balanchine dancer—Sallie Wilson—and Balanchine would choreograph the rest of the ballet, using his own company, except for a section he would choreograph for Paul Taylor. For once, those traditional foes, a classical-ballet choreographer and a modern-dance choreographer, would be working together in amicable conjunction. That evening, Balanchine's studio, as usual, held an assortment of other visitors, among them two composers, Leon Kirchner and Hershy Kay, as well as an old Russian-émigré friend of Balanchine's who had dropped in to see what Balanchine was up to. During the session, a brief mix-up occurred when Balanchine inadvertently skipped a couple of bars in putting two of his dance passages together. Upon discovering his lapse, Balanchine coolly took it in stride; there was no indication that it bothered him to be discovered in such an error by an audience containing a rival choreographer and a couple of composers. First he tried to see how it would go if he stretched out the preceding dance phrase to incorporate the missing bars. "No, that doesn't work," Balanchine said. "I'll have to make something new to put in there." And he did, forthwith. Miss Graham—whose own manner of choreographing was far more emotional and who, according to her friend Agnes de Mille, sometimes dismissed all the dancers from the room when things were not going well and communed with God and her soul—shook her head in wonder at this manifestation of Balanchine's aplomb.

Throughout the rest of the session, she leaned forward intently, following every move. At the end, after Balanchine had had the dancers do a run-through of what he had choreographed so far, she turned to me, for I happened to be seated next to her, and said, "It's like watching light pass through a prism. The music passes through him, and in the same natural yet marvelous way that a prism refracts light, he refracts music into dance."

During the company's season, when Balanchine was not only choreographing new ballets but also supervising the preparation of old ones, he would generally teach company class at eleven and then work in the rehearsal studio the rest of the day. He would take a little time off for dinner, and then he would stand in the wings to watch the performance. Because of the complexity of the company's daily rehearsal schedule—with an active repertory during a given season consisting of some thirty or forty ballets—Balanchine could never count on having the full cast of any new ballet he was choreographing for more than a couple of hours at a time. Unable to work consecutively from beginning to end, he had to make his ballets the way directors make movies, working first on one section, then on another. As a further complication he often choreographed more than one new ballet at a time. So in alternate sessions during the day he might move back and forth between quite disparate works in progress—going, as he did during the memorably creative season of autumn 1957, from a complex, astringently witty, and uncompromisingly avant-garde ballet like *Agon* to a sprightly, untroubled novelty like *Square Dance,* and from the romantic lyricism of the *Gounod Symphony* to the flashy brassiness of *Stars and Stripes.*

*Before the premiere of **Donizetti Variations** in 1960, Balanchine and Kirstein confer on production details.*

While Balanchine was working on his choreography and transmitting it to the dancers, he concerned himself little with nuances of performance. The last few days before the premiere, he usually concentrated on that aspect: getting his ensemble to approach his idea of perfection. Balanchine's style demands unusual precision and energy, and as he worked on his dancers' performance techniques he could be constantly heard exhorting them to more vigor, to more clarity in their attack on every movement. "Audience must be made aware that leg is *your* leg and is going right *there!* Bam!" he admonished them, slamming down his own leg to emphasize his words. When he was engaged in this refining process, the studio resounded with "Bams!" and "Pows!" and similar exclamatory explosions, uttered in a voice that was charged with energy, though it did not go up many decibels in volume. Balanchine's intense vision of beauty as the end result of all this was always present, however, and no one was permitted to forget it. "Isn't it selfish of you," he chided one corps de ballet member, "to expect three thousand people to sit and watch you lift your leg if you're not going to do it beautifully?"

To make a point, Balanchine was capable of producing an apt illustration or a vivid, often surprising metaphor. "Don't forget," I heard him tell a principal dancer, "that Carpentier was the most lyrical boxer who ever lived, but Dempsey knocked him flat in no time." She nodded, apparently discerning a vital truth for herself in this odd bit of information, and immediately attacked her dancing with as much vigor as if she herself were training for a match with Dempsey. To illustrate why another principal dancer's performance of a particular passage was not altogether satisfactory, even though she was dancing it absolutely correctly and in tempo, he told her a little story about Louis XIV, who one day, it is said, emerged from his palace with the intention of taking a ride somewhere and found that his carriage was just arriving. It reached the palace door at the instant he came out. The king did not have to wait a second for it, or even slow down his stride, but he was nevertheless highly offended. As he swept into the carriage, he complained to the coachman, with majestic indignation, "You *almost* made us wait." The dancer laughed at the story, and Balanchine said, "So you see, to be correct, to be perfectly on time is not enough. You must be *luxuriously* perfect if you want to satisfy."

On the whole, however, Balanchine's pedagogy, like his choreography, was essentially nonverbal. "You think, then," a dancer would ask him, "that it should go like this?" and she would perform the passage in

∽ *Choreographing the hornpipe section of* Union Jack *in 1976.*

question. "Ye . . . es," Balanchine would reply, "but maybe a bit more like this," and he would dance it himself the way it should be. When he performed a dance phrase for his company, he would not do the steps in full scale or finished form, but the effect was always astonishingly telling. He evoked an essence as easily as a master painter might with a hasty pencil sketch. Maria Tallchief said that when he was teaching her the role of the Swan Queen in his revised version of the second act of *Swan Lake,* she used to watch him do her part and think, "I'll *never* look that beautiful." Similarly—though apropos of a very different kind of role— Jerome Robbins recalled, "As a dancer, I got some of the best notices of my life for the role of Tyl in Balanchine's ballet *Tyl Ulenspiegel,* but I never came anywhere near the gusto and earthiness that he achieved when he was demonstrating it for me in rehearsal."

Eventually, in the course of preparing a new ballet, Balanchine would dance every step of all the parts—those of all the soloists and all the groupings of the corps de ballet. In a sense, when one witnessed a performance of the New York City Ballet, one was seeing a whole ensemble of Balanchines, in various sizes and shapes, and some critics considered this a fault or limitation in the company. The matter is not so simple as this would suggest, however, for what a ballerina might have picked up from watching Balanchine dance her part for her was a heightened awareness of her own special style and qualities, which his keen eye had perceived, and which he had rendered in clarified form for her. Still, all his dancers were always acutely responsive in copying and appropriating the qualities he sketched out for them. An instance of just how responsive they were occurred when he was choreographing *Bourrée Fantasque* in 1949. When he had the ensemble repeat for him a section that he had created the preceding week, he was perplexed to see that all the movements were being danced in a peculiarly cramped and agonized way. When he questioned the dancers, they insisted that this was the way he had shown the steps to them. He could not figure it out until he recalled that the week before he had been suffering from bursitis; the company had apparently picked up all his aches and pains and magnified them into a bursitic *Bourrée Fantasque.*

Having done his best in the preparation of a work, Balanchine did not fret as the time for its premiere neared. "Somehow it will all work out all right," he would say reassuringly when one of the usual emergencies arose shortly before curtain time, and, one way or another, it nearly always did. "Somehow" was one of Balanchine's favorite words. A recollection that Jerome Robbins sometimes summons up to help compose himself when he is getting jittery as an opening night approaches is that of Balanchine a few hours before the premiere, in 1954, of his version of *The Nutcracker*—the costliest work the New York City Ballet had ever put on till then. At five o'clock that afternoon, with the curtain due to go up at eight-thirty, it was learned that the costumes were still not ready. Balanchine and Robbins hastened over to the workshop of Karinska, the noted costume-maker, to see what could be done about this crisis. When they got there, Balanchine, discerning at a glance that everybody in the shop was working feverishly to get the job finished, spoke not a word of exhortation or reproof. He simply sat down among the seamstresses, took up an unfinished costume, threaded a needle, and began stitching a ruffle. Robbins found himself following Balanchine's example. "After a while, I looked over at him," Robbins recalled. "Here it was only about three hours before curtain, and there sat Balanchine, sewing away as if he

෴ **Harlequinade** *rehearsal. Balanchine shows Villella how to take a fall.*

didn't have a care in the world. I said to him, 'How can you be so calm?' He just smiled and went on sewing."

When the curtain rose for the premiere of one of his new works, Balanchine usually watched from the wings. What he saw on those first nights seldom wholly satisfied him—not compared with what he had pictured in his mind as he worked on the ballet. "It's like coffee," he once said to me. "It never tastes as good as it smells." At the end of the ballet, after everyone else had taken repeated bows—soloists, ensemble, conductor— the audience might get a glimpse of Balanchine in the spotlight.

Usually he emerged onstage in the grip of a couple of his dancers, like a culprit apprehended at the scene of his crime. His appearance always brought forth the most thunderous ovation of the evening, to which he responded with a quizzical smile, a shrug, and a nod of acknowledgment. Then he quickly ducked back behind the curtain. Some in the audience who did not know Balanchine were heard to surmise that his diffident stage manner was a studied performance—like that of the nineteenth-century composer who, after the premiere of one of his operas, always had to be dragged bodily onto the stage, struggling valiantly to get away while muttering to his captors, "Pull harder!" Those who knew Balanchine somewhat better disagree with this; the way he took a curtain call, they say, accorded with the engagingly modest, unpretentious manner in which he invariably comported himself when they met him off-stage. The few who knew him very well, however, while agreeing that he did not put on an act and that his everyday behavior was equally unpretentious, say that modesty was not the explanation but just the reverse— a kind of monumental self-assurance. He was so sure of himself and his work that he did not need to boast or to bathe his ego in applause. "He seems as soft as silk, but he's as tough as steel," said Lincoln Kirstein, the general director of the New York City Ballet, who for fifty years was Balanchine's most devoted patron and partisan. "He's the most secure man I've ever met in my life. He has authority to the nth degree." It was Balanchine's feeling that in seeing his new ballet the audience had seen what he wished to show of himself and that it was irrelevant, and also not very interesting, to follow the ballet with a display of his own person onstage. He felt about this rather as Joseph Conrad felt when he was asked by the *Bookman* for a photograph of himself that it could publish; Conrad replied, "My face has nothing to do with my writing."

Taking a curtain call with Patricia Wilde after the first performance of **Native Dancers in 1959.**

R. Charles   St Pétersbourg.

CHAPTER TWO

Childhood in Russia

ime was when a young ballet dancer, if not so fortunate as to be a Russian to start with, was expected as a matter of course to adopt a Russian stage name. (So Hilda Munnings became Lydia Sokolova, for instance.) Balanchine may have been the only Russian in the dance world who had to do the opposite. He was christened Georgi Melitonovitch Balanchivadze at his birth, which took place in St. Petersburg on January 22, 1904. The change to "Balanchine" was made twenty years later, at the request of Serge Diaghilev, when the young man joined that autocratic but inspired impresario's Ballets Russes in Paris. Diaghilev thought the name too difficult to pronounce. Strictly speaking, "Balanchivadze" is a name of Georgian, rather than Slavic, derivation. It was from his Georgian forebears that Balanchine inherited his physical characteristics—his black hair, intense dark eyes, hawklike features, and wiry frame—and also, as he would occasionally later assert, his type of artistic temperament. "We Georgians are not Russians in culture, not at all," he sometimes declared, in his Russian-flavored accent. "We are Mediterranean people, like Italians."

Another important influence of a non-Slavic sort was that of the city in which he was born. In its fashions, its values, its style of thought, its very appearance, St. Petersburg was the most European of Russian cities—as it continues to be today, though bearing Lenin's rather than Peter's name. Italian architects—Rastrelli, Rossi, Guarenghi—worked here in the service of the czars, creating great, baroque marble palaces, set amid carefully laid-out gardens and broad, handsome streets. Even

About age five.

25

the ordinary buildings along the streets, of brick or the local granite, were generally plastered and painted in Italian colors. Many a visitor to this city has found himself reminded by its appearance of Rome—but a Rome without the *dolce far niente,* a Rome icebound for months of the year, above whose Italianate palaces the strange lights of the aurora borealis glimmer of a bitter winter night.

Of his mother's origins Balanchine knew very little in detail, and of his father's not much more. One thing he was sure of: neither of his parents was of aristocratic lineage. He had never heard tell of any princes among his ancestors, or even counts—and he found this quite distinguished him from nearly all the other Russians he met in exile. His father, Meliton Balanchivadze, was born in Kutais. He was a composer and won a measure of fame, if little fortune, by collecting and arranging the folk songs of his native Caucasus region. "The Georgian Glinka," he was sometimes called. His compositions included an opera entitled *Tamara the Wily,* numerous choral works, a mass, and other church services.

Meliton Balanchivadze was a convivial, elegant gentleman, something of a bon vivant, who on festive occasions was often called on to play the role of toastmaster because no one in his circle was as gifted as he at improvising flowery speeches of tribute. This was not hypocritical of him; he liked people very much and, with the aid of a little wine or vodka, could readily believe that they were as distinguished and as delightful as he said they were. If his had been a less convivial nature, he might have left a more substantial body of achievements as a composer; but maybe not. Cold sober, at some time early in his life, he may have taken the exact measure of his talents and come to the conclusion that since he would never be one of the immortals of music, it would be a pity to deprive himself, during his mortal span, of such passing gratifications as the world had to offer. His friends were mostly fellow Georgians. There would always be a good deal of hearty drinking, for which Georgians are renowned, whenever they got together, and much singing of Georgian folk songs. Among his friends he numbered not merely fellow artists but also people of varied interests, including such political figures as Tseretelli and Chkheidze, who were later to play leading roles in the short-lived Kerensky regime. Balanchivadze very much enjoyed political discussions. He professed liberal, antimonarchical tenets, but he was not a political activist himself. He engaged in these discussions in the manner of a Chekhov character, as one of the amiable and harmless distractions of a civilized man.

~ *Georgi's father and mother.*

He was thirty-six at the time of his marriage to Georgi's mother, Maria Nikolayevna Vassilyeva; he had been married once before, had two teenage children, and was a widower. Maria Nikolayevna was a blond, petite, blue-eyed girl little more than half his age. A native of St. Petersburg, where they met, she was of unpretentious background. Her education, typical for a girl of her class, had not left her overly burdened with erudition, but she was sensitive to the arts and could play the piano better than passably.

From this marriage three children resulted, each a little more than a year apart in age. Georgi was the middle one; he had an elder sister, Tamara, and a younger brother, Andrei. They lived in a modest apartment, for Balanchivadze earned little from his music. Despite their straitened circumstances and the frequently expressed wish that they could somehow get their hands on just a bit more money, the family seems to have lived quite happily—happily, that is, until disaster struck, in the way that in fairy tales disaster most loves to strike, disguised as a fabulous piece of good fortune that bestows upon poor misguided mortals everything they have wished for and more. Going gloomily to the bank one day to cash in his last savings bond, Balanchivadze was informed by an excited clerk that his bond's number had been drawn in the state savings lottery and that he had won the top prize, a sum amounting, in present terms, to perhaps as much as several hundred thousand dollars, tax free. Here were riches far beyond the Balanchivadzes' dreams.

There followed, after the first delirious jubilation, such a series of ridiculous and distressing chastisements as the Brothers Grimm themselves might have plotted. First off, Balanchivadze alienated most of his friends by passing out presents. Those to whom he had given five hundred rubles were mortified at learning that others had received a thousand; those to whom he had given a thousand thought it curiously selfish of him not to have made it two thousand, or anyway fifteen hundred. A white carriage horse that a man with a luminously honest face sold to the Balanchivadzes (to go with an elegant carriage they had bought to go with their fine new twelve-room flat) turned out to be not a carriage horse at all but an old circus trouper. It danced and cavorted whenever it heard a band and kept trying bravely, despite the encumbering carriage behind it, to show how cleverly it could prance on its hind legs. One day, in the middle of the city, it threw over the whole equipage, itself and all, smashing the carriage and shaking up the occupants.

Surprised at how expensive life had suddenly become, Balanchivadze heeded the advice of people who urged him to put part of his new fortune into some sound business; he opened a handsomely decorated Georgian-style restaurant in a fashionable quarter of St. Petersburg. This venture soon proved to be a costly mistake, because the hospitable Balanchivadze could never bring himself to charge even the slightest of acquaintances for their meals, and they, in turn, never affronted him by offering to pay. To recoup his losses, Balanchivadze then invested in a factory that would produce foundry vats by a new process. This proved to be not merely a blunder, like the restaurant, but totally ruinous, and he was sent to prison for two years on a charge of willful bankruptcy. His wife did not tell the children where he was (they learned this only after they were grown) but led them to understand that he was off in the Caucasus gathering folk songs. Balanchine well remembered the day his father returned. The boy, then about six or seven years old, was with his family on the porch of a house they had moved to in the country. Glancing up, he saw his father coming in at the garden gate, dressed as elegantly as ever and carrying a single red rose in his hand. "Oh, look!" Georgi's mother cried. "Here's your father back from—back from the Caucasus!" And they all rushed down the path to embrace him.

Balanchine retained few coherent memories from that first period of his life in St. Petersburg, the five years or so during which his family experienced unexpected affluence and impending doom. He could recall being taken on walks by his nurse to a park not far from their flat, holding primly onto her hand as they crossed the broad street. One of his very earliest memories, dating from when he was about two years of age, was of being on a stage, with an audience staring at him. Taken by his mother to some holiday performance or fete, he happened to get separated from her in the crowd and wandered tearfully about until a stranger, perhaps an official of the fete, noticed his plight. The next thing he knew he had been carried onto the stage by the stranger and, wretched with embarrassment, was being held up to view, like an umbrella or hat that has been found about the premises, for the owner to come forward and claim. The interval that ensued before his mother rescued him from the stage, probably of the briefest duration, remained in his mind as an agonizing eternity. The episode could not be considered an auspicious presage of a theatrical future.

An incident from his infancy that he did not remember but often heard recalled was one that occurred in 1905, when he was little more than a year old. His mother had taken him and his sister to the park, where they played for an hour or so. Throughout that time his mother noticed a well-dressed, wealthy-looking man sitting on a bench close by, reading and enjoying the sunshine. He was still seated there when she gathered up her children and left, but no sooner had she done so, as she learned from the papers the next day, when revolutionaries threw a bomb that killed him. He was, the papers revealed, a high-ranking diplomat. The papers also quoted the captured assassins as saying that they had waited in ambush in the park for a long time before throwing the bomb, because they had wanted to avoid harming some innocent people who were near their intended victim—a woman, they said, with two small children.

More vivid often than the serious or important events of childhood are those sensory impressions, usually slight or ordinary in character, which for some reason make an indelible mark. So, for Balanchine, the St. Petersburg of his childhood was a wispy cluster of such images: the rattle of droshkies' wheels on the wooden pavements, the cries of street vendors, the pealing of the church bells on High Easter; the mingled pleasurable aromas of coffee beans, spices, and rope tar at a merchant's shop his mother sometimes took him to; the strangeness of waking up one night many hours after he had gone to bed and finding it still light as day

∽ *The house near Lounatiokki.*

outside—one of those midsummer nights it must have been when the sky scarcely darkens before dawn, what the St. Petersburgers call a "white night."

The country house to which his family moved when Georgi was small was about a three-hour ride by slow train to the northwest of St. Petersburg, in what is now Finland but in those days before World War I was part of the Russian empire. It was near the village of Lounatiokki, in the vicinity of Viipuri. This property was all that remained to the Balanchivadzes from the fortune they had won. Built of logs in indigenous, rustic style, the house was rough-hewn but spacious. It had ample grounds, where the family raised most of the food required, and was surrounded by woods—pine, white birches, and mountain ash. Here Georgi had fewer restraints than in the St. Petersburg flat. He and his brother and sister could play outdoors all day. He was free, as he grew older, to roam in the woods. In season he would gather the mountain-ash berries and bring them home, to be made into jam. Sometimes the family would go out into the woods and spend the entire day on a mushroom-gathering expedition; Georgi soon became expert at identifying the edible varieties. He enjoyed also working in the family's vegetable garden and in the large strawberry patch at the side of the house. It was an active, bucolic life for the boy, and on the whole a happy one, though the bucolic life has tragedies and bitter lessons of its own for a child. He had for a pet a little pig. A smart animal and sweet-natured, it used to follow him about wherever he went, even accompanying him on walks in the woods. He was more fond of that pig than of any other pet he had as a boy. But the pig grew; the time came for it to fulfill its barnyard destiny and become bacon. Georgi's heart was broken as he was thus brought up against one of the basic facts of life: man's inhumanity to pig. It made a vegetarian of him for a while.

Reading and writing, arithmetic, the Bible, and a little history were taught him by a tutor. When he was five, he was started on the piano, taught at first by his mother and then by an imposing, bespectacled German lady who, when satisfied with his efforts, would at the end of a lesson ceremoniously open her handbag and take out a piece of chocolate, smelling of face powder, which she would confer on him as if it were the Iron Cross, First Class. He did not at all want to learn the piano at first; practicing was a bore. But his mother was firm with him and put him to bed without supper when he balked. Then one day, as he was thumping mechanically at a movement of a Beethoven sonata, something of the potential beauty and grandeur of the music suddenly came glimmering through to him. It brought tears to his eyes. He could not fathom what it was all about, but he felt it. From then on, though he still often preferred romping outside to sitting down to practice, the most deadly element of boredom—meaninglessness—had been removed for him. Before long, he began to show considerable aptitude for the instrument. In the evenings, he and his mother would often play four-hand music together. The other children would join in. His sister, Tamara, played the violin, and his younger brother, Andrei, who later in life would become a composer, early showed talent for the piano also. One might have expected that it would be the composer father rather than the mother who would serve as the children's mentor and companion in music, but the father was not at home much; aside from his spell in prison, he was often on tour with a choral group he had organized. Nor would he have had the necessary patience. Forty-two when Georgi was born, he remained a rather distant figure to his children, one who, despite his amiability and his kindness to them, inspired them more with awe than spontaneous affection.

Even as a young boy, Georgi possessed a keen eye for feminine beauty. There is no way of measuring such a faculty, but it is probably as much a part of the precocious endowment of a future ballet master as an ear with absolute pitch is for the future composer. Lounatiokki had not much to offer in the way of pulchritude, but it was not wholly a wasteland; there was, glory be, the village dentist. A blonde in her twenties, she was the first woman he ever thought beautiful. Even when she was causing him agony, he could not help appreciating her charms. Going to the dentist was thus an even more acutely ambivalent experience for him than it is for most people.

Little diversion of a cultural nature was available in that remote region of the country. In the woods near the village was a rustic theatre, where an occasional troupe of players would perform. Georgi was taken to the theatre by his mother a few times, but the performances made little impression on him. Once, though, while taking a walk alone through the woods at the age of about eight he came upon the empty theatre and, on impulse, made his way into it through a trapdoor he found underneath the stage. He wandered through the dressing rooms, intrigued by the props and costumes and makeup boxes. And he stood on the stage, looking about him in the gloom of the unlighted theatre, strangely excited. He was aware of a curious sense of wonder and mystery now such as he had never known when he had been there before as a regular part of the audience.

A moment of strange wonder it was for the boy but no epiphany, no revelation that the theatre was to be his destiny and the stage the place where he would someday work a magic of his own. His parents had it all settled by that time that Georgi would have a military or naval career, as had several of his relatives. His half-brother, Apollon, was a captain in the army, and one uncle was a colonel. Throughout his early boyhood bewhiskered uncles and uncle types would eye him appreciatively, appraising his military potentialities. "Look at that back!" one of them used to roar admiringly. "Just look at that back, would you! The boy's a born officer, I tell you. He'll wear a uniform beautifully."

Georgi found the idea of becoming an officer agreeable enough. At times, though, he thought it would be even more splendid to be a priest, as were a number of his father's kin—most notably an uncle who was the bishop of Gori, in Georgia (from whence, incidentally, also came Joseph Stalin—a stray from the bishop's pastoral flock). To the boy's mind no field marshal could equal a bishop when it came to sheer pomp and display. The Orthodox Church, with its antique ritual, its Byzantine panoply and sublime music, appealed strongly to both the mystical and the

In motley—Tamara, Georgi, Andrei.

theatrical sides of his nature, and one of his favorite childhood pastimes was to play bishop. Dressed in such ecclesiastical costume as his fancy could improvise, he would spend hours in his room before an altar composed of a stack of chairs, pretending, with portentous gestures, that he was presiding over high mass. More thrilling to him than any visits to the theatre were the occasions when, in St. Petersburg, he and his family would attend services at the great Cathedral of Our Lady of Kazan. Modeled in architectural style after St. Peter's of Rome, the cathedral was noted for its superb choir of two hundred boys' voices; the pianissimo they could produce, seeming to float in the heavens, always sent chills along Georgi's spine. Sometimes, adding to the emotions he was experiencing would be the awareness that the choir was singing music composed by his own father. It was in this cathedral that Georgi witnessed the most impressive scene of his early childhood when he was present at his uncle's investiture. It was a ceremony of burial and resurrection. He heard a solemn requiem being intoned and saw a great black cloth being draped over his uncle, who lay face down, arms spread, before the altar. The secular man was being interred. Then the boy saw his uncle emerge —transformed, as it were—clothed in his new vestments until at last the priest stood before them in all his new glory.

When Georgi was nine, he and his mother and sister took the train to St. Petersburg one day. His mother was planning to enroll him in the Imperial Naval Academy. The sister, Tamara, was to try out for admittance to the ballet section of the Imperial Theatre School. At the naval academy, Georgi's mother was given the disappointing news that the rolls were full and that he would have to wait a year before his application could be considered. The three then went over to the ballet school, hoping that Tamara would meet with better luck. Both she and her mother had their hearts set on the girl becoming a ballerina—another Pavlova or Karsavina, rich and famous, dazzling the whole world with her art and beauty. In the St. Petersburg region, and for miles around, many of the parents of young girls were infected with this dream in those days—much as in Odessa, as Isaac Babel tells it in his story "Awakening," the parents of little Yiddish boys dreamed of making violin prodigies out of them.

This was to be Tamara's second try for the ballet school. She had been turned down the previous year. Without *protektsia*—some influential sponsor—it was difficult to gain consideration, for there were so many seeking admittance. At the academy, when they arrived there this day, they found about a hundred and fifty girls and fifty boys trying out for the twenty or so openings. As the Balanchivadzes were waiting on a hall bench, one of the school officials, who was acquainted with Georgi's mother, stopped to chat and, in the course of the conversation, suggested that Georgi might as well audition, too, since he wasn't doing anything else that day. He did not need to point out that a career in ballet was considered in the Russia of that time (as in the Soviet Union today) an honored and respected one for a man to pursue; but he did remark that there was nothing to lose, for if it did not work out the boy could still go ahead and apply once more for admission to the naval academy the following year.

Georgi's mother agreed. Times were hard for the Balanchivadzes now, and here at least was a chance for a free education for the boy. So Georgi joined the other boys in line.

The audition was a lengthy but not a demanding procedure. The young candidates were not expected to demonstrate any abilities in the dance; they were assayed in terms of health, physique, carriage, general air and appearance, and such other subtle considerations as the examining board had evolved through the years. First each child was given a medical examination. Then each one in turn had to walk back and forth across a large room under the penetrating scrutiny of the judges. Among the judges was the famed prima ballerina Olga Preobrajenska, then nearing the end of her long, glorious dancing career. Ignorant though he was of ballet, Georgi had nevertheless heard enough about Preobrajenska to be awed at finding himself in her presence. He had never felt more awkward than he did that day whenever he was called back into the large room and requested once more to walk back and forth in a natural manner. Yet something about his looks—his vitality, the elegance and strength of his slim young body—caught the discerning eye of the ballet-school judges. Preobrajenska, in particular, seemed interested and spoke to him in friendly fashion when he made his last appearance in the auditioning room.

At the end of the day it was announced that he was one of the eight or nine boys chosen. His sister, to her grievous disappointment, was again turned down. Though pleased for her brother, she might well have been piqued enough at the ironic turn of events to wish she could show him up by trying out for the naval academy. Thus it was, at any rate, through a whimsical combination of circumstances, that Russia lost a naval officer and the world gained a master of the dance.

CHAPTER THREE

Monkey—A Student

So Georgi's feet were set on the path of his destiny. He took one frightened look down it and turned tail. He promptly ran away from the ballet school.

In the light of history, we may savor now the irony of this action on the part of one who was to prove himself so devoted to the art of the dance and so consequential a figure in it. A child is not impelled by historical perspective, however, but by his immediate feelings and impulses. Georgi had never seen a ballet in his life and had only a dim idea what the word even meant. The whole thing had happened so suddenly and without transition; his mother had left him at the school and, with Tamara, had gone off back to their home. He felt as miserable and bewildered as a dog whose master has taken it to some strange city and then abandoned it.

Fleeing the school, he ran through the streets of St. Petersburg until he managed to make his way to the apartment of a maiden aunt—his Aunt Nadia. "What's this?" she exclaimed on opening the door, alarmed at the sight of the boy's forlorn, desperate appearance. "What's this?" She took him in, made him tea, and listened to his plaint. She was kind but firm. He would have to go back to the school, if the authorities would take him back after this misdeed. There was no question of acceding to his wishes, no matter how strongly he felt; his elders knew best what was good for him. For such a breach of discipline Georgi could well have been expelled. The first year at the school was a probationary one. With so many seeking admittance, only those who showed themselves eager as

Andreyanov, Georgi's teacher, as he appeared in Swan Lake.

37

well as apt were retained. But the authorities heeded the pleas of Georgi's aunt and agreed to give him another chance.

Georgi was not grateful to his aunt for her intervention—not then, at any rate. The whole first year he was intensely miserable. The postures and movements that he was spending grueling hours trying to learn seemed to him useless and absurd; he would never master them, he was sure, and did not want to even if he could. In most of his academic subjects—French, arithmetic, Russian grammar, and literature—he did poorly also, excelling only in the classes in music and religion. On top of that, he did not get along with the other students. He had a trait, when nervous, of sniffing perceptibly, a twitch of his upper lip that showed his front teeth; his classmates promptly nicknamed him "Rat."

Nevertheless, he somehow survived the probationary period and was promoted to permanent status. Then, in his second year, when he was ten, something happened to him that had the force of a revelation, transforming everything for him and causing him to view his school experience in a new light. He appeared in his first performance.

It was the custom that students from the school, from the second year on, were used in some of the ballets put on by the Imperial Ballet Company at the famous Maryinsky Theatre. This provided the youngsters with invaluable professional apprenticeship while also making for a piquant supplement to the already vast resources of a company numbering some two hundred dancers. Court coaches, emblazoned with the czar's double-eagle emblem and each with a liveried coachman in front and behind, transported the children on those occasions from the school to the Maryinsky stage door. Six children rode in each coach. The night Georgi took his first part the carriage he rode in was one of a cavalcade of ten. The ballet that evening was *The Sleeping Beauty*. Georgi was in the garland waltz in the first act and also appeared as a cupid on one of the carriages in the last act. When he was not onstage he stood wide-eyed in the wings. The lush, poignant Tchaikovsky music; the fairy-tale story; the miraculous stage effects, of cascading fountains, walls of flame that suddenly sprang up from nowhere, a boat that seemed to sail forever across the lake of an enchanted forest, and great trees and shrubbery that grew before one's very eyes, until the bewitched palace, so full of life and gaiety a few moments before, was all overgrown and the garden colonnades entwined about with vines; the dancing, such as he could hardly believe possible even as he watched; the sumptuous theatre itself, with its glittering chandeliers and gold, white, and peacock-blue decor—all worked magic on the boy's imagination. So this was what ballet was! This was what it was all for, the rigors and demands of the school! The sudden light of insight was like that he had experienced when a few years before he had first apprehended the beauty of the Beethoven sonata he was practicing, but magnified now by all the circumstances.

That night, as he watched the dancers—Karsavina, Andreyanov, and all the others in the great company—the boy was stirred by the realization that every one of them had gone through the very same schooling as he, in the same building and with many of the same teachers. He admired these dancers and wanted to emulate them. In his mind at that time there was no soaring ambition to become someday a great choreographer, with an academy and a company of his own. Even in fantasy he would not then have been so bold. For the moment, all he could think of was that if he worked with all his might and tried his very best, perhaps he could earn the chance to dance with the imperial company as often as it put on a ballet that called for children from the school.

It had been August 1913 when Georgi Balanchivadze was enrolled in the ballet school. In Europe the guns would soon begin to thunder. Surprisingly, ballet, theatre, and opera continued to flourish in Russia throughout the war. At the ballet school, the children devotedly sweated away at their exercises—striving to perfect their arabesques and entrechats, their fifth-position turnout and rond de jambe en l'air, their courtly bows or curtsies—as deeply absorbed in their own cosmos as novices in a Tibetan monastery, and just about as remote from everyday reality. One day a week they did without sugar, as a contribution for the soldiers at the front. Beyond that, as some of them have since wonderingly recalled, they were scarcely aware that the war was going on at all.

The design and location of the school building served to foster this atmosphere of remoteness and self-absorption. Theatre Street, on which it was situated, was not far from the busy Nevsky Prospect, but it was a short, spacious, and tranquil cul-de-sac of a street. The width of the street at one end was taken up by the Alexandrinsky Theatre, the great imperial theatre for classic drama. One side of the street was occupied by a building housing the ministry of culture, where the lord chamberlain had his offices. The school building occupied the entire other side. Designed in baroque style by the Italian architect Rossi, its proportions were palatial—with spacious, high-ceilinged, elegant rooms. This whole palace of a building housed in all perhaps sixty girls and forty boys. One lived amid an atmosphere of space and grandeur, with an abiding sense of being especially privileged.

There were two floors to the building. The girls had their quarters on the first floor, the boys on the second. Boys and girls attended the academic classes together, but their dancing classes, with the exception of those in adagio and in ballroom dancing, were held separately. The academic classrooms were on the second floor, as was also a small jewel of a church. Downstairs was a completely equipped little theatre just for student use, where concerts, plays, and dance performances were frequently put on. On this floor were also two huge rehearsal rooms and a smaller one. When ballets were being prepared for production, the distinguished artists of the Maryinsky would rehearse in the largest of the rehearsal rooms. The students were not supposed to loiter about the hall then and peer in, but most of them could not resist doing so whenever they got the chance. Peering through the crack in the door at these glamorous and superbly proficient beings, they were in a sense spying on their own future and wondering if it was really possible that they would ever attain it. It was on one such occasion that Felia Doubrovska, who was a promising soloist with the company, having graduated from the school the year that Georgi Balanchivadze entered it, first saw him. She noticed him watching her and the other dancers at rehearsal. It was his eyes she noticed—the intense, searching scrutiny of his gaze, perfectly polite but completely merciless. "There's a little boy," she thought, "who doesn't miss a thing."

As a student at the ballet school, young Balanchivadze wore the same sort of uniform (dark blue with a velvet collar) that would have been issued to him if he had qualified for one of the imperial military academies. The chief distinguishing mark was the collar insignia; the ballet student wore a silver lyre—the symbol of Apollo, leader of the Muses. The regimen of the school was as firmly regulated as a military academy as well. Corporal punishment was not administered, but an occasional cuff might be given by way of pedagogical emphasis or as a mnemonic aid. One teacher used to rap the children with his knuckles on offending parts of their anatomy when correcting their postures. He wore a couple of heavy rings on the hand he taught with, and there was seldom a time during his first years at school when Georgi did not have a bruise somewhere on his body.

Georgi, seated, during his second year at the ballet school, with his brother, Andrei, who had begun attending a technical school.

Despite this, he did not feel abused. In retrospect, he considered himself to have been extremely fortunate in his teachers. For his classes in mime, acting, and makeup he had as his teacher the remarkable Pavel Gerdt, whom the *Dance Encyclopedia* describes as "probably the greatest classic dancer and partner of all time on the Russian Imperial stage." In 1913, when Georgi entered the school, Gerdt was sixty-eight years old and still making memorable appearances in character roles on the Maryinsky stage. His mime classes were, for Georgi, a significant and fascinating experience. Under Gerdt he learned how one can transform oneself to fit the role being played. In the student plays that were performed in the school theatre—such plays as Chekhov's *The Bear*, Ostrovski's *The Storm*, and Griboyedov's *Woe from Wit*—he was often cast to play the roles of old men, because none of the other boys could carry the parts off so convincingly.

For the classic dance, Georgi's main teacher throughout most of his years at the school, and the one he admired most, was Samuel Constantinovitch Andreyanov. A tall, blond man in whom grace and elegance were combined with strength and indubitable but unostentatious virility, Andreyanov was then in his thirties and at the height of his powers as a dancer. As a teacher, he had a reputation for bringing out the best in his pupils, of whom he was considerate without ever being condescending. He never sought to woo their friendship. There was no chumminess between students and teacher, but they felt, nevertheless, great affection for him—an affection founded on deep respect.

In some other fields of endeavor, we are accustomed to seeing youngsters of talent asserting their independence from an early age and rejecting their mentors as fools or tyrants, from whom they must escape if they are to fulfill themselves. That is the standard early-chapter theme in the biographies of certain kinds of artists. But the situation is very different in a specialized, difficult craft like ballet, in which a student, no matter how sublime a soul he may feel himself to possess, must manifest his achievements in terms of specific details. A young ballet student is not likely for a moment to think himself better than his teachers, for he can readily see by a glance in the mirror how vain that notion would be. At the school on Theatre Street in St. Petersburg the students knew that they were not being taught by mere theoreticians; those who were showing them what to do were, the youngsters understood, the best in the world at it. A bond of tradition linked students and teachers together as those of the older generation passed on to the younger, as if in apostolic succession, the mysteries and subtleties of their art.

In his early years at the school Georgi was lonely, even in the midst of so many other children and with his days so occupied. He had no close friends among the others for some time. Alexandra Danilova, who was in the class just above his, has recalled that her first impression of him was of a shy boy who kept himself rather aloof from the others. She thought there was something very distinctive and mysterious about him and said she promptly fell in love with him, though she wouldn't have dreamed of letting him know it then. Even as a boy he had extraordinary self-control. He did not show his feelings. His slim Georgian body was possessed of great energy and of more strength than one might have guessed; he loved to run and jump and dance, but he did not much care for the boisterous horseplay some of the other boys enjoyed. Some of them made him a butt because of this. One boy in particular set himself the task of trying to provoke him into losing his temper. Eventually he succeeded. When at last Georgi lost his patience, he threw himself on his adversary so violently that he broke the other boy's collarbone. It was the only fight he had in his school years, and it was the only time his schoolmates ever saw his temper out of control. There were not many such times in his life. It may well be that the extraordinary outward calm of manner he cultivated throughout his life stemmed from the intuition that his nature may have been too turbulent to go unleashed.

Music was his greatest satisfaction. Throughout the school building there were a number of pianos; whenever he had a few spare moments, he would sit down and play. Music was a compulsory subject at the academy. Each student was expected to learn to perform passably on the piano or the violin, but there were none, not even in the higher grades, who could play so well as he. Soon he was being chosen by senior students to be their accompanist at the dance performances each had to give in order to graduate; this was considered a signal honor for so young a lad as Georgi and brought him to the attention of the faculty and influential personages who attended these graduation examinations. It also gained him respect and admiration from the younger fellow students who had been at first puzzled by him and therefore, in the way of children and other primitive tribes, hostile to him.

Soft-spoken and unpretentious in manner as he was, he yet seems to have conveyed an air of authority from early on, as if there were something special in store for him. Perhaps he thought so, too. For a parlor game, he wrote an acrostic of his name that later on his schoolmates remembered and liked to quote:

> *Fate smiles on me.*
> *I am Ba.*
> *My destiny in life is fixed.*
> *I am Lan.*
> *I see the keys to success.*
> *I am Chi.*
> *I will not turn back now.*
> *I am Vad.*
> *In spite of storm or tempest.*
> *I am Ze.*

In his third year at the school he performed his first ballet role at the Maryinsky that was considered worthy of mention in the program's cast of characters. The part was that of a monkey in the ballet *Pharaoh's Daughter*; he had to clamber about in the treetops while Kschessinska, *prima ballerina assoluta* of the Maryinsky, tried to shoot him down with bow and arrow. His billing on the program read: "Monkey—A Student." This ballet was his favorite work for a time. He enjoyed immensely scrambling about high above the stage and leaping from branch to branch; here was a part, he felt, for which he had a special affinity. He considered himself privileged to be on the same stage as Kschessinska, whose technical abilities were extraordinary and whose presence was regal—as well it might be, since she had been the mistress of Czar Nicholas II himself, before his accession to the throne, and was then the consort of the Grand Duke André. Kschessinska was not Georgi's favorite of the Maryinsky ballerinas, though. Best of all he liked Karsavina and Elizaveta Gerdt, the wife of his teacher, Andreyanov, and daughter of Pavel Gerdt. Some critics thought Elizaveta Gerdt's dancing too cool—too "vegetarian," as the critic Volynsky put it—but to Georgi's eye it possessed a crystalline purity that was near perfection. Of the male dancers he saw at the Maryinsky, he most admired Andreyanov and Vladimirov; both seemed to him truly noble figures.

As time went on, Georgi was given a variety of opportunities. He danced in a mazurka in *Paquita,* a part, incidentally, in which Nijinsky, as a boy, had made his first appearance on the Maryinsky stage a decade before; he was one of a group of boys who performed a delightful Spanish character dance in Fokine's *La Jota Aragonese,* which that choreographer staged at the Maryinsky in 1916, and he was a street vendor in *Petrouchka*; with broad dramatic flair he played the role of the child prince in *The Nutcracker*, as well as, earlier on, the king of the mice. Whether he was onstage or watching from the wings, those ballet evenings enthralled him. The lavish resources of the czar were available to the Maryinsky, and the ballets in the repertory—*Paquita, Esmeralda, The Corsair, Swan Lake, Pharaoh's Daughter*, and the rest—were, if nothing else, extraordinary as sheer spectacle. They were, as they were intended to be, a distraction fit for a king.

All this—the theatre, the school, the ballet company—existed, Georgi was brought up to think in those years, to gratify and glorify the czar. Without the czar, he could not imagine that there would be any ballet in Russia, but then he was not able to imagine Russia without the czar. Georgi himself, as a student at the Imperial Theatre School, was considered a member of the czar's own household. In 1916, on December 6— Czar's Day—he, along with other students who had appeared in the ballet that evening, was conducted, after the performance, to the royal box and presented to the czar and members of his family. The czar patted Georgi on the shoulder, bestowed a vague, gentle smile on him, and gave him a silver box, ornamented with the imperial crest and filled with chocolates. Some children were so awed that they almost swooned; they kept their chocolates as sacred relics, until they crumbled moldily away. Georgi Balanchivadze was thrilled, too, but he ate his chocolates.

If Georgi Balanchivadze was not aware then that a great revolution was brewing, he was not the only one. Many of those whose profession it was to keep informed about political and social matters did not anticipate that upheaval. Even after it began, most people were slow to recognize the significance of what was happening. On March 8, 1917, that historic day when the Russian Revolution broke out, the chief topic of conversation among guests at a dinner party at the French Embassy in St. Petersburg, the topic that aroused the most fervor and debate, according to the memoirs of the French ambassador, Maurice Paléologue, was which of the exquisite ballerinas who had graced the Maryinsky stage could be considered the very finest—Pavlova, Karsavina, or Kschessinska. And a friend of Kerensky's recalled standing on the Troitsky bridge late one night in November of that year, as Bolshevik troops bombarded the nearby Winter Palace in the crucial action that was to topple the Kerensky provisional government and bring the Bolsheviks to power, and being told by an acquaintance that it was a shame he had missed Chaliapin in *Don Carlos* at the Maryinsky that night—the basso had been in glorious voice.

With the triumph of the Bolsheviks, the ballet school's isolation from the harsh realities of the world outside came to an end. One day Red sailors came through the dormitories looking for czarist agents and counter-revolutionaries. Not long afterward the school itself was shut down, and the ballet company disbanded, as a decadent, counter-revolutionary institution, a vain burden on the honest masses, an unwanted luxury, and an offensive symbol of the despised old regime. The students were turned out to get along as best they could.

Georgi was then not quite fourteen. For a short while he lived with his mother, brother, and sister in an apartment on Bolshoi Moskovska Street, next to the lodgings his Aunt Nadia occupied. His father had gone to Tiflis, where he became the minister of culture in the brief-lived Georgian Republic that was established in the spring of 1918. Early that year all of the family except Georgi managed to make their way to Tiflis to join him. Georgi was left with his Aunt Nadia to be available in case the school should reopen. He would never see his parents or sister again.

To help support himself and his aunt during the times of terrible privation now being endured, Georgi put his hand to whatever he could. He worked as a messenger and then as a saddler's assistant, his job being to stitch the canvas pieces of horses' girths and bellybands. Evenings, for a while, he worked as the house pianist for a small, shabby movie theatre in a remote part of the city, to accompany the flickery, silent one-reelers of the German comic dandy Max Linder, the best-known predecessor of Charlie Chaplin. These labors of Georgi's were not for money, money having become meaningless, but for whatever scraps of food his employers could spare or for whatever he might be able to trade for something to eat—some matches or some soap, perhaps, that might be bartered for a crust of bread; or some coffee grounds that he might succeed in trading for potato peels with which to thicken a watery soup.

His plight was not unique. Nearly everyone was desperate. One day Georgi witnessed a sight he never forgot. A near skeleton of a horse, drawing a wagon, dropped dead in the street—perhaps from exhaustion, possibly from some disease. Nobody stopped to inquire. From all the houses on the street people rushed out with knives and began hacking up the corpse, for meat. Within a few minutes there was nothing left. By the middle of 1918 few cats or dogs were to be seen in St. Petersburg—or rather Petrograd, as it had become. Most pets had gone into the stew pot. Rats were abundant, though; for them conditions were ideal.

Sometimes Georgi, along with one or another of his friends from the school, would creep under cover of darkness to the army barges docked along the Neva to pilfer what rations they could. Once Georgi and a companion stole a large fish, which the other boy hid in his blouse. As they left, strolling past the Red Army sentry with careful casualness, the fish suddenly revived and began flopping about inside the boy's blouse. They took to their heels, the other boy beating his bosom with his fist to stun his plunder, and Georgi's heart leaping in his own breast, like the fish, as he ran.

It was ludicrous but no game. Martial law was in effect, and they could have been shot as looters. Civil war raged. There were barricades in the streets. More than once Georgi, as he went about the city, had to duck into a doorway to avoid stray bullets from some skirmish or riot. At one time, when it looked as if the White forces, supported by a British gun-boat on the Neva just outside of Petrograd, were about to launch a full-scale attack on the city, Georgi and other boys his age were marched out to one of the city squares, given a rudimentary training in the use of arms, and told where to report if the attack materialized. Fortunately for him, he never had to put this hastily acquired knowledge to use.

One wonders what effect his experiences during this period must have had in the shaping of his character. Undoubtedly self-sufficiency, re-sourcefulness, and adaptability were fostered in him then, and the lesson that most people never have to learn: that simply to survive can be a considerable achievement. It is likely that a strong strain of fatalism in Balanchine's character was reinforced during those years, and a kind of ultimate aloofness and untouchability that friends sensed despite his good humor—an emotional independence which, in the opinion of some who knew him, amounted to an indifference so fundamental as to be cruel.

Whenever he could during those days, Georgi would go over to The-atre Street. An army unit was stationed in the school, but the street was the meeting place where he could expect to find his friends and former schoolmates, among them such as Leonid Lavrovsky, who in later life was to become chief choreographer of the Bolshoi Ballet, and Pyotr Gusev, who became head of the Bolshoi's choreographic school. They would look to see if any notices had been put up regarding the reopening of the school and would share with each other rumors they had heard. From there they might go off together through the city to scrounge for scraps of food. One day, when they had begun to give up hope of ever seeing it, they found posted on the wall the notice they had been looking for: the announcement that the school was to reopen. This had been brought about through the efforts of Anatole Lunacharsky, the Bolshevik commissar for education, who was a man of considerable culture and who happened to be something of a balletomane. Lunacharsky managed to convince Lenin that such arts as ballet and opera were not *inherently* decadent or all the other contemptuous things the Bolsheviks had said they were, but rather could be considered a sublime heritage of the Russian proletariat, which the aristocracy had stolen from the people and perverted, and that, when properly used—that is, for propaganda purposes—these arts could be as valuable to society as a pig-iron factory. This interesting conversation may well have occurred amid the gilt and fluted splendors of a palace that the Grand Duke André had built for Kschessinska, for the Bolsheviks had taken the ballerina's palace over and made it their party headquarters. It had been from Kschessinska's balcony that Lenin, upon winning power, had made his first important address to the public. Among the crowd in the street below on that momentous occasion had been young Georgi Balanchivadze, thoroughly bewildered by the changes that were taking place.

His bewilderment continued during the first performances he appeared in after the school and theatre were reopened. For a time the dancers— these former members of the czar's household whose education had included such refinements as how much more profound a bow one makes to a grand duke than to a simple duke—were called on to perform only at Communist party meetings, some of which were held in the Maryinsky Theatre, with the functionaries at a long table on the stage and the rest of the delegates seated in the auditorium. Bits of ballet—the hoop dance from *The Nutcracker,* perhaps, or the Hindu dance from *Bayaderka*— would be served up as postludes to four or five hours of debate on, say, the menace of Menshevik deviationism. It was all very strange. While waiting to dance, Georgi would stand in the wings intently observing what was going on, just as in the very same place a few years before he had stood watching *The Sleeping Beauty.* The debates—grim, involved, devious, tedious—scarcely worked the same magic on him; but they made an impression. Years afterward, he could, on occasion, give a telling imitation, both ludicrous and frightening, of a Trotsky harangue he once heard from the Maryinsky wings.

Eventually regular performances were resumed at the Maryinsky, renamed now The State Academic Theatre for Opera and Ballet. Under the circumstances, it was remarkable that the Bolshevik government was willing to allot any portion of its meager budget for such activities. There was no fuel to heat the theatre, even when the temperature dropped below zero. The audience sat bundled in fur and sheepskin coats, stamping their booted feet to warm them; the dancers, in their flimsy costumes, were in constant danger of being frozen to the spot whenever they held a pose, and as they moved about, clouds of steam puffed from their mouths and nostrils. At the school, the boys were sometimes given the day off to go out and hunt for wood to burn. They made shirts out of the velvet draperies as their clothes wore out. For food, it was a feast to celebrate when they could get horse lungs, neck, or heart for a stew. "Everything was free in those days—streetcar rides, food, goods—because the millennium was here, the ideal society had been achieved," Balanchine later wryly recalled. "The only trouble was that there wasn't anything. No streetcars, no food, no nothing."

Instead of being transported luxuriously to the theatre in court coaches on performance nights, the children now were expected to walk. It was good revolutionary discipline for them. In time, the authorities relented—this may have been Lunacharsky's doing again, or that of the new theatre director, a scholarly Communist with the apologetic-sounding name of Excusovitch—and the old court coaches came back, but stripped of the double-eagle emblem. One day, Lunacharsky himself took a hand in the process of helping these former protégés of the czar adjust to the new conceptions of society. He took the children to a showing of D. W. Griffith's *Intolerance,* translating the subtitles into Russian for them as the film went along. Thus, in an environment that was an incongruous and unresolved mixture of the old and the new—of royal modes and revolutionary ferment, of classes in the elegant, aristocratic, and thoroughly artificial conception of movement known as ballet carried on amid near-starvation conditions on behalf now of Marxist materialism and the proletarian masses—Georgi Balanchivadze pursued his last years at the school.

A reminiscence of him as an upper-grade student during those curious years after the revolution was set on paper for me in 1963 by Vera Kostrovitskaya, senior instructor of classical ballet at the school, who some forty years before had been a fellow student, in a class three years below Balanchivadze's:

"I remember," she writes, "a slender youth with a fine, pale Georgian

Graduation picture of the class of 1921. Georgi is standing, second from right.

face, straight dark hair and irreproachably polite and modest manners. He never teased us little ones nor despised us but acted as if we were equals and of the same age, though in those early years a difference of three classes was enormous. Among the students he was noted for his extraordinary understanding of music. He could never pass with indifference by any musical instrument. The minute he came down to our floor of the school the sounds of a piano would be heard from one of the big rehearsal halls—that would be Balanchivadze improvising or playing the most difficult compositions while waiting for the rehearsal to begin. Sometimes, in the evening, we would secretly climb the stairs to listen to Balanchivadze playing Liszt, Chopin or Beethoven in the boys' quarters above us. Whatever he played, one could always feel a sort of special, exciting inspiration. There was no doubt that Balanchivadze was a young man of many talents, though it was not yet clear how his talents would further develop."

To Georgi Balanchivadze himself it was not yet clear either how his talents would develop or how he wanted them to. Upon graduation from the school, with honors, in 1921, he was taken into the ballet company as a member of the corps de ballet; but at the same time he enrolled in the Petrograd Conservatory of Music—which happened to be located just across the street from the theatre—and for the next three years, while carrying on his dance activities, studied musical theory and piano. He was at the time strongly tempted to become a musician rather than a dancer. Such hesitation on the part of a young man on the threshold of his career, before finally committing himself to what later would seem to have been inevitable, is not at all unusual. Fokine, at the same point in his life, studied painting for a year, feeling that the dance, as institutionalized in the Russian ballet, was not taken seriously enough to be thought of as a career for one who wished to be a true artist. He had circulated a questionnaire among the members of the ballet company asking them for their definition of ballet, and he was much discouraged by their responses. "Pornography, pure and simple," replied one dancer.

If Fokine could have his doubts about a ballet career at a period in Russian ballet history when the institution was so securely established, how much more reason did Balanchivadze have to be doubtful, graduating as he did at a time when all was in upheaval. In the state of flux that then prevailed, the direction of the theatre and school was lax and irresolute as to policy; rehearsals were irregular; remuneration for the dancers was scant. Occasionally, some members of the company would get together to talk about the situation, saying to each other, "We must all do what we can to preserve ballet," but not all of them were so certain, when they thought of it, that there really ought to be any place for so antiquated a form as ballet in a revolutionary new society. Georgi himself was by no means sure, his own dance ideas at the time of his graduation being also of a revolutionary nature, far from the classical ideal.

All that aside, if Georgi could have become a worthwhile composer, that is what he would rather have been than anything else in the world. All his life, composition was for him the loftiest of the arts; he was sure that the highest seats in heaven were set aside for the great composers. At the conservatory, he tried his hand at composition, urged on by encouraging letters from his composer father, but he was dispassionately perceptive enough to recognize that he would never be a composer of significance. All this intensive musical training, such as no other choreographer has ever had, was to prove invaluable to him when the dance reclaimed his undivided allegiance. Musically, he might, if he had chosen, have become a conductor or a pianist, once he had given up his dream of composing, for he possessed talent enough. Fortunately, he did not. As Igor Stravinsky later said on this point, "The world is full of pretty good concert pianists but a choreographer such as Balanchine is, after all, the rarest of beings."

CHAPTER FOUR

First Choreography

Balanchine could never remember when he first decided he would become a choreographer or that, in fact, he ever consciously made such a decision. The deed preceded the wish. "In the old days," he once said to me, "you first were a choreographer and then you became one"—meaning that you made up dances long before thinking of yourself as destined to be anything special, whereas nowadays artistically inclined youths have been known to announce themselves as would-be choreographers before they have taken a single dancing lesson. He was sixteen when, on the occasion of one of the school concerts in the little theatre there, he made his first serious choreographic essay, a love duet, set to "La Nuit," Anton Rubinstein's duet for violin and piano. When I asked Balanchine about it many years later, he thought it was he who danced the first performance with a girl whose name he could not remember. Pyotr Gusev has said, however, that the piece was created for him and Olga Mungalova. It became part of their repertory when they became professional dancers, and the work survived in the Soviet Union for many years. At its first performance, it created a minor furor. One straitlaced staff member condemned it as a "scandal of eroticism" and favored dismissing Georgi from the school. Of this work, Balanchine commented to the British ballet devotee and critic Arnold Haskell, during an interview some thirty years later, "As I remember it today, it would be perfectly suitable for presentation in a young ladies' seminary. I thought it very daring at the time." The outraged puritanism of the staff member who wished Georgi disciplined was not shared by the head of the school, who was taken by the work and was strongly impressed, not only

At twenty.

53

by the abilities the dance revealed but also by the initiative Georgi had shown in conceiving and carrying out this project all on his own. Such creative enterprise on the part of a student was a rarity in that academy. The director told the other upper-grade students that he hoped Balanchivadze's example would inspire some of them to creative efforts of their own.

Whether others were inspired by his example or not, Balanchivadze himself continued to make up dances now at every opportunity. He choreographed a duet to Fritz Kreisler's *Schön Rosmarin,* which was performed in the spring of 1920 at the ballet school's graduation performance. Shortly afterward he choreographed another romantic duet— *Poème,* to music by Zdeněk Fibich—that he danced with Danilova. He designed the costumes himself. Danilova's was of a light-blue transparent material. One of Balanchivadze's schoolmates, Marietta Frangopulo, who eventually became the curator of the academy's museum and library in Leningrad, saw this duet danced and four decades later wrote: "There are some themes and impressions which are remembered throughout one's life. The dance to Fibich's 'Poem' is one of those—it remains in my memory as something beautiful and poetic." Kostrovitskaya also recalled it in her reminiscence of Balanchivadze. "The choreography of the beginning of this piece," she wrote, "was extraordinary for that epoch: Balanchivadze came out on stage carrying Danilova, who was weightlessly reclining on his shoulder and arms." Equally innovative and memorable was the choreography of the end, with Danilova lifted high in arabesque as Balanchine carried her off. "One had the impression," Kostrovitskaya wrote in an account included by Yuri Slonimsky in a memoir of Balanchine he wrote in 1975 for *Ballet Review,* "that she herself, without a partner's support, was gliding through the air away from the audience to finish 'singing' her dance somewhere far, far away." The piece won great public success. It was given at numerous concerts, and the audience always demanded it be repeated as an encore.

Another of his early essays was a duet to a waltz he had composed. A performance of this piece, incidentally, received a mention in a Leningrad periodical, *Theatre and Art News,* June 11, 1922. This is the first review to be found in print of a Balanchine ballet. ". . . on the last night, a special attraction was *Valse,* music and choreography by G. M. Balanchivadze, executed by A. D. Danilova and the author. The first name speaks for itself; G. M. Balanchivadze proved to be a talented composer, choreographer and dancer. Such a combination is a rare one, promising him much in the future." The performance mentioned here took place at one of the pavilions in the suburbs where concerts and dance programs were often given during the summer. In addition to their appearances at the State Theatre, the company's dancers frequently performed at various benefits and other entertainments. There was one Red Army charity performance around that time at which the former prima ballerina of the Maryinsky, Olga Preobrajenska, was the featured artist. A great favorite with the populace, she was then over fifty but still full of verve. For her partner on this occasion, she chose the young Balanchivadze—a great honor for him—and the two of them whirled through a tarantella, while the audience cheered. Her honorarium for the performance was a loaf of bread. She gave half to her young partner, who accepted gratefully. Years later, when I asked him what Preobrajenska was like then, he said, "She was a little old woman with no neck, like a monkey. It was very nice dancing with her. She had a profound mind. She was like a cardinal."

A year or so after his graduation, Balanchivadze gathered a group of about fifteen young dancers and began preparing a program that was to be the first in a series called Evenings of the Young Ballet. The group included such youthful talent as Alexandra Danilova, Lydia Ivanova, Leonid Lavrovsky, Pyotr Gusev, Vera Kostrovitskaya, Nina Stukolkina, Nicholas Efimov, Olga Mungalova, Tamara Gevergeva, and Mikhail Mikhailov—most of them fledgling members of the state ballet company, a few still students. He was aided in organizing this project by a gifted young painter named Vladimir Dimitriev. Another who participated was Yuri Slonimsky, later to become an eminent Soviet ballet critic, who was in those years one of Georgi's closest friends. His friendship brought Georgi not only companionship, encouragement, and advice but also an occasional and most welcome meal at the home of Slonimsky's parents, including—the Slonimskys being Jewish—one memorable Purim feast.

For the forthcoming ballet program, the young dancers sewed their own costumes. They met in their spare time, whenever they were free from performances or rehearsals at the State Theatre, and worked till late at night on the new dances Balanchivadze was choreographing. "We had confidence in Balanchivadze," one of them later said. "Gentle and shy as he was, he yet had authority among us." They felt they were creating something such as had never been seen before.

It was an extraordinary period for the arts in Russia. There was no

Two moments from Marche Funèbre—Stukolkina kneeling, Kostrovitskaya on points. These pictures are among the earliest photographs extant of Balanchine choreography.

censorship, tradition had been dethroned, experimentation was applauded. Mayakovsky, Esenin, Pasternak, Babel, and others were expressing themselves spontaneously in new literary forms; Malevitch and Kandinsky were developing the conceptions of abstract painting they had asserted, and, indeed, it was in Petrograd in 1919 that the very first abstract canvas—Malevitch's White on White—was exhibited; Prokofiev was composing some of his freshest scores; stage designers were experimenting with constructivism and other unusual approaches to theatre decor; Eisenstein was making Potemkin. Not until Lenin's death and Stalin's consolidation of power did the arts become bureaucratized and fettered to a rigid ideology. Later Soviet histories invariably deal with this pre-Stalin period in solemnly patronizing terms: "a rash and turbulent era . . . novelty for its own sake . . . individualist self-indulgence . . . deformations of natural beauty, distortions of reality," and so on. Yuri Slonimsky—an older and more conservative Slonimsky than the one who collaborated with Balanchine on the Evenings of the Young Ballet—

strikes the conventional note in his work *Bolshoi Theatre Ballet,* published in 1952: "In the 1920's Soviet Ballet went through all the phases of barefoot naturalism, strident constructivism, unnatural plastic expressionism and erotic orientalism. But time and reality, as usual, exposed the fallacy of the then prevailing conceptions."

The first program of the Evenings of the Young Ballet was to be in the form of a demonstration in three parts, the last and longest part of the evening being devoted to Balanchivadze's works—among the new ones being dances to some of Ravel's *Valses Nobles et Sentimentales;* a composition of Balanchivadze's own entitled *Extase;* and, as the young choreographer's major opus to date, *Marche Funèbre,* to the music of Chopin. The program was grandly entitled "The Evolution of Ballet: From Petipa through Fokine to Balanchivadze." Pretentious titles treating the new epoch as the culmination of all history were common in those days. The funny thing is that this one turns out to have been not so farfetched.

Of the influences that formed Balanchine choreographically, Petipa's was undoubtedly the most significant. From Petipa were derived such characteristics of Balanchine's mature work as the frank delight in the classic dance for its own sake, the elegant grace of deportment of the dancers, the conception of ballet primarily as a means of giving pleasure and not as a vehicle for transmitting a portentous message. As manifested in Balanchine's ballets, however, these characteristics were usually presented in a distinctly contemporary manner, generally without the framework of the elaborate story or spectacle in which Petipa embedded his moments of dance. The aspects derived from Petipa were, in Balanchine's work, transformed, concentrated, intensified, accelerated, modernized.

It was to be some years before Balanchine developed to the point of acknowledging or revealing these traits or the influence of Petipa, or of recognizing Petipa's ideals as, in part, his own. In his school years and as a beginning dancer, classicism had not much interested him. His preference as a youngster had been for the more flamboyant national dances. Virtually nothing of Petipa showed in *Marche Funèbre, Extase,* or the other dances the young choreographer was devising for his first program of the Young Ballet. The Petipa material was then present within him, but buried. He had stored Petipa up in his very muscles, having danced in nearly all the Petipa ballets, since they were predominant in the Maryinsky repertory. Though in time he would draw on this glittering heritage for his own purposes, it was only natural that, as a youth demonstrating his capabilities for the first time and during an epoch of revolution, he should seek to assert himself in quite different ways.

Fokine did not influence him much, with one significant exception. A number of Fokine ballets were in the Maryinsky repertory, and Fokine himself, after breaking with Diaghilev, returned to the Maryinsky, where he worked from 1914 to 1918, when he left Russia for the last time. It was during that time that Balanchivadze, age thirteen, had the opportunity to work under Fokine's direction in *La Jota Aragonese*. The Fokine ballet that affected young Balanchivadze most, though, and planted a seed in him, was *Chopiniana* (or *Les Sylphides*, as it is known outside of Russia). Seeing this ballet as a youth, Balanchivadze was captivated and intrigued. He had never before seen a ballet that evoked a mood just by dancing, without any story, and he kept puzzling over it, trying to figure out what it meant and, in accordance with his training and experience, supply a more literal reading of it than was intended. At that time, as a boy, he took it for granted that all ballets were required to tell a story; later in life he was to make the storyless ballet his most characteristic medium. In this respect, *Chopiniana* is more characteristic of Balanchine's own main line of development than of Fokine's. For this was one of the few storyless ballets Fokine made in his life; he did it, as he has said, just to show that he could if he wanted to; the rest of his career was devoted to his efforts to give ballet *more* explicit content and meaning, not less.

For Fokine, and for his generation, one of the most powerful of experiences had been that of seeing Isadora Duncan dance, when she first visited St. Petersburg in 1905. She left Fokine and other members of the ballet company questioning their own approach to the dance. They had learned to be cool, formal, professional. Isadora, in her filmy drapes and rapt air, offered the virtues of inspiration, improvisation, freedom, soul. For them the dance was theatre, for her ritual. They regarded the dancer as an entertainer, she as a high priestess. They found her very convincing. Balanchivadze too saw Duncan, but she did not make that sort of impression on him. It was 1922 when he saw her. She had come to Russia at the invitation of Commissar Lunacharsky to establish a Duncan school of the dance, for which Lunacharsky had promised in a rash moment to put a thousand children at her disposal, a promise he did not find it convenient to keep. In 1922, at the age of forty-four, she was still an extraordinary personality, with a fervor for complete revolution that none of the Bolshevik leaders could match. Swathed in her red Marseillaise scarf, she went about Moscow and Petrograd, accosting the Bolshevik leaders and calling them bourgeoisie in disguise because she found them listening to operas and giving receptions amid elegant salons, such as Kschessinska's palace. "Give me your children," she would cry to the astonished Bolsheviks, "and I will teach them to dance like gods—or you may assassinate me!"

Nevertheless, despite the vividness of her personality, she was past her peak as a dancer. To Balanchivadze's eyes she was unbelievably ludicrous and incompetent. In an interview printed in *Horizon* magazine many years later, he cruelly summarized how she had appeared to him: "To me it was absolutely unbelievable—a drunken, fat woman who for hours was rolling around like a pig. It was the most awful thing." Balanchivadze could not believe that she had ever been a good dancer. For him inspiration was never a satisfactory substitute for technique.

If there was an avowed and discernible influence on the choreography of the youthful Balanchivadze then, it was that of Kasyan Goleizovsky. Little known in the Western world, Goleizovsky attained both fame and notoriety in the Soviet Union during the turbulent twenties. A product of the St. Petersburg imperial ballet academy, from which he graduated in 1909, Goleizovsky served as *premier danseur* of the Bolshoi Ballet until, becoming dissatisfied with the aesthetics of classical ballet, he resigned to establish his own school in Moscow and found a chamber dance group to put his dance conceptions into practice. Like Fokine, he had felt acutely that the classic ballet, as it was then institutionalized in Russia's major theatres, had become superficial and devoid of any significant creative impulse—sustaining itself only by the technical excellence of the performers, the sumptuousness of decor and spectacle, and the chic unconcern of the kind of languid, aristocratic audience it attracted. He preached—and with all the fervor of a gospel preacher—the development of an art of pure dance, one exalting the human body and revealing itself not in a chain of stereotyped steps but in fluid, unfolding motion. To this end, he chose for his dances not the kind of rhythmically obvious music that classical ballet had almost always preferred but subtle, sensuous music of a complicated rhythmical nature—Scriabin, Debussy, Richard Strauss, Prokofiev. His troupe danced barefoot and scantily clad; in an art form in which the human body is the expressive medium there should be as little costume hiding and encumbering it as possible, he declared. The choreography utilized fluid, plastic, sometimes acrobatic movements. The effects achieved were startling and, according to many contemporary accounts, sometimes extraordinarily beautiful. Golei-

zovsky himself was a strange, powerful figure—romantic, temperamental, iconoclastic. It was undoubtedly he who was most in the critic Slonimsky's mind when he damned in retrospect the dance directions of the twenties, for he was certainly the most prominent innovator of the times. A work of his, *The Legend of Joseph the Beautiful*, was produced at the Bolshoi in 1925, creating a great sensation, but not long after that the heavy hand of Soviet conformism began to make itself felt, and Goleizovsky was pushed from the great state stages into obscurity.

Balanchivadze saw a performance in Petrograd at the old Hall of the Nobles by Goleizovsky's group in 1921, when he was just graduating from the ballet school. Some of the older members of the audience were scandalized by what they saw that evening, but on Balanchivadze an immediate and overwhelming impression was made. After the performance he rushed backstage to congratulate Goleizovsky and tell him how moved he had been. It was this occasion that gave Balanchivadze the impetus to found his own chamber group of the Young Ballet some months later, and the images of Goleizovsky's dances were very much in his mind as he worked on his own choreography for the forthcoming performance. "Seeing Goleizovsky was what first gave me the courage to try something different on my own," he later said.

The performance for the first program of Evenings of the Young Ballet was scheduled for June 1, 1923. As the date approached, the youthful participants scarcely took time out to sleep, so engrossed had they become in this adventure. For their theatre, they somehow obtained the hall of the Duma, or city parliament, on the Nevsky Prospect—an enormous round hall with steep banks of seats entirely surrounding the space used for the stage. It had been turned, after the revolution, into a hall for conferences and lectures; Mayakovsky, Esenin, and Blok had appeared there and read their poems to the public. For their first performance, Balanchivadze and his associates had done little to advertise other than prepare a poster; they consequently did not expect much of an audience. But word got around. To the astonishment of Balanchivadze and the others, the hall was filled with spectators. A great many young people were present—students, actors, artists, even young workers. "The success was so great that we could hardly believe it," recalled Kostrovitskaya. As the performance went on from one new work to the next, the audience's excitement grew. None of the spectators seemed able to watch

∽ *With Tamara Geva in 1923, dancing his pas de deux* Etude, *to music by Scriabin, or possibly* Enigma, *to music by Arensky.*

with calm indifference. From some of the older, conservative members of the audience came whistles of disapproval. The younger people cheered vociferously, cried out for encores, and demanded a bow from the choreographer.

As an event in the life of the city, this performance created a sensation such as nobody had anticipated. "The whole town started talking of Balanchivadze," wrote Kostrovitskaya in her memoir of him. The attention being paid him was additionally stimulated now by a severe condemnation of him and his works, penned by Akim Volynsky, the most learned and distinguished ballet historian and authority in all of Russia. As a critic, Volynsky was consistent. He had witnessed Fokine's first effort in 1905 and had hated that, too.

Instead of accepting this rebuke like a chastised schoolboy, as he was supposed to, Balanchivadze penned a counterattack of his own. This article was not a defense of his own choreographic works, but a scathing discussion of Volynsky's—for the critic had made the mistake recently of opening up a choreographic school of his own and thus laid himself wide open to the kind of treatment he had been accustomed to meting out to others. Balanchivadze called his article "How Mr. Volynsky Flogged Himself," parodying a phrase from Gogol's *The Inspector General*. It appeared in the magazine *Teatr,* and the cover of that issue, December 11, 1923, consisted of a photograph of Balanchivadze.

The face that gazed from the cover of *Teatr*—intense, poetic, with brooding dark eyes and disheveled hair—was that of a young Byron or Chopin. It was a look assiduously cultivated by the nineteen-year-old Balanchivadze, as well as by many of his artistic contemporaries—particularly those of the group he belonged to who liked to call themselves The Feks, an abbreviation standing for The Fabricators of Eccentricities, Incorporated. Balanchivadze carried the Chopinesque style through by dressing in black garb, letting his hair grow long, and cultivating dark, mournful circles under his eyes. With the pervasive hunger and physical deprivation of the era, it was not difficult to acquire dark circles under one's eyes, but some of Balanchivadze's friends thought he was not above using the makeup pot to add to the effect on dramatic occasions.

One problem he had, though, was that his natural gaiety, liveliness, and risibility kept asserting themselves just at a time when a true Chopin would have been a very model of romantic melancholy. It wasn't so easy

G. M. Balanchivadze, as he appeared on the cover of Teatr *for December 11, 1923.*

ТЕАТР

ЕЖЕНЕДЕЛЬНИК

НОМЕР 11

Г. М. БАЛАНЧИВАДЗЕ
...возрождению „Молодого балета".

...ена 30 коп. золотом

11 декабря 1923

to be gloomy, try as one might. Among his friends he was as cherished for his spontaneous flights of humor and fantasy as he was for his more serious activities. One fanciful exploit of his was an episode that took place at the State Theatre, where he was then a corps de ballet member with an occasional small solo role. In the ballet *Esmeralda* he was given the part of a tramp to play. When he appeared onstage, it was to be seen at a glance that he had made himself up to look exactly like the artistic director of the theatre, one V. P. Rapoport, a short man with a large head, adorned on the pate with long hair and at the chin with a dapper goatee—in appearance and mannerisms very much resembling a Spanish grandee in an operetta. Balanchivadze had not merely managed to look like Rapoport but while doing his dance succeeded in suggesting Rapoport's mannerisms as well. Throughout this impersonation stifled sobs of laughter could be heard from what had been the czar's box in the theatre but which after the revolution had become the box assigned for the use of artists of the opera and ballet companies. Fortunately for Balanchivadze, Rapoport had enough of a sense of humor not to punish him for his impertinence.

As behooves a romantic youth, Balanchivadze was passionately in love in those days. The object of his ardor was a flaxen-haired girl, two years younger than he. Her name was Tamara Gevergeva (a name that was eventually changed, for professional purposes, to Geva). Only fifteen when they met, she was a beauty. Tartar and Turkish blood on her father's side and Swedish on her mother's mingled in Tamara to striking effect. She was tall and had a breathtaking figure; her face was Nordic in its features but with an exotic hint of the Oriental about the cheekbones and eyes. Her personality was vivacious, and she was interested not just in dance but in other arts as well—poetry, drama, music, painting.

She was taking evening classes at the ballet school. One evening a slim, graceful young man, with aquiline features and long dark hair, came into the studio with the school's director during a class on ballroom dancing. The young man asked the instructor if he could join the other boys for the quadrille. Somehow, with scarcely a word, he took command of the lesson and began inventing patterns and combinations. What had begun as a stiff, formal lesson, she later wrote, "became a lark." The young man seemed to her "a combination of poet and general." That was her first meeting with Georgi Balanchivadze.

They began filling small dancing engagements together at one or another of the little nightclubs that had sprung up about the city during the past year, since the proclamation of N.E.P. (the New Economic Policy permitting a temporary return to private enterprise in modest form). Tamara had a pleasant singing voice, of the German cabaret type; at some of the clubs she would sing and Balanchivadze would accompany her at the piano. These engagements brought them in a little much-needed income.

At Tamara's home, when he called on her, Balanchivadze found a welcome and stimulating environment. Her father, Levko Gevergeyev, was an interesting figure. He had made a fortune in czarist days from the manufacture of gold lamé for ecclesiastical vestments and from the sale of other religious items; it was not the sort of trade that could be expected to survive a materialistic revolution. Gevergeyev's interest in these religious objects had always been pecuniary and aesthetic, for his own father had been a Mohammedan and he himself was a freethinker. A leading authority on the theatre, he had assembled during his lifetime one of the world's finest collections of theatrical memorabilia and had built an experimental theatre next door to the nine-story building on the Grafsky Pereulok, where he lived and had his factory. He had long been a patron of the arts. After the revolution, when the state confiscated his property, Gevergeyev—as a result of a petition on his behalf by a long list of young intellectuals whom he had befriended and aided—was allowed to remain in it and was appointed director of the museum he had once owned. His home continued to be, after the revolution, a center of the arts and a meeting place for the avant-garde. Here Balanchivadze met Mayakovsky and many others of the artistic world.

Gevergeyev took to young Balanchivadze from the start, thinking him gifted and very promising. Sometimes when Balanchivadze came to the house for Tamara, her father would meet him in the living room and suggest he play a little Wagner on the piano for him before Tamara was summoned from her room. Gevergeyev adored Wagner and considered himself, by this means, to be correcting a deficiency in the youth's education, since Balanchivadze had heard very little of Wagner's music up till then. Gevergeyev would seat the young man at the piano, set before him the score of *Tristan und Isolde* or *Parsifal* or *Tannhäuser* and say, "Come on, my boy, let's hear those sublime opening chords." Balanchivadze would commence, while Gevergeyev, with eyes closed, would settle back in rapture. When, after a time, Balanchivadze would stop, Gevergeyev would open his eyes in surprise and say, "But how can you break off at *that* point, with every chord and tension unresolved?" Or he'd say, "Go on just a little further, will you. I want you to see what a marvelous thing Wagner is about to do here."

With a discreetly concealed sigh, the young suitor would play on and on, while elsewhere in the house waited the fair, white Tamara. One evening he had to play through the whole of *Siegfried* before Tamara's father would let him go. It was an ordeal like that of Jacob, who had to labor twice seven years before being rewarded with Rachel. For Balanchivadze each of these evenings with Wagner was at least seven years long. The ordeal left its mark. He could never stand Wagner thereafter.

As for young Balanchivadze's intentions toward Tamara in those days, they were probably—shall we say?—dishonorable. After all, what other intentions could a self-respecting Bohemian have in the revolutionary new society where bourgeois conventions had been cast off? One day, though, Gevergeyev detained him and Tamara as they were going off, hand in hand, to a dancing engagement, and said to them, "Look here, you children, why don't you two get married?" They stared at him in astonishment. He could see how much they were attracted to each other, he went on, and it would make him feel easier if they would take his suggestion. Then he wouldn't have to worry about what they were up to, or whether he should try to play the stern father and forbid them to see each other, particularly since he doubted he could make that stick. It would be easier for them, too. They wouldn't have to have furtive meetings—they could live right here at the house. "If the times were different, I wouldn't even permit such a thing, let alone suggest it. But these are very strange times. One must adjust as best one can. So—what do you say?"

The two young people looked at each other, trying to keep straight faces. To have this solemn idea popped at them like that—it was really very funny! "Well," said Balanchivadze after a moment, with an impulsive gesture, "why not?"

"Yes," echoed Tamara, "why not?"

"Good!" said Gevergeyev. "That's a load off my mind."

The next day they went out and found a dingy, cluttered bureau where a bored Soviet functionary scribbled a few words on a piece of paper for them. In accord with Georgi's wishes, they followed this with a religious ceremony. And so the two "children," as Gevergeyev had called them, Tamara not yet sixteen and Balanchivadze all of eighteen, became husband and wife.

* * *

Throughout 1923 and the spring of 1924, Balanchivadze continued his choreographic efforts in a variety of forms and for whatever stages he could find. He was in great demand. He staged the Milhaud-Cocteau *Boeuf sur le Toit* as a pantomime for the Petrograd Free Theatre. For the Alexandrinsky Theatre he did a dance in silhouette for Ernst Toller's *The Broken Brow* and dances and pantomime for Shaw's *Caesar and Cleopatra*. For The Carousel, an intellectual cabaret that had opened in Petrograd, he devised movement for poems set to music. For a charity concert given at the State Theatre he and his new wife danced a duet he had composed to music by Arensky. He called it *Enigma*. It was danced barefoot and was most likely the first such number ever performed on that august stage. The Maly Opera Theatre had engaged him as a ballet master, and he staged the dances for that company's production of *Le Coq d'Or*, which was given its premiere on December 11, 1923. All of this activity took place while he continued to perform as a dancer in the State Theatre's ballet and opera productions and while also working as a rehearsal pianist at the school three hours a day to earn additional income.

By now, he had become interested in Stravinsky's music. He had begun rehearsing *Pulcinella* with his Young Ballet group, and he was eager to choreograph a major work for the State Theatre company. He asked an administrator at the State Theatre for permission to stage *Le Sacre du Printemps*. "We'll see," the administrator said.

Late in 1923, another program of the Evenings of the Young Ballet was presented at the Duma hall, this one even more experimental than the first. The program featured, in addition to various dance works, a presentation of Alexander Blok's strange, mystical poem *The Twelve*, about the twelve Red Guards, at whose head Christ takes His place at the end. To stylized movement choreographed by Balanchivadze, a chorus of fifty voices chanted this and other poems, without music. The performers were dressed in national costumes. For the dancers, such novel movement concepts posed difficult problems, but as one of them—Nina Stukolkina—later wrote, "We young people believed in Balanchivadze's talent and were ready to perform any and every one of his conceptions as a ballet master."

The authorities of the State Theatre were less enthusiastic, however, as were the city's conservative balletomanes and critics such as Volynsky. To them, such work as Balanchivadze's and Goleizovsky's represented a kind of heresy, a dangerous threat to the precious traditions they strove to preserve amid the chaos of the revolution. The authorities let it be known that they disapproved of their company dancers participating in such outside activities as the Evenings of the Young Ballet. The young dancers seemed not to have been cowed, for they continued to give frequent performances in and about Petrograd. A review of one of these performances in the May 20, 1924, edition of *Krasnaya Gazeta* speaks of Balanchivadze as still searching for a style and speculates on his future:

"Yesterday's performance gave the full measure of the creative range of the young ballet master from strict classical adagio to fox-trot. His program to date has been based on his able combination of both extremes. It is difficult to see at what stage of his artistic career he will finally find himself but his creative efforts have already brought a fresh impact to ballet which will continue to make itself felt and the influence of which cannot be halted.

"Balanchivadze is sometimes daring, even audacious, but his audacity contains real creation and includes real beauty. Balanchivadze has not been as successful in his staging of national dances as he has in classical and abstract dances. His national dances lack color, brightness and strong temperamental movements. In classical dancing he overburdens the choreography with plastic poses at the expense of the dance itself, but he manages to produce such beautiful and unexpected effects that one cannot help overlooking his shortcomings."

Slonimsky, in his *Ballet Review* memoir, made note of how innovative Balanchivadze was from the start and what a strong influence he had on his contemporaries. Into the classical ballet vocabulary Balanchivadze introduced elements from the popular dance, from acrobatic acts, from the cabaret, from Goleizovsky, and even—thinks Slonimsky—from Isadora Duncan. Among his innovations were the high lifts, which later became a cliché of Soviet choreography.

If not checkmated by State Theatre disapproval, young Balanchivadze did nevertheless feel himself in check at that time. It was apparent he could expect no encouragement for doing the kind of work he wanted to do under the auspices of the state. It is possible that despite the extreme physical hardships of life in Russia at that period and the increasingly baleful political atmosphere, he might not have chosen to become an exile from his homeland if only he could have been assured of the prospect of being able to work to the fullest extent of his powers there, but this is speculative, for leave Russia he did, and for good, on July 4, 1924.

His departure was made possible by a man named Vladimir Dimitriev (no relation to the young painter mentioned earlier). A former baritone in the Maryinsky opera company, Dimitriev was shrewd and capable, and possessed influential connections in the new bureaucracy. During the N.E.P. period, he had been a croupier at a government gambling casino and had managed to save some foreign exchange. Somehow, he was able to get permission to organize and take abroad for the summer vacation period a small group from the State Theatre, who would be known as the Soviet State Dancers. The group was to include three singers, a conductor and five dancers, the latter being, beside Balanchivadze, Tamara Geva, Alexandra Danilova, Lydia Ivanova, and Nicholas Efimov. Lydia Ivanova was considered as promising a future ballerina as any young dancer to have appeared in many years. She and Danilova were rivals. On June 16, just before the permission for the group to depart was received, she was drowned in a mysterious accident when a boat in which she was paddling on Lake Ladoga was run down by a lake steamer. It was a great loss and cast a pall over the joy the others felt at learning that, after many delays, their exit permits had at last been granted.

The group hurriedly packed to leave before the authorities could change their minds; the packing consisted of putting their costumes into wicker baskets and wrapping their meager personal belongings in brown paper to carry as bundles under their arms. None of the young performers talked openly of this trip as a chance to get out of Russia for good. Quite likely, Dimitriev knew full well what he was going to do from the time he devised the scheme, but the dancers—young and ignorant of the world as they were, and accustomed to living from day to day without trying to shape the future—may not have admitted even to themselves that they harbored such a thought. Nevertheless, as they went to board the ship— a German steamer that was to carry them across the Baltic Sea to the East Prussian port of Stettin—there was more tension among them than a mere vacation tour would warrant. A petty immigration official caused them anxiety at the dock by examining their papers with such leisurely skepticism that they were certain the ship would go off without them. Even when they were aboard and under way, it was a while before they felt secure enough to relax. Danilova, the daughter of an artillery colonel, did not breathe easy, she later said, until the ship had got well beyond the range of the guns at the Russian naval bastion at Kronstadt.

After seven years of semistarvation in revolutionary Russia, the travelers could scarely believe their eyes when they went down to supper and saw on every table baskets of bread and rolls, accompanied by dishes of butter. "It was such a beautiful sight—all that beautiful bread just sitting there like that, so casually, with nobody guarding it—that I almost wept," Balanchine recalled. For the next two and a half days, the group gorged their way across the Baltic Sea. By the time they reached Germany their abiding hunger was somewhat appeased—at least, they had taken the edge off it.

No advance bookings had been made for them. They had not much money and knew nobody, and none of them could speak German. Berlin was quite deserted, since many people were away on vacation. Still the Russians were delighted with everything they saw. To the rest of Europe Berlin was then a drab city, still impoverished from the war. To Balanchivadze and the others, though, it looked dazzlingly prosperous, and to their eyes the dowdy Berliners appeared incredibly chic. They shopped for some clothes here. Balanchivadze tried to buy a hat, but before he was able to find one to fit him he had to go a barber to get his mop of hair shorn. The money that they had brought quickly disappeared. While they were pondering how one went about obtaining a dance engagement in Germany, a telegram arrived from the Soviet Union, ordering the group to return at once. It was a fateful moment of decision. The conductor and the three singers chose dutifully to go home; the young dancers and Dimitriev chose at that point to defect. The Soviet State Dancers company, as they still called themselves, were now down to four; it was a grandiloquent title for a troupe consisting of four youngsters, no scenery, and only a few sleazy homemade costumes.

The resourceful Dimitriev managed to arrange a tour of Rhineland resorts, where they danced wherever they could find an audience—summer theatres, beer gardens, private parties, and even a lunatic asylum. In the autumn Dimitriev got them booked for a month into the Empire Theatre in London, a variety music hall. Among the variety acts they did not make a great hit; they had not learned anything about vaudeville house tempo and their costume changes between dance numbers were too slow. While they were there, an American impresario who was considering booking them wired his British agent and asked him to take a look at their program; the agent did so and wired back that they weren't worth bothering with. The Empire management had come to the same opinion and after two weeks dismissed them.

With no work permit now, they had to leave England. It was early November. They took cheap rooms at a small hotel on the Place de la République in Paris and tried to figure out what to do next. They had just enough money, if they were cautious, to last two weeks. Several days went by, while they became increasingly nervous and gloomy—all except Balanchivadze. He, according to Geva's later account, remained calm and philosophic, as if assured that destiny had plans for him.

At that point a telegram arrived. It was from Serge Diaghilev, who had heard of them and managed to track them down. Ever seeking replenishment for his Ballets Russes, Diaghilev had been particularly interested to learn that among this small troupe was a choreographer, for he was then at odds with his current choreographer, Bronislava Nijinska. The telegram invited them to audition the next day.

The audition was held in the handsome salon of Misia Sert, Diaghilev's confidante and patron. In the salon, waiting majestically for the young Russian dancers, sat Serge Diaghilev, that extraordinary figure who had made a unique impact on the cultural life of Europe and who, as a personality, has been an endless source of speculation and fascination. "His dancers called him Chinchilla," wrote Jean Cocteau, "because of a white streak in his hair, which was dyed deep black. He wrapped himself in a pelisse with an opossum collar and sometimes fastened it with safety-pins. He had the face of a bulldog and the smile of a baby crocodile, with one tooth sticking outside. If he ground his teeth, it was a sign of pleasure, fear or anger. . . . And his moist eyes as they looked downwards were curved like Portuguese oysters."

On Balanchivadze at that first meeting Diaghilev did not impose himself in quite such vivid detail. Balanchivadze noted then simply an impressive-looking gentleman with false teeth and a perfume or hair tonic that was scented with almond blossoms. To tell the truth, the young man was not aware of how awed he should be at this encounter. He had not heard a great deal about Diaghilev or his company while in Russia and assumed as a matter of course that Diaghilev's company was bound to be inferior to the great Maryinsky company in which he had been trained. Danilova was of rather the same mind. She was quite huffy at being asked to dance for an audition—she, a Maryinsky soloist! Still, they complied, and Diaghilev was pleased with what he saw. He asked Balanchivadze if he could make opera ballets very fast—a question that stemmed from the fact that the Ballets Russes had recently been taken under the patronage of the princess of Monaco, with the company dancing in the opera performances at Monte Carlo as well as giving evenings of ballet there. Balanchivadze had made only one opera ballet in his life,

Serge de Diaghileff

but he replied yes, he could—*very* fast. "Good!" Diaghilev said. Within a week, Diaghilev offered to engage all four members of the Soviet troupe in his company as dancers, and they accepted.

A few days later, in London, where the Ballets Russes was having a season at the Coliseum, Diaghilev put a part of the company at Balanchivadze's disposal for the day and, as a test of his abilities, asked him to prepare a demonstration of one of his works. Balanchivadze taught the Diaghilev dancers his *Marche Funèbre.* Ninette de Valois was one of the dancers who took part in this, and she remembers the purposeful competence with which the young man approached the task assigned him. At the end of the day, Diaghilev arrived at the rehearsal hall with his entourage and demanded to see what had been prepared. Imposing, inscrutable, his familiar monocle in place, Diaghilev sat through the performance, taking in every detail. When it was over, he swept out without a word, leaving Balanchivadze and the dancers in total ignorance of his reaction to their efforts. It must have been favorable, however, for shortly afterward, when Nijinska decided to leave the company, Diaghilev let it be known that the newcomer was to take her place. Thus it happened that at the age of twenty-one Georgi Melotonovitch Balanchivadze—or George Balanchine, as he would henceforth be known— found himself ballet master of the most famous and remarkable ballet company in the world.

Serge Diaghilev.

CHAPTER FIVE

Ballet Master to Diaghilev

*I*n a rare moment of retrospection, Balanchine once commented that his education had occurred in two stages. The first took place in Russia, where, at the ballet school and at the Maryinsky Theatre, he learned to love ballet, developed a profound respect for its history, tradition, and fundamental principles and, most significant of all, acquired a mastery of all aspects of ballet technique. The second stage began when he had the good fortune to be taken into Serge Diaghilev's Ballets Russes as the company's ballet master. It was during his four and a half years with Diaghilev that Balanchine's aesthetic outlook was shaped, his canons of judgment were established, his taste was refined— that, in short, he became an artist as well as a technician.

At the time he joined the Diaghilev troupe, he was clearly a young man of extraordinary gifts, but as yet raw—talented but without taste, as Diaghilev told him not long after he had engaged him. Diaghilev remarked that the music Balanchine had used till then—Scriabin and such—was not really very good music. Diaghilev also pointed out that in what he had seen of his choreography false, crude, or disappointing effects often marred passages of great beauty, and he added that Balanchine was like someone who carefully prepares an elegant and delicious meal for his guests and then, when they are waiting for just the right wine to go with it, brings them a big jug of water.

From the very start, though, Diaghilev treated Balanchine with respect, despite the difference in their ages. Since Balanchine had just come out of Russia, Diaghilev was eager to hear all that he had to say

In Venice, 1926.

75

about what was going on there and what was happening to ballet. He was particularly interested in Balanchine's accounts of Goleizovsky's new productions, with their unorthodox, sculptural effects, and questioned Balanchine closely about them. "Diaghilev greatly enjoyed these conversations," wrote Serge Grigoriev, who was the company's *regisseur* (or stage manager) throughout its entire existence. These conversations with Balanchine reinforced Diaghilev's conviction that Balanchine was going to be a good risk as the company's choreographer. "At the same time," wrote Grigoriev, "he perceived, what was less welcome to him, that Balanchine's ideas were already, so to speak, crystallized, and that he would consequently prove too independent to act as a mere instrument for the realization of Diaghilev's own conceptions." Since Fokine, none of the other choreographers—Nijinsky, Massine, Nijinska—had ever made any ballets before coming under Diaghilev's wing. As choreographers, they were entirely Diaghilev's creation. With Balanchine, Diaghilev could see, it was not going to be like that. He could teach Balanchine much, but he could not mold him as he had the others.

Still, for Balanchine, what an education it must have been! As Arnold Haskell has written, "For twenty years the Diaghilev Ballet was the only company that counted. Its history was the history of ballet. . . . It was, in fact, far more than a ballet company, it was a whole artistic movement." From the moment of its first Paris appearance in 1909, it made itself felt as a major influence on European culture. It is remarkable how many memoirs written by people not of the dance world contain an account of the author's discovery of the Ballets Russes as one of the major revelations of his life. The company was the darling of the smart set—Coco Chanel, Misia Sert, the Comtesse de Noailles, Lady Ripon, Lady Abdy, and the rest—but it also spoke to the intellectuals of the day, who treasured it for being in the forefront of the avant-garde, winning spectacular victories for important new movements in other arts besides the dance. A Diaghilev premiere in Paris was always an event of electric excitement. There was in the air the feeling, possibly snobbish but with more justification than most snobberies, that *everybody* who mattered was seated in that audience—the *haut monde,* the artists, the intellectuals. With tense anticipation they awaited the curtain's rise, wondering what new discoveries Diaghilev was going to reveal; what new trends in art and fashions in style were about to be set; what new reputations would be made; what scandals perpetrated.

The center of a creative ferment, the company brought to light a host of major talents. At one time or another, almost every European painter of genius, as well as a number of brilliant composers, worked for Diaghilev's Ballets Russes. The list of painters who created scenery and costumes for ballets just in the four and a half years that Balanchine was its choreographer includes Rouault, Utrillo, Miró, Gris, Ernst, de Chirico, Braque, Derain, and Tchelitchev. At first, young Balanchine rather took these colleagues for granted. They were simply the painters around the place, as far as he was concerned. Not having had much experience with the pictorial arts, he did not know any better. When he was told that *Le Chant du Rossignol*, a ballet that originally had been choreographed by Massine but that Balanchine was to restage as his first major ballet assignment, had sets and costumes by none other than Henri Matisse, Balanchine replied carefully, "Oh, *really?*" and tried not to reveal that he had never heard of Matisse.

One of the things for which he was always grateful to Diaghilev was that the latter took some pains to develop Balanchine's knowledge and appreciation of painting. Diaghilev believed that a choreographer should be cultivated in all the arts. For Diaghilev himself, paintings were not merely a pleasure but a passion, a necessity. When he stood before a picture, he seemed to be not just looking at it but imbibing it. During the first two summers he was with the company, Balanchine spent part of the time with Diaghilev in Italy, and when they were not engaged in planning the coming season's new works, Diaghilev would take him along with him to museums and churches. The party would generally include Serge Lifar, the handsome but still awkward young dancer who had become Diaghilev's favorite after the defection of Massine, and Boris Kochno, Diaghilev's secretary, an intelligent, striking-looking young man, somewhat of a dandy, who was doing most of the librettos at this time and whose opinions Diaghilev valued highly. They went to Florence, Venice, Siena, Assisi, Ravenna, and Rome. Diaghilev always carried his Baedeker with him. He was as inseparable from his Baedeker, Kochno has written, as a priest from his breviary. "He pored over it in the train and as soon as he arrived in town would set off to see the pictures he knew so well already as if late for a romantic rendezvous."

Balanchine appreciated the fact that Diaghilev seldom lectured him about how he was supposed to react to the paintings he showed him, but would merely usher him up to some picture and command, "Look!" Then he would leave Balanchine alone to gaze at it. Gradually some of the paintings began to become meaningful to Balanchine and give him pleasure. He grew especially fond of Perugino. Once, Diaghilev led the group into a part of the Vatican that, he said, was adorned entirely by paintings by Raphael. They looked about. "That one," said Balanchine diffidently after a while, pointing to the central painting in the ceiling, "looks to me more like a Perugino."

Lifar scoffed at Balanchine's assertion. "Don't quarrel," said Diaghilev. "Let's look at the book." He turned to the pertinent section in his Baedeker and read it aloud. The book said that the paintings in this section were all by Raphael with the exception of one in the ceiling, which was by Raphael's master, Perugino. Diaghilev congratulated Balanchine, who felt quite pleased with himself at this small triumph.

Considering his youth when he joined Diaghilev's Ballets Russes, Balanchine might well have been forgiven if he had panicked upon being suddenly entrusted with choreographic responsibility for a company of such intimidating reputation, but he met the challenge coolly. Even at that age, he was a thorough professional, and he had perceived at first glance something that the public had not yet noticed—that the company, though it offered manifold delights in the way of scenery, new music, avant-garde librettos, and overall style of presentation, really did not dance very well. At that period in its history the Diaghilev group had only forty dancers—a handful compared with the huge ensemble Balanchine had been accustomed to at the Maryinsky. The soloists were good, but the corps de ballet was ragged. Diaghilev, who had never set up a ballet school of his own, had always counted on getting new dancers from the great Russian companies, but with the revolution that source of supply had been cut off, except for an occasional defector. That was one of the reasons, Balanchine concluded, that Diaghilev came to focus so much attention on decor and costumes; he was trying to distract the public from the inadequacies of the dancing.

At first, Balanchine's appointment as ballet master had been greeted with grumbling and passive resistance on the part of some members of the company, who were loyal to Nijinska and not disposed to welcome a callow stranger in so authoritative a role. Before many rehearsals, though, he managed to gain their confidence and allegiance. "Easy brilliance, strong individualism, humor, and a rare intelligence"—these were the traits that Ninette de Valois, who was a soloist with the Ballets Russes at the time Balanchine joined the company, noted about him then. Others in the company recalled his unfailing courtesy and spontaneous charm, his gaiety and his lack of temperament. Though he was sparing of praise, he was easy to get along with. In these respects he was an agreeable contrast to some of the other choreographers the company had known: the brooding, withdrawn Massine; the unhappy, severely disturbed Nijinsky; and especially Fokine, who frequently flew into rages and threw chairs about during rehearsals.

Among those who have recorded their memories of Balanchine during his early days with the Ballets Russes is Vladimir Dukelsky, a young Russian composer who never fulfilled his early promise in serious music, but who later, under the name of Vernon Duke, became a successful writer of musical comedy and film scores. Dukelsky was working on his first commission for Diaghilev, the score for a ballet to be called *Zephyr and Flora,* when Balanchine joined the company. In a volume of breezy reminiscences called *Passport to Paris,* he wrote that his first memory of Balanchine is actually quite dim because he was so charmed by the sight of Tamara Geva, Balanchine's wife—with her pale skin, fair hair, cool blue eyes, and lissome body. This was at a rehearsal of *Scheherazade.* "She startled Grigoriev, the stern disciplinarian, by wearing pink Russian boots to rehearsal; since *Scheherazade* is a character, not a classical, ballet, he let it pass. She also wore a pink ribbon in her lemon-blond hair and had seductive little wrinkles at the corner of her mouth when she smiled—I never saw a prettier girl." To George Balanchine he paid little attention at first. "Unaware of George's prodigious gifts as a choreographer I thought he was merely an inevitable nuisance in his lucky role as Tamara's husband." Dukelsky, who was just enjoying his first splash of fame as a composer and who fancied himself a Beau Brummel, promptly began ogling Tamara and trying to start a flirtation. Soon, however, he began to be aware of Balanchine as well, and when he did, he developed a great admiration and affection for him—which did not stop Dukelsky from continuing to flirt with his wife. After all, thought Dukelsky, they were men of the world, weren't they, and twenty-one (just barely, both of them)? They became good friends, a friendship that was to endure many years. Dukelsky delighted in Balanchine's sense of fantasy and his untranslatable humor; he called him "a Tiflis pixie." He enjoyed watching Balanchine making his way by mimicry in countries where he did not know the language, and usually, though not always, succeeding in communicating his meaning. He remembered one occasion when they were dining together in Florence, and Balanchine wanted a glass of milk, which was not to be found on the menu. "On all fours, he made a stupid face and uttered several heart-rendering 'moos'; the waiter smiled, snapped his fingers, nodded repeatedly, and, a few minutes later, triumphantly produced a large steak."

Bedazzled as Dukelsky was in those days by the lure of money and worldly success, he was impressed by Balanchine's casualness about such matters. He was also struck, as were most composers who knew him, by Balanchine's rare musicality; and he could not help regretting that his *Zephyr and Flora* was being choreographed by Massine, who, though now on cool terms with Diaghilev, had been engaged for this occasion as guest choreographer. He would have much preferred Balanchine. "Massine had no musical intuition; he didn't know or feel why a certain passage was right, another wrong," he wrote. "He never guided me the way Diaghilev did, by talking, or the Balanchine way, by sitting down at the piano and improvising the sort of music he needed."

Ballet dancers—even the vainest, most narcissistic and hysterical of the breed—are first and foremost professionals. Ultimately, a choreographer wins a company's allegiance not by compliments and pleasing ways but by his abilities. From a capable choreographer dancers will patiently tolerate almost any kind of treatment; the only thing they will not put up with is incompetence. The members of the Ballets Russes thought it was very nice that Balanchine was such an agreeable young man, but what most endeared him to them at the start of his tenure was the freshness and imagination, the easy inventiveness, with which he carried out the first chore Diaghilev gave him—to revise the opera ballets that the company had to dance during the winter season at Monte Carlo as a way of earning its bread and butter at its home base. Dancing in opera ballets had always been drudgery for the company, but Balanchine managed to make it a pleasure, and Ninette de Valois remembered that they were all grateful to him for this liberation. "How refreshing was his originality!" she wrote in a volume of reminiscences called *Come Dance with Me*. "I can remember taking part in many small duets and ensembles arranged by him for the various operas: he charged those dreary experiences with new life and interest, and no demands on him could curb his imaginative facility. His great musical sense never failed to make the most of the material offered to him, even when confronted with that outlet so universally dreaded by all choreographers—the opera ballet."

Diaghilev was also gratified by the results. In the two months of the 1925 opera season, Balanchine made dances for twelve operas—including the world premiere of Maurice Ravel's *L'Enfant et les Sortilèges*. That season it became quite the thing at Monte Carlo to attend the opera just for the dancing.

Later, Balanchine would acknowledge that he had learned a lot about his craft from those opera chores, particularly from working on Verdi operas. "From Verdi's way of dealing with the chorus," he said, "I learned how to handle the corps de ballet, the ensemble, the soloists— how to make the soloists stand out against the corps de ballet and when to give them time to rest."

Part of Balanchine's job was also renovating the older ballets in the company's repertory. One such assignment was *Swan Lake*. He put in the waltz, revised the pas de trois, and made a new beginning. Some of the steps he used were what he remembered from the Maryinsky, but he shifted things around to make the production less static and more pleasing. This version of Ivanov's original choreography for act two of *Swan Lake* became the standard and eventually hallowed one-act version of the ballet for the West.

One of the earliest assignments Diaghilev gave Balanchine, and with much urgency, was to recruit new dancers from Russia, young people whom Balanchine thought talented. Balanchine got in touch with six or eight of them. Some were interested, and negotiations went on for several months, but it proved impossible for any of them to get permission to leave the country.

During his first year Balanchine choreographed two major ballets. The first, which made its debut in Paris on June 17, 1925, was Balanchine's new version of *Le Chant du Rossignol*, made necessary because Massine's version of it, five years before, had been forgotten by the dancers and had never been much liked anyway, receiving only two performances. Balanchine's choreography matched well the enchantment of the fairy-tale libretto and the mysterious, modern lyricism of Stravinsky's score, and the ballet was never out of the Diaghilev repertory thereafter.

Among other features, *Le Chant du Rossignol* was noteworthy as the ballet in which Alicia Markova, then fourteen years of age, made her debut. She danced with much success the part of the Nightingale, in a role that Balanchine had fashioned especially to suit the ethereal fragility of her style and appearance. "I think I could claim," she later wrote, "to be the first Baby Ballerina discovered by Balanchine." She recalled that Balanchine was instrumental in Diaghilev's engagement of her. She had danced several times for Diaghilev at the studio of her teacher Astafieva in London during the previous winter. Diaghilev was much taken by her,

Alicia Markova as the Nightingale in Le Chant du Rossignol.

but the decision as to whether he would engage her was still pending when, one day, she received an urgent call to come to the studio again. This time Diaghilev brought Balanchine with him. "I remember dancing for them for about two and a half hours on end, with Mr. Balanchine asking me to do all kinds of difficult technical and acrobatic steps, which, strange to say, however difficult, I was able to accomplish. I felt he seemed very intrigued and interested, and rather amused; and later I learned he had told Diaghilev I would be right to create the role of the Little Nightingale in Stravinsky's ballet, which was to be the first work he was to choreograph for the Diaghilev Company."

Dealing with a child ballerina created unexpected problems from time to time. One such arose in connection with her costume. A magnificent white costume had been made for her, in accord with Matisse's sketches. When Alicia saw it, she burst into tears. She had been told that she was going to be a nightingale, and a nightingale wasn't white. It was a drab little brown bird, and she wanted a drab little brown costume. Nobody was able to pacify her, not even her governess or mother. But Balanchine had a little talk with her and managed to cheer her up and reconcile her to the sumptuous white costume. He had a nice way with children, perhaps because he was not too far from one himself then. He was, after all, only seven years older than she.

The second Balanchine ballet of the year, *Barabau,* a knockabout farce, was about as different a ballet from *Le Chant du Rossignol* as could be imagined. "These two works," wrote Boris Kochno in his handsome historical survey *Le Ballet,* "the one solemn and lyrical, the other Italian buffoonery, inspired by popular song, allowed the young choreographer to show the diversity of his gifts." *Barabau* was a setting by the youthful new composer, Vittorio Rieti, of an old Italian nursery rhyme. It used a vocal chorus, had sets by Utrillo, and was danced by Woizikowsky, Lifar, Sokolova, Danilova, and Tamara Geva, plus various peasants and soldiers. Most of the dancers wore false noses, padded bottoms, and coarse peasant garb. *Barabau* brought a fresh breath of pure garlic to the ballet stage. It was probably the first ballet that was funny enough to set an audience to laughing aloud. The dancers were surprised to hear such a sound coming from the other side of the footlights. *Barabau* was given its first performance at the Coliseum in London on December 11. Though it was to prove popular on the Continent thereafter, the English did not take to it. "Merely vulgar and rather tedious," was Cyril Beaumont's verdict. "As a whole," he wrote, "'Barabau' filled me with misgivings as to the wisdom of Diaghilev's choice of Balanchine as choreographer."

The English audience did not care to be shaken up by new things very much. They had rather a rigid code of propriety concerning what they expected ballets to be like, and they felt rather put off and wounded if Diaghilev's company offered them anything different. They tended to be sentimental about the older ballets, including those which, now properly wooled up in their thoughts by nostalgia, they had at first rejected as too experimental. They liked best to see their old favorites, danced by their favorite dancers. That was nice; that was cozy. Diaghilev had decidedly mixed feelings about the English audience. "He valued his English friends above others," wrote Arnold Haskell, one of his biographers, "and knew that he could rely upon them; he valued the fidelity of the public, and at the same time he deeply resented the conservatism that prompted it." The Paris audience was much more fickle, but Diaghilev cared far more what Paris thought. In Paris the decor and costumes were the chief focus of interest, followed by the music. London tended to be more interested in the dancing, the dancers' personalities, and the story.

Elsewhere, on tour, there were still other reactions. Each city seemed to have its own preferences. Least predictable was Berlin. There what had been warmly greeted one year might be received with apathy the next.

It had been only two years before Balanchine's advent that the company had found its haven at Monte Carlo, under the patronage of the Princess Héritière of Monaco. Before that the company had been very much itinerant entertainers, lugging their baggage with them, going from one crisis to another, and never being sure that the whole enterprise was not on the verge of collapse. The Monte Carlo arrangement provided a substantial measure of security. From November or December until May, Diaghilev's company would be in residence at Monte Carlo, where it would present a season of its own, dance in the opera ballets, and prepare new works. In late May or early June, its all-important Paris season would take place, followed by a couple of weeks in London. After that the company might disband for its annual summer vacation period of two months. When it reassembled, there would be a tour of such cities on the continent as Diaghilev had been able to arrange, with perhaps another week or two in London, and then once more it would settle in for the winter at Monte Carlo.

A wonderful place to work, Monte Carlo was, for the Diaghilev company: a haven, a storehouse, a laboratory, a resort. Balanchine loved the place from the first moment he saw it—the sea, the mimosa, the flowered hillsides and winding streets, the café terraces and the little shops, with whose proprietors he became friendly. He was at home there. Life for him in those days was by no means all art and high purpose. Sometimes Diaghilev told him that he worked too hastily. But then the rehearsal hall was in a windowless basement of the opera house, lit only by electricity. "Outside it was so beautiful, and I was young," Balanchine later recalled. "There were times when I would finish up a task more quickly than I should have, because I couldn't bear to linger in that dungeon another minute." During one slack period, he and Grigoriev thought they were safe in cutting the morning rehearsal sessions short and giving the company the time off, because Diaghilev never attended those rehearsals; he usually rose late, chatted in his hotel with Grigoriev for a while, and about one o'clock emerged from his hotel. But somebody betrayed them. Grigoriev arrived at Diaghilev's hotel one morning to find Diaghilev already up and dressed. He had decided to attend Balanchine's rehearsal, he said, and to make sure that Grigoriev would not dash ahead and warn Balanchine, he asked Grigoriev to wait and go with him. When they reached the rehearsal room, the porter there of course told Diaghilev that everybody had left half an hour before. No comment was made by Diaghilev, but none was necessary. Balanchine cut no rehearsals after that.

Balanchine and Tamara Geva lived at first in a pension at the Hôtel de Prince. Dimitriev, Efimov, and some of the other members of the company also stayed there. The food was good, and lunch, following the morning rehearsal, was a leisurely, pleasant, often merry affair. In the evenings, after a performance or the evening rehearsal, there might be little parties at the apartment of one or another of the dancers—though often by that time most of the dancers were too exhausted from their day's work to do anything but sleep. At these parties Balanchine would often be called on to improvise at the piano or he might strum a guitar and sing, in a lugubrious voice, bawdy and nonsensical lyrics to mournful Russian tunes. Sometimes he would prepare a gala meal. He had discovered in himself, once he began to appreciate French cuisine, a talent as a chef, and he became eventually quite noted for this within the company.

They had good times, but it was not all the high brilliant gala that romantic accounts have suggested. They worked exceedingly hard, these dancers. The standard salary for those below the top rank of stars was only 1,500 francs a month, or about sixty dollars. Balanchine, because of his additional duties as ballet master, was paid 2,500 francs. Each month Balanchine, Tamara Geva, Danilova, and Efimov would contribute a fifth of their salaries to Dimitriev, in accord with a contract they had signed with him. After this, not a great deal was left to live on. Most of the Diaghilev dancers lived rather like sharecroppers, begging advances from the management and always in debt to it. Meanwhile the smart set were nightly tossing away fortunes in the casino, which incidentally was supposed to be off limits to the dancers and other entertainers, a rule that had been put into effect shortly before the war as a consequence of a gambling spree by Chaliapin, during which he lost his entire season's fee. During all his years in Monte Carlo, Balanchine only once slipped into the casino. This was one evening just after he had been paid his monthly salary, which he found amounted, after he had given Dimitriev his share and paid back what he had borrowed from the management, to a total of twenty francs. It seemed better to Balanchine to be completely penniless than to hoard such a pittance. He walked into the Casino, tossed his twenty francs down on number thirteen, and, without waiting for the wheel to spin, turned and walked out again. A moment later, an ac-

quaintance who had observed this rushed after him to give him the hand-ful of money Balanchine had won; the wheel had turned up thirteen. Delighted, Balanchine took his winnings and paid his rent. He never tried his luck again.

The glittering soirees in Paris and London, around which legends have accumulated, were not attended by most of the Diaghilev company, ex-cept on the occasions when they were invited to dance for the guests. For such chores, they got no extra pay, had to put out from their own pockets for taxi fare back to their hotels late at night, and were lucky if they even got fed. Only the brightest luminaries among them were lionized guests at such parties. Balanchine was not in that category. The choreographer was all-important to the company, but he was not, in those days, a star or public personality unless he also happened to be the leading dancer or Diaghilev's special protégé. Once, not long after Balanchine had joined the company, one of Diaghilev's coterie of patrons, Lady Abdy, was be-ing honored at a fete at Claridge's. Diaghilev asked Balanchine to come to the affair and stage Lady Abdy's various entrances with all due ele-gance and theatricality. When Balanchine attempted to pass into Clar-idge's that evening, the doorman barred the way. Balanchine said he had been invited to the gala for Lady Abdy. The doorman looked him over with an expert eye and sniffed disdainfully. When Balanchine persisted, the doorman called two large policemen who expertly tossed him into the rain-filled gutter. Balanchine argued no more but made his sodden way home. In later years as Balanchine became better known, he would occasionally be invited, as a guest, to such affairs; but he never enjoyed them and sought to avoid them whenever he could. Unlike Nijinsky, Massine, or Lifar, he would never play a dazzling part in the glamour of the Diaghilev epoch. The chic world would never fawn on him; Picasso would not sketch him; the papers would not be full of fascinating stories concerning his latest tantrum or exploit. It caused him no regrets. He could well do without all this.

With Diaghilev—"*cet homme charmant et terrible,*" in Debussy's apt characterization—his relations remained friendly but always rather for-mal. Their mutual respect was tinged with a certain mutual wariness. Balanchine, it was obvious from the start, was one of those men who, as Diaghilev chose to put it, "had a morbid interest in women." This left him out of some of the opportunities that Diaghilev reserved for his fa-vorite, but it simplified life immensely. He was spared the hysteria that

In front of the rehearsal studio in Monte Carlo.

went with the favorite's role. No detectives would shadow him, at Diaghilev's behest, as they once did another of Diaghilev's ballet masters when Diaghilev began to suspect the latter of infidelity—and with a woman, at that. Balanchine's private life would be his own.

After the success of his first year, Diaghilev counted on him for two or three new ballets a year, along with such other occasional dances, divertissements, and ballet revisions and refurbishments as might be required. His facility was considered extraordinary; only Fokine could be compared with him in this respect. One of the most popular of his ballets for Diaghilev, *Les Dieux Mendiants,* or *The Gods Go A-begging,* was one that Balanchine put together backstage in just a week's time during the 1928 London season, choreographing it in spare moments between rehearsals and performances of other ballets. With Handel music arranged by Sir Thomas Beecham, it had been intended by Diaghilev as no more than a complimentary gesture toward his faithful English audience; but the ballet unexpectedly turned out to be a success that delighted audiences everywhere, even Paris.

Of the other ballets he did during the first half of his tenure with Diaghilev his most applauded works were *The Triumph of Neptune* and *La Chatte. The Triumph of Neptune* was another work that was specially created to please the British audience. It had a book by Sacheverell Sitwell, music by Lord Berners, and sets and costumes designed in the style of the nineteenth-century English toy theatres. The ballet, in its twelve scenes and fantastic, sensational plot, evoked the atmosphere of the Victorian pantomime. With its jolly jack-tar and bustling London streets, its clowns and fairy queen and apotheosis of Britannia at the end, it captured an English essence—"the puerile romanticism," as the Russo-French dance critic Levinson wrote, "of a race of grown-up, laughing children."

La Chatte, the following season, was very different from this tribute to sentimentality. It was a thoroughly modern statement. The constructivist sets, of transparent talc against a background of black cloth, were by Gabo and Pevsner. The story was an Aesopian fable, though turned upside down in a way that really destroyed the fable's point if anybody had stopped to consider it, and the dancers in their gleaming cellophane costumes resembled science-fiction characters. Paradoxically, despite all the novel elements, the ballet succeeded in suggesting, more powerfully than a traditional treatment might have, a quality of classic mythology,

Lifar's entrance in La Chatte.

an ancient Greek ideal of physical beauty. According to Grigoriev, Diaghilev liked this ballet a great deal, comparing it as an achievement with one of his early favorites, Fokine's *Le Spectre de la Rose*. In *La Chatte* Serge Lifar achieved his first important triumph. As a dancer, he had come a long way in just four years from the apologetic, awkward youth who, in 1923, had tagged along, uninvited, when Nijinska sent to Russia for some of her promising students. "Who is the boy who has no sense of rhythm and no ear?" Diaghilev asked when he first saw him, but Lifar was allowed to stay with the company on sufferance. Driven by ambition, he worked as probably no other dancer has ever worked, for none of the other great ones ever started so late. He practiced his parts incessantly. Long after Balanchine had begun yearning to get out of the rehearsal hall and into the sunshine, Lifar could be heard begging him, "Please, George, go over that bit just once more with me, won't you!" Maurice Tassart has described him well:

"He did not command quite as much elevation as did Nijinsky, and his *batterie* was not nearly as clean. But he had the same grace and radiance, and undoubtedly much more fire and dramatic power. In addition to this, he was taller, with a much more beautiful figure: broad shoulders, narrow hips, perfectly shaped legs. His strange, unforgettable face was both childish and diabolic. Far from trying to soften his Asiatic features, he emphasized them deliberately when he had his naturally upturned nose surgically flattened in 1928."

Though Lifar never succeeded in overcoming all his technical faults, Balanchine was able to conceal and even exploit such inadequacies as remained and provide for him the kind of movements—something of a daring synthesis between the classic dance and the suppleness of the circus and music hall performer—which were his most superb expression. "It was Balanchine who provided Lifar with the necessary outlet for his talent," wrote Pierre Michaut. "Here was the ideal dancer for Balanchine's choreographic compositions."

Originally, Balanchine himself was called on to do considerable dancing for the Diaghilev company as well as choreographing. How good a dancer he was has been the subject of some dispute. Ninette de Valois has dryly dismissed his dancing as having been "less than indifferent." He resented this imputation fiercely, whereas criticism of his ballets provoked nothing more than a careless shrug from him. He used to say he did not see how anyone could be a choreographer without having been a first-rate dancer, since the choreographic ideas are all communicated by demonstration. A choreographer who had not himself been a strong dancer could expect to find himself overpowered by the dancers he had to work with, he said. He had no doubt that he, himself, had been a wonderful dancer, though in character roles, not as a *danseur noble*. While at the Maryinsky, he had won acclaim for his performance of the hoop dance as the Jester in *The Nutcracker*. Danilova and many other of his colleagues concurred as to his abilities. They said that his leaps were prodigious—that, in fact, they never saw anybody, except Nijinsky, with better elevation. "He could jump like a flea," recalled Danilova once, "and he could dart and whirl about the stage like a string of firecrackers. I never saw anybody dance a better *Lezginka* than he." And Cyril Beaumont, in his book *The Diaghilev Ballet in London*, singled out as one of the outstanding dances of *The Triumph of Neptune* the "remarkable solo by Balanchine as the Negro, Snowball; a dance full of subtly contrasted rhythms, strutting walks, mincing steps and surging backward bendings of the body, borrowed from the cake-walk, the whole invested with a delicious humour derived from the mood of the dance, a paradoxical blend of pretended nervous apprehension and blustering confidence."

Balanchine was also often used in mime roles. One such was the monstrous Kostchei in *Firebird*—a role Balanchine does not seem to have taken as seriously as intended. Wrote Kochno in his *Diaghilev and the Ballets Russes*, "His capers often won him sharp reprimands from Diaghilev, because some evenings, in interpreting this evil genie . . . Balanchine would make him a hilarious character and send the audience into gales of laughter with his pranks."

Early in 1927, shortly after the season in which *The Triumph of Neptune* was given its premiere, he suffered a severe knee injury during rehearsal. He had to have an operation, and his leg was in a cast for a month. It was fortunate that Balanchine had choreographic talent, or all his years of rigorous training would thus have come to nothing, for he had difficulty with strenuous roles after this operation and for quite some time could not even kneel with ease. "Good! Now I won't have to work so hard," Balanchine remarked when he first learned the bad news that his knee would never be strong again—an unexpected reaction but not an inexplicable one. It is similar to Pablo Casals' exclamation when, at the age of twenty-one, a rock injured his left hand: "Thank God I won't have to play the cello anymore!" It was a cry of relief from the agonizing burden of responsibility his talent meant. "My intimate enemy," Georges Enesco used to call his violin. How much more intimate is the enemy for

the dancer, whose instrument is his own body!

Of the various performances Balanchine gave as a dancer, the one least likely to be forgotten by those who saw it took place about a year after he had joined the company, when he danced Alicia Markova's role of the Nightingale in *Le Chant du Rossignol*. The work had been scheduled as a command performance for the Princess Héritière of Monaco, whose favorite ballet it was that season. At the last moment little Markova fell ill. None of the dancers knew her part, except the choreographer Balanchine. So Diaghilev waved aside Balanchine's demurrals and ordered him into the breach.

Le Chant du Rossignol is based on the fairy story about the emperor of China, dying of melancholy, whom nothing whatever can cheer, until at last he is given a nightingale in a cage, who sings for him with such exquisite, innocent joy that his heart is touched, and he revives. Markova, in the cage, looked delicate and winsome, a wisp of a thing. She may have weighed all of eighty pounds in those days. By comparison Balanchine, at about one hundred and forty, was a great hulk. Clad in an improvised nightingale's costume, sewn together in haste backstage, he just barely managed to squeeze into the cage. Pressed against the bars, with his muscles rippling and bulging, he looked—one witness recalled—more like an ape in a cage than a nightingale, a white-faced ape with a beak. Tchelitchev, who was present, thought he looked like a stuffed rabbit. As soon as the maidens of the Emperor's court glimpsed this apparition, they began to titter. Grigoriev, the company's stage director and disciplinarian, was playing the dying Emperor. "Shut up, girls!" he threatened under his breath, as he languished feebly on his couch. "I'm going to fine you all a week's pay." But then, opening his eyes, he caught sight of the caged Balanchine and choked with laughter himself. It was hard on his melancholy. Once the cage has been brought on, the Nightingale is supposed to hop out lightly and dance for the Emperor. Balanchine wormed his way out and began his solo. Being a superb mimic, he managed to look fourteen years old, and ethereal—suggesting many of Markova's mannerisms. Diaghilev all the while was rolling about in his box with mirth at the sight. Had it been Paris, instead of Monte Carlo, Diaghilev would have cancelled the performance rather than substitute a man for Markova, but he did not care much what the Monte Carlo audience thought. The princess, it is said, witnessed the whole performance gravely. Afterward she is supposed to have re-

Balanchine in his Snowball costume, on the roof of the Lyceum Theatre, London, in 1926.

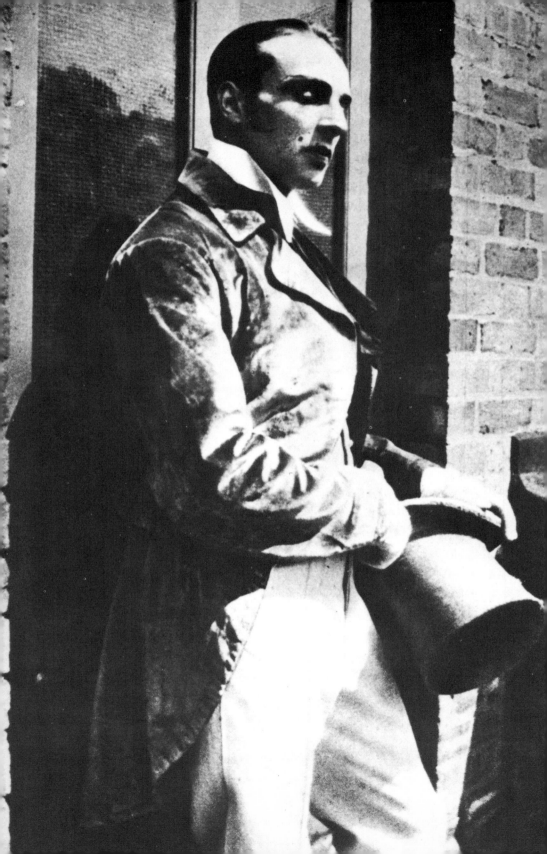

marked judiciously that Mr. Balanchine was very good but that she still preferred the little Markova girl.

In the summer of 1927 Balanchine's marriage to Tamara Geva, which had been growing increasingly shaky for some time, came to an end. She was restless and bored with the narrow world of ballet. She was not, as most of the others were, a graduate of the Russian ballet academies, and she had interests other than the dance. She was eager to get about more, to see more of the world, to live. To her mind, Monte Carlo was a dull place. It annoyed her that Balanchine was so satisfied with things. "What are we going to do tonight?" she would ask. "Why do we need to do anything?" he would reply. Then they would quarrel. Once Dukelsky came along in the midst of such a quarrel, just as she was walking out in a huff. He promptly proposed that they elope to Nice. She said it was a splendid idea. He hired a horse carriage and off they went. After about ten minutes, though, she decided that perhaps it wasn't such a good idea after all. Dukelsky sheepishly agreed and, feeling like an ass, had the carriage driver turn around and deliver her back to her husband. But the time eventually came when she could no longer contain her restlessness. She let Balanchine know that she was leaving him, and the company as well. She joined the Balieff's Chauve-Souris and traveled with it to America, where she later made a theatrical career.

Balanchine was wounded by her leaving him, but not mortally. He even made a couple of solo dance numbers for Geva to take with her to the Chauve-Souris—his kind of dissolution settlement. Their marriage had been impetuous. He was young; he had by now come to accept change and rootlessness as part of his life, and he did not, as a matter of principle, show his feelings. They healed before long anyway, his wounded feelings. The balm for this healing process, if it was needed, was supplied by the charming Alexandra Danilova, in whom he had long taken delight, as a fascinating dancer as well as person. For Danilova, Balanchine had just made perhaps the finest role she had danced so far—The Fairy Queen in *The Triumph of Neptune*. Other brilliant roles would follow. What better love tokens could a choreographer offer a ballerina!

ᘓ *In costume for his part in* **Carnaval.**

CHAPTER SIX

Apollo and Prodigal Son

efore the war, Diaghilev created a vogue for Russian ballet, but after the war he merely created a vogue for vogue."

Constant Lambert's cutting summation has its truth; though, like most aphorisms, it leaves out much. Certainly, the history of the Diaghilev Ballet in the postwar years for the most part reflects a restless search for novelty, for modernism at any cost. The watchword of the epoch was the fiat that Diaghilev had issued when Cocteau, having undertaken to prepare a scenario for a new ballet, asked what his employer would like him to do. "*Étonne-moi!*" Diaghilev replied. And Cocteau tried his very best to astonish him, as later on did Boris Kochno and nearly everybody else in Diaghilev's service.

It was a period in which the artists around Diaghilev deliberately cultivated the banal and the trivial for shock effect. Thereby they caught the spirit of the postwar age, antiheroic and contemptuous of bourgeois morality as it was, and distrustful of all causes—the era of "So what?" The clever person cultivated his disbelief; he did not commit himself, his emotions, or his faith to anything, if he could help it.

Lambert's witticism leaves all that out—the psychological effect of the war—and it imputes to Diaghilev more power than he actually wielded, powerful as he was. When Diaghilev in 1921 sought to go against the times with a revival of a full-length classical ballet, *The Sleeping Beauty*, he suffered a financial disaster that almost destroyed the company.

Joining the Ballets Russes at the end of 1924, Balanchine naturally participated in the making of the clever modernistic works that were the

Lifar as Apollo, with Tchernicheva (left) and Doubrovska.

97

vogue. Sometimes he did them very well, as with *La Chatte*. At other times, as with *La Pastorale*—a complicated ballet in twelve scenes concerning the romance between a Telegraph Boy and Movie Star who meet while she is in the midst of making a film—the results were less notable.

It is a question how congenial all this kind of thing was to Balanchine's nature. He was adaptable and bright, and he was a child of this era; but it is likely that he was not wholly at ease in the atmosphere of smart cynicism and delicious triviality. Presently he found his own way out of the confusion of the times. This artistic salvation came with the creation of *Apollo* (originally *Apollon Musagète*) in 1928. "I consider *Apollo* the turning point of my life," he has said. Here, for the first time, he struck the unmistakable Balanchine note. At the height of the jazz age, he turned to classicism—or, rather, he evolved a new classicism, which serenely embodied the classical virtues of clarity and grandeur and yet in spirit and in style of movement was more up to date and adventurous than the run of ultramodern ballets. With *Apollo*—"a work of capital importance in the arts of the twentieth century," it has been called—Balanchine started out on what was to be one of the major lines of development in his career.

The ballet had its premiere in Paris on June 12, 1928. As usual, there were last-minute improvisations—such as the lovely pas de deux for Apollo and Terpsichore which, according to Nikitina, Balanchine choreographed in half an hour at the Studio Wacker in Paris—but most of this ballet was prepared with special care at Monte Carlo during the preceding spring, and with a clear sense on the part of all concerned that something new and significant was being made. Nicolas Nabokov, a young composer whose *Ode*, choreographed by Massine, was one of the other new works of that season, has given a vivid account in his autobiography, *Old Friends and New Music*, of a glimpse he had of *Apollo* in preparation. The occasion was his first sight of Balanchine, with whom he was shortly to become close friends. Nabokov had just arrived in Monte Carlo, having come to work on *Ode*. At the rehearsal hall, when he entered, looking for Diaghilev, he saw the massive figure of André Derain, whom he already knew, leaning against the upright piano. Diaghilev was seated to the left, and next to him was a funny-looking little man with thick glasses and a crooked goatee, who was dressed in a disheveled manner and giggled in a bleating voice. This odd figure, as Nabokov learned, was André Bauchant, a primitive painter whom Diaghilev had commissioned to do the sets in order to avoid, he said, a false

Hellenism. Bauchant, whom the Paris art dealers were pushing as a successor to Rousseau, always had his pockets bulging with photographs of his work. If someone said anything in Bauchant's presence about a cucumber, according to Derain, Bauchant would immediately pull out a photograph and say, "Here's a still life of mine with a cucumber. Won't you buy it?" If someone mentioned that he was going to America on the *Lafayette*, Bauchant would pull out of his pocket a *Lafayette Meets Washington*. On that particular day Diaghilev was in bad temper with Bauchant because on walking into Bauchant's studio he had found him painting a still life instead of working on the *Apollo* sets. But at the moment of Nabokov's arrival, Diaghilev was completely absorbed in what was going on in the center of the floor—so absorbed that he did not even look up to greet Nabokov.

"There, in the center of it," writes Nabokov, "a group of three ballerinas were clustered around and over a male dancer. The ballerinas were Tchernicheva, Doubrovska, and Nikitina. . . . The male dancer was Serge Lifar. That group's pose has since become famous in the annals of choreographic classicism: Lifar knelt among the three ballerinas, who dipped forward and their necks stretched upward so that they looked like three drinking swans whose precarious balance was maintained by a trembling hand firmly clutching Lifar's shoulder. In front of the group stood its inventor, the slight and incredibly young-looking George Balanchine, Diaghilev's recent discovery, his new choreographic genius."

After a moment Diaghilev turned around and greeted Nabokov curtly. Without waiting for an answer, he pointed at Balanchine, and Nabokov heard him saying to Derain, "What he is doing is magnificent. It is pure classicism, such as we have not seen since Petipa's."

The events with which *Apollo* deals are simple, compressed, evocative: Apollo is born, discovers and displays his creative powers, instructs three of the Muses in their arts, and then ascends with them to Parnassus. The theme is creativity itself—Apollonian creativity, vigorous but lucid, untortured, civilizing. Edwin Denby, a poet and former dancer who has written some of the most perceptive dance criticism of our time, has said of this ballet:

"Extraordinary is the richness with which he can, with only four dancers, create a sustained and more and more satisfying impression of the grandness of man's creative genius, depicting it concretely in its grace, its sweet wit, its force and boldness, and with the constant warmth of its sensuous complicity with physical beauty. 'Apollo' is an homage to the academic ballet tradition—and the first work in the contemporary classic style, but it is an homage to classicism's sensuous loveliness as well as to its brilliant exactitude and its science of dance effect. . . . And it leaves at the end, despite its innumerable incidental inventions, a sense of bold, open, effortless and limpid grandeur."

It was Stravinsky's music for this ballet that showed Balanchine the way to the technical and aesthetic discoveries he made in *Apollo,* and to Stravinsky he gratefully admitted his indebtedness. Balanchine later recalled that in his previous ballets it had been his practice to heap all styles of movements together, as in a sort of goulash. The score that Stravinsky provided for *Apollo*—restrained, disciplined, yet uncommonly lyrical—taught Balanchine the most useful lesson of his career: that he, too, could clarify his art by reducing all the multitudinous possibilities to the one possibility that was inevitable, that he could, as he later put it, "dare to not use all my ideas." As he studied the score, which left with him a strong impression as of a white-on-white canvas, Balanchine for the first time realized that, like tones in music and shades in painting, gestures have certain family relations, which as groups impose their own laws. All the choreography he did thereafter, said Balanchine, was affected by this realization.

It was characteristic of Balanchine and of his work that his greatest choreographic discoveries should come by way of a musical experience. He would seldom, in the course of his life, be able to do first-rate choreography to second-rate music. Many choreographers are just the opposite; they find it intimidating and inhibiting to have to cope with a musical masterwork. It was also typical of Balanchine that he frankly gave pride of place to the composer. "A choreographer can't invent rhythms," he once said, "he only reflects them in movement. The body is his medium and, unaided, the body will improvise for a short breath. But the organizing of rhythm on a grand scale is a sustained process. It is a function of the musical mind." Already, at the time he began work on *Apollo,* he had come to admire Stravinsky's music immensely. When he heard it, he felt moved to try to make it visible. If he himself could write music, Balanchine felt, that was the way he would want it to sound.

In Russia five years before, Balanchine had been intrigued enough by the score of *Le Sacre du Printemps* to ask the State Theatre for permission to stage it, and as soon as he had heard *Pulcinella,* he had begun trying to make dances for it. Appropriately, his first major assignment for Diaghilev had been the restaging of Stravinsky's *Le Chant du Rossignol.* But

Apollo was the first ballet in which he and Stravinsky worked together. Stravinsky, who had in the past not been easily pleased by what choreographers had done to his music, was this time altogether satisfied. The choreography for *Apollo,* he wrote, with its "groups, movements and lines of great dignity and plastic elegance as inspired by the beauty of classical forms," was exactly what he had wished for when he had composed its music. Thus, with *Apollo,* began what was to become the most exquisitely matched and notable collaboration in the history of ballet.

The premiere of *Apollo* at the Théâtre Sarah Bernhardt, with Stravinsky conducting, was a gala event, and for many in the audience, a profound experience. Gordon Craig wrote that he found the ballet so beautiful that he left the theatre during the intermission that followed it, without seeing the rest of the program, because he wanted to retain its loveliness in his memory as long as possible. As Apollo, Lifar was superb. Backstage, after the performance, Diaghilev kneeled down and kissed his leg in homage. "Remember it, Seriozha, for the rest of your days," Diaghilev said to him. "I am kissing a dancer's leg for the second time in my life. The last was Nijinsky's after *Le Spectre de la Rose.*"

Nobody offered to kiss the choreographer's leg. He would have laughed if anybody had tried. There was no need for extravagant gestures. Balanchine knew well what he had achieved and what had happened to him in the course of making this ballet, and he was content.

For all its success, *Apollo,* surprisingly, proved to be the cause of the one serious disagreement that Balanchine had with Diaghilev. At the next performance after the premiere, Diaghilev peremptorily ordered Terpsichore's variation cut out. He said it was boring. Balanchine protested indignantly. Of the three Muses' variations, Terpsichore's was not only the loveliest but also the most personally meaningful to Balanchine—his testament to the goddess of the dance. Balanchine told Diaghilev that it was not the variation that was boring but the dancer, Nikitina, whom Diaghilev had insisted on casting for the part.

Balanchine had from the start very much wanted the part to go to Danilova, but Lord Rothermere, the newspaper magnate who had provided the financial assurance for the London appearances of the Ballets Russes during the previous two seasons, had urged Diaghilev to give Nikitina the part. Nikitina was Lord Rothermere's favorite. He made her one of his "adopted daughters" (he had two), as she relates with filial piety in her memoirs, and he gave her one of his Rolls-Royces (he had eight). He was very good to her and, on her account, to the Ballets

Apollo. *Lifar with Danilova in the original production (below). Above, Lew Christensen as Apollo in 1937.*

Jacques d'Amboise with the three Muses—Allegra Kent as Terpsichore—about 1960 (below). Above, Peter Martins with Karin von Aroldingen, Kyra Nichols, and Heather Watts in 1982.

Russes. But unexpectedly, just before the 1928 season opened, Lord Rothermere had withdrawn his patronage. Diaghilev, who could be petty on a grand scale, now could no longer stand the sight of Nikitina and addressed cutting remarks to her in front of the whole company.

Balanchine felt that Diaghilev, not wishing to admit that he had been wrong and venally motivated in the first place, was now taking his revenge on the role. He threatened to quit. Angry words were exchanged. Diaghilev refused to alter his stand. The second performance proceeded without Terpsichore's variation, but when it came to the place where the variation should have been, some members of the audience who were aware of what had happened began to shout their disapproval. Ultimately, the variation was restored, with Danilova alternating with Nikitina in the Terpsichore role and doing a somewhat different version.

It was not long after this quarrel that there occurred the episode in regard to Balanchine's contract which Grigoriev mentions in his book. One day shortly after the summer holidays, Grigoriev, aware that Balanchine's contract was about to expire, asked Diaghilev if he had remembered to renew it. At this question, Diaghilev began heaping abuse on Balanchine. He was very much of a mind, Diaghilev said, not to renew his contract at all.

Grigoriev was shocked and astonished but discreetly forbore to ask questions. He said merely that he wished to know if Diaghilev intended to retain Balanchine. If so, then he would go ahead and make the contract arrangements himself. After a pause, Diaghilev said, "Do as you like."

To Grigoriev, these words came as a great relief, and he hastened to get Balanchine safely under contract as soon as possible. There had been a time, some sixteen years before, when on being warned by Benois that the company was in danger of losing Fokine, Diaghilev had been able haughtily to reply, "That's not so great a calamity. What is a ballet master? I could make a ballet master out of this inkwell if I wanted to." But those times were past. There had been too many painful crises in the intervening years resulting from the threatened departure of a choreographer for Diaghilev to repeat so haughty an assertion now. Nor would he again be so glib about how easy it was to make a ballet master. By now he, and all concerned, were well aware that a good choreographer was rarer than diamonds, and that for the company to lose its ballet master was calamity indeed.

By the following season, it was Grigoriev's impression that the breach between Diaghilev and Balanchine had been healed and that they had resumed the correct and formally friendly relationship they had always maintained. Grigoriev felt certain that Balanchine would have gone on working for Diaghilev after that if Diaghilev had lived. Balanchine himself said later that he thought so. There were others, however, who, noting a growing sense of independence in Balanchine, were sure it would have been merely a question of time before an irrevocable rupture developed between him and Diaghilev. By 1929, Kochno wrote in *Le Ballet,* Balanchine seemed already to have "emancipated himself," so that it was necessary to be thinking about his eventual replacement if the company was not again to find itself in the disastrous situation caused by Massine's departure in 1921.

Some lively and pertinent memories of Balanchine are those which Danilova has supplied. Because Balanchine did not have a divorce from Tamara Geva, they were unable to marry, but they thought of each other as man and wife. They lived in a pension in Monte Carlo, and they had also taken a two-bedroom apartment in Paris as a year-round base, sharing it with Dimitriev. Recalling their four years together, Danilova, long afterward, touched on many of Balanchine's traits, some of which had two sides for her—his spontaneous generosity, which to someone who was sharing his life could also be ranked as frightful improvidence; his honesty, which could sometimes be painful, and which on occasion turned into stubbornness and pride; his evenness of temper, which made him easy to be with but difficult to engage deeply. She remembered with appreciation his simple but helpful wisdom about things that mattered. "I used to worry about how much money other dancers were being paid and what parts they were getting. He told me to just sit down and think about what I wanted to do, never mind worrying about others." Envy was not one of Balanchine's characteristics. Herself of an effervescent nature, Danilova enjoyed Balanchine's gaiety and fantasy. He liked to clown. At one period it amused him to wear a billboard around the apartment instead of a dressing gown.

Despite his generosity to strangers—to anyone, as Danilova pungently put it, "who would cry in his pocket"—he could be forgetful about those nearest to him. Once, she felt hurt because she got no flowers from Balanchine on a night when she was dancing one of his parts for the first time. It had not occurred to him that she might expect them. When their friend the conductor Roger Désormière reproved him the next day for his negligence, Balanchine clapped his hand to his head and, rushing off, spent all his money on a bouquet of a hundred roses for her for the second night's performance.

"I think, perhaps," she said, "he had not learned in those days how to love another human being. Perhaps if he had not been separated so much from his family, he might have learned that—and learned not to bury his feelings. And there was all the upheaval of the revolution we lived through, affecting him and all of us. In a way we were like little wild animals. We were forced to bring ourselves up, to improvise our lives— and that left its mark."

Of the ten ballets that Balanchine made for the Diaghilev Ballet only two have survived. One is *Apollo.* The other is *Prodigal Son,* which had its first performance on May 21, 1929, in Paris, just three months before Diaghilev's death, and was the last new ballet to be presented to the public by him. It was one of two new works that Balanchine choreographed in 1929; the other one, *Le Bal,* with music by Rieti and interesting but perhaps overwhelming sets and costumes by de Chirico, was given its premiere in Monte Carlo a few weeks before.

For *Prodigal Son* Diaghilev commissioned Georges Rouault to design the decor and the costumes. It was Rouault's first theatrical commission. He stayed at the Hôtel de Paris in Monte Carlo for many weeks while this ballet was in preparation and often attended rehearsals. A small, rather shabby, gray-faced man, he would sit and watch with interest but would say very little. Once, during an intermission in the rehearsal, he showed Balanchine and some of the other members of the company how to balance a chair on his nose, and did it very skillfully. When Diaghilev would ask how the designs were coming along, he would reply, "I'm thinking." As time went by, Diaghilev grew increasingly anxious about the designs. He kept asking Rouault to show him some of the sketches, but Rouault always put him off. Rouault, as Diaghilev must have been aware when he engaged him, was extremely loath to show a work until it was finished, and it was always a great struggle for him to concede at last that a painting might be finished; he liked to keep a painting by him for years, pondering it and every now and then adding a brush stroke. Finally, Diaghilev could wait no longer. From the hotel's concierge, he obtained a key to Rouault's room, into which he stole one day while Rouault was out. There, according to Balanchine's account of the epi-

Balanchine and Doubrovska in a performance of Le Bal. *Here he strums her leg like a guitar.*

sode, Diaghilev found hundreds of sketches lying about. He snatched up a handful. From this loot, used as a rough guide, the company's scenic artist, the extremely capable Prince Shervashidze, was able to execute the ballet's two magnificent sets, so unmistakably Rouault in their profundity of spirit and their somber, glowing palette of color; and also from these sketches Vera Soudeikina (who later became the wife of Igor Stravinsky) was able to derive the basic conceptions for the costumes.

Prodigal Son was yet another new kind of work for Balanchine to attempt. In many respects, it was a novel experience for the whole company. It seemed a surprising return, though utterly different from them in approach, to the emotionality and passion of the early Diaghilev ballets of twenty years before. How strange the members of the company found it during rehearsals, after years during which Diaghilev had firmly suppressed any signs of histrionics or emoting he detected in their performances, to be now urged, even implored, by him to give free play to their feelings. In this ballet Diaghilev took a greater personal interest than in any he had prepared in years. It was a return to the kind of close supervision of the early years, for which he had been famous. Perhaps it was that the subject was closer to Diaghilev's heart than the chic, clever ballets he had been conjuring up to keep ahead of the vogue. "*Assez de musiquette!*" he had been heard to say of late—"Enough of this music-hall triviality!" Perhaps, as Grigoriev has suggested, he felt his supervision was required because he had doubts as to whether Balanchine, whose previous ballets "had been almost entirely devoid of drama and feeling," could cope with what was required in this one. "Gifted though Balanchine undoubtedly was," Grigoriev wrote, "his approach was almost exclusively intellectual, and any manifestation of emotion was foreign to him."

New also, for a Diaghilev ballet, was the biblical theme and the religious spirit. The Soviet musicologist Nestyev, in his biography of Prokofiev, who composed the score for *Prodigal Son,* finds Diaghilev's choice of a biblical theme symptomatic. "In seeking 'eternal themes,' in turning to artistic devices of the remote past, the artists of the West sought to save themselves from the complete intellectual and artistic degeneration toward which their rootless experimentation was inevitably leading." Though Nestyev's tone is slighting, his point has some validity. *Prodigal Son* anticipates the trend toward religion and orthodoxy which characterized much art in the thirties and forties. It was Diaghilev's fate to be in the forefront of the vogue, even when he thought he was turning his back on vogue.

Doubrovska in Prodigal Son, *with Dolin and Woizikowsky as the two friends.*

Prodigal Son derived in theme and action from the parable in St. Luke. For clarity, some unessential elements, such as the good elder brother who remains at home while the sinful prodigal wanders, were omitted. The libretto was, as usual, by Kochno. Balanchine and Kochno often argued over the librettos. Balanchine favored making the story for a ballet as simple and clear as possible. Kochno liked to invent witty complications that were a delight to read but impossible to dance. "Paper will withstand anything," Balanchine would say to him, "but a stage is different. Not every idea is suitable for dance." Or sometimes Kochno, at a loss for an action, would simply write "*Promenade*"—leaving Balanchine with numerous measures of music to fill up, somehow or other. "It's all very well for you to write '*Promenade*,'" Balanchine would say in exasperation, "but meanwhile *I've* got to figure out something interesting for the people up there on the stage to be doing all that time." On this occasion, however, the libretto Kochno prepared was fairly straightforward. For some of the action, such as the Prodigal's return, Kochno drew on a Pushkin story, "The Stationmaster," in which are described in detail several engravings, depicting scenes from the biblical story, which hang on the walls of the little post station, somewhere in the middle of Russia.

Thus *Prodigal Son* had a biblical theme, but as seen through Russian eyes and filtered through Russian souls, and, as Balanchine choreographed it, one that was expressed in a thoroughly twentieth-century manner. His choreography was symbolic and expressionistic. It conveyed the central significance of each action and situation poetically—though the poetry was often the poetry of the grotesque—but never with a literal or naturalistic gesture. For this ballet Balanchine turned away from the classical vocabulary he had employed in *Apollo,* but he remembered the lesson he had learned about unity of tone. This time his palette of movement contained borrowings from gymnasts, circus performers, and acrobats. In an interesting article, "Acrobatics and the New Choreography," published in *Theatre Guild Magazine* shortly after *Prodigal Son's* premiere, Agnes de Mille discussed some of these devices and the uses to which Balanchine had put them: the circus trick employed in the duet between the Siren (Doubrovska) and the Prodigal Son (Lifar)—"one of the most important seductions to be found on any modern stage," she wrote—in which Doubrovska wraps herself around Lifar's waist like a belt and then slides slowly down his body to the floor where, as he sinks down beside her, their limbs intertwine in an inextricable tangle; or the tumbling stunt used to hurl her up to the shoulders of her depraved attendant revelers, where, from a height of ten feet, she stands looking down at her subdued lover, towering over her prey; or the back-to-back scuttlings of the inhuman revelers among whom the Prodigal Son has fallen; or the father's lifting up of his returned son from the dirt at the end and folding him tenderly in his cloak, like a child. Such steps and movements had not been seen on a ballet stage before, but they had been introduced by Balanchine not for show but to communicate inexorably the heart of the matter. There are very few modern works, in any art form, that can match this ballet's horrifying sense of degradation or the tenderness and wonder that the scene of redemption and forgiveness at the end achieves.

As usual there were last-minute inspirations at rehearsal. It was only at the final rehearsal that Balanchine got the idea of having the revelers be hairless, with bald pates—a most effective gargoyle touch. And it was just a few hours before performance time that he improvised the boat scene near the end when, finding himself at this point with music but no movement choreographed for it, he had the revelers turn over the long

⟲ *The boat scene from* **Prodigal Son,** *as performed by Yvonne Mounsey in the New York City Ballet's 1952 production.*

table and use it as if they were sailing away in it, with the Siren, her body bowed backward and her long magenta cloak stretched out behind her like a sail, in the pose of a figurehead. The dancers were not to suggest an actual departure at that point, but a charade of a departure: "This is how we'll sail away with our gold." Balanchine planned to change that part the next night when he had time, but it looked so good he kept it.

There were also last-minute altercations and emotional crises. Prokofiev, when he arrived in Paris in mid-May for the final rehearsals and to conduct the premiere, was appalled at what he saw. He hated Balanchine's stylized choreography. It was not at all what he had expected. He had envisioned the whole thing being done naturalistically. He wanted it to be "real"—with real wine to drink and real cushions to lounge on in the orgy, as in the orgy in the ballet *Scheherazade* twenty years before. And the characterizations were not what he had had in mind. According to his biographer Nestyev, Prokofiev had thought he was writing music not for a Byzantine whore as the Siren but for a delicate maiden—"a fragile young girl with a sad exquisite grace." The only thing he liked was the final repentance scene. He complained strenuously to Diaghilev, but Diaghilev sided with Balanchine.

An unpleasant episode over money also occurred. In those years royalties to the creative artists involved in ballet were paid through La Société des Auteurs et Compositeurs Dramatiques. There were royalties for the composer and for the librettist, but none for the choreographer. The composer's work and the librettist's could be printed, and hence copyrighted, whereas the choreographer's work, for lack of a system of accepted notation, had not been made subject to copyright laws. After *Apollo*'s premiere, Stravinsky had voluntarily decided to give Balanchine a sixth of his royalties. To those who knew how tight Stravinsky always was with money, this was an indication of how much he liked the choreography. After Prokofiev's arrival in Paris, Balanchine, impoverished as he then was, asked Prokofiev if he would do as Stravinsky had done and include him in some share of the royalties. Prokofiev was outraged. As Balanchine later recalled the scene, when he told me of it, Prokofiev shouted at him, "Why should you get money? Who are you? You're nothing but a lousy ballet master. Get out!" Balanchine apologized for having broached the subject, and left. For the rest of his life, he never again used a Prokofiev score.

Throughout the rehearsals of this ballet the company had been unusually wrought up, and tension grew as the first night approached. Doubrovska, whom Balanchine affectionately used to call his guinea pig because he liked to try out his most unusual new steps on her, was feeling uneasy because her poses and movements were so suggestive. She had never danced anything like that before. Lifar was suffering in his soul even more than usual, first because his beloved Serge Pavlovitch Diaghilev had turned against him of late, and second because he simply couldn't fathom what the role was supposed to mean—he couldn't *feel* the part. In one of his many memoirs—this one a book purporting to be a biography of Serge Diaghilev—Lifar has related how at long last, in the course of several agonized minutes on his bed in his hotel room just before the curtain went up, he "created" the "Prodigal Son." It is worth quoting at length.

In it, he tells first how, an hour before curtain time, Diaghilev's cousin and factotum, Korebut-Kubetovitch, called at his hotel to fetch him, and how, racked by doubts and torments as he was, he refused to go. He wasn't going to dance tonight, he told the poor cousin, he simply couldn't. Seven-thirty arrived. Then eight, then ten after eight.

The seduction scene from **Prodigal Son**—*with Yvonne Mounsey and Francisco Moncion.*

Korebut-Kubetovitch's face was white with anxiety. Lifar lay on his bed, suffering:

> *A terrific struggle was going on inside me. Somberly, sadly, I thought of Serge Pavlovitch, he who was my spiritual father, and of our relations together. I thought of the past, that life I had offered up as a sacrifice to him, uselessly and so unnecessarily. Why? To what end? Then visions out of the remote past came thronging around me. I saw myself in Kiev, on my father's threshold, returning from my first unsuccessful effort, to fly abroad. . . . I, a prodigal son, waiting for dawn to dare to enter my home. . . . The love, tenderness and care Serge Pavlovitch had lavished on me, the manner in which, through him, I had become an artist; all, all rose before me again, and a feeling of intolerable poignancy, of pity for the ailing, weary, aged old man—for suddenly he had begun to seem much older—sent a wave of endless commiseration pulsing through my being. Was it possible I could betray him? . . .*
>
> *The memory of things past, my sudden vision of the old man, merged*

into one vision of . . . The Prodigal Son. I am that prodigal son of his. . . . In my ears there sounded Prokofiev's music. Suddenly I saw light. I began to understand. From out of the depths of chaos and turmoil emerged the creative instant of clear and calm perception.

I leaped out of bed.

"Let's be off to the theatre. I have created my Prodigal Son. . . . It is myself."

His performance that night did, in fact, move the audience to tears. Balanchine later said that Lifar was, without doubt, the most exciting Prodigal Son of all those who had ever danced the role, as he was also the most impressive Apollo; but Balanchine laughed at Lifar's account of his creation of the part. He commented, when I drew it to his attention, "His performance would have been just as good, whether he had ever discovered or not that the Prodigal Son was really him in disguise, because he had been given interesting steps to perform and had been rehearsed very carefully." It was a characteristic Balanchine comment—cool, practical, unsentimental, antiheroic—concerned with technique rather than feelings. If he, himself, had been emotionally affected while working on *Prodigal Son*, the world would never know, for it would have been unlike him to admit it. As for Diaghilev, he valued Balanchine's technical mastery but, like Lifar, had no qualms about admitting his feelings. He told Balanchine he had been moved to tears by *Prodigal Son*. He said it was the best thing Balanchine had done.

On the night of July 26, 1929, the company concluded its London season. At Diaghilev's request, the entire company had assembled backstage so that Diaghilev could bid them farewell for the summer. He was going to Paris and then, by stages, to his beloved Venice, while the company was scheduled to leave the next morning for a performance at Ostend. When all were gathered, Diaghilev came onto the stage and gave a little speech, courteous and charming as only he could be. "You are leaving tomorrow," he said, "and I shall not see you again until the autumn. I wish you all to have a good rest and return to work refreshed and invigorated. We have a busy year before us. All my contracts are signed, and for the first time in our whole career we have an uninterrupted series of engagements already fixed. I thank you for the excellent work you have done, which has been largely responsible for any success we may have had. Good-bye—and good luck."

Lifar in **Prodigal Son.**

With that he passed among them and shook hands with each member of the company. Among Balanchine's memories of that night there persisted an olfactory one that, in some way, suggests the complex quality of the whole ballet enterprise—the fragrance of the almond-blossom pomade that the fastidious Diaghilev always used, mingled with the dusty smell of the backstage props and scenery and the acrid odor of the dancers' sweat. Diaghilev looked ghastly that night. His cheeks were as pale and lifeless as dough; his eyes, under which were dark circles, glittered feverishly. His massive head drooped and he moved with painful effort, as if his body were a burden too great for him to carry. When he spoke it was in a voice so low Balanchine had to strain to hear him.

Yet his appearance, though awful, did not alarm Balanchine or the other members of the company that night as much as perhaps it ought to have, for they, and Diaghilev's other acquaintances, had by now become accustomed to Diaghilev's continued ill-health. He was terrified of death, which no one might safely mention in his presence, and he took all the elaborate precautions of a superstitious hypochondriac. He would wipe his hands with a handkerchief to get rid of the germs after opening a door; rather than cross a black cat's path he would turn about and walk all the way around the block; when he rode in a carriage he worried about the possibility of catching glanders from the carriage horse; he was in constant anxiety whenever he had to cross the channel, for a fortune-teller had once told him he would meet death by sea; he wrapped himself up with the greatest care against drafts, which he could discern in rooms where no one else might be aware of even the slightest breath of air stirring. Yet he willfully neglected the simpler safeguards his physician had prescribed to cope with the actual ailment from which he suffered: diabetes. On an impulse he would stuff himself with chocolates or drink a bottle of champagne, even though he had been ordered to avoid sweets and alcohol; and, despite his obvious exhaustion, he would stay up till the early-morning hours at a party with his latest young protégé rather than admit that his sick, aging body required rest. To this, too, all who knew him had by then become accustomed. They assumed his extraordinary will would always revive his flagging flesh when need be, just as for twenty years, through all vicissitudes, it had animated his Ballets Russes. They were used to seeing startling changes in his appearance within a few hours, brought about by the sheer force of his spirit. "He could look the oldest man in the town when you met him at noon," wrote Gordon Craig, "and at eight, when the curtain was about to go up, he would look the youngest." They imagined he would somehow go on this way indefinitely.

The morning after that leave-taking scene backstage the company proceeded to Ostend, and from there to Vichy, where it performed for a week before an audience of fashionables and notables, a number of whom had been following the company with adoration since its inception. August 4 was the last night there, after which the company was scheduled to disband for the summer vacation. No novelties were performed that evening, but cherished favorites—an all-Massine program: *Cimarosiana*, *Le Tricorne*, and, for the closing ballet, *La Boutique Fantasque*, with Danilova, Tchernicheva, Balanchine, Woizikowsky, and Lifar as the principal dancers. Balanchine danced a mazurka in this ballet. At its close there were clamorous ovations, fortified by resounding basso "bravos" from Chaliapin, who had attended every evening of the week, and repeated curtain calls.

From Vichy Balanchine went back to England, where he was to choreograph a dance sequence for a film called *Dark Red Roses*, produced by Sinclair Hill, which, as it happened, was to be the first talking picture made in England. A romantic melodrama, the film concerned a sculptor who suspected his wife of infidelity with a musician; the dance sequence in it was used as is the mousetrap play in Hamlet—as a kind of fantasy reenactment of the crime to be played out before the eyes of the guilty ones at a party. The dance Balanchine made of this was a quasi-Oriental affair, to music from Mussorgsky's *Khovanchina*, and the dancers were Balanchine, Lydia Lopokova, and Anton Dolin. During part of the time he was in England in connection with this film, Balanchine was a guest of Lopokova and her husband, the economist John Maynard Keynes, at their country home in Sussex. Balanchine was extremely fond of Lopokova. Before her marriage, when she was a member of Diaghilev's company, she had been Diaghilev's most delightful comedienne. She could be very witty and even wise, in a piquant, spontaneous way; Balanchine thought of her as a kind of small, merry wizard. Keynes, too, for all his erudition, was of a high-spirited temperament—enough so as to move him to dance the cancan with his wife at Bloomsbury parties on occasion—and Balanchine always remembered his visit there with great pleasure. With Keynes he got along beautifully, for Keynes loved to talk about ballet and Balanchine loved to talk about economics, on which subject he held decided, if rather whimsical and untutored, opinions. One afternoon, when he happened to find himself in Keynes' study, Bal-

A scene from the movie **Dark Red Roses**—*Balanchine (with sword), Lopokova, and Dolin.*

anchine caught a glimpse of a paper dealing with economic theory that Keynes was working on. It was covered with formulas and calculations of which Balanchine could not make head or tail; he resolved to make no more pronouncements on economics to Keynes.

The dance sequence for *Dark Red Roses* was to be filmed on August 19. Dolin, Lopokova, and Balanchine went out to the film studio at Isleworth in the late afternoon, got into costume, and waited for the director to give them their call. In French, Russian, and tags of English they sat chatting as they waited. Lopokova had a few lines to say in the film before the dance began—a conventional compliment addressed to the sculptor, to the effect of, "I wish I could do as well with my feet as you with your hands." She was conscientiously reciting it over and over, for she was afraid she was going to get it backward when the scene was shot. Balanchine was doing his best to mix her up by inventing absurd variations on her lines. "I wish I could do with my toes as well as you can do with your nose," and the like. With such help, the more she rehearsed, the more mixed up she got, to the hilarity of Balanchine and Dolin.

In the midst of this a news vendor came around with the afternoon papers and Dolin walked over to get one. On the front page, as he glanced casually at it, Dolin saw a small picture of Diaghilev such as might accompany an announcement of some surprising new spectacle that that prince of surprises and splendors was planning. But there were to be no more such announcements. Crying *"Serge Pavlovitch est mort!"* Dolin ran back to where Balanchine and Lopokova sat and showed them the paper, with its brief item carrying the information that Diaghilev had died in Venice from diabetes in the early hours of the morning. "Big Serge, poor, poor Big Serge," murmured Lopokova, her eyes full of tears, "he was so tired, so very tired." Not talking much, the three of them, sad figures in their exotic costumes, sat on in the gloom and damp chill of the studio until two-thirty in the morning, when, at long last, the call came for them to do their dance before the cameras.

Soon those who had been Diaghilev's associates would begin to vie as to who could claim to be his true and sanctified spiritual heir. In Venice, at the funeral, Lifar would throw himself into the grave, like Hamlet, and he and Kochno would compete in their lamentations. Such was never Balanchine's style. He recoiled instinctively from hysteria. He would make no contribution to the various cults of Diaghilev that would arise. Then, and always, Balanchine distrusted cults—even cults celebrating undeniably exceptional persons, including, when that time would come, cults about himself. All such expressions, he felt, inevitably generated enough spuriousness to contaminate whatever was being thus celebrated. On the other hand, he would certainly not go to the other extreme, as some of Diaghilev's collaborators—such as Fokine and Benois—would do and assert that Diaghilev had made no creative contribution to ballet at all but had merely been a skillful, parasitical exploiter of the artists he had been fortunate enough to garner. A score of years later, at the request of *Dance News*, Balanchine contributed an appreciation of Diaghilev and an evaluation of the role he had played. He wrote:

> *Perhaps it is only today, almost twenty years after his death, that all contemporary choreographers begin to realize the true proportions of the enormous artistic debt we all owe to Serge Diaghilev. If we analyze the work we have done since his death in 1929, we see that we are still following in his footsteps, still adhering to the principles laid down by him during the twenty years he guided the fortunes of his unique Ballets*

Russes. Were he alive today, Diaghilev would probably find a new direction in his beloved art form, a new approach to the creation and presentation of ballet. He was always twenty-five years ahead of his time.

Diaghilev had the capacity to see not only the potentialities inherent in an artist, be he choreographer, composer, designer or dancer, he also knew what work, what style, what period suited that artist best. Great though it was, his genius for discovery would not have been so overwhelming had he not had that innate and cultivated taste which alone distinguishes true artistic quality from a sense for novelty and craftsmanship.

If I were to describe Diaghilev simply, I should say that he was a man of high culture. It so happened that he was a great ballet impresario, a patron of the arts, but he could just as easily have been a statesman, an ambassador: he could have held any post that required knowledge, intelligence, culture, taste. He was at home in world literature, music, painting and sculpture. He spoke three languages with the fluency and in the idiom of the native. Never a professional musician, he could read a musical score as one reads a book.

Stravinsky has described Diaghilev's intimate musical knowledge in his Autobiography *and Nicolas Nabokov, who also composed his first ballet for the Ballets Russes, has written of Diaghilev's great understanding of music in his book* Old Friends and New Music. *Never a choreographer or a dancer, Diaghilev knew what was exactly right and what was wrong about a particular ballet or in any portion of it. Never a painter, he possessed an unerring and intimate knowledge of art.*

These qualities made Diaghilev a creator, a real producer. He was not just the director or manager of a ballet company who guessed what the public would accept and what it would reject. He did not follow the public; the public followed him. He did not really care very much whether people agreed with him or not. What mattered to him was the work done by the best and most suitable choreographer, musician, designer and dancers. If they succeeded, their work was a success. Diaghilev so inspired the artists who worked under his direction that it is not too much to say that any ballet created for his company bore his personal stamp as well as that of the composer, painter and choreographer. . . .

During his five years with Diaghilev, Balanchine, as has been said, had remained on rather formal terms with him as far as their personal relationship was concerned. Still, that night at the Isleworth film studios, as he sat sadly waiting for the camera call, with the newspaper on the floor at his feet, he mourned Diaghilev with a keen sense of personal loss. How could he not? This man had been his great benefactor. He had reposed confidence in him at a time when Balanchine was but a youth, had recognized the promise of his inherent talents, and had provided him the conditions and opportunities for realizing them; he had taken pains to educate him and cultivate his sensibilities; he had, in short, helped transform him from a craftsman of ballet to an artist. For all this Balanchine was grateful then and remained so all his life. "It is because of Diaghilev that I am whatever I am today," he said.

CHAPTER SEVEN

Rootless Years

How important Diaghilev was to his Ballets Russes became unmistakable at his death. Without him the ballet company collapsed. Diaghilev himself had never been wealthy. He had been, in Cocteau's phrase, "a sublime pauper," dependent on the favors of his rich patrons for the realization of his luxurious fantasies. For years the duns had followed him about, waiting to pounce. At his death they seized what they could lay their hands on of the heavily mortgaged sets and costumes. A deluge of unpaid bills washed away Diaghilev's dance empire; his dancers were left stranded.

For Balanchine, the five years with Diaghilev had been an amazingly productive time. In addition to the ten ballets for the Ballets Russes, he had made dances for thirty-two operas at Monte Carlo as well as an unknown number for provincial French opera houses in the off season; he had choreographed at least eleven dance numbers as occasion or concert pieces for various dancers or other companies; he had done his first film choreography, and he had done his first musical revue choreography.

But that was all behind him. He couldn't live in the past. What was he to do now? He was twenty-five years old and needed a job. Almost immediately, a notable opportunity appeared. A few weeks after Diaghilev's death, Balanchine was approached by Jacques Rouché, the director of the Paris Opéra, and invited to stage a new version of Beethoven's two-act ballet, *Les Créatures de Prométhée,* as part of the centenary commemoration (two years late) of Beethoven's death, which France was then

Errante, *to the music of Schubert's* **Der Wanderer,** *as seen here in a 1934 production with* **William Dollar** *and* **Tamara Geva.**

123

observing. The Prometheus ballet was to be the Opéra's major event of the year; more than that, it was to be, Rouché hoped, a decisive effort toward the achievement of his ambition to resurrect the glory of French ballet at its ancient home. In centuries past the ballet of the Paris Opéra had been the most admired in the world; it had served as the very model of what ballet should be. But it had been in sad decline since the latter half of the nineteenth century. No one took the Opéra ballet seriously anymore. People attended the performances not to look at the ballet but to be seen themselves. The house lights were not even turned off during the performance. The spectators could sit in their boxes and chat and wave at their friends; during lulls in the conversation they could divert themselves by ogling the girls onstage. Season ticket holders were permitted to wander about backstage, where they might pinch from behind what they had ogled from in front. Rouché—a wealthy, dapper, bearded little man who looked himself like a *boulevardier*, like one of the *vieux abonnés* he despised, but was actually a man of considerable discrimination and artistic integrity—had long wished to change all this, but first, he reasoned, he had to produce ballets that were actually worth looking at and taking seriously. That was what he hoped Balanchine would do for him. He told Balanchine that he would like him to become permanent *maître de ballet* and assured Balanchine that the position—the most prestigious potentially in the Western ballet world—could be his if he wished to take it.

Balanchine was not at all sure at the moment that he wanted to become the Opéra's ballet master. He relished the prospect of having a big stage to work on, like that of the Maryinsky, where ingenious scenic effects were possible, and of having at his disposal a large company, well trained in the fundamentals of the classic dance, with a constant supply of new talent from the Opéra's ballet academy. But he did not look forward to the rest of what went with the position—the politics, the intrigue, the social calculations, the herculean efforts involved in effecting any changes and innovations in so bureaucratic and hierarchical an institution. For these aspects he had little talent or inclination. He lacked the ferocious, obsessive ambition for "success" it took.

But no decision was required as yet. The immediate question was *Les Créatures de Prométhée,* and Balanchine had no hesitation about accepting the engagement to stage that work, even though one of his friends, Eric Wollheim, who had been the British agent for the Diaghilev company, urged him fervently to have nothing to do with it. *Les Créatures de*

Prométhée had been a bad-luck ballet from the moment that Salvatore Vigano had commissioned it from Beethoven, he told Balanchine, and recited a long list of disasters associated with it throughout its history.

Balanchine began choreographing the ballet in late October. Within two weeks he fell desperately ill with pneumonia. At one point it was doubted he would live. French physicians in those days still treated pneumonia by cupping, an ancient form of bloodletting; thick glass cups, inside which burned tapers, were clapped to the patient's flesh, which turned bruise-colored when they were removed. It was supposed to draw out the inflammation. Balanchine managed to survive both the pneumonia and the treatment, only to learn, as he convalesced, that he had developed pleurisy, the consequence, quite likely, of the malnutrition and other hardships endured during the postrevolutionary years in Russia.

As soon as Balanchine was able to receive visitors, an aide of Rouché's called on him, wanting to know if he was going to be able to continue with the Prometheus ballet: time was growing short. Balanchine told him there was no chance of that. He urged that Lifar, who had the leading role in the ballet, be given the opportunity to finish choreographing it. Up till then, Lifar had choreographed only one ballet in his life, Stravinsky's *Renard*, with acrobats and dancers doubling in the roles, which the Ballets Russes had presented, with only moderate success, the previous May. The Opéra management had qualms about entrusting a major work to such a tyro but accepted Balanchine's recommendation, having no alternative except to cancel the ballet. Surprisingly, Lifar proved diffident. "Do you think I can do it, George?" he kept asking anxiously, as he paced, pantherlike, about the small bedroom where the ailing Balanchine lay.

"Certainly you can," Balanchine assured him. Still so weak he could barely keep his head propped up on the pillow, he wished that Lifar would just sit still for a bit.

"I mean, George, do you *really* think I can?"

"Of course. Don't worry about it. I'll help you in any way I'm able."

Recovered from his brief siege of humility, Lifar agreed to try. The two settled between them that Lifar could enjoy sole credit on the program as choreographer and that Balanchine, who was going to need all the money he could lay his hands on for his medical expenses, could keep for himself the 10,000-franc fee for which he had contracted with Rouché. (Lifar was to receive a substantial fee from the Opéra for his dancing.) In the two weeks before he had fallen ill, Balanchine had sketched the basic plan of the ballet and made a start on the choreography. Now, as work on the ballet resumed, under pressure to make up for lost time, Balanchine's bedroom became a workshop. Designers, musicians, personnel from the Opéra—all came and went, each with some urgent problem requiring attention. Daily, Lifar would appear at Balanchine's bedside to show him how the choreography was progressing. Balanchine would make comments and suggestions, interlarded with words of encouragement and reassurance.

This went on for some days until Balanchine's doctor, who had been grumbling about the strain to which his patient was being subjected, put a stop to it. The pleurisy, it was discovered now, had turned into tuberculosis. Balanchine would have to go to a hospital right away. By this time the ballet was taking shape. Lifar was growing in confidence. He no longer needed Balanchine.

The tuberculosis sanitarium that the doctor recommended was in the Haute-Savoie, amid pine woods and within sight of Mont Blanc. There, in that Magic Mountain environment—a self-contained world, introspective and remote, with its own values and concerns—the next three months of Balanchine's life were passed. He was supposed to lie as still as possible, this young master of the art of movement; to eat as much food as he could, even though he had little appetite; to avoid the direct rays of the sun—these were the main prescriptions of his treatment. Swaddled in blankets against the biting winter cold, he spent his days on the veranda outside his room, his gaze absently taking in the prospect before him—the snow-covered fields, the dark-green pine masses, and the austere and formidable mountainside, over whose ice fields the blue cloud shadows wandered. He was feverish most of the time and in a vague state. Time flowed by in dreamlike fashion. These months were an interval of suspended animation for him. He had no visitors. He did very little reading, or even thinking. No ideas for ballets occurred to him. He had never been able to do much away from a studio. For his imagination to be stimulated he had always needed, besides music, to have the dancers he was going to create for right before his eyes—assembled in the mirrored studio, waiting, idle but expectant, for the choreographer to make use of them. Up there in the mountains the world of ballet seemed as far away as the moon.

Still, all of his expectations were centered upon returning to ballet as soon as he was able. No other life could be imagined now. When the sanitarium's doctor wished to perform a pneumothorax operation on him, Balanchine flatly refused to allow it, for fear his career would be jeopardized. The unsuccessful knee operation had left him suspicious of surgery, anyway. If he were left now with only one lung, as well as a damaged knee, how could he ever expect to carry on the strenuous physical activity that choreographing required? The doctor was less concerned about that question. His interest was to preserve Balanchine's life, which was more threatened than Balanchine was aware of at the time; but seeing that Balanchine was adamant, he gave up trying to persuade him.

Shortly after this Balanchine's fever abated. He grew stronger. By the middle of December he was well enough to be taking walks about the sanitarium grounds and into the woods, and early in January he was considered sufficiently improved to be permitted to leave the sanitarium. Portions of both lungs had been permanently impaired, the left lung so badly that it did at some point, then or shortly afterward, spontaneously collapse. For the time being, the progress of Balanchine's illness had been arrested, but for many years afterward he was to be harassed by symptoms indicating that the infection had not been completely suppressed. He would start out a day feeling healthy and vigorous, but then in the afternoon he might find himself suddenly feverish and weak and liable to break out into a clammy perspiration at the least exertion. This condition he accepted as something he would have to live with; he tried not to let it interfere with his work, or with his pleasure either, for that matter. It was a source of amazement, to those who knew him, that he was able to pursue so taxing a career under such a handicap.

The next few years were to be rootless ones for him—years in which he would wander from one place to another, putting his hand to whatever he could. They were years in which he was without security, yet also, characteristically, quite without care on the whole. If he worried, he seldom showed it. On leaving the sanitarium, he went directly to Paris. Unacclimated as yet to the real world of the flatland, after his sojourn on the Magic Mountain, he found himself at first affected by a rather eerie sense of unfamiliarity amid the familiar sights, as if Paris or he, or both, had altered in some subtle way during his absence.

The next day he sought out Lifar. They greeted each other convivially. With great enthusiasm Lifar told Balanchine about the success he had scored with Prometheus at the ballet's premiere at the end of December. There had been a dozen curtain calls. What a triumph! Balanchine was pleased to hear of Lifar's success. After a while Lifar asked Balanchine what his plans were for the immediate future. Balanchine replied that he was in need of work and was thinking of talking to Rouché about the ballet-master job that Rouché had spoken of to him before he fell ill.

Lifar did not seem to think that was a very good idea. "They don't like foreigners here, you know," he said.

"What about you—and Efimov? Aren't you foreigners?"

"Well, we're here already. But I don't think they want any more."

Balanchine got the impression from that conversation that even if he could manage to overcome the Opéra's antipathy to foreigners and become engaged as ballet master, he would not find the atmosphere congenial. With a shrug, he said he guessed he would forget about it and would look for something else—he was sure something would turn up somehow. Lifar heartily wished him the very best of luck. They shook hands and parted. Not long afterward, the Opéra announced the appointment of its new ballet master: Serge Lifar.

Why Balanchine never pursued the position further if he had wanted it, at least to the extent of discussing it with Rouché, is difficult to explain—except that it was in keeping with his character that in some situations he would be diffident about pushing himself forward, while in others he would assume a dominating role without question. Once he had turned his back on the Opéra prospect, he suffered no regrets. He was a fatalist by nature—a lighthearted fatalist. He believed that since human beings were incapable of foreseeing all the circumstances and surprises that destiny had in store for them, it was a waste of time to try to plot out one's future. To calculate too finely is to presume on God's role, and he who does so can expect to meet with frustration, disappointment, and humiliation. The revolution he had experienced combined with the mystical religious training of his childhood to reinforce this philosophy in him. All that a person ought to do was make the best of whatever turned up. "As a human being, you cannot know in advance what will be best for you," he always said. All his life such would be his attitude. Like ballet itself, he would live intensely in the present, with no laments for the past and little regard for the future. He would never carry insurance. When insurance men would call on him, he would tell them, with an air of grave plausibility, that he would be happy to do business with them if their company would reverse its usual procedure, paying him a lump sum right off, to use while he was young and able to enjoy it, and letting him repay it bit by bit in his old age. They would depart, perplexed, and never call on him again.

As for the Paris Opéra, hindsight suggests that Balanchine would probably not have been content with the conditions he found there, and may well not have been able to function effectively. Whereas Lifar turned out to be just what the institution needed, a triumph of personnel placement, in effect. In him the Opéra obtained not only a capable enough choreographer and the most compelling male dancer of his epoch, but also just the kind of flamboyant and strenuous public personality the situation required. His love of the limelight, his flair and appetite for publicity, his copious memoirs and treatises on ballet, his feuds and well-advertised but happily bloodless duels, all enabled him to become himself something of a French institution, like Brigitte Bardot. Indeed, so well known was he to become that in France his name would eventually pass into the language as a lower-case noun. When a French paratrooper would put on his long underwear under his uniform, it would be his sergelifars he was getting into. Such is fame.

Meanwhile, to return to January of 1930 and Balanchine, he had said confidently that something would turn up, and within a few days something did in the shape of an offer from the English showman, Sir Charles B. Cochran, who was about to put together his *Cochran Revue* of 1930. After quickly choreographing for Nemchinova's little company in Paris a ballet to music by Poulenc called *Aubade*, Balanchine crossed the channel for England. There, in a period of about eight weeks, he prepared five ballets for the revue. Balanchine experienced no distress at finding himself working for a showman now, for Cochran was a unique figure—one of the great showmen of the century. In his time he staged a wide range of spectacles—revues, Shakespeare, contemporary comedies, Ibsen, prizefights, rodeos, religious pageants—all with zest and with exactly the quality of taste each required. "Cochran was the center of elegance and excitement in the theatre, with just that touch of toughness that brought in the crowds—and the money," recalls Beverley Nichols, who was the author of the book and some of the songs for the 1930 revue.

Cochran's revues had a flavor all their own. International, lavish, chic, they had the esteem of the intellectuals as well as the white-tie-and-tails set. His revues, Cochran said, "are not for the tired businessman." His aim, he declared, was to be "intelligently amusing." He commissioned sets from such artists as Derain and Bérard, and he engaged some of the finest Diaghilev dancers, including Nikitina, Lifar (who also choreographed one ballet for the 1930 revue), and Efimov. He had the taste to hire superlative talent, and the sense and modesty not to interfere with his employees.

The ballets in these revues could only be miniatures, because the Pavillion Theatre, though a charming theatre, possessed a stage not much larger than a dining table. The backstage area was equally cramped. It had only one narrow entrance to the stage; if a scene called for hoop skirts, the costumes had to be hung from the flies and lowered onto the performers before the curtain went up.

In these circumstances Balanchine managed to make works of art out of the miniature ballets he created and to achieve quite magical effects. They were ballet quintessences. Cecil Beaton, the designer and photographer, wrote in his book, *Ballet,* about the impression these numbers made on him at the time. He recalled attending the *Cochran Revue* several times to see them, thankful to find ballet being kept alive in some form or other after the demise of the Ballets Russes. One of the ballets that particularly caught his fancy was a carnival ballet called *Luna Park,* with music by Lord Berners, in which the dancers were sideshow freaks. The ballerina, Nikitina, was reduced to one shapely leg; Serge Lifar had been given two extra pairs of arms; and there was a two-headed man and other such attractions. Balanchine had obviously had a fine time working out the choreographic possibilities of those odd appendages and parts. "It was all very strange, and, in its peculiar way, beautiful," Beaton wrote.

Making a virtue out of necessity was always one of Balanchine's fortes—in ballet, as in his life as a whole. So, in one of his ballets for the *Cochran Revue* Balanchine triumphed over the confined area of the Pavillion stage by devising a work in which the dancers did not move about at all. *In a Venetian Box,* it was called, set to the music of the pizzicato movement of Tchaikovsky's Fourth Symphony. In this miniature work an ensemble of female spectators are seen as they sit watching a play; they weep, laugh, applaud, gossip, and look about them. The choreography featured only the movements of their arms and upper bodies, yet succeeded in maintaining variety and interest. The young dance critic of *The New York Times,* John Martin, then in Europe for a summer visit, wrote an appreciative review of the ballets in the Cochran show, singling out *In a Venetian Box* as a particularly delightful and subtly realized conception.

ᕈ *Lifar in a moment from* **Luna Park** *in the* **Cochran Revue** *of 1930.*

* * *

There was some talk in those days of Balanchine going to America to work. In an interview John Martin had with him, Balanchine was quoted as saying that he was sure he would be in the United States by the autumn, though he had no specific offers or projects in mind. A few months before this, the *American Dancer* had carried the report that Balanchine was slated to join Anna Pavlova's troupe on its American tour in the coming season. In fact, Pavlova and her husband, Victor Dandré, had met with Balanchine in Paris just before he fell ill and had asked him if he would create some of his "modern" ballets for her, but when he showed her some of his conceptions, she found them, predictably, not at all to her taste. What she was looking for really was a modern *Dying Swan*; neither Balanchine nor any other choreographer could provide her with such a fowl.

America seemed to beckon to the expatriate Russian; he thought of it as the country of the future; but all talk of his going there was premature. Instead, Balanchine made his way next to Copenhagen, to take up for a season the duties of guest ballet master for the Royal Danish Ballet. He stayed in Copenhagen from August 1930 until the following January. It proved to be not a very stimulating sojourn for him, or very satisfying for the Danes either. His assignment was to stage six works from the Diaghilev repertory: Fokine's *Scheherazade* and *The Legend of Joseph*; Massine's *The Three-Cornered Hat* and *La Boutique Fantasque*; and his own *Apollon Musagète* and *Barabau*. He would have preferred making new ballets to restaging old ones, even his own old ones; he tended to lose interest in a ballet quickly once he had completed it. For their part, the Danes, whose company is to this day a kind of wonderful living museum of the dance—the only one in the world that tries to present a whole repertory of ballet almost exactly as it may have been danced a hundred years ago—did not take to Balanchine's approach, which was always vitally contemporary even when he was paying homage to tradition. He freely altered all of the ballets he staged in Denmark, and for *The Legend of Joseph* he did completely new choreography from start to finish. Summing up Balanchine's tenure in Copenhagen, Svend Kragh-Jacobsen has commented in his historical work, *The Royal Danish Ballet*, "He did not make the impression his ability had promised."

From Denmark Balanchine made his way back to England. There he did a couple of numbers for Cochran's 1931 revue and also did a stint for Sir Oswald Stoll, the impresario of the Coliseum. In Sir Oswald's variety show, the little troupe of dancers that Balanchine had gathered ("16 Delightful Balanchine Girls 16," the billing ran) performed various "popular" ballets, which were supposed to furnish relief of a sort between the clowns and trained-dog acts. Some of the relief was unintentionally comic, the comedy being supplied by the efforts of the inept Coliseum orchestra to cope with the music.

Working for Stoll was not so satisfactory as working for Cochran. Still it paid handsomely. Best of all, it permitted Balanchine to live in England. England pleased him. "It is very dignified life here," he was heard to say approvingly. Cravatted and bowler-hatted, he used to go riding in Hyde Park on Sundays. He had his suits made at Anderson and Sheppard, and he learned to roll an umbrella. With umbrella impeccably rolled and trousers impeccably baggy, he fancied himself the very model of an English gentleman.

If he could have had his way, he would have been happy to settle in England. The Depression had begun to make itself felt in the theatre world though, and he found himself out of work. Without a job he could not get his residence permit extended, even though John Maynard Keynes interceded for him with the authorities; and so, with regret, he had to take leave of England and return to Paris.

With the money he had earned from his engagement at the Royal Danish Ballet, Balanchine had bought his first car, a sporty, green Willys roadster, which he had had imported to Copenhagen from the United States. When he had moved on to England, he had had it shipped after him. Now that he had to depart from England, he tried to take it along with him to France; but when he debarked at Calais, he found himself in a dilemma. He could not bring the car into France because, impoverished as he now was, he could not pay the import duties. He couldn't leave it at the dock, because he couldn't pay the storage fees. From this dilemma Balanchine neatly freed himself by making a present of the car to the nearest bystander. That's the way the money went. He lived, during those odd-job years following Diaghilev's death, sometimes like a prince, sometimes like a pauper. Saving or budgeting was not in his nature. When he worked and had money, he indulged his fancies, gave presents to friends and casual acquaintances, entertained with parties and banquets in the grand manner. Between jobs he seldom knew where his next meal was coming from.

Alexandra Danilova was waiting for Balanchine's return in their Paris apartment. When he arrived, she was particularly distressed to learn what he had done with the car, because she had just bought herself a complete outfit to go with it—green hat, green shoes, green dress, green bag. All that Balanchine had to offer her as a present was a bottle of toilet water he had bought in London. She regarded it with astonishment. Her blue eyes sparkled with icy incredulity, her proud neck arched regally. She looked magnificent. "Toilet water? To Paris! How very kind of you—I can see you've been thinking of me night and day." And she took the bottle and threw it at his head.

On that *opéra bouffe* note the curtain was rung down on their romance. It had in any case been fading away. Both had enjoyed other companionship during the frequent periods of separation from each other. Since his illness, Balanchine had been feeling that he was not so interesting to Danilova as he had once been. For her part, she had been chafing increasingly at the insecurity of their lives. The following year she married an Italian engineer, Giuseppe Massera, hoping to find a source of stability outside the world of the theatre, but the marriage did not long endure.

During the autumn of 1931, not long after Balanchine's return to the Continent from England, still another major opportunity materialized for him. He was asked by René Blum, the director of the theatre at Monte Carlo, to become the *maître de ballet* of a new company that Blum was organizing. Periodically, since Diaghilev's death, there had been rumors and announcements of new ballet troupes being formed to fill the gap left by the disappearance of Diaghilev's Ballets Russes; Blum's company—the Ballets Russes de Monte Carlo, as it was to be eventually called—would be the first such actually to come to fruition. In addition to Balanchine, Blum early solicited as collaborative talents Boris Kochno, Christian Bérard, and André Derain, For his *regisseur* he engaged Serge Grigoriev. And as a managerial colleague he took on, to his ultimate regret, Wassili Grigorievitch Voskresensky, a one-time military police and cossack captain better known to the world by his assumed name and title of Colonel W. de Basil.

A tall, gaunt man with thick-lensed glasses behind which gleamed cold, shrewd eyes, de Basil was a strange but powerful personality—a man of great energy and resourcefulness, with a reservoir of charm he could turn on at will and a natural propensity for the devious and the Machiavellian. He had little cultivation in the arts and next to no knowledge of ballet, but he did possess an instinctive theatrical flair. In recent years he had been associated with Prince Zeretelli in bringing performances of a Russian opera company to Paris, and in 1931 he had arranged for the appearance in Monte Carlo of a small troupe of dancers who had taken part in the Zeretelli opera. As soon as he got word of Blum's venture he hurried to Blum to offer his services. By that time Blum had already succeeded in establishing the basis of the organization. All that de Basil brought to Blum, as Blum later wistfully noted, was "vague promises of backing and contracts," yet so compellingly did he work on Blum that, almost before Blum knew what he was doing, he found himself taking de Basil into partnership and bestowing on him the title of codirector.

Balanchine had little to do with de Basil at first. His early dealings were with Blum, for whom he had great respect and with whom he was in excellent rapport. Blum, who was a brother of the French Socialist leader Léon Blum, was a gentle amateur of the arts—sensitive and cultivated. If de Basil was a character who would have been at home in the pages of a Dostoyevski novel, Blum could better have been imagined gracing the world of Proust. Indeed, he had been one of the earliest admirers of Proust's work at a time when that author was unknown and had helped make possible the publication of the first volume of *À la Recherche du Temps Perdu.*

It was Balanchine's conviction that the new ballet company should be *new* in almost every way. He did not wish it to rely on the Diaghilev repertoire or to present itself to the public as the true inheritor of Diaghilev's beaver-trimmed mantle. As he saw it, if Diaghilev had left any heritage, it was the message that one should dare to be oneself. Diaghilev was noted for his lifelong, almost phobic reluctance to repeat or even imitate himself. Sharing this feeling, Balanchine wanted to see the new company demonstrate its independence boldly from the start. He was averse to using the word "Russe" in the company's name, since it suggested a speciously glamorous link with the past. He would have preferred that the company forthrightly call itself Ballets de Monte Carlo.

Full of enthusiasm and ideas, Balanchine went out looking for dancing talent to recruit. The general expectation was that he would be signing on as many of the former luminaries of the Diaghilev company as he could round up, but Balanchine had different ideas. By chance, one day when he was in Paris, he met Danilova. She had heard the news of the new company being formed and was agog. Naturally she assumed that she would figure prominently in it. "When will we be starting, George? You'll be needing me, won't you?"

"No, Shoura," Balanchine replied. "I don't think so."

"But why not?"

"Because, frankly, you're too old."

"Too *old?*" Danilova cried, momentarily more astonished than outraged.

"That's right," Balanchine said. "For the kind of ballet company I have in mind, much too old."

At that time Danilova was twenty-seven years of age. She was just reaching her peak. Ahead of her were to be more than twenty years of glory and adulation, during which time she would reign as the prima ballerina of the era, at least outside of Russia. So it is understandable that Balanchine's words left her fuming. The fact was, however, that compared with the ballerinas Balanchine planned to employ, the twenty-seven-year-old Danilova did, indeed, seem venerable. While in Paris on this occasion Balanchine had discovered three prodigies, children of Russian émigrés, whom he had engaged. These were the trio upon whom American publicity agents were before long to pin the label of "the baby ballerinas"—Irina Baronova, who was twelve; Tamara Toumanova, who was thirteen; and Tatiana Riabouchinska, who was all of fourteen. The first two were pupils of Preobrajenska and the latter a student of Kschessinska. They could perform feats of virtuosity with innocent ease. Apparently nobody had told them that fouettés were supposed to be difficult. Though by St. Petersburg standards they were much too young for leading roles, Balanchine intended to feature them prominently in the new works he planned to create for the company.

Toumanova and Riabouchinska were to join the company in Monte Carlo when it began rehearsals after the start of the year. Baronova meanwhile was to have a part in the Offenbach operetta, *Orpheus in the Underworld,* which Balanchine staged in December 1931 at the Theatre Mogador in Paris. "The sensation of the evening," as André Levinson wrote after that work's highly successful premiere, "was the tiny child Baronova, who went through the final galop like a whirlwind."

Baronova herself, in an article she wrote some years later, gave an amusing and rather touching account of what being a "baby ballerina" was like. "At the age of twelve I found myself in the magical and hard-working world of ballet. In the years to come I found out that the hard work was always there but the magic was not always present. Of my debut at the Mogador Theatre I shall always have the happiest of memories. It was a delightful operetta; working with Mr. Balanchine was sheer joy, and all of us were madly in love with him. To show my admiration, I used to buy little bags of sweets (he loved sweets) and shyly offer him some; and to my delight he not only took a sweet but invariably grabbed the whole thing, which by then was rather a sticky little bag."

She remembered Grigoriev's perplexity when she arrived at Monte Carlo and was introduced to him as the newest member of the cast for whom he, as *regisseur*, would be responsible. "You are such a child, my angel!" he exclaimed. "Oh, dear, what am I going to do with you?" And she also recalled that in Monte Carlo a favorite off-duty diversion for the baby ballerinas, when they were away from the rehearsal hall where they had each been striving their utmost to appear as sophisticated and mysteriously glamorous as a Russian ballerina is supposed to look, was to go to Pasquier, the famous tea shop, and have a competition to see who could eat the most pastries. "Sometimes I would win by eating twelve pastries or more in no time at all, and I must confess without much effort."

It was, of course, most incongruous. Sometimes they seemed mere children, no different from other schoolgirls; at other times they never seemed to have had a childhood at all. In the ballets he created for them Balanchine succeeded in making a remarkable synthesis—a new artistic essence—out of these incongruities. He achieved this most tellingly in *Cotillon*, a ballet to music by Chabrier, with sets by Bérard, and which featured Toumanova, pale and mysterious, with her long black hair hanging down her back. Here dazzling choreography, which showed off the technical precocity of Toumanova and the others in the ballet, was combined with a wistful, bittersweet atmosphere, shy yet sophisticated, and somehow terribly poignant even in the midst of exuberance. *Cotillon* was a heartbreak ball that seemed to express, for all its tenderness, the insecurity and desperate gaiety of one moment of time, over which hovered a sense of fatality and doom. A. V. Coton, in *A Prejudice for Ballet*, has written: "As a creation of atmosphere—in the absolute sense, not an atmosphere of a time and place—nothing else in ballet compares with 'Cotillon.'" Some who saw it still regard it as Balanchine's masterpiece.

In addition to *Cotillon*, Balanchine fashioned two other new works for that first season: *Le Bourgeois Gentilhomme*, with music by Richard Strauss and scenery by Benois, which proved an agreeable but not memorable ballet; and *La Concurrence*, with music by Auric and decor by Derain, who was also responsible for the conception of the ballet. A madcap ballet depicting the rivalry of two tailors, who go to shameless extremes

to lure customers from each other, *La Concurrence* won favor from the start; it provided Baronova with an opportunity to show her talents and featured an extraordinary burlesque variation for Woizikowsky, in the role of a ragged tramp. There was one other new work, *Jeux d'Enfants*, which Massine prepared, as guest choreographer. With these as the showpieces of its repertory, the Ballets Russes de Monte Carlo made its debut on April 12, 1932, in the elegant, small theatre in Monte Carlo.

Out front the fashionable audience was delighted by what it saw. Behind the scenes, however, the picture was less delightful. Ballet companies have, of course, always been famous for the amount of intrigue that goes on in them, but those with which de Basil got involved were to be notorious in this regard. He thrived on intrigue. It was as salubrious an atmosphere for de Basil as a dank cellar is for a fungus culture. From the moment of his arrival at Monte Carlo he had begun his own intricate backstage ballet of maneuvering and finagling—fostering rumors, setting factions of the company against each other, elaborating schemes whose aims were never quite what they appeared. Steadily he managed to gain increasing control over the company's affairs; soon he seemed to have his hands in everything. Years later Balanchine was asked, on one occasion, to characterize de Basil. "De Basil was an octopus," Balanchine replied. Then he added, after a moment's thought, "A crooked octopus, and with bad taste."

René Blum had a fine automobile. Before long, de Basil could be seen riding about in it. He had persuaded Blum that the car should be considered part of the enterprise. Not long after that he got Blum to give him a bill of sale for it. "You know what?" Blum said wistfully to Balanchine one day, "De Basil has just bought my car from me with my own money." In that way, during the next few years, the entire enterprise was to pass from Blum's ownership to de Basil's. In a power struggle the gentle amateur of the arts was no match for the former cossack officer.

Frequently, during the company's formative months, de Basil would come to Balanchine with a receipt for ten thousand francs (or some such sum), which he would ask Balanchine to sign. Balanchine would ask why he should sign a receipt for money he had not received. De Basil would then give a complicated explanation, not exactly plausible yet somehow very nearly persuasive, to the effect that this would in some manner or other facilitate de Basil's raising funds for the company's use and thus enable it to put on more splendid and costly ballets. Balanchine always

Tamara Toumanova in Cotillon.

demurred. He was sure, however, that other of his colleagues—particularly Bérard, who would amiably sign anything put before him—did sign such fictitious receipts for de Basil; and he suspected that de Basil used them as a way of obtaining money from Blum.

On one occasion Balanchine had strong words with de Basil when he learned that de Basil had solicited fifty thousand francs from a young American would-be ballerina, giving her to understand that by making this contribution she could hope to get ahead in the company and get good parts from Balanchine. Balanchine was offended at the suggestion that roles in his ballets were for sale and, beyond that, outraged that de Basil had apparently left the impression with the girl that some of her contribution was to end up in Balanchine's pocket. De Basil seemed surprised and rather amused that Balanchine should get worked up over such a trifle. He shrugged, adopting his suavest man-of-the-world tone. "She's a rich girl, with nothing better to do with her money. Why get yourself all upset? You are an artist—you have your beautiful ballets to create. Leave these onerous money problems to me. That's what I'm here for. Ah, my dear Balanchine, you have no idea what an expensive luxury a ballet company is."

Balanchine also had words with de Basil about the latter's encroachment on the artistic policies of the company. Increasingly, he sought to alter the fundamental image of the company on which Balanchine and Blum had agreed. De Basil wanted to risk no commercial failures. He was eager to exploit to the hilt all the company's Russianisms. He aimed to peddle nostalgia, dressed up in what Balanchine regarded as phony glamour. The core of de Basil's clientele and patrons was to be all the White Russian exiles, weeping in their champagne for a Mother Russia such as never was. And additionally he sought to clutch Diaghilev to his bosom as a sacred relic, and to present the Ballets Russes de Monte Carlo to the world as nothing other than a kind of miraculous resurrection of Diaghilev's troupe.

All this was most uncongenial to Balanchine. Under such conditions he might have been expected to assert his principles and quit. He debated it; and while he was debating, de Basil quietly replaced him as *maître de ballet* with Léonide Massine. This took place in June, during the company's Paris season. The first that Balanchine heard of this transaction was when Danilova telephoned him one day to say that she was perplexed, for she had just been asked by Massine to join the Ballets Russes de Monte Carlo with top billing and she wondered why Balanchine was giving up his position. Danilova professed great indignation on Balanchine's behalf when she heard what he had to say about how he had been treated by de Basil, but she would have had to be less than human if she had not also experienced a certain delicious satisfaction at one aspect of the turn of events: the company she was now being courted to join was, after all, the same one her former lover had told her she was too old for the year before.

Even if Balanchine and de Basil had not been at odds, there were a number of respects in which it was clearly more advantageous to the Ballets Russes de Monte Carlo to have Massine as *maître de ballet* than Balanchine at that time. Of the two choreographers, Massine was then the bigger name. His ballets had wider appeal than Balanchine's. He appeared to have yet unlimited potential ahead of him as a choreographer and had a magnetic presence as a dancer. In addition, he brought with him, in his negotiations with de Basil, the rights to a number of the old Diaghilev sets and costumes, which he and an American theatrical agent named E. Raymond Goetz had acquired.

For one brief season, after his break with de Basil, Balanchine had the chance to try to put into practice something much closer to his conception of what he thought a ballet company should be—experimental and creative, international in its cultural orientation, and with no "Russe" in its name. Les Ballets 1933 it would be called.

It started out in January of that year amid an atmosphere of dedicated poverty, with a pittance of 25,000 francs to work on. The chief collaborators with Balanchine at first were Kochno, who had withdrawn from the Ballets Russes de Monte Carlo after Balanchine's dismissal, and Derain. There was also a handful of dancers from the Monte Carlo company, of whom the most prominent were Toumanova, Lubov Rostova, and Roman Jasinski. No one was being paid more than bare subsistence, but they met daily to prepare Balanchine's new ballets, and their enthusiasm was so great that they refused to worry about whether money could be raised to present the works to the public. They would put them on somehow, they vowed. Derain suggested that they buy a wagon which he would decorate, just as Toulouse-Lautrec had done for La Goulue, and that the troupe would travel around in it to fairgrounds and public squares, giving performances wherever they alighted.

Around this time the wealthy, young British socialite Edward James came along. James was looking for some token of affection to give to his estranged wife, the Viennese dancer and mime Tilly Losch—for whom Balanchine had choreographed "What Is this Thing Called Love?" in the 1929 Cochran revue—and he decided to make her a present of a ballet company, in which she could display her talents. A ballet company as a present for one's loved one is a more princely gift than a diamond necklace from Cartier's. The one season Les Ballets 1933 existed—in which not more than a score of performances were given—was to cost James over a million francs. It is to be hoped that James enjoyed the ballets that resulted from his largesse, for he gained little in the way of domestic or other bliss. He found himself harried and maligned by various disappointed composers and artists, who thought they should have been commissioned to contribute their precious efforts to the venture, some of whom he had to buy off to obtain respite; he had his face slapped on the stage of the Savoy Theatre in London after the curtain fell one evening by Lifar, who called him "an amateur," an incident which precipitated one of the celebrated bloodless duels and near-duels of Lifar's history; and within a short while his marriage to Tilly Losch broke up for the last time, culminating in one of the more sensational divorce suits of the era.

With the arrival of the bountiful James on the scene, Balanchine's little Cinderella troupe found itself suddenly able to have almost everything it could wish for. A number of other dancers were engaged, including Diana Gould (who later married Yehudi Menuhin) and Pearl Argyle, of whom Balanchine was briefly, and rather shyly, enamored. A brilliant group of designers, librettists, and composers was assembled, among whom, in addition to Derain, were Tchelitchev, Caspar Neher, Bérard, Bertolt Brecht, Kurt Weill, Darius Milhaud, and Henri Sauguet. In collaboration with such stimulating figures, Balanchine, applying himself to the task at hand with his typical calm but intense concentration, regardless of whatever hysteria or emotional turbulance might be in the air, produced in a remarkably short time six new ballets—*Errante, Songes, Fastes, Mozartiana, Les Sept Péchés Capitaux,* and *Les Valses de Beethoven.* These, together with a brief oratorio, *Job,* by Nicolas Nabokov, made up the entire repertory.

By the night of the company's premiere, which took place in Paris on June 7, the atmosphere of dedicated poverty in which the troupe had begun its work had been long forgotten. The fashionable and avant-garde intellectual elements of Paris had adopted the much discussed, though as

William Dollar with Holly Howard and Annabelle Lyon in the 1934 production of Errante.

yet unseen, new company as their pet of the hour. The season was held in the glittering Théâtre des Champs-Élysées—a far cry from the painted wagon Derain had romantically suggested a few months before—and the opening night turned out to be one of the poshest social events in years. *The New Yorker*'s correspondent, Janet Flanner, wrote in her Paris letter shortly afterward:

"The French are still fond of dancing. As proof, the opening of the newly organized 'Les Ballets 1933' at the Champs-Élysées was the most brilliant first night of *tout Paris* since the *ouverture* of Comte Étienne de Beaumont's 'Soirées de Paris' in '24, which was probably the most brilliant première since Diaghileff's 'Sacre' in the spring of '13. Which was probably the most brilliant debut since Fanny Elssler's at the Opéra in 1834, which was probably the most brilliant first night since the court ladies of Louis XIV applauded themselves as ballet girls in Lulli's 'Triumph of Love,' by special request. For four hundred years Parisians have been regally addicted to ballet, and if the 1933 group lacked Bourbon appreciation, it enjoyed Ritz royalty, much more tastily dressed."

Yet, for all that, Les Ballets 1933 fell flat. There was a moderately appreciative response for the lighter, more conventional works, but the public, with only a few notable exceptions, did not take to the three more experimental and more consequential ballets—*Errante, Mozartiana,* and *Les Sept Péchés Capitaux.* The first they found scandalous, the second dull, and the third disagreeable. Paris' most distinguished and thoughtful ballet critic, André Levinson, wrote a lament in the newspaper *Candide,* grieving over the course that Balanchine's career seemed to be taking. "By a phenomenon as regrettable as it is curious," Levinson wrote, "this artist, having proved himself last year by guiding his world in the direction of a choreographic classicism rejuvenated by fortunate audacities, abdicates his role of leader and resigns himself to the auxiliary role of a kind of illustrator who comments, by vague dance steps, on the musical concepts of composers or the pictorial concepts of designers." In trying to satisfy so many contrary and uncongenial demands on his talents, Levinson wrote, Balanchine seemed plunged in perplexity, "totally disoriented, riddled and shaken up by contradictory esthetics. . . . It is for us to hope that this almost total eclipse of a choreographer in whom we had founded the most justified hopes is only temporary; moreover it is necessary that he be taken in hand again by a patron capable of orienting his vacillating will."

During the same time that Les Ballets 1933 was appearing at the

Champs-Élysées, de Basil's Ballets Russes de Monte Carlo, in direct competition with the new company, was presenting its Paris season at the Théâtre du Chatelet. To add to Balanchine's mortification, his former company was acclaimed as sheer delight and far better in nearly every way than it had been the previous year, when he had been its *maître de ballet*. In London the ballet war continued, with Balanchine's company opening at the Savoy on June 28 (with the addition to the repertory of a Lifar ballet, danced by Lifar and Nikitina) and de Basil's company opening at the Alhambra on July 4. The results were the same there as in Paris. Les Ballets 1933 could sustain only a few performances and then had to capitulate, leaving the Ballets Russes de Monte Carlo triumphantly in charge of the field.

In London Balanchine's company was to disband in mid-July. Balanchine was at loose ends once again. The four years since Diaghilev's death had been restless ones for him; the future seemed to hold no promise of any greater stability. There were job possibilities on the horizon, but nothing that he craved. He had been making ballets for thirteen years, since his first choreographic effort at the age of sixteen. Most of the ballets he had made had already vanished, never to be seen again, and as far as Balanchine could judge, the few still in repertory were shortly doomed to follow the others. Balanchine did not mourn them. By its nature, ballet is the most ephemeral of the arts. It is like ice sculpture or sand painting, threatened with dissolution from the moment of its creation. The awareness of its mortality contributes to the poignancy of the spectator's experience. Balanchine always accepted this, without distress, as a fundamental condition of his art. "Ballets are like butterflies," he would say. "Who wants to see last season's butterfly?"

But not to be able to engross himself in new creation, not to have a company for whom he could fashion the next season's butterflies—that would be the great frustration for him. He sat backstage at the Savoy one night after a performance, despondently weighing his possibilities. He had just danced *Errante* that night, substituting for the injured Jasinski, and he was exhausted as well as in a state of uncertainty.

It was at that point that the American, Lincoln Kirstein, entered his life.

CHAPTER EIGHT

But First a School

Since childhood, Lincoln Kirstein had been enamored of ballet. As a nine-year-old, when his parents refused to take him to see a performance of Diaghilev's company in Boston, during the one American tour it made, he harbored vengeful fantasies of running away and becoming a famous dancer. The scion of a wealthy, mercantile, Jewish family, he was born in Rochester, New York, and brought up in Boston from the age of five. His father was a partner in Filene's, the department store. His mother furnished and decorated their big house on Commonwealth Avenue in emulation of Mrs. Jack Gardner's Fenway Court. The walls were hung with green silk, and the house abounded in neoclassical art; Lincoln loved growing up in it. For the most part, he was encouraged in his early interest in the arts, and he never did know why he wasn't allowed to see the Diaghilev company on that occasion, although he suspected later on that it was because in the ballet *Scheherazade* the black slave Nijinsky made love to a white harem queen.

When he was ten years old, he bought his first work of art; at twelve, he saw Pavlova and her troupe dance at Symphony Hall (a dilettante older cousin took him; they went five nights running); at fourteen, he wrote a play, set in Tibet, which he managed to get published. During his fifteenth year, he spent the summer in London, where his older sister Mina had taken a house. He mingled with the Bloomsbury set—David Garnett, Lytton Strachey, John Maynard Keynes and his wife Lydia Lopokova, E. M. Forster, and the Sitwells—and heard lots of clever gossip as well as much talk about the arts.

Lincoln Kirstein, about 1934.

147

In 1926 he entered Harvard, after working for a year in a stained-glass factory to get some "practical experience." There, he essayed various arts, showing some talent in all of them: he won a prize for freehand drawing, wrote and published a novel, played the piano better than competently, collected artwork, wrote articles on painting and photography, and was one of the cofounders of the Harvard Society for Contemporary Art, which is generally credited with being the germinal source out of which grew New York's Museum of Modern Art. And, while still in college, he helped establish the highly regarded literary quarterly *Hound and Horn,* which he later edited.

But it was ballet that gripped him most. He first saw the Diaghilev company in London in 1924, when he was seventeen. "The first blaze of its great adventure was over. A small theatre housed the company, and it was by no means a good season. But I never knew that," he later wrote. "It was exactly as if I had come home to that splendid country for which I knew I had been destined, but which up to that time I could not seem to find." Every season thereafter he traveled to Europe to see the ballet, and soon he began noting appreciatively the works that Balanchine (just three years older than Kirstein) was creating. "Ballet became an obsession with me," he wrote. "Far more than the ordinary influence or attractions of Harvard, the ballet seemed my real education. As time passed, I was increasingly magnetized toward some direct participation in it."

This growing conviction that ballet was to be his special destiny was reinforced by an episode that occurred when he was twenty-two. It was August of 1929, and he was a tourist in Venice. He was searching through the back alleys one hot morning for a church in which El Greco might have worshiped. As he approached it, he found a barge of black and gold moored to the church steps. Entering the church, he perceived in the gloom a bier, blanketed with heaped-up flowers, below a great Byzantine iconostasis of burnished bronze. "Suddenly he became aware of mourners, and the fact that this was, indeed, a funeral," he wrote in *Hound and Horn,* portraying himself in third-person form. "Faces, somehow familiar, ignored him as he passed out into the sunlight, and leaving, heard the first words of the Greek Orthodox service for the dead. Not until three days later, reading the London *Times,* did he learn that he had unwittingly attended, in San Giorgio dei Greci, the obsequies of a great Russian."

It was the funeral of Serge Diaghilev. The episode affected him strongly; he dwelt on it in detail in the novel *Flesh Is Heir,* which he wrote two years later. That he should have been led to that scene at just that moment seemed to him no mere chance but a sign that fate was making to him, perhaps even a revelation of a role he might someday assume.

Preparing himself, he plunged into extensive research in the history of the dance, the fruits of which appeared in his book *The Dance* a few years later, which was described at the time of its publication as the most comprehensive history of the dance to date. He also helped Romola Nijinsky with her biography of her ill-fated husband. And at the age of twenty-five Kirstein—six feet three inches tall, ungainly, self-conscious, and cerebral—began taking elementary ballet lessons from Mikhail Fokine in New York, exposing himself to the derision of that great but by then embittered ballet master.

"How can Kirstein be a director of a ballet company?" Fokine some years afterward commented scoffingly to Anatole Chujoy, the editor of *Dance News*. "He took some ballet lessons from me, and he can't get his feet off the floor." To this, Chujoy replied that, after all, Diaghilev had never taken a ballet lesson in his life—a reply not likely to impress Fokine, who nursed the aggrieved conviction that, as a ballet company director, Diaghilev had been a baleful influence. For Kirstein, taking these lessons was the act of an intellectual deciding that he ought to be less intellectual in his relationship with so physical and immediate an art as ballet—a groping attempt to share to whatever extent he could the experience of the working ballet practitioners.

When Kirstein set sail for Europe in the summer of 1933, he was ready to make his decisive commitment to ballet. He had some money of his own. When he graduated from Harvard in 1930, his father had said to him, "Look here, I'm going to leave you a lot of money. Do you want it now or when I die?" Lincoln answered, "I want it *now*." And his father thereon gave him his share of his inheritance. In addition, he carried with him tangible assurances of financial assistance from friends and relatives, particularly Edward M. M. Warburg, of the banking family, the classmate with whom he had collaborated in founding the Harvard Society for Contemporary Art. "I felt that I was about to put all the pieces together in my puzzle—pieces I had been unconsciously collecting for the previous ten years," he wrote. The pieces fitted together into a vision, one that, in the perspective of history, was of imperial grandeur. He wanted to bring ballet to America. He was not content to have some Russian or Russianesque company tour here, but, rather, it was his idea to have ballet take root and prosper as a vital, indigenous art in the United States—to establish a ballet academy, a ballet company, a ballet repertoire, and a ballet audience. Such a transplanting had succeeded only three or four times in the three hundred years since the first ballet company was chartered by Louis XIV, and each time it had taken a monarch with ample coffers to achieve it. Each time, too, it had been effected by the importation into the new country of a great ballet master from the old, who brought the art with him, like Prometheus bringing fire.

Even before Kirstein saw what Balanchine had wrought in Les Ballets 1933, he knew that it was Balanchine he wanted as the instrument of his ambition, and what he saw that year reinforced his conviction, despite the audience's lukewarm response. "Why did I choose Balanchine?" he asked in a retrospective article he wrote for *Theatre Arts* in 1958. "Because I was in love with dancing and had seen 'La Chatte' in 1927 and 'Apollon Musagète' the year following. No one else could do dances like these. There was no question of choice, even if Fokine, Massine, or Lifar had been accessible to me, which they were not (although subsequently they might have been); I knew that what Balanchine made meant ballet to me, because ballet was about dancing to music, not about painting to pantomime."

Still, all was not as clear and inevitable at the time as it became later in retrospect. In 1933, for all his ardor, Kirstein was beset by uncertainties and acutely conscious of his youth and inexperience. Was it folly to have the ambitions he had? What was he letting himself in for, in seeking to transplant ballet to America? How much would it cost, and where would the money come from, once the initial commitment and his own inheritance were used up? How was a venture like this managed? What else was involved beyond engaging a ballet master? Certainly Balanchine was the ballet master whose work intrigued him most, but did that necessarily make him the right man for the job? Was he available? Would he be interested? What would he be like to work with?

That summer in Paris, Kirstein looked for advice. He frequented the studios of Pavel Tchelitchev, who was working on the designs for Balanchine's *Errante,* and listened to that mystical spellbinder talk about art, theatre, ballet, the cosmos. Tchelitchev dazzled him. He told Kirstein that Balanchine was the best ballet master of the lot, even though he had no taste or visual sense, but that was all right because he, Tchelitchev, would supply all the taste the enterprise required. Kirstein also saw much of Virgil Thomson, the composer-critic, who, as Kirstein put it, "undazzled" him. With his cool, realistic insights into the politics and finances of the ballet world, Thomson "showed me the skull beneath the skin," Kirstein wrote. Still, Thomson paid Kirstein the compliment—somewhat to Kirstein's surprise—of acting as if he thought what Kirstein wished to accomplish could, in fact, be accomplished. And Kirstein talked a lot with Romola Nijinsky, who knew intimate details about everybody in the ballet world. She told him Balanchine was madly in love with Tamara Toumanova, but that Toumanova's mother thought her daughter was too young to marry. All Kirstein's advisers warned him about Balanchine's ill health. He would be dead in three years, Romola Nijinsky told Kirstein; a clairvoyant had given her the exact date of his death. In his diary, Kirstein made due note of this. "However," he wrote, "much can be accomplished in three years."

It was Romola Nijinsky who arranged the initial meeting of the two men. She took Kirstein backstage after a performance of Les Ballets 1933 at the Savoy Theatre in London. That was the night when Balanchine, at short notice and despite his bad knee, had been required to step in and dance Jasinski's role in *Errante*. Seeing how weary Balanchine looked, Kirstein made no attempt to discuss his plans then. A few days later they talked briefly when they met at the rented house of a New York art dealer. Shortly after that, at Kirstein's invitation, Balanchine called on him at his hotel, and there, in the parlor of the small hotel—"dusty with propriety and full of provincial beauties who had come up to London to be presented at court," as Kirstein remembered the scene—the two of them talked, conversing in French. Two more dissimilar young men it would be hard to imagine—the one wealthy and dilettante, earnest and torrentially articulate, and the other buoyant by nature, distrustful of solemnity about his craft, and with scarcely a penny to his name. That afternoon in the parlor, Kirstein poured out his admiration for Balanchine's creations, his grand dreams for the ballet in America, his lofty ideals for the future of the art, his ardent hope that Balanchine would join him in the endeavor. Balanchine said that he would like to try it. As far as he was concerned, Europe had become a museum; in America he sensed the promise of new possibilities. He would dearly love to go to a country, he said, that produced girls as wonderful as the movie star Ginger Rogers. Fervently, Kirstein promised Balanchine that by the time he was forty he would have a company and a theatre of his own. Balanchine replied, "But first a school."

After Balanchine left, Kirstein sat on in the parlor, his imagination soaring even higher than before. At the next table, having tea, were three young women in white court dress, with plumes in their hair—just returned, most likely, from the court photographers. "I could not discover whether they were the three Muses of Apollo or the three Fates," Kirstein wrote. "My mind jumped forward in time and I saw the completed school achieved and functioning, and even more, a great stage swarming with dancers the school had trained, situated somewhere in America. It was exasperating to think concretely of ways and means to make the mirage a miraculous reality."

Balanchine arrived in New York aboard the *Olympic* on October 18, 1933. With him was Vladimir Dimitriev, for Balanchine had insisted, as a condition of his own acceptance, that Dimitriev should be in charge of the school's administration. Balanchine still felt a debt of gratitude to Dimitriev for the enterprise he had shown in organizing, nine years before, the little ballet exodus from the Soviet Union; and, though he was no longer the inexperienced youth he had been then, he still looked to the older man for guidance on practical matters.

The times could scarcely have been less propitious for an attempt to introduce into the United States so exotic, costly, aristocratic, and useless an amusement as ballet. The arts were expected—according to the dominant critical and intellectual attitude of the Depression period—to be committed in the social struggle, to portray reality in all its harshness, or at least to be earthy and "of the people." Classical ballet certainly did not meet any of those conditions. Modern dance seemed closer to the earnest temper of the time than classical ballet. Actually, there were comparatively few people in the United States, even among the sophisticates, who had ever seen any ballet. Famous ballet stars and their troupes—Pavlova, Mordkin, Bolm, Fokine, and others, including Nijinsky and the Diaghilev Ballets Russes—had made American tours or given performances in this or that large American city, with varying degrees of acclaim, during the past twenty years; but there was no settled tradition of ballet in the United States, no significant standard of reference. People who had never seen ballet naturally did not feel that they were missing anything, while among its devotees the snobbish conception prevailed that Americans could never master ballet techniques and simply did not have the "soul" for ballet.

Initially, the plans drawn up by Kirstein, in consultation with his wealthy young colleague, Warburg, had called for the new institution—

the School of American Ballet, as it would be known—to be established at Hartford, Connecticut, under the auspices of the Morgan Memorial Museum there. The theory was that the school should be conducted in a sheltered, tranquil atmosphere, like that of a university, sufficiently remote from New York to be unaffected by that city's pressures and demands, by the ambitions and crises under which the performing arts labor there. The museum, in addition to offering the ballet school the dignity of its sponsorship, would be able to make available to it a completely equipped auditorium and excellent classroom facilities. It seemed, in theory, a most advantageous arrangement. Kirstein, who had worked very intensively and persuasively to effect it, was entitled to feel satisfied with himself at having these details all worked out in time for Balanchine's arrival. There was, however, one major factor that he had neglected to take sufficiently into account: Balanchine.

After having received his training in the capital city of Russia and gone on from there to show his wares in Paris and London and other great cities of Europe, Balanchine did not fancy the idea of now settling down in a provincial American town, whose name he had never even heard before. This was not what he had come to America for. He and Dimitriev announced to the flabbergasted and crestfallen Kirstein that they would rather return to Europe than go to this Hartford place. They might well have done so if Balanchine had not fallen seriously ill at that point, with a recurrence of tuberculosis. Gravely ill, he spent several weeks in bed following a treatment prescribed by a Russian doctor he had met. The treatment was to stuff himself with as much food as he could, particularly fats—as much as a pound or more of butter at a meal. In a month he gained thirty pounds. Presumably the treatment worked, for he did recover, though subsequently he used to wonder what this diet may have done to his liver. During the time Balanchine lay ill, Kirstein and Warburg frenziedly revised their plans. They had begun to get an inkling of the crisis-ridden existence they had let themselves in for in getting mixed up with ballet, in aspiring, as they put it in one of the many grandiose public announcements they issued, "to further the tradition of classical theatrical dancing in order to provide adequate material for the growth of a new art in America." Reluctantly they gave up their carefully secured Hartford connection. After some search, they found a classroom on the fourth floor of an old building on Madison Avenue at Fifty-ninth Street. The classroom was in a studio that Isadora Duncan had once occupied. Balanchine was disappointed by the makeshift quarters. His talk with Kirstein in the London hotel had left him in two quite contrary states of mind. On the one hand, he hadn't really expected anything to come of that conversation, since he had never even heard of Lincoln Kirstein before he met him. At the same time, though, he firmly believed—based on popular mythology and the movies he had seen—that whatever Americans decided to do, they did on a giant and opulent scale. An American ballet academy, therefore, would be like West Point. He had some things to learn about America. Fortunately, he was endowed with the capacity to make do and bide his time.

The official opening date for the School of American Ballet was January 1, 1934, and classes began the next day. Thirty applicants auditioned; twenty-five were accepted. Some of these were pupils of Catherine Littlefield, of Philadelphia, who had given them good training. Only three were male. Dimitriev had the title of director of the school. Balanchine was chairman of the faculty, which consisted of just two other members. One was Dorothie Littlefield, who was to teach the junior grade. The other was Pierre Vladimirov, a former partner of Pavlova's and Nijinsky's successor as *premier danseur* at the Maryinsky. It was by chance that this distinguished dancer became available to the school. At the time the school was being formed, he happened to be in New York, as a member of a small troupe that Lifar had brought to America, and became dissatisfied with it. Balanchine had always admired Vladimirov greatly and thought it very lucky that the school had been able to obtain his services. Ballet is an art of example. No textbooks can supplant the living presence of a teacher, who embodies tradition.

Among the students enrolled was sixteen-year-old Ruthanna Boris. Years later, after a career as a soloist and choreographer, she recalled her first days at the School of American Ballet. "We were all shy with Balanchine. He was a great figure to us, and handsome. He had beautiful sideburns. Most of us instantly decided we were in love with him. He asked me to do a double turn. I said I couldn't. 'Certainly you can,' he said. I got halfway around when suddenly I felt a whack on my behind, and I spun all the way around before I fell down in surprise. It was the first time in my dance training that anyone had laid a hand on me. Our training hitherto had been aloof, impersonal, very proper. That wasn't the Russian way, which involved whacking, pushing, tugging, touching, poking, lots of physical contact. It was a whole different way of communicating, and very electrifying. Suddenly I found myself doing things I had never thought possible."

∿ *The first known photograph showing Balanchine working with American dancers—June 1934, at White Plains.*

An interesting relic of those early days of the School of American Ballet is a snapshot, which is the first photograph taken, so far as is known, of Balanchine rehearsing American dancers. Dated June 1934, it shows him out in the open air, on a small, tree-rimmed stage, preparing a group from the school for its first performance. Looking at the snapshot, one can readily see why it was felt that ballet dancing was no activity for Americans. It just does not seem possible that anything remotely like a ballet troupe could ever emerge from this hodgepodge of chubby, self-conscious young women in homely, one-piece bathing suits. A couple of them have their arms upraised in an ethereal attitude and appear to feel pretty foolish about it. Another has a hand clapped to her head, as if she were asking herself, "Now what was I supposed to do on count three?" Still another suggests a shopper in a department store; her feet hurt, but she won't give up. A hefty woman with a bandanna on her head, standing at one side of the group, half-crouched, with her legs apart and solidly planted, looks more like a prospective linebacker for the New York Giants than a future ballerina. Balanchine is to be seen in the midst of this forlorn, chaotic scene, tugging at one of the young women in an effort to haul her approximately into position. He is the only person in the picture who does not seem to be aware of the manifest hopelessness of the whole enterprise.

If it is strange to reflect that the brilliant New York City Ballet developed out of so unpromising a beginning, it is almost as astonishing to realize, as one looks at this funny picture, that the ballet Balanchine was working on with that group must have been *Serenade*—a work of enduring loveliness, which is today to be found in the repertory of many companies throughout the world. *Serenade* was the first ballet that Balanchine created in the United States, and the first of any consequence ever created for American dancers. It was a choreographic tour de force. Balanchine devised it as a lesson for the students in his school's advanced class. He wanted to show them how the fundamental steps they were painfully trying to master can become transformed, when shaped by a choreographer, into something more than routine exercises, and he also wanted to bring home to these novices that ballet, for all its ancient heritage, is a living, contemporary art, not to be worshipfully thought of, as most people thought of it then, merely in terms of *Giselle* and *Swan Lake*. So, with a string serenade by Tchaikovsky for his music, he improvised choreography around his students. The first evening he worked on it, seventeen young women were present, so he choreographed the opening scene for seventeen, demonstrating how that awkward number of dancers could be arranged on the stage in an interesting manner. The next evening, only nine were present, and the third evening six; at each session he simply choreographed to the music with whatever students he had. Male students began attending the classes, and he worked them in. At one point, where the women were supposed to rush out, one fell down and began to cry. He choreographed the incident right into the ballet. Another evening, someone showed up late. That went in, too. Subsequently, when Balanchine decided to make a stage work of *Serenade,* he elaborated some parts, dropped others, and made the whole thing more theatrical and dramatic, embodying in it an elusive suggestion of a story about ill-fated lovers. What *Serenade* is really about, though, is not that hint of a story; it is about the classical ballet itself—how the young, inexperienced, unsophisticated dancers we see on the stage achieve mastery of the art, and how they are refined and transfigured in the process. So it opens with the dancers standing in diagonal rows, as if in a classroom, with one arm upraised, feet together and toes pointed forward. Then, on a chord, they open their feet to the first position. This is the most elementary movement in ballet, yet Martha Graham, whose own career in the dance was a long revolt against formal ballet, once said that at that moment, the first time she saw the work, tears sprang to her eyes. "It was simplicity itself," she said, "but the simplicity of a very great master—one who, we know, will later on be just as intricate as he pleases."

In Balanchine's first American ballet, Edwin Denby has written, Balanchine was devising, intentionally or unintentionally, an approach to ballet that would be natural for American dancers. The problem was that Americans were as yet too self-conscious to dance in the grand classical manner, and Balanchine tackled it by making the company as a whole more important than any individual stars. Denby writes:

"He had to find a way for Americans to look grand and noble, yet not be embarrassed about it. The Russian way is for each dancer to *feel* what he is expressing. The Americans weren't ready to do that. By concentrating on form and the whole ensemble, Balanchine was able to bypass the uncertainties of the individual dancer. The thrill of 'Serenade' depends on the sweetness of the bond between all the young dancers. The dancing and the behavior are as exact as in a strict ballet class. The bond is made by the music, by the hereditary classic steps, and by a collective look the dancers in action have unconsciously—their American young look. That local look had never before been used as a dramatic effect in classic ballet."

Balanchine sometimes liked to say that such exegeses as Denby's were "too fancy" and that all he had been trying to do was teach his students "some little lessons" and make a ballet that would conceal their individual inadequacies. Maybe so—yet *Serenade* always remained a ballet of special importance to him. It was not allowed to slip casually into oblivion, as happened with many other lovely Balanchine ballets. From time to time over the years Balanchine would turn to *Serenade* and work it over in one way or another—adding some elements, omitting others, consolidating or expanding individual roles. The ballet seemed to serve him as a certain archetype, or perhaps a kind of journal or copybook, in which some of the maxims he cared about might be set down. I remember standing with Balanchine at the rear of the center aisle, at City Center, watching a New York City Ballet performance of this ballet one evening in 1959. When the curtain came down and I expressed my admiration for the work, Balanchine replied, with evident pleasure, "Yes, it stands up not too badly—considering it's twenty-five years old. For a ballet, that's a long time to last."

We went across the street to a café during the intermission. Over a drink Balanchine began talking about some of the dramatic themes in *Serenade*. The angel episode, he said, had been suggested to him by a

Serenade, as danced by the New York City Ballet about 1960.

statue of Eros he once saw. "It's like fate," he went on about that part of the ballet. "Each man going through the world with his destiny on his back. He meets a woman—he cares for her—but his destiny has other plans."

I listened in some amazement as Balanchine went on in this vein, for I had never before heard him discussing the literary content of any of his plotless works, or even admitting that they had any. "That's fascinating," I commented. "Did you tell any of that to your dancers when you were choreographing the ballet?"

Balanchine drew back in mock horror. "God forbid!" he said.

The first performance of *Serenade* was at an "invitation only" affair on the estate of Felix Warburg—Edward Warburg's father—near White Plains on June 10, 1934. A few months later Balanchine and Kirstein decided that the school's students were now ready to perform before the general public. A separate corporation was established for the performing group, which took the name of the American Ballet. Whereas the ballet school was subsidized chiefly by Kirstein and his family at this point, with assistance from Nelson Rockefeller, who was a friend of Kirstein's, the funds to support the performing company now came mainly from Edward Warburg, supplemented by donations from Mrs. W. K. Vanderbilt and some other benefactors. Warburg took the title of director of the American Ballet; Balanchine, naturally, became ballet master; Kirstein had himself put down as secretary. Actually, for some years, Dimitriev— scrupulous, morose, hardheaded—had a large say in the management of the company, as well as running the school. He intended to wring a profit from the enterprise and viewed his main function as protecting it from the follies of everyone else involved in it. To his mind, Kirstein and Warburg were dilettantes and financial idiots but useful because they had wealthy fathers. Of Balanchine, he seemed fond—as fond as a misanthrope can be of another human being. He treated Balanchine like a gifted child, who could be indulged but only within limits.

After a couple of out-of-town tryout engagements, the American Ballet played its first season in New York—two weeks at the Adelphi Theatre, beginning March 1, 1935—with a small repertory of Balanchine ballets. Four were new—*Serenade, Transcendence, Alma Mater,* and *Reminiscence*—and added to those were *Errante* and *Dreams* from Les Ballets 1933. For these performances, the company numbered twenty-six dancers from the school, plus two guest artists—Tamara Geva and Paul Haakon. Among members of the company featured in these ballets were

William Dollar and Gisella Caccialanza in Alma Mater.

Leda Anchutina, Holly Howard, Gisella Caccialanza, Elise Reiman, Anabelle Lyon, Charles Laskey, William Dollar, and Eugene Loring.

The new company and Balanchine's new ballets aroused no great enthusiasm among either the public or the critics. In 1952, in his book *Modern Ballet,* John Martin, *The New York Times'* dance critic and for many years the only dance critic of consequence in the United States, was to write: "The bringing of Balanchine to America in 1933 was an event of considerably greater moment than anybody realized at the time except perhaps Lincoln Kirstein, who brought it about." But in those earlier years, when Balanchine and the American Ballet were first trying to get established in the United States, Martin was not merely lukewarm on the subject of Balanchine but actively antipathetic. His reaction to the ballets presented during that first appearance in New York was that *Errante* was "cosmic nonsense"; *Dreams* was "scarcely worth the labor that has been spent on it"; *Transcendence,* though of greater interest than *Dreams,* was "largely incomprehensible" and manifested a "straining for choreographic novelty"; *Alma Mater* was amusing but little more than a revue sketch. Best he liked *Reminiscence,* a frankly derivative collection of divertissements in the old Russian-ballet manner. Of *Serenade,* Martin wrote: "It is a serviceable rather than an inspired piece of work. No doubt Mr. Balanchine had his problems in devising choreography for an inexperienced company, but whatever the reasons, *Serenade* lacks spontaneity to a great extent." In his initial reviews and subsequent estimates, Martin repeatedly attacked Balanchine's approach as precious and decadent, an example of the kind of "Riviera esthetics" that America should be spared. "While every region is entitled to whatever decadences it pleases, there is nothing to be gained by our importing them." At this point, he wrote, the very best thing that the American Ballet could do would be to get rid of Balanchine, with his international notions, and hire a good American dance man. For the next decade and more, Martin's reviews and articles expressed variations on that theme.

The criticism that Balanchine was not American enough to be entrusted with nurturing a truly American school and style of ballet was one that was frequently heard in those days. Even Balanchine's admirers kept urging him to do more ballets with American subjects. Kirstein, himself, felt the attraction of folklore themes, as did many city intellectuals then. The ones who did not were the American folk, who were, on the whole, leaving the farm as fast as they could or mechanizing it to resemble an agricultural factory. Early on, Kirstein commissioned his friend e.e. cummings to write a libretto for an *Uncle Tom's Cabin* "choreodrama," and got Warburg to commission Ben Shahn to design costumes and sets. When the libretto was written, Kirstein read it to Balanchine, in his own French translation. Balanchine said it might be a very nice poem, but it didn't impel him to make dances. Actually Balanchine had a lively interest in Americana, but not as ballet subjects. He had taken to America from the moment of his arrival and felt at home in it. He liked the way it looked and smelled and sounded. He felt in tune with its tempo, its vigor, its directness. His intuitions as to what being a twentieth-century American meant would prove truer and more persuasive eventually than the notions of his folklore-loving critics and allies. One of the things he found congenial about America was that, like Russia, it was unfinished. Most of all, he liked the way the people moved—their athleticism and unself-conscious freedom of gesture, which showed in their games and daily activities, if not yet in their dance. The long-limbed girls he found a pleasure to behold, and he compared their configuration favorably with the Boucher cherub kind of body, which had been the standard model of the dancers at the Maryinsky when he was young. "The land of lovely bodies," he called America.

Friends of Balanchine from that period remember that, unlike most expatriate Russians, he was seldom nostalgic for the old country, nor could he be heard, as was something of a practice among the intellectual Russians, continually praising Paris at the expense of New York. His closest friends and companions tended to be Russians, as would always be true for him—among them, in those days, Tchelitchev, Nicolas Nabokov, Dukelsky, Nicholas Kopeikine, the company's rehearsal pianist, and George Volodine, a dancer. In addition to these, he soon came to know a great number and quite extraordinary variety of people around New York. People were attracted to him—"perhaps," as one who knew him for a long time said, "because he doesn't misunderstand what they say or do but always watches attentively for the truth." Or, perhaps, simply because he was playful, easy to be with. Despite being continually surrounded by people who considered themselves his friends, or who simply enjoyed being with him, he struck some who knew him as essentially a lonely person—with the loneliness of those who think they do not need others and who avoid deep involvements. He could be spontaneously kind, but without ever giving up an abiding aloofness or detachment. "If one of Balanchine's friends got into trouble," one of his associates once said, "Balanchine would always be ready to help, with all the money he had or with whatever he could do for him, but he wouldn't weep over him." There was in his makeup what one friend called "a gentle ruthlessness," which enabled him to pursue his course through life with fewer detours than most people experience. Kirstein liked to describe him admiringly as "sinister." To reporters and others who inquired as to what Balanchine was like, Kirstein would often say, "He's Georgian, you know—just like Stalin." In his book *The Dance,* completed not long after Balanchine had settled in America, Kirstein characterized his nature more thoughtfully: "His personal experience has tended to make him a philosophical anarchist. The only order in his creative life has been accidental, its only logic, chance encounters with music, with a painter, or a dancer. He has been criticized for a lack of continuous principle, an absence of interest even in his own career's consecutive development. He is not given to talking, writing, thinking, or in any way expressing himself, except by the dancing he directs for the theatre which is his world."

A characteristic of Balanchine's that impressed all who knew him was his decisiveness. When something had to be done, he simply made up his mind and did it—and never fretted about it afterward. This applied to just about everything except letter-writing. He had, his whole life, an almost physical aversion to writing, so that he would telephone long-distance almost anywhere rather than write a letter and, when pressed to write, would invent improbable and ingenious reasons for avoiding it. He could not even bring himself to write a letter of condolence to his mother, when he learned in 1937 that his father had died. Finally, Kopeikine wrote it for him. If he could help it, he even avoided reading letters people sent him. Vittorio Rieti, who had moved to America shortly after Balanchine and resumed a friendship with him that had originated during their collaboration for Diaghilev, noted that Balanchine's mailbox would always be full of unopened mail. Inquisitive by nature himself, Rieti could hardly bear Balanchine's indifference. "George!" he would exclaim. "Aren't you going to read your mail?" "I will—I will," Balanchine would reply with a wave of his hand. "Not now—later."

His living quarters were not pretentious. During his early years in New York, he seemed restless in this regard—as if looking for a place to settle, but not finding it. He lived in a series of small apartments on the East Side of New York, not far from the school. He would furnish one and fix it up, and then, after a few months, begin looking for another place. Early he acquired a car, which, characteristically, he bought on impulse one day, without making any detailed inquiries or doing any comparison shopping. The friend who was with Balanchine on that occasion commented, "I spend more time buying a tie than you just did buying a car." In this automobile, Balanchine and friends, and often one or another of the young women from the school, enjoyed driving out to Connecticut or Long Island on a Saturday or Sunday. Their favorite objective was to try to find, out in the American countryside, some restaurant where they could get a nice Russian glass of tea.

Though Kirstein's advance announcements, at the time the school had been established, had stressed that no attempt would be made to rush into the production of ballet programs until some considerable maturation period had elapsed, neither he nor Balanchine had had the patience to abide by this. In the fall of 1935, they set out with their small, inexperienced company and their modest repertory of ballets on what was planned to be a fourteen-week tour of America. The tour got as far as Scranton, Pennsylvania, and then collapsed, when the company's theatrical manager suffered a nervous breakdown and suddenly it was discovered that there were no funds to meet any of the expenses. It was a disillusioning experience, but those involved with the company did not despair. They were brimming with optimism for the future. That summer, just before the tour began, there had occurred what seemed at the time the greatest piece of good fortune imaginable: the Metropolitan Opera had invited the American Ballet to become the Met's resident ballet company, with Balanchine as ballet master. Kirstein afterward wrote: "The invitation was so unexpected, the opportunity seemingly so wonderful, there was scarcely any thought of refusal." It appeared to offer the company, at one stroke, almost everything it could desire: a home, and a distinguished home at that; steady employment; an audience; and the chance—so Balanchine and Kirstein assumed—to present evenings of their own repertoire as well as dances and ballets for the operas.

At that time, in 1935, the Metropolitan had just undergone an administrative shake-up. Giulio Gatti-Casazza's long reign as director had ended, and Edward Johnson was to take his place. Johnson was himself a former opera singer and reportedly intended to give more consideration to the artists' viewpoint than the opera's management hitherto had done. Johnson told the members of the ballet company that he hoped they would bring "freshness, youth and novelty" to the Metropolitan. Nobody listening to him seemed to have greeted this skeptically, or stopped to consider the incongruity of such qualities as freshness, youth, and novelty at the Met as it was then constituted. As Kirstein was later to recall, in a caustic pamphlet entitled *Blast at Ballet*: "I was so enchanted to work in the dusty labyrinth of that palatial mortuary under the cracked gilt plaster, powdery scenery and bundles of rotting costumes, that my *zeal* exceeded a crusader's. I had not yet learned the first rule of diplomacy: *Surtout point de zèle*."

Balanchine, being less demonstrative and voluble, did not show his feelings so openly, but he was, if anything, even more enchanted than Kirstein. To work in such a setting was what he had trained for as a boy. Opera houses would always arouse memories of the Maryinsky in him; when he entered one, he always felt as if he were returning home and assuming his heritage. Stimulated by the splendid prospect he envisaged for his company in these grand new circumstances, he found himself brimming with creative ballet ideas that he was eager to demonstrate as soon as possible. He could scarcely wait for the season to begin. In Kirstein's words, "Everything proceeded on our part with a fatal and precipitate enthusiasm."

It did not take long to discover that the ballet company's relationship with the Met was not going to be the happy and fruitful one they anticipated. As soon as Balanchine saw the dressing area assigned to his dancers—a dingy, cheerless, cramped portion of the basement—he realized in what low esteem the Met held its ballet troupe. Everywhere he turned, during the season, he encountered other reminders. The Met begrudged every penny the ballet company cost it. It kept nagging at the dancers not to wear out so many pairs of ballet shoes, and it fussed over the cleaning bills for the costumes. To economize, the Met's management never let the dancers rehearse with the orchestra; all they had was a pianist. That was the way things had always been done. For *The Bartered Bride* the conductor had made cuts in the orchestra score, but nobody bothered to tell Balanchine. The result at the opera's performance was, of course, chaos. The critics wrote that the dancers couldn't keep step.

From the outset the Met's management and Balanchine quarreled over his conceptions of the dance. The management complained that the divertissements and ballets Balanchine devised for its operas showed no respect for tradition. To this Balanchine coolly replied, "Of course not. The tradition of the ballet at the Met is bad ballet." The Met, he went on, had always used ballet in the opera the way a diner uses a napkin—to wipe his mouth before resuming his meal—whereas he wanted to provide dances that would be tasty dishes in their own right.

As things worked out, though, the only dishes of his concocting that satisfied the management and the critics were the dances he did for *Carmen* and the kermis ballet in *Faust*. ("I think Balanchine must have composed it in a deep sleep," Kirstein said of the latter effort.) The reason for Balanchine's success in *Carmen,* according to Irving Kolodin in his history of the Metropolitan Opera Company, was that the surroundings in *Carmen* were neutral in quality so that there was no clash between the style of the dancing and that of the staging. In other, more stylized operas a violent clash was felt.

The essence of the more knowledgeable criticism of Balanchine's work at the opera house was that his dances were not properly subordinated to the overall intention of the operas. Some years later, in summarizing Balanchine's tenure at the Met, Kolodin wrote: "Balanchine could have made a fresh and vital thing of the danced portions of a Metropolitan production; but the production itself would have to be fresh and vital before such a departure could be regarded as adjunct rather than intrusion."

Even if the Met had been willing to attempt new productions at that time, it is possible that there would still have been manifest a basic incompatibility between the style of movement Balanchine used and that of the singers. This is a point that Virgil Thomson made in his later analysis of what had gone wrong with the marriage between Balanchine and the Metropolitan. "Balanchine's ballet style employs a dynamic, explosive, sharply precise kind of movement, full of enormous tension and vigor. That was the style that the Russians had been developing since they imported classical ballet from France, and the style that Balanchine brought to America with him. But the style of movement employed by the singers and other stage figures in the opera houses of the West comes directly from the Franco-Italian manner and uses slow, broad, much softer gestures. I don't think Balanchine himself was aware of what a contrast the two styles made."

The difficulties encountered with the management over the opera ballets were disconcerting enough, but the greatest blow to Balanchine and Kirstein was the discovery that the Met had no intention of scheduling regular evenings of ballet, as other great opera houses of the world did. Balanchine was flabbergasted, for he thought there had been a clear understanding on this matter. The fact that his company had a repertory of ballets suitable for performance had seemed one of the main reasons why the company had been invited to enter the Metropolitan in the first place; certainly that had been the decisive reason for the company's acceptance of the invitation. But when Balanchine and Kirstein broached this subject after joining the establishment, they were informed that the Met regarded evenings devoted to ballet as a luxury that could not be afforded. "There is simply no budget for the extra orchestra rehearsals that would be required," they were told repeatedly whenever they sought to advance their proposals.

To salvage something under these conditions, Balanchine contrived to have his company create some works to music the orchestra already knew, and thus could play without extra rehearsals. He arranged *The Bat* to the music of Johann Strauss' *Die Fledermaus*. The public found it delightful, and it was presented many times. Another work, created to meet these exigent circumstances, was *Concerto*, which represented the dancer William Dollar's first venture into choreography. It was to the music of Chopin's Piano Concerto in F Minor, another piece that the orchestra had in its repertory. John Martin was invited to attend a piano rehearsal of this work (no orchestral rehearsal could be afforded, of course), but he was turned away when he presented himself at the stage door. The custodian at the door knew his Metropolitan Opera House, and he could not believe that a critic of *The New York Times* could really be interested in seeing dancing there.

A frustrating, disagreeable relationship it was from the start, and harrowing for all concerned—for the Met as well as for Balanchine and his company. Balanchine must have been a great trial to the Metropolitan. Theretofore, it had always employed humbler dancing masters who modestly accepted their place in the Met's scheme of things. Balanchine, for all his quietness and elegant breeding, was never afflicted with an ounce of humility, and he had never hesitated to speak his mind. The Met can hardly have enjoyed learning that its ballet master, in a statement to the press, had said that New York's music critics knew nothing about dance and not much more about music, nor can it have been much amused by Balanchine's reply to a reporter's question about how he had prepared his dancers for performing with an opera company: "Generally, I instructed my dancers to dance all over the place. The dancers must pay no attention to the singing chorus. I advised them to kick the chorus if they got in the way." Such flights of brash humor were not calculated to endear Balanchine to the officials who ran the joyless, unprofitable business known as the Metropolitan Opera. To them, the very enthusiasm with which Balanchine and Kirstein approached their work seemed an appalling and vaguely menacing breach of the standards of decorum customarily observed in the gloomy gilt sanctuary on Thirty-ninth Street.

As early as the first *Aïda*, the insiders were saying that Balanchine and company were done for, as far as the Met was concerned. The general expectation, shared by Balanchine, was that at the end of the season the Met, with a sigh of relief, would bid them farewell. No such announcement appeared. Instead, there came the surprising announcement that during the experimental, popular-priced spring season (an innovation of Edward Johnson's), which was to take place right after the close of the regular season, there would be featured a new production of Gluck's *Orpheus and Eurydice*, staged and choreographed by George Balanchine, danced by members of his company and with decor by Pavel Tchelitchev.

What led the Metropolitan suddenly to offer so fair a chance to one toward whom it had hitherto been so grudging? It is hard to say. At the time there was much intramural conjecture about the Met's motives. Some of the speculation imputed a devious malice to the Met management, which would have done credit to the Borgias; they had decided, it was said, to let Balanchine commit suicide in public and were going to relish seeing him measure out and administer his own poison. But it may not have been at all like that. The Met's management may have been sincerely seeking to give Balanchine's talents a fuller trial, under more ample and flexible conditions than the regular season afforded. They were skeptical, but still . . . And it would not cost the Met much, for Edward Warburg had agreed to share the production costs.

At any rate, here was a great opportunity at last for Balanchine and his young company. He and his colleagues decided to put into this work all their long-nourished conceptions as to the ideal form of presentation for lyric theatre. It was to be a revolutionary treatment of an opera: all beauty. No fat, ungainly singers would clutter up the stage. The actions and passions of the timeless legend, to Gluck's sublime music, would be conveyed visually through the "nebulous precision," in Cocteau's fine phrase, of the ballet. The singers—soloists as well as chorus—would be in the pit, out of sight, along with the orchestra.

As for the conception, Kirstein wrote that they sought to present what was most living for the present epoch in the Orphic myth. They visualized it, he said, as "the eternal domestic tragedy of an artist and his wife. . . . We saw Hell as a concentration camp with flying military slave-drivers lashing forced labor; the Elysian Fields as an ether drama, a desiccated bone-dry limbo of suspended animation, and Paradise as the eternity we know from a Planetarium arrayed on the astronomical patterns of contemporary celestial science."

The leading spirit in the formulation of these ideas was Pavel Tchelitchev, who evolved set designs and costumes for the opera that recalled in their quality and atmosphere Piero della Francesca's paintings and at the same time suggested surrealistically something of the present workaday world. Febrile, intense, exceedingly articulate, Tchelitchev was a visionary with an intense compulsion to systematize his visions. On top of a surrealist's perceptions of the world, he erected a medieval structure of logic. He could hold forth hypnotically, if not always comprehensibly, for hours on subjects that obsessed him. Balanchine would listen to him as spellbound as a child being told a fairy tale. He had a lasting influence on Kirstein, who collected his paintings and organized exhibitions of

them and wrote monographs on him. "It was Pavel Tchelitchev," Kirstein later recalled, "who showed me that theater was an amazing amusement of measurable importance, neither more nor less. His standards of taste, ingenuity and genius were icily professional; he was only interested in virtuosity; as he said: the coloratura style." On Balanchine also, Tchelitchev's personality was a powerful stimulant during the preparation of *Orpheus and Eurydice,* as it had been when they worked together on *Errante* for Les Ballets 1933, but on the whole Tchelitchev's influence on him was not so marked or lasting as it was on Kirstein, for Balanchine was less susceptible than Kirstein to abstract ideas and systematizations— or, indeed, to words of any sort. Also, Balanchine had a suspicion that despite all the ardor of his fine language about ballet and the lyric theatre, Tchelitchev did not really care much for dancing—at least, not anywhere near so much as Balanchine. No painters ever did, it seemed. Many painters, Balanchine sometimes thought, would really have preferred it if the dancers would only dance behind the set instead of in front of it; that way they would not distract from the exhibition. Still, Balanchine thought Tchelitchev's designs for *Orpheus and Eurydice* very beautiful—as beautiful, in fact, as any set designs he had ever seen.

On this occasion, as always, the chief stimulant and deepest fount of inspiration for Balanchine was the music. He listened, during the intense, excited conferences that would sometimes go on far into the night, to the ideas propounded by Tchelitchev and Kirstein, but the voice to which he gave most heed when it came time to choreograph was that of Christoph Willibald Gluck—poignant, passionate, grave, and noble. *Orpheus and Eurydice* had long been perhaps his favorite of all operas. For Gluck's music Balanchine created, in Kirstein's words, some of his "most accomplished erotic patterns, touching and electric encounters, and noble plastic groups."

Lew Christensen was cast as Orpheus. Tall, blond, handsomely proportioned, musical, and technically gifted, he was America's first *danseur noble.* Daphne Vane was cast as Eurydice and William Dollar as Amor. There were only three weeks to create, prepare, and rehearse the opera, but all concerned, down to the members of the corps de ballet, gave themselves over completely to the work. For those three weeks they lived and breathed it. At last came the day—May 19, 1936—and the company was ready. The music began, the curtain went up, the dancers performed, in Balanchine's opinion, to near perfection.

᭡ *Pavel Tchelitchev.*

Nothing like this had ever been done at the Metropolitan Opera—and the official consensus of opinion was that it was awful, a most devastating failure. The critics called it silly, arty, bogus, irrelevant, and ugly, and the most inept performance they had ever seen at the Met. They acted as offended as if they had been personally insulted. If New York had been Paris, there might well have been boos and catcalls from the audience, and all the rest of the furor of a *Sacre du Printemps* scandal; as it was, there were merely titters, yawns, scowls of frigid disapproval, and polite applause.

Some few among the audience were deeply impressed. One was Glenway Wescott, who wrote a letter to *Time*, taking issue with that magazine's sarcastic and flippant review. Wescott called it "the only original undertaking of the opera association this season," and said: "By virtue of the strange new scenes and 20th-Century dances, I was more deeply moved by the old myth and music than ever before. . . . Balanchine is a very great man, I think. If I were to make a list of the dozen most exciting and inspiring things I have seen in the theatre, three of his choreographic works would be on it: Apollon Musagète and The Prodigal Son and Errante."

But those of Wescott's mind were in the minority. The management of the Met permitted *Orpheus and Eurydice* a total of two performances, and then dismissed it forever.

If the Met had been seeking Balanchine's destruction as diabolically as Kirstein was certain it was, it had his head on the block now. Yet the ax was withheld for the time being. The American Ballet was permitted to return for the 1937-38 season but was manifestly there on sufferance only. Clearly the company's days were numbered. The atmosphere of the dusty caverns backstage at the Met could not have been grimmer for Balanchine and his dancers that year.

Despite all, during what remained of his tenure at the opera house, Balanchine managed to wangle one more opportunity to show his work in gala style on the Metropolitan stage—an opportunity once more made possible by the generosity of Edward Warburg, though this time with no cooperation at all from the Met's management. The occasion was a Stravinsky-Balanchine festival, presented in the spring of 1937—featuring *Apollo* and two new ballets: *Le Baiser de la Fée* and *Card Game: A Ballet in Three Deals*. The latter work had been specially commissioned from Stravinsky for the occasion. Stravinsky himself conducted a sev-

Lew Christensen in Orpheus and Eurydice.

A cutthroat poker game as publicity for Card Game—Warburg, Stravinsky, Balanchine, and Dollar (back to camera), with the four Queens of the ballet as kibitzers: Hortense Kahrklin, Leda Anchutina, Ariel Lang, and Annabelle Lyon.

enty-piece orchestra, hired from the Philharmonic, not from the Met's pit, and, as publicity, had himself photographed playing poker with Balanchine and Warburg. This time, to everybody's surprise, the presentation came within a hair of breaking even at the box office. The public was delighted, and the critics called it the most brilliant evening of ballet ever seen in New York.

This success, however, did not alter the fundamental incompatibility between Balanchine and the Metropolitan Opera, and in March 1938 they parted company. "The Met is a heap of ruins," Balanchine angrily told the press as he left, "and every night the stagehands put it together and make it look a little like opera." As a parting shot, he added, "The Met is always saying it wants something new. Why don't they put together all the first acts that the box-seat patrons who always come in late never see, and make a new opera from them?" He was in a rage—a rare thing in his life. The crassest of the Broadway producers for whom he later worked never shook his famous aplomb as the Met did. He could adjust himself amicably to the quirks and demands of commercial entrepreneurs, since he knew in advance how little their business had to do with making art as compared with making money. From the Met he had expected something different.

If it was artistically impossible for the American Ballet to function in collaboration with the Met, it was financially impossible for it to function alone. Shortly after the Stravinsky-Balanchine festival, Warburg ceased to be a patron of ballet. The art had never been his primary interest, as it was Kirstein's, and had cost him around a hundred thousand dollars in less than three years, which was fairly steep for a side interest. He had caught ballet as one might catch the measles—and now he had got over it.

So, in the middle of 1938, the American Ballet went out of existence.

CHAPTER NINE

An Ace Job on the Terp Angle

For the better part of the next decade, Balanchine spent much of his time being a Broadway and Hollywood dance man. He may have been too arty for the Metropolitan Opera, but he was a hit with Sam Goldwyn and George Abbott. He quickly established himself as the best in the business and had more offers of shows than he could handle. On Broadway, he was thought of as a real pro—quick, adaptable, easy to work with, and possessed of an inexhaustible supply of clever and original dance ideas. *Variety* bestowed its succinct accolades on him: "George Balanchine has done an ace job on the terp angle." A lot of the shows he choreographed made big money, among them *On Your Toes, I Married an Angel, Babes in Arms, The Boys from Syracuse, The Merry Widow, Rosalinda, Louisiana Purchase, Song of Norway,* and *Where's Charley?* His movies included *Goldwyn Follies, I Was an Adventuress, Star-Spangled Rhythm,* and the filmed version of *On Your Toes.* Along the way, during this tinsel era in Balanchine's life, he and Stravinsky—that capable team—joined forces to do a project for Ringling Brothers Circus. This was in November 1941. The circus first engaged Balanchine, and then he made a long-distance call to Stravinsky, who was at his home in Los Angeles, to enlist his collaboration. Their dialogue is worth preserving:

"I wonder if you'd like to do a little ballet with me," Balanchine said, after Stravinsky answered the phone, "a polka, perhaps."

"For whom?"

"For some elephants," Balanchine said.

Tamara Geva and Ray Bolger in the "Slaughter on Tenth Avenue" number in On Your Toes.

177

"How old?" asked Stravinsky cautiously.

"Very young," Balanchine assured him.

There was a pause. Then Stravinsky said gravely, "All right. If they are very young elephants, I will do it."

The score that Stravinsky subsequently delivered—*Circus Polka*, it is called—bears the dedication: "For a Young Elephant."

The *jeux d'esprit* that resulted from this Stravinsky-Balanchine collaboration was first performed in Madison Square Garden on April 9, 1942, with a troupe of fifty elephants in tutus and fifty circus starlets, and featured Zorina riding Modoc. The costumes were by Norman Bel Geddes. Everybody thought this ballet a very chic and clever thing—everybody, that is, except the elephants, they being essentially middle-class creatures, suspicious of novelty. Balanchine gaily told a reporter when he started on the project, "Elephants are no harder to teach than ballerinas," but he knew better. No elephant, perhaps no creature in the world, will work as hard or as patiently as a ballerina—particularly a ballerina in a Balanchine company. The elephants trumpeted their annoyance at the choreography Balanchine gave them, even though he tried to keep it as elementary as possible, and they flapped their ears in pain at the Stravinsky music. Their trainer was much relieved when the circus, after cashing in for a season on the publicity the number had received, dropped it from the show; he had been muttering from the start that if they kept on making his beasts do things like this, he would end up with a herd of neurotics on his hands.

The first musical comedy to feature Balanchine choreography was *On Your Toes*, which had its premiere on April 11, 1936. A few months before that Balanchine had made his initial contact with Broadway by way of a couple of dance numbers he did for the Shuberts' *Follies*, a show starring Fannie Brice and featuring a young comedian named Bob Hope. At considerable expense the Shuberts had brought Josephine Baker from Paris, and it was Balanchine's assignment to fashion some dances that would display to advantage her dusky elegance and her talented, world-famous *derrière*. As much as anybody else, Balanchine admired this *derrière* of hers, but there was little original he could do for it. It was already, so to speak, institutionalized and not to be tampered with. Balanchine's contribution was not of much consequence to the *Follies*, which scored no great hit as a show.

On Your Toes, though—a show that has come to be regarded as something of a milestone in the history of musical comedy—was a different story. Here Balanchine could give freer rein to his abilities; his participation was an integral ingredient to the work as a whole. Produced by Dwight Deere Wiman, *On Your Toes* had music by Richard Rodgers and lyrics by Lorenz Hart. The dancing stars were Tamara Geva and Ray Bolger, in a role so strenuous that it would nightly exhaust him to the point of collapse, but which, by way of compensation, was the role that would first bring him into prominence. The story dealt with backstage life in the ballet world, a new theme for Broadway, with a gangster fable woven through it.

At the time Balanchine worked on this production, he was still ballet master at the Metropolitan Opera. Richard Rodgers has recalled how intimidated he was at first at the prospect of collaborating with Balanchine. "I expected fiery temperament," Rodgers has said. "He had bushy black hair, gleaming eyes and an aquiline profile. He was Russian, artistic, a genius. I was scared stiff of him. I asked him how he worked. Did he make the steps first and have music written to fit them, or what? He answered, in the thick Russian accent he had then, 'You write. I put on.' For me, that was marvelous. I went ahead and wrote the score, and I never had to change or cut a note of it as far as he was concerned."

Rodgers had some uneasy moments, though, when he first sought Balanchine's reaction to the music he had written for the big *Slaughter on Tenth Avenue* ballet, which was to be the show's climax. It was his most ambitious piece of show music, and he desperately wanted Balanchine to be impressed by it. Rodgers and the show's rehearsal pianist played a two-piano arrangement of it for Balanchine at the pianist's apartment one day. Throughout their performance Rodgers kept eyeing Balanchine anxiously to see how it was going over. Balanchine listened with an expressionless countenance. When they finished, he stood up and started out of the apartment. Rodgers trailed after him, thinking wretchedly that at least Balanchine might have commented, "Better luck next time." As they waited for the elevator, Rodgers could stand the uncertainty no longer. In the primitive English he, and many of Balanchine's acquaintances, employed with him in those years, when Balanchine's command of the language was limited, Rodgers asked, "You don't like?"

"What you mean—I don't like?" said Balanchine.

"You don't say anything," pointed out Rodgers.

"Am too busy staging," said Balanchine, touching his forehead. "I love."

Far from being difficult, Balanchine turned out to be, as Rodgers recalled, "a pleasure to work with—untemperamental, logical, objective. In all the shows I worked on with him, I never once heard him speak above a normal conversational tone—not even when everybody else was succumbing to hysteria. With most other choreographers I've known, it was like asking them to give up some of their living flesh if they were told that, for one reason or another, one of their dance numbers wouldn't work. But Balanchine would just take it in stride and cheerfully produce on the spot any number of perfectly brilliant ideas to take the place of what came out."

Before *On Your Toes*, the playbill credit line for the dancers in musicals had always read, "Dances by——." Balanchine asked the producer, Wiman, whether his billing might read, "Choreography by George Balanchine." This was an unfamiliar word in the United States in 1936. Wiman said he feared the public would not know what it meant. Balanchine replied that maybe it would intrigue the public to see a new word, and Wiman agreed to make the experiment.

The change in the credit line was the least of Balanchine's musical-comedy innovations. Balanchine was able to rid musical comedy of the notion that a dance number was a couple of showy soloists backed by a line of high-kicking showgirls; this dreary nonsense he replaced by genuine choreography. To musical comedy Balanchine brought, it was generally agreed, an elegance, sophistication, and range of reference—all conveyed subtly and with a light touch—such as Broadway had not previously known. In addition, his dances in *On Your Toes*—particularly the memorable *Slaughter on Tenth Avenue*—were the first ever seen in a Broadway musical that were not just interludes but functioned as an essential, active aspect of the plot. This paved the way for what was done by Agnes de Mille a few years later in *Oklahoma!* Thus Balanchine began a trend in American musical comedy that helped make it one of the brightest of this country's theatrical forms.

This is not to suggest that Balanchine at the time thought of himself as engaged in a historic mission labeled "The Reform of American Musical Comedy." He would have been the last person in the world to take such an approach. If his conception of the very finest achievements of classical ballet was that they are by nature ephemeral, iridescent bubbles in the air, if he wasted no energies mourning over the fact that such masterworks of his as *La Chatte* or *Cotillon* had lived for only a few performances and then had disappeared forever, how much less likely was he to be engrossed with delusions of immortality in regard to the entertainments he was now designing for the commercial theatre. Still, in all that he did for Broadway he did not stint himself and used all the skills required. As ever, he took the job seriously and himself lightly.

To the show-going public Balanchine's approach was a refreshing change; to the dancers in his shows it was an absolute liberation. "If the rules of Equity permitted," Brooks Atkinson wrote in 1940 in his *New York Times* review of *Cabin in the Sky*, "probably the dancers would be glad to pay Mr. Balanchine something for the privilege of appearing under his direction, for he has released them from the bondage of hack dancing and ugliness." Many of the dancers considered their association with Balanchine something of an educational experience. Ray Bolger, who performed in three shows that Balanchine choreographed, once commented to me that working with Balanchine was like spinning from Juilliard to the Louvre to the Royal Academy of Dramatic Arts to Stillman's Gymnasium.

Among Balanchine's personal traits, perhaps none made such an impression on those who worked with him as his gentle, mannerly demeanor and his even temper—a deportment so different from the general run of behavior in the frenzied world of show business as to inspire some beholders with awe. This effect was registered most markedly, perhaps, on the occasion, in 1942, when Balanchine did his stint for the circus. Connie Clausen, who was one of the circus' fifty starlets that year, has described, in a charming book of reminiscence of her circus experiences entitled *I Love You Honey, But the Season's Over*, the impression Balanchine made from the moment he appeared at the circus' headquarters at Sarasota, Florida, to begin work on his elephant polka. "Balanchine's romantic good looks and soft-spoken courtesy were such a contrast to the cigar-filled faces of the circus men and the sarcasm of Mr. Anderson [the musical director] we'd have walked into a cage full of hungry lions for him," she wrote. Backstage life at the circus, Miss Clausen had found, had little glamour, but was crude, callous, and rather menacing; she was terrified of the elephants and just about as scared of the elephant trainers with their steel hooks, led by the fearsome Walter McClain. "In Balanchine's presence," she noted, "Walter McClain's manner changed. To our astonishment he broke into a wide smile and held out his hand. If Balanchine was abashed by the elephants, by McClain or his crew of tattered assistants, he gave no sign. He maintained then (and always) an almost formal politeness. At first it bewildered, then delighted the men, and, I sometimes suspected, the elephants as well."

Working with Modoc.

A starlet was to perform with each elephant. The girls had to learn how to mount onto the elephant's trunk and balance gracefully there. Over and over Connie Clausen worked at it, during that first rehearsal, with the elephant Ginny, with which she had been paired, and its trainer, Dooley. Before long she was bruised, scratched, weary, and frustrated. Balanced high in the air, after she had fallen some twenty-two times, she was just beginning to think she had finally mastered the task when suddenly her foot slipped and she crashed to the ground once more. "Dooley winced. Walter McClain spat. Ginny looked bored. And Balanchine, who suddenly appeared on the ring curb, said in his gentlest voice, 'You must try to land on the balls of your feet, my dear.'"

Another trait of Balanchine's much appreciated by his colleagues and an asset to the shows he worked on was his sense of humor. Some of his best musical-comedy numbers were spoofs, like the trio for two tap dancers and a ballerina on her points in *The Boys from Syracuse,* and the riotous burlesque of the old classic war-horse of a ballet *Scheherazade* in *On Your Toes.* A feature writer for a New York newspaper wrote wonderingly about the *Scheherazade* parody at the time. He seemed perplexed, even a bit shocked, by the willingness of this noted ballet master to poke fun at one of the accepted classics of his art. The newspaperman's attitude was indicative of the prevalent attitude in those days. Americans did not like ballet, but they were solemn about it. Balanchine loved ballet, so he did not need to be solemn. The real connoisseurs of ballet enjoyed his *Scheherazade* parody, as they did nearly all of his musical-comedy work. As Denby wrote, apropos of *Song of Norway* in 1945, "Balanchine's Broadway choreography does not falsify ballet as most musicals do on the grounds that adulteration is the first principle of showmanship. Balanchine's numbers are simplified ballet, but of the purest water."

It was the success of *On Your Toes* that aroused Samuel Goldwyn's interest in Balanchine and brought Balanchine to Hollywood for his first American film. Here, it seemed, was just the dance director Goldwyn was seeking for his new picture—a choreographer of international repute who could also do smash-hit dancing. Goldwyn had aspirations for this picture—*The Goldwyn Follies*. It was to be not just a colossal; it was to be an *artistic* colossal. He offered Balanchine twelve hundred dollars a week to stage the dances, a sum that Balanchine thought both artistic and colossal. It was the most money he had ever made. One of Balanchine's terms was that the dancers should be selected from his American Ballet Company, then still in existence. Goldwyn agreed to hire twenty-five members of the company for the five months or so it would take to make the film, and to provide adequate facilities for them—which meant fitting out a ballet school on the set, complete with mirrored walls, hardwood floors, dressing rooms, showers, and all the other necessary appurtenances. In that kind of thing, there was no problem from Goldwyn, who, unlike the Metropolitan Opera, was not niggling about money. When the time came, he turned his studio's workmen loose on the project and they built a complete ballet school in one day. In the grandeur of such gestures Goldwyn reminded Balanchine of a Russian nobleman of the days before the serfs were emancipated.

As the film's ballerina, Goldwin engaged Vera Zorina, who was then starring in the London production of *On Your Toes*, and who was a soloist with the Ballet Russe de Monte Carlo, where she had been a protégée of Massine's. Goldwyn hired Zorina for the *Follies* on the strength of the rave reviews she received for *On Your Toes*, without requiring the customary screen test. Then he grew nervous and cabled to London for "shots of what I have bought." When these rushes arrived, Goldwyn was so delighted with what he saw that he expanded Zorina's role in the film beyond merely a dancing part. She was then twenty years old and one of the most beautiful women in the world. Born in Berlin, of Norwegian extraction (her real name was Eva Brigitta Hartwig), she had long blond hair, an oval face with high cheekbones, gray eyes, and a generous, expressive mouth. She was slim and long-limbed. She dressed with flair, and she was witty and intelligent. It would not take long, once Balanchine began to work with her, before he would become entranced by her.

In the weeks before his departure for Hollywood, Balanchine was as busy as he had ever been in his life. It was then that he was preparing the Stravinsky festival at the Met. At the same time he was choreographing *Babes in Arms*, a Rodgers and Hart show, for Wiman, with a cast of talented youngsters headed by Mitzi Green. He would work part of the time at the Metropolitan Opera House, fashioning intricate choreography to match the most advanced Stravinsky music; then he would rush over to the Shubert Theatre and turn out a clever dance number to Richard Rodgers' popular strains. The Stravinsky project was his great challenge and delight, but even so, as a professional, he did not slight his musical-comedy assignment, or speak patronizingly of it. Both at the Met and at the Shubert, during those hectic weeks, he was as creative as was appropriate to each situation. Among the dances he did for *Babes in Arms* was an engaging fantasy called *Peter's Dream*, which was the first dream ballet to be seen on Broadway. It set off a vogue; for some years thereafter the dream ballet became virtually an obligatory feature of American musical comedy. *Babes in Arms* opened, to much acclaim, on April 14, 1937 (it was to have a run of 380 performances—the first Rodgers and Hart show to play more than a year). The Stravinsky festival took place two weeks later. Balanchine knocked off for a few days' rest and then set out for Hollywood.

He made the journey by train, accompanied by his pianist friend Nicholas Kopeikine. On his arrival at the railroad station in Los Angeles, he was met by a bevy of press photographers and studio publicists. His appearance and deportment perplexed them. Soft-spoken, smooth-skinned, with a grave countenance in which dark eyes gleamed impishly under haughty eyebrows, he appeared younger than his thirty-three years. Somehow he did not look quite like their notion of a fiery Russian ballet master. As usual, the press set about enthusiastically to rectify reality. They tried to get him to pose in various melodramatic attitudes, more in accord with their notion of a Russian genius of ballet, whatever that might be. Balanchine courteously refused. He had discovered by now, as he commented to a friend, that if you were a Russian in America it was automatically taken for granted you were a genius. That would not be so bad, he added, if Americans didn't also assume that all geniuses were crazy or dumb.

Frustrated, the photographers suggested to Balanchine that he should at least smile for them. He replied that it was too early in the morning; he did not feel like smiling.

"But everyone smiles!" the photographers said.

"I am not everyone," he retorted. "I am myself. Only one person."

He and Kopeikine had rented a house on North Fairfax Avenue, not far from Hollywood Boulevard. It was a white, two-story house—not palatial by any means, but ample. Its best feature was a pleasant garden. Balanchine took great delight in being able to have slices of lemon from his own trees in his Russian tea. Goldwyn, if he had been disposed to quibble over money, could probably have persuaded Balanchine to come to Hollywood for a lesser salary simply by promising him fresh lemon slices in his tea. Such gratifications always meant more to Balanchine than money. The heaped stalls of fresh fruit and vegetables at the markets also pleased him exceedingly. On one of his first shopping trips he bought a wheelbarrow-load of fruits and vegetables that he wheeled home himself, refusing to let the store deliver it because he wanted to be able to feast his eyes on it all the way home. He was also charmed, as might be expected, by the profusion of pretty, lightly clad young women to be seen wherever his eyes chanced. As he drove about town, he would make joyful noises. "Ah, look at that *tsoupoulia!*" he would exclaim, employing a concocted Russian word meaning a young chicken. And for a particularly attractive young woman, he would make a U-turn to prolong his sight of her. He wouldn't be trying to pick her up; he was just feasting his eyes. These pretty, long-legged, uninhibited-looking young American women, swinging along Hollywood Boulevard, were his potential material. He was as happy as a sculptor in a choice marble quarry. And there was much else he liked about the place. The warm dry climate was good for his health. The balmy air, the vivid flowers and foliage, the broad vistas, with the mountains nearby and the sea not far away, and the leisurely tempo of life there, at the time, were a welcome contrast to New York City. It all made Balanchine feel, he used to say, somewhat as if he had been transported to the ancestral Georgia he had never known.

Shortly after his arrival in Hollywood he was summoned to his first conference with Samuel Goldwyn. It is a shame that the conference was not filmed, for it was sheer farce. Goldwyn had heard that Balanchine did not understand English very well, so he had asked George Gershwin, who was under contract to write the music for the *Follies*, to act as an interpreter. Goldwyn, of course, spoke pure Goldwyn. When Goldwyn had delivered one of his utterances, Gershwin would turn to Balanchine and convert this into pidgin English, along with the facial gestures one might use when talking to a very bright two-year-old. Ira Gershwin, who was present, could not bear it. "George!" he exclaimed to his brother. "What kind of language are you using? Even Balanchine can't understand you!" Balanchine demanded to have an interpreter of his own, to deal with Goldwyn's interpreter.

Gershwin had looked healthy and vigorous at that conference. His face, shaped rather like a ram's, with large, forceful features, had a good tan. His intense black eyes were keen and alert. He had been taking pains to keep himself in condition—playing golf, taking long walks with his wirehaired terrier, and getting in a weekly tennis match with his Beverly Hills neighbor, Arnold Schönberg. His chief physical worry till recently had seemed to be his thinning hair, for which he spent half an hour a day having his scalp massaged in a contraption the size of a refrigerator that he had purchased. Of late, though, he had begun to suffer from headaches. The *Follies* was to be his last motion-picture job for a while; he was planning to move back to New York and devote himself to some serious composing—another opera, a symphony, perhaps a string quartet.

Shortly after the meeting with Balanchine and Goldwyn, Gershwin's headaches grew so painful that he began to find it difficult to concentrate. He laid off work, but the headaches did not abate. Once he reported a strange and disagreeable smell, like that of burning rubber. He felt increasingly tired and vague, though the doctors could find nothing organically wrong with him. Balanchine called at his house one day, near the end of June, to see how he was coming along and to discuss with him plans for the ballet they were supposed to create together for the film. He found Gershwin in bed, in a darkened room. Gershwin talked with him feebly for a few minutes in a strange, faraway voice. Balanchine came away distressed and full of foreboding. Within a few weeks after this, George Gershwin, aged thirty-eight, was dead—of a brain tumor.

Before his headaches became acute, Gershwin had written five songs for the *Follies,* including "Love Walked In," one of his most attractive tunes, but he had not done any of the ballet music. It had occurred to Balanchine even before Gershwin's death that Gershwin's *American in Paris* suite might be suitable for ballet, and now together with Ira Gershwin he worked out a libretto. In this project Balanchine intended to put into effect his ideas about ballet in movies. The possibilities of the medium intrigued him, and the opportunity to try out some of his conceptions had been one of the temptations that had lured him to Hollywood. A movie ballet, he felt, ought not to be merely a stage ballet on film. It need not be a continuous dance observed from a fixed angle, as the stage required, but could be a montage of dance shots, photographed from whatever angle or distance one wished. And it could employ effects the stage could never achieve, especially in the realm of fantasy, which seemed to Balanchine a quality particularly suited to the film medium.

The *American in Paris* ballet was conceived of as a fantasy quest. The milieu was to suggest the Paris Exposition, through which an American, portrayed by the tap dancer George King, would search for Zorina, the girl of his dreams. Seductive, tantalizing, ever elusive, she would manifest herself now here, now there—at one moment in a Spanish pavilion, another time in a Ferris wheel, yet again high overhead among the stars of the zodiac in a planetarium—always just beyond reach, and vanishing each time just as the American was about to take her in his arms.

After three weeks of preparation, the day came for Goldwyn to see a run-through of it. Goldwyn arrived at the studio's stage 2, accompanied by his entourage. With him were Adolphe Menjou and the Ritz Brothers, who had roles in the picture, Alfred Newman, the musical director and Fred Kohlmar, who was Goldwyn's assistant. Balanchine's old friend, Vladimir Dukelsky, now known as Vernon Duke, was also present, having been hastily called to Hollywood from New York to complete the musical score. Kopeikine was at the piano. Balanchine, in shirtsleeves and slacks, was bustling about, making certain that all was in readiness. Little sets representing the various scenes were scattered here and there on the vast soundstage, and Balanchine moved about from one to another, arranging his ballet company members in various groupings.

Goldwyn sat down in his director's chair, and all settled back to enjoy the ballet. The music began. In about two minutes, Balanchine said briskly, "That's the first bit. Now the next part will be shot over here." All had to pick up their chairs and move to another of the little sets. A couple of minutes later they had to move again. Goldwyn tried to protest.

He did not want to keep moving around, he said, his arm hurt him. His arm was in a sling, the result of an injury sustained—so rumor had it—by pounding on the desk while reprimanding a subordinate. But Balanchine, all afire with enthusiasm for his project, brushed Goldwyn's protestations aside. He insisted that Goldwyn had to see each scene exactly the way the camera would see it. Goldwyn was not used to having his wishes, or even his whims, ignored by his employees. "It was a rare sight," wrote Vernon Duke in his memoirs, "to see the man, piloted by George, made to crouch and squat, the better to view a couple wriggling on the floor or peep straight into a dancer's navel—'that's where camerra vill be shott!' George would exclaim triumphantly."

As this went on, Goldwyn's face grew redder and grimmer. All at once, he said, "All right, thank you very much."

"But you have not seen it all," protested Balanchine.

"I've seen enough." And Goldwyn, trailed by his entourage, swept out.

Furious, Balanchine dismissed the company from the soundstage and followed, a few minutes afterward, to Goldwyn's office. There Goldwyn told him he simply could not comprehend what Balanchine was trying to do and that he did not intend to risk a hundred thousand dollars on an experiment. It might turn out to be a very artistic and beautiful ballet, Goldwyn said, but even so he was sure it was not for the general public. "The miners in Harrisburg wouldn't understand it."

"I'm not President Roosevelt," Balanchine retorted. "What do I care about the miners in Harrisburg?" As an afterthought, he added, "Besides, there are no miners in Harrisburg. I know because I've been there."

With imperial finality, Goldwyn said that he was sorry but the ballet was out. With equal finality, Balanchine replied that then *he* was sorry but he was out, too, and stalked from the office.

For several days Balanchine went into seclusion while Goldwyn's staff sought to find him. At last the designer Richard Day, a good friend of Balanchine's, managed to track him down and persuade him, for the sake of the whole ballet company, whose contracts depended on him, if for no other reason, to return to the studio and meet once more with Goldwyn. As far as the *American in Paris* ballet was concerned, the ensuing meeting with Goldwyn did not alter matters. Goldwyn was still reluctant to risk the experiment. Now, however, instead of handing down fiats to Balanchine, as a lowly subject of his empire, Goldwyn treated him as a respected colleague. As a favor, he begged Balanchine, for his first Hollywood effort, not to try to be too radical in his film techniques. "This time I'd like you to make for me a ballet I can put a chair in front of and enjoy, without having to worry about how it's going to work out and how much it will cost if it doesn't. Be guided by me this first time, George, and after that you can have all the freedom you want." Goldwyn could be very convincing when he tried.

The ballet that Balanchine made as a substitute was the famous water-nymph ballet, to music by Vernon Duke. An updated *Swan Lake* in concept, it began with the beauteous nymph, Zorina, suddenly emerging from a pool at a garden party. One of the guests, William Dollar, falls instantly in love with her. They have a pas de deux of a romance which, alas, must come to an end—as all such ballet romances must. In ballet, people are always falling in love with nymphs or birds, and having to suffer for it. The art form is better suited than any other for expressing the unconsummatable. So at the end the nymph returns to her watery element, and the human lover is left forlorn beside the pool. Numerous surrealistic effects were employed in the staging, but the whole thing, as Balanchine had promised, could take place before Goldwyn's eyes, without scene changes, and without his having to squat or squint. At the run-through, Goldwyn was extremely pleased. His only doubt came at the very start when, as he was taking his seat, his eyes fell on a large, non-naturalistic representation of a horse, which was the most prominent feature of the set's background. It was a touch that Balanchine had suggested to the designer, who had modeled it after the horse in de Chirico's set for the Balanchine ballet *Le Bal*, of the Diaghilev days.

Goldwyn grimaced at the sight of it. "I don't think I like that horse," he groaned. "It doesn't look human, somehow. Jascha, look at that horse," he said turning to Jascha Heifetz, who happened to be present because he was performing in another film that the studio was making at that time. "What do you think?"

"I love it," Heifetz replied. "I think it's wonderful."

So the horse stayed.

During the filming of this ballet Balanchine was able to demonstrate that his conceptions were not the vague ambitions of an amateur. His acute eye and trained powers of visualization enabled him to plot with easy instinct the camera setups required. Working with the excellent cameraman Gregg Toland, he completed the filming of the ballet ahead of schedule in six days of shooting, with as many as eighteen camera setups a day, which the old hands on the lot considered very fast. So sure of himself was he that he never bothered, while filming a scene, to have protection shots made—that is, shots from more than one vantage point. This took nerve. It saved some time and money, but Balanchine would have been in trouble if the scenes had not turned out as well on film as he had imagined they would.

Goldwyn was not only delighted with the results but all his life remained devoted to the water-nymph ballet as the finest example of dance on film. He often showed it to guests at dinner parties and spoke proudly of his initiative in bringing the greatest choreographer of the age to Hollywood. The water-nymph ballet won much praise from ballet critics as well. Balanchine himself thought that probably the best thing about it was the de Chiricoesque horse and that otherwise, though pleasant, it was not particularly novel or exciting. It was not what *American in Paris* might have been or what Balanchine had hoped to do when he set out for Hollywood. He never did get the chance to experiment that Goldwyn had promised. This was the only Goldwyn movie he worked on. The producers of the other films he did dance numbers for in the years immediately following this proved even more unwilling than Goldwyn had been when it came to trying new techniques.

During those years when he was producing dances for Broadway and for Hollywood, Balanchine made lots of money and spent it all. He drank the best champagne, tooled around town in one of the first MGs seen in America, bought two grand pianos for the living room of his posh apartment on Central Park South, built a house on Long Island, near Northport, and courted Vera Zorina with trinkets from Cartier. He spent a lot of his spare time with a racy, fast-quipping Broadway crowd—with Larry Hart, Vernon Duke, and his agent, Milton Bender, who was known as Doc, having been a dentist before becoming a Broadway agent, a profession he had given up because, as he said, making a decent living at it was like pulling teeth. There would be noisy parties at Hart's apartment, where there was always something doing, or weekends at the Northport house, or at Westport or the Cape. He lived high and had a lot of fun. When he had a nightmare, as he occasionally did, he would call up Salvador Dali and tell him about it, and Dali would give him an expert opinion as to whether his nightmare was an interesting effort or just run-of-the-mill stuff.

On Christmas Eve of 1938 Balanchine and Zorina were married. The marriage came as something of a surprise, for the newspaper columnists

~With Vera Zorina on the set of The Goldwyn Follies.

had lately been linking her name with various glamorous figures, most particularly with Douglas Fairbanks, Jr. She was, that year, the toast of Broadway for her role in I Married an Angel—a Rodgers and Hart show, with choreography by Balanchine, which had great charm. Balanchine had fashioned her dances with imagination and loving care, to show her off to best advantage. He had also painted her dressing room at the theatre himself, because he thought it too dingy for her. There was no doubt about his adoration. He was moonstruck—as passionately in love as he had ever been in his life. Time and again he proposed, and then one night, to his astonishment, wonder, and delight (in that order), she said yes. Without any public announcement, they slipped over to Staten Island on the ferry right after the Christmas Eve performance of I Married an Angel and were married by a judge in St. George.

A small Christmas party had been planned for that evening at the Manhattan apartment of Mrs. Hartwig, Zorina's mother. Zorina and Balanchine arrived long after the other guests had assembled, but they did not tell anybody present why they were late. Supper was served, with champagne, and then Christmas presents were exchanged. Balanchine's present to Zorina was a package that when opened was seen to be a raincoat—obviously a very cheap one, such as could be picked up at a drugstore. "Oh, a raincoat!" Zorina exclaimed. "Just what I wanted." Balanchine suggested that she try it on. As she unfolded the garment, there fell out from inside it an ermine coat, whose individual skins Balanchine had spent weeks selecting and matching, and which he had then had specially made up for her. Zorina found she liked it even better than the raincoat. The gesture of wrapping a precious gift in an unprepossessing exterior was an example of Balanchine's playfulness, but it also had its symbolic aspect. Whatever assurance he may have had about his inner worth, Balanchine was always surprisingly diffident about his outer appearance. He did not consider himself a handsome or romantic figure, even though the young girls in his ballet company had sighed over him. He thought of himself as rather a shrimp, with a beaky nose and rodent-like front teeth. He nicknamed himself Malaross and would sign himself that way in some of his letters to Russian friends—on those rare occasions when he wrote. "Malaross" was a pun. The word is generally used to mean an inhabitant of "Little Russia" or the Ukraine, which Balanchine, a Georgian born in St. Petersburg, never was. But literally it means "undersized," and that was how he regarded himself, though, in fact, he was of average height.

The bliss of Balanchine's conquest of Zorina did not last long. In fact, it seemed to him that, though he had won her hand, he had not conquered her affections. Their marriage in its essence was, one of Balanchine's friends said, rather like Balanchine's scenario for the *American in Paris* ballet, in which Zorina was the elusive will-o'-the-wisp, always just out of reach of her tormented lover. During the seven years this marriage lasted, Balanchine was as nearly wretched as he had ever been in his life. Frequently they would separate, and then he would beg her to try again. Sometimes he could be seen standing in the street outside her apartment late at night, unshaven, haggard, thoroughly wretched, waiting for a glimpse of her. He was in such despair that some of his friends thought he might do himself harm. At one time he talked his problems over with a psychiatrist. The consultation took place in the fall of 1940 aboard a small steamer returning to New York from Cuba, where Balanchine had gone to recuperate after the opening of *Cabin in the Sky*, and the psychiatrist—a Russian—was a fellow passenger with

In the country near Westport, Connecticut, about 1939.

whom Balanchine had struck up an acquaintance. Vernon Duke, who had done the music for that show, accompanied Balanchine on the cruise, and he noted with amusement one aspect of these shipboard psychiatric sessions: it was a rough voyage, and the doctor, whose stomach was queasy, lay down as well as the patient while they talked. Duke thought there might be a new analytic technique in the making there. From the psychiatrist, Balanchine got the advice that he needed to be more assertive toward his wife, whereupon he composed a long, high-handed letter to her, telling her what a great man and great choreographer he was and how lucky she should feel at being associated with him. But Balanchine was not able to hold the high-handed pose for long. Such advice could not help him because it was false to his nature. Once back on dry land, he did not seek further psychiatric treatment, the process of introspection and self-contemplation being so alien to him. Eventually, by a route opposite to the one the psychiatrist had advised, he found a way of making some peace with his frustrated desires. This was the route of abnegation and humility, and it was shown to him by a friend of his father's, a Georgian, now living in America, to whom Balanchine once went for advice. This friend, a devout member of the Greek Orthodox faith, was an old man and, Balanchine thought, a wise one. "Aren't you selfish?" the old man said to him, after listening to Balanchine tell of his unhappiness. "You think only of yourself. What makes you think you have a right to be happy, anyway? And above all, what makes you think you have a right to demand that another person love you? No human being has a right to demand love from another—that is the height of conceit and arrogance." These words took hold, and they seemed to help.

To blame all of Balanchine's unhappiness during those years on unrequited conjugal love would be an oversimplification. That was an important element, but his unhappiness was compounded by many other ingredients as well. For one thing, he had begun to run into his share of Broadway flops—such forgettable shows as *Keep Off the Grass*, *The Lady Comes Across*, and *Dream with Music*. For another, though he had been fortunate in his colleagues in the first shows he had done—people like Rodgers and Hart, and the producer Dwight Deere Wiman, who was a gentleman and who treated Balanchine with deference and respect—he now began to find himself working for much cruder Broadway types, who tried to push him around and meddle with his dances. Typical of this genre of Broadway producer was Harry Kaufman, of the Shubert enterprises, who produced *Keep Off the Grass*. Kaufman came into a rehearsal once, during an adagio moment, and almost swallowed his cigar in horror. "George, what are you doing? Why the slow motion?" he exclaimed.

"I'm building toward a climax," Balanchine replied.

"Please, George, you're killing me with that slow motion," cried Kaufman. "I want you should start with the climax. Give me nothing but climaxes."

It did not make life pleasanter during those days to find himself suddenly, after having lived prosperously for several years, stone broke and having to borrow money from Larry Hart to live on. Naturally, he could not get rich from flop shows. And even on the hits now he had bad luck. *Cabin in the Sky*, for instance, won great acclaim and was considered a smashing triumph, but it was not a money-maker. It was one of the first Broadway shows to be built around an all-black cast—including Ethel Waters, Todd Duncan, Rex Ingram, and Katherine Dunham and her dancers. Balanchine put more of himself into *Cabin in the Sky* than any other show he did. He tried to persuade Samuel Goldwyn and others to back it, and he himself sank several thousand dollars, his last savings, into it. He not only choreographed the dances, but he also staged the entire production.

Even if he had kept on earning fat sums and had continued to find the most understanding and congenial of producers to work for, by that time the challenge and interest that the commercial theatre had originally posed had been exhausted for him. The whole epoch was not one he would care to relive. He had adapted himself philosophically, even lightheartedly, to Broadway and Hollywood much of the time, but it was not the life he would have chosen by preference. "I'm like a potato," he once said to me, in one of the homely metaphors he would produce from time to time. "A potato is pretty tough. It can grow anywhere. But even a potato has a soil in which it grows best. My soil is ballet."

Undoubtedly, the worst and most fundamental of all his frustrations during that time was not having a ballet company. Those years without a company were years in which it was impossible for him to work at what he did best. Without a troupe of trained dancers, a choreographer, it has been said, is as frustrated as a painter without brushes, oil, or canvas. Balanchine, characteristically, preferred a livelier comparison to describe this situation. He said it was like being a lion tamer with no lions.

During the years that Balanchine was out of serious ballet, his absence was not mourned by ballet's powers-that-be as much as one might suppose. Kirstein, of course, regretted it and was bitterly disappointed at the waste of Balanchine's talents. A friend remembers Kirstein gloomily proclaiming to him one day—in French, for heightened effect, no doubt—"*Balanchine, c'est un homme perdu.*" But there were others who saw no reason to lament the way things had worked out. In 1938, for instance, when Balanchine staged the dances for *I Married an Angel,* John Martin wrote an article about it for the *Times* that lavishly praised the show's choreography and at the same time suggested that this light commercial stuff was the sort of thing that Balanchine was really cut out for. Late the following year, Balanchine found himself left on the sidelines when Ballet Theatre was organized. Eleven European and American choreographers were invited to contribute ballets to the new company; he was not. Balanchine was the only choreographer of note in the Western world who was not asked to participate. The reasons he was passed by have never been clarified. Power politics, with which the ballet world is rife, undoubtedly played a part, and the founders of Ballet Theatre may also have been motivated by the apprehension that Balanchine might prove too dominating a personality to work in tandem with other choreographers. All the more galling it must have been to Balanchine to be thus excluded, however, as he saw that ballet was beginning to catch on in the United States at last. The founding of Ballet Theatre marked a big stride forward for ballet in the United States, and it was organized on a far larger scale than the humble enterprise of Balanchine, Kirstein, and Warburg five years before. Endowed by Lucia Chase, a New England heiress, who over the years thereafter pumped vast sums into her venture, Ballet Theatre was to prove the dominant company on the American scene for the next decade.

Throughout his Broadway years, Balanchine never ceased regarding himself as a ballet master, not a showman. He had a deeper allegiance to ballet than he had to the Shubert enterprises. One day he met Edwin Denby on the street in New York and, in the course of the casual conversation that ensued, suddenly declared, "We must save ballet."

"But it is immortal," Denby replied.

"I don't mean the dance," said Balanchine. "I mean ballet."

It was then the age of Tudor. The psychological ballets Antony Tudor was doing for Ballet Theatre were being received with great excitement and acclaim. Tudor's work was a continuation of Fokine's revolt against the formalism of classical ballet. His productions stressed emotion and literary content, employing a style of movement that relied on mimed gestures and set up tensions by deliberately working against the recognized classical line or model of movement. In a Tudor ballet the characters whose steps were from the classical vocabulary were intended to be recognized as conventional, inhibited, cold people; and these often danced in a peculiarly rigid way. Balanchine's aims were the direct opposite of all this. To him the classical technique was not a constriction but a liberation—a way of freedom from the drabness and compromises of workaday reality. He wanted to show the grandeur and grace that was potential in the human form. "I would like to show," he said once, "that these bodies of ours, which most of the time are used for dull, ordinary things, can be beautiful—really beautiful." Least of all did he want to use ballet as a vehicle for self-expression. "If I were feeling suicidal," he remarked at one time, "I would never try to express this in a ballet. I would make as beautiful a variation as I could for a ballerina, and then— well, then I'd go and kill myself."

Always, during this period of his life, whenever he got the chance to do a ballet, he seized the opportunity. In 1941 Balanchine choreographed *Balustrade*, with Toumanova, Roman Jasinski, and Paul Petroff as the leading dancers, for a company known as the Original Ballet Russe. Its music was Stravinsky's *Violin Concerto*, its sets and costumes were by Tchelitchev, and it enjoyed but three performances in all. Stravinsky, who worked closely with Balanchine and Tchelitchev on this project and conducted the orchestra for the performances, was delighted with the result. He called it "one of the most satisfactory visualizations of any of my theatre works." The critics, though, heaped scorn on it. John Martin wrote that it was a sad state of affairs that "while gifted American artists are starving in the effort to bring their work before the public, there is money available for the production of European importations of this calibre." Despite this reception, the making of *Balustrade* was for Balanchine a happy occasion, as he collaborated once again with artists he admired on a project to which he could give himself wholeheartedly.

Perhaps Balanchine's most fruitful interlude during the period of his stint in the world of the commercial theatre came later on in 1941 when the American Ballet company was temporarily revived, for the purpose of carrying out a specific mission. The mission was a goodwill tour of Latin America. The idea for this project came from Nelson Rockefeller, who had recently been given an appointment in the State Department as coordinator for Latin American affairs. He suggested it to his friend Lincoln Kirstein, who naturally recruited Balanchine. The aim of the project was to reveal to the people of South America, through a medium that transcended the language barrier, that the North American colossus had a soul and was not just a grasping imperialist. The government would agree to underwrite all the operating expenses of the tour if Kirstein could raise the production costs—which he readily promised to do. The dancers were recruited from the School of American Ballet and from a chamber dance group, Ballet Caravan, which Kirstein had been sponsoring and working closely with during the past three years. Among the dancers, the one whose abilities most stimulated Balanchine was Marie-Jeanne, a ballerina of amazing brilliance, speed, and precision. Utilizing these attributes of hers, Balanchine choreographed two new ballets for the tour—*Ballet Imperial* and *Concerto Barocco*. These ballets were not only two of the most luminous and achieved statements in dance Balanchine ever made but were also of considerable importance in Balanchine's development. This was the first time he dared to make ballets that were purely dance compositions, with no apologies and without even the hint of a plot. This was what he had been moving toward for some years. He said it was, oddly enough, Fokine who gave him the courage to dispense with the last vestige of the plot element. Balanchine saw a Ballet Theatre production of *Les Sylphides* the previous year, one that Fokine himself had carefully supervised, and was struck once more by its beauty. "Of all the Fokine ballets," he told himself, "*this* is the one that really lasts—this one which is an exception to all of Fokine's theories. If he could do it, why can't I?"

The South American tour, which lasted four months, was only moderately successful. The South American audiences did not find the company or its repertory very glamorous. There were sizable deficits at the box office, and numerous petty difficulties and problems along the way. Kirstein, in his gloomy fashion, once described the South American tour as "a disaster," but it was not. It was the first attempt the American government had made in the direction of sponsorship of the performing arts and, as such, laid some of the groundwork for the State Department's cultural exchange programs. If nothing else, it provided the excuse and the conditions for the production of two of Balanchine's greatest ballets.

After this tour, the company disbanded once more. Balanchine went back to work in the commercial theatre. His spirits were somewhat refreshed by the creative interlude; he was more at peace with himself now.

൭ Concerto Barocco, *as performed by the New York City Ballet in 1950, with Diana Adams and Tanaquil Le Clercq as principals.*

In the shows he was engaged to do after this, he found some that were enjoyable enough, as well as lucrative—particularly a number of operettas, such as *Rosalinda*, *The Merry Widow*, and *Song of Norway*, which allowed him more scope for dancing than the typical Broadway musical and which, incidentally, were extremely successful.

From 1933 on, the Ballet Russe de Monte Carlo—one of the offshoots of the company that Balanchine had helped to start and been fired from by de Basil—had been making frequent tours of America, under the sponsorship of S. Hurok. By 1944, this company, now controlled by Serge Denham, was in run-down condition, and that year Denham asked Balanchine to help liven it up. Balanchine agreed. The effect on the company was that of a magic potion; the moribund company suddenly blossomed again. As George Amberg has written in his book *Ballet in America*, "The one single individual who miraculously rejuvenated the Ballet Russe de Monte Carlo was George Balanchine." In addition to supervising the staging of a number of his older works, he choreographed five new ballets—*Night Shadow, Danses Concertantes, Raymonda* (assisted by Alexandra Danilova), a new version of *Le Bourgeois Gentilhomme*, and a *Pas de Deux* for Danilova and Frederic Franklin to the music of the entr'acte from *Sleeping Beauty*—and reformed the company's dancing in general, replacing about half of the old Russians with eager young Americans, most of them graduates of his School of American Ballet, and letting the company know, in his authoritative way, quiet but formidable, that he did not wish to see any more of the shoddy, slack dancing it had been trying to get by with. For two years Balanchine worked enthusiastically with the Ballet Russe. It can be considered the return of that potato, Balanchine (to use his own figure of speech), to his native soil of ballet.

The sleepwalker carries off the dead poet in Night Shadow—*Margrethe Schanne and Henning Kronstam in the Royal Danish Ballet production.*

CHAPTER TEN

Second Beginnings

alanchine never considered allying himself permanently with the Ballet Russe, because no matter how much the company improved its dancing, it was fundamentally oriented toward the box office. It picked up its living from one-night-stand tours of the country—a ballet dancer's idea of hell—and had to shape its repertory to compete successfully in the hinterlands with traveling circuses or local revival meetings; there had to be big-name stars and plenty of tried-and-true terpsichorean fireworks. Continual touring dictated the expediency of employing only a small orchestra, which limited the range of ballets the company could put on. It also made it difficult for the company to maintain peak standards of performance. In addition, Balanchine did not find working for Serge Denham, the company's general director, congenial. Their tastes differed, they had different conceptions of ballet, and Denham, a former banker, kept asserting himself in matters that Balanchine regarded as peculiarly his own province as ballet master—a province Balanchine always jealously guarded. It was inevitable that eventually Denham and Balanchine would part. For some years after Balanchine left the Ballet Russe, in 1946, the company managed to go along in good style on the momentum he had given it, and then it deteriorated again.

The immediate reason for Balanchine's departure from the Ballet Russe early in 1946, however, was not any particular climactic disagreement with Denham. It had to do rather with Lincoln Kirstein's discharge from the military. For three years Kirstein had been away in the army, serving as a member of the Monuments and Fine Arts section. For his

ᐤ *Maria Tallchief in* **The Four Temperaments.**

203

∾ *Tanaquil Le Clercq (far right) taking class at the age of nine.*

work in ferreting out art treasures the Nazis had hidden away he had been awarded a citation and promoted from private all the way up to private first class. He returned to civilian life with plans for a new venture into ballet and with about two hundred and fifty thousand dollars, a recent inheritance, burning a hole in his pocket. Immediately he sought out Balanchine to enlist his help in disposing of this money in the most stimulating and productive way. "As millionaires go," W. H. Auden once commented, "Lincoln Kirstein is really a very *poor* millionaire, but he's been more effective than many richer ones because he's used his money with such discrimination, as well as passion." Balanchine once said, after years of association with Kirstein, "Lincoln is a true Christian, even though he won't admit it. He gives you money and runs away before you can thank him."

Throughout the years since Kirstein had brought Balanchine to America, the two men had maintained their rapport even during periods when they saw each other little. The abiding link between them, after the American Ballet company had collapsed in 1938, was provided by the school they had established together. The school, as it patiently went about its task of teaching an ancient code of movement to young American bodies, asserted their mutual faith in the future of ballet in America, regardless of individual setbacks or mischances. Kirstein had always maintained an office in the school building, and Balanchine had always been the chairman of its faculty, even though there had been stretches of time when, busy with musicals and movies, he had not done much teaching himself. The school had flourished. It had survived a crisis in 1940 when Kirstein had bought out the director, Dimitriev, with whose financial policies he had increasingly disagreed, and incorporated the school, as he had always wanted to do, as a nonprofit educational institution. Kirstein then became president and director, but its administration, for all practical purposes, was placed in the hands of its executive secretary, Eugenie Ouroussow, who had been with the school since its founding.

As part of its new policy, after its reorganization, the school in 1941 had instituted a scholarship competition—awarding scholarships to the five most promising children who applied. One of the scholarships went to a long-legged, eleven-year-old girl named Tanaquil Le Clercq. Balanchine, chief judge at this competition, had been charmed by her poise and fine configuration. "She looks like a real ballerina already," Balanchine commented, "only very small, as if you were looking at her through the wrong end of a telescope." By 1946, the school's enrollment had grown to more than two hundred, and it even included some boys— a handful only, for most Americans still regarded ballet dancing as a sissy occupation for men and feared that in a ballet school their dear sons would be bound to catch an incurable case of homosexuality. Among the boys at the school, the most promising was an eleven-year-old lad, Jacques d'Amboise, now in his third year at the school, who could leap like a gazelle and had an open, ingratiating personality. His parents had not intended to enroll him as a ballet student, but at first had just sent him along to keep his sister, Ninette, company when she took her lessons. After class, though, it would turn out that young Jacques was able to demonstrate everything he had seen his sister trying to learn and could do it easily and naturally, with a broad grin on his face. He did not know it was supposed to be hard; he thought it was just fun. So his parents bowed to his wishes and enrolled him as well as his sister. At the school, in whose classes he was doing his best to acquire, as was expected of him, the noble, elegant bearing of a courtier or prince, he could often be seen, when his own class was over and he was waiting for his sister to

Balanchine with pupils at the School of American Ballet in 1946. The boy is Edward Villella, age ten.

finish, lying slouched, his hair rumpled, on the floor in some corner reading comic books and looking like any American kid who has just come in from playing ball. Then there was another boy, a new lad—Edward Villella by name. He was ten and had just started taking classes. He was small but handsome and had a sturdy, manly air. But it was too soon to tell how he would develop.

Second beginnings are often more difficult than first tries. One has acquired more wisdom and experience, but often more inhibitions as well. One sees all too clearly now along the path the pitfalls and booby traps of which one had been blithely unaware when setting out in earlier days. Is it worth all that pain and trouble? a man may ask himself at this point. Balanchine and Kirstein thought it was, but they were chary of repeating the mistakes they had made a dozen years before. They wanted to avoid the hazards and distracting preoccupations that went with box-office ventures and the commercial theatre; they wanted nothing to do with that whole rat race. So they decided to form an organization that would cater only to an elite subscription audience. Working with them in this project from the start was the conductor Leon Barzin. This new organization, which was to be called Ballet Society, would have as its aim, as its announcement stated, "the encouragement of the lyric theatre by the production of new works." It would not perform works in the standard repertory, since it needed to make no concessions to mass tastes. In addition to new ballets, it would put on chamber operas and other kinds of dance beside the classical. Among the chamber operas it would present would be Gian-Carlo Menotti's *The Medium* and *The Telephone*—the latter being a work that Ballet Society commissioned. The society also planned to publish books and monographs on the dance, to award fellowships to gifted young dancers or to choreographers, and to commission dance films.

Ballet Society's first performance took place November 20, 1946. It was given in the auditorium of the Central High School of Needle Trades. It would have taken considerable effort to find a more unlikely setting than this bleak hall for the presentation of ballet or lyric theatre. The chairs were hard, the stage was merely a raised surface with a curtain, there was no orchestra pit. The fifty members of the orchestra were seated in full sight at floor level, partially obstructing the spectators' view of the stage, and the conductor, on a small raised platform, presented a further obstruction to vision. "The whole thing," recalled Anatole Chujoy, in his detailed history, *The New York City Ballet*, "looked hopelessly amateurish, provincial, and depressing." The audience was kept waiting for half an hour for the first curtain, during which time the sound of hammering and other construction work could be heard going on behind the curtain while the orchestra tuned up and practiced difficult passages over and over. "The evening was getting to be as uninspiring and untheatrical as one could imagine," wrote Chujoy. Then the curtain went up. "The long wait, the uncomfortable seats, all the impedimenta of the auditorium and stage were immediately forgotten, for there was magic on the stage: *The Spellbound Child* (*L'Enfant et les Sortilèges*) by Maurice Ravel."

A work of fantasy, in an English translation of Colette's text by Jane Barzin and Lincoln Kirstein, the opera was staged by Balanchine in a manner similar to what he had done at the Metropolitan Opera with Gluck's *Orpheus*. That is, the singers sat offstage with the musicians, and the action was portrayed by dancers. "There were forty-three dancers on the stage," noted Chujoy. "How they ever got on or, having got on, did not spill into the audience, will remain Balanchine's secret."

The other work on that first program, after the intermission, was the premiere of one of Balanchine's most astonishing ballets, *The Four Temperaments*. The score for this ballet came into being in an unusual way. A few years before, during his Broadway-Hollywood heyday, Balanchine found himself running out of ideas as to how to spend all the money he was earning. He had a sporty car, two grand pianos, a country place on Long Island, and, as he said, "I didn't need another cigarette case." He got to wondering how much it would cost to commission a piece of music—from Paul Hindemith, say. Balanchine had no ballet company at the time, and he was not looking for music he could choreograph, merely something for his own pleasure that he would enjoy listening to and playing over on the piano. He inquired of Hindemith's agent how much that composer's fee would be for a work of perhaps half an hour in length for piano and strings. The agent's reply was five hundred dollars, which seemed to Balanchine a great bargain. Hindemith was too busy to undertake the commission at the moment, but one day in 1940, about a year after Balanchine had broached the matter, Balanchine got a letter from the agent saying that Hindemith, then in residence at Yale, had some free time; if Balanchine still wished to have a composition, on the terms discussed, the first part could be delivered to him one week from that date. On the promised date the music arrived. It received its first hearing in Balanchine's apartment on East Fifty-second Street at Fifth Avenue, at one of the little Sunday afternoon "musicales" he liked to give. At the piano was Kopeikine. The "orchestra" was made up of a few of Balanchine's musician friends: Nathan Milstein, Samuel Dushkin, Leon Barzin, and Raya Garbousova. Edvard Fendler conducted. That performance alone, Balanchine thought, gave him more than his five hundred dollars' worth. He first began seriously to think of using the score for dance in 1941 when the temporarily revived American Ballet was preparing for its State Department–sponsored tour of Latin America. At that time he and Tchelitchev worked out a conception quite different from the present one. It was to be called *The Cave of Sleep*. Tchelitchev designed sixty fantastic costumes, derived from the anatomical principles of Vesalius. His designs, he assured Balanchine, would wipe out everything else—music, choreography, dancers. The project was abandoned because Hindemith objected to the concept and it would have been exorbitantly expensive. The 1946 performance for Ballet Society used costumes designed by Kurt Seligmann. They were elaborate, bizarre, and cumbersome. A few years later Balanchine got rid of them and found that this ballet made its best effect and showed up most clearly when danced simply in black-and-white practice clothes against a bare blue cyclorama.

The Four Temperaments, as Balanchine's first ballet for Ballet Society, was a presage of things to come. Unlike anything that had ever been seen in ballet before, it opened a realm of new possibilities that he subsequently explored in such ballets as *Opus 34, Ivesiana, Agon, Episodes, Movements for Piano and Orchestra, Stravinsky Violin Concerto,* and *Kammermusik No. 2.* It seemed to demonstrate that ballet could do anything that modern dance could do—and more. Inexorable yet not gloomy, austere yet somehow finally joyous, *The Four Temperaments* had the radiance achieved by a work of art that makes a definitive statement. It seemed to manifest a force that was new to ballet, a kind of ruthlessness—even in its degree of concentration and in its impersonality—that projected a meaningful attitude toward life in the mid-twentieth century. There also seemed to be in *The Four Temperaments* a new sort of content—for the so-called "abstract" ballets of Balanchine do have real content even if they do not have plot. "Balanchine's ballets are all full of the most extraordinary encounters and events," Jerome Robbins once commented. "In *Apollo* the three Muses suddenly become horses pulling Apollo's chariot, and then an instant later they are lovely goddesses again. In *The Four Temperaments* at the end, where there are those great soaring lifts, I always feel as if I am watching some momentous departure—like interplanetary travelers taking their leave of the world." Even without a metaphorical science-fiction interpretation, *The Four Temperaments* was a ballet of the future. The audience in the auditorium of the Central High School of Needle Trades that November evening in 1946, favorably disposed toward Balanchine, thought they liked what they saw; but it would be some years before *The Four Temperaments* achieved the status of acknowledged masterpiece.

For the critics at the time, Ballet Society was a most peculiar venture, and they did not know what to make of it. Kirstein and Balanchine carried the exclusiveness of their policy so far that they did not even invite the press to attend their performances. This made for an odd situation, with the critics buying their own subscriptions, sneaking into the auditorium on performance nights and then, half apologetically, writing what were, on the whole, laudatory reviews—which they were not at all sure the haughty management would welcome. *Time* magazine titled its article about the organization "Ballet Underground." A deliberately im-

The Four Temperaments, as performed by the New York City Ballet in the 1980's. Shown here are Bart Cook (upper left), Heather Watts and Tracy Bennett (upper right), Adam Lüders (lower left), and Bart Cook, Maria Calegari, and Adam Lüders (lower right).

practical venture, the Ballet Society was a typical expression of Kirstein's—and, to a lesser extent, Balanchine's—noble but unrealistic struggle to establish ballet on purely artistic terms, untainted by the box office. As a ballet impresario, Kirstein was no Hurok. Profits revolted him. When a booking agent once came to him and showed him how he could make money by taking his ballet company on tour with a reduced ensemble and orchestra and a popularized repertoire, Kirstein said caustically, "Sir, I am not in ballet to make money."

To many, then, Ballet Society appeared to be just another of Balanchine's and Kirstein's impetuous, quixotic forays. But a few observers saw that it was part of a grand plan and was potentially significant. Chujoy remembered that back in 1937 Kirstein had outlined to him a plan for an organization very similar to the Ballet Society he had now formed. Since 1934 Balanchine and Kirstein had worked together to de-Russianize ballet as an art—to establish it as something that American practitioners could do well and that American audiences could enjoy in a natural way. Now, as Denby noted, they were trying to decommercialize it as theatre—as the most effective, even if troublesome, way of keeping it civilized. "I have here reported the Society's lucky beginning at quite disproportionate length," Denby wrote in an article in April 1947, "partly because it is a new, much talked of enterprise, partly because it may well, after several years of trial and error, turn out to have been the origin and foundation of the sensibly organized, exciting American ballet company we need now so badly."

Each new epoch of Balanchine's creative life seems to have been associated with a new wife or love—always a dancer under his aegis, always young and not yet fully formed, either as person or dancer. As models do for a painter or sculptor, they served the choreographer as both reality and potentiality—with the poignant addition that they were also the raw material out of which the finished work of art would be formed. Patiently, willingly, they allowed themselves to be used by him in the explorations of his craft. It was their job; they were married to their work, as he was to his. That one young woman should be supplanted in this role by another in the course of time had begun to seem by then, as with Picasso's succession of wife-mistress-models, an outward manifestation of the constantly renewed youthfulness of the artist's creative powers. "Grow old along with me, the best is yet to be" was not a likely motto for Balanchine. He lived only in and for the present. Caring intensely as he did about physical beauty, as joined in the great dancers with an Olympic athlete's prowess, Balanchine always suffered to see this masterful beauty fade. No Elizabethan sonneteer was ever more pained by time's encroachments and ravages than he. Sometimes he would avoid meeting with beautiful dancers whom he had known in a bygone era because he cherished a precise and acute image of their beauty in his memory, which he could not bear to have spoiled for him by their present appearance.

For the era in his life initiated by his active return from the commercial theatre to the world of ballet, the young woman who would play the central part in his life was to be Maria Tallchief, whom he married on August 16, 1946. Balanchine was forty-two years of age at the time of their marriage, Maria Tallchief was twenty-one. Their marriage lasted five years, ending with her being granted an annulment. The grounds for the annulment were that she wanted to have children but Balanchine did not. These grounds were generally assumed to be simply a convenient pretext for the legal action, but it is a fact that during her subsequent marriage, to a Chicago businessman, she did have a child, and it is also a fact that Balanchine did wish that the ballerinas in his company would suppress the urge to procreate. "Any woman can become a mother," he said, "but not every woman can become a ballerina."

At twenty-one Maria Tallchief was already striking looking, with black hair, pale olive skin, and beautiful, large, dark eyes. Her young face had a mysterious, somber gravity; it had the look of a Mayan mask. Born in Fairfax, Oklahoma, of an Osage Indian father and a mother who was of Irish, Scottish, and Dutch ancestry, Maria grew up in Beverly Hills, California, where her family moved when she was eight. As a child she studied the piano intensively and also took ballet lessons from Bronislava Nijinska in Hollywood. On her twelfth birthday she gave a recital at which, for the first half of the program, she played the Chopin E Minor Concerto and for the second half she danced. Her musicality was part of her attraction for Balanchine, a personal bond as well as a trait of crucial importance in one of his ballerinas. They often played four-hand piano together. He was also very taken by her Indian heritage. This charmed him. It made him feel that in marrying her he was becoming really American—John Smith marrying Pocahontas. When, a few months after their marriage, he crossed the country by train to join her in Los Angeles, where she was vacationing with her family, and to work with Stravinsky on *Orpheus,* Balanchine was quite agog when the train, passing through Oklahoma, went by an Indian reservation. "Look, those

are my new relatives!" he proudly told Nicolas Nabokov, with whom he was making the trip, and then for hours regaled Nabokov with Indian lore—all this in Russian, of course. Most of all, in regard to Maria Tallchief, Balanchine was attracted by her appearance and her potential abilities, by the way she moved—and by the way he saw that she would move after he had worked with her. Still with a little tender plump flesh on her, not pared down to the bone yet, the way Balanchine said he liked his dancers, she had a high chest and straight back, and she moved like a tiger. Under Balanchine's tutelage and in his ballets, she would win world renown.

For her part, she stood in awe of Balanchine. He was the master. She had said that she was astonished when he proposed, for he had not previously showed any lover's ardor, and when he had turned his eyes on her, in the rehearsal hall, she had not been aware that these might be melting glances he was bestowing, but was rather painfully conscious of all the flaws he must be noting. There was no thought of refusing him, just as in the rehearsal hall there was no thought of refusing to attempt whatever he demanded of her.

To the general public, by this time, Balanchine's marriages were beginning to be a subject of some fascination, viewed through the golden haze of glamour. The public had begun to picture Balanchine as having the personality of a Don Juan combined with a pinch or two of Pygmalion and more than a trace of Svengali. This reputation quite surprised him. He had never concealed his interest in beautiful women or his admiration for them—indeed, his ballets so glorified the ballerinas that he had been scolded by some critics for neglecting the male dancer—but he did not think of himself as a rake, or even as a particularly dashing figure. He did not leave any of his wives; it was they who left him, he said. Outside of the world of ballet, where he moved with absolute assurance, he was often not merely reserved but diffident. Some of his friends suspected that a certain element of insecurity about himself in relation to women was what led him always to choose young women from his company—as if he felt the need to bolster his role as lover by that of ballet master. But it may have been merely chance and propinquity that made this pattern in his life. Balanchine himself once gave a reporter a more whimsical explanation of why he always married dancers. "If you marry a ballerina," he said, "you never have to worry about whether she's running around with somebody else or anything like that. You always know

Maria Tallchief in Orpheus.

exactly where she is—in the studio, working." With all his ex-wives, he seemed able to maintain an amicable relationship. A friend who dropped into the school one day was intrigued to observe all the ex-wives lined up at the bar, calmly taking class together.

On February 26, 1947, shortly before the third program in Ballet Society's first season, Balanchine sailed for France on the *America*. He had received an invitation to be guest ballet master at the Paris Opéra for the coming season. Lifar had been dismissed after the liberation of Paris on charges of collaborating with the Nazi occupation. For the Opéra, Balanchine staged his *Serenade, Apollo,* and *Le Baiser de la Fée,* and he choreographed one new work, intended as a tribute to the Opéra ballet. Deeming it fitting that the music for this new ballet should be by a French composer, he decided to make use of a little-known work by Georges Bizet—his Symphony in C Major, which Bizet had written at the age of seventeen but had never published for fear that it would be thought too derivative of the symphony by his teacher, Gounod; it had only in recent years been discovered. Balanchine took just two weeks to choreograph this ballet—*Le Palais de Cristal,* or *Symphony in C,* as it later became known—but he caught ineffably its essential qualities: the youthful freshness of the allegro movements, the moon-drenched romanticism of the adagio movement. In this plotless, classical ballet the music supplies all the continuity required. Balanchine's musicality made for the happiest matching imaginable of music and dance. Few people who have seen this ballet can hear the music thereafter without seeing once again in their mind's eye some of the visual images Balanchine conjured up for it.

As guest ballerina that season, Balanchine had the services of Tamara Toumanova. A world-famous figure, she was no stranger to Paris, which had been applauding her performances since her "baby ballerina" days and hailed her now as "the black pearl." The other guest artist being presented was an unknown quantity to Paris—Balanchine's new wife and protégée, Maria Tallchief. She made her debut at the Opéra dancing Terpsichore in *Apollo* at a gala evening attended by King Gustav of Sweden, and she danced the Fairy in *Le Baiser de la Fée.* She was the first American to dance at the Paris Opéra since Augusta Maywood appeared there in 1839. Tallchief made a good impression on that great stage; she was recognized as showing great promise. Balanchine even told her that she had danced "not too badly"—which, from him, was high praise.

In addition to staging his ballets, Balanchine restored discipline, which had been deteriorating. As usual, he kept a sharp eye out for new talent. He broke Paris Opéra protocol by giving such youngsters as Claude Bessy, Liane Daydé, and Jacqueline Moreau more important parts to dance than their official rankings at the time indicated. At the Paris Opéra, as at the court of Louis XIV, it was not the custom of those of upper rank to dance on equal terms with those of lower. In general, the members of the Paris company respected Balanchine but were somewhat disconcerted by his reserve. They were used to Lifar making a great fuss over them, and some missed that kind of excitement. *"Il ne s'est pas penché sur nous,"* one of the Opéra's ballerinas later said, when asked how Balanchine had treated them. He did not hover over them.

Once more, as in 1929, it is likely that Balanchine would have stayed on at the Paris Opéra permanently if he could have had his choice. Balanchine thought of himself by now as very much an American. He had received his citizenship papers in 1939 and, like his fellow naturalized American patriot, Stravinsky, would not permit criticism of the United States to go unanswered, but he had to find a place to work, to have the opportunity to make his ballets and show them to a public. Ballet Society was giving only four programs a year to a small audience and was in precarious financial state. If it continued and he got the Paris post, he thought it might be possible to divide his time between Paris and New York.

But his wishes in regard to the Paris Opéra were once more of no consequence. At the Opéra that season Balanchine found himself in the midst of a spider web of intrigue, buzzing with rumors, machinations, plots, and counterplots. Lifar's adherents were constantly active in his behalf. Instead of Lifar being condemned as a collaborator, they felt he should be treated as a hero for having held the Opéra ballet together during the occupation. Actually, Lifar was neither hero nor collaborator; he was simply someone who needed at all times to bask in the applause of an audience. Not long after Balanchine arrived at the Opéra to take up his duties, a petition signed by nearly a thousand people was presented to the minister of fine arts, asserting that the Opéra needed a permanent ballet master, not a guest, and not a foreigner. No names were mentioned, but none needed to be: the message was clear. At the end of that season Lifar, cleared of all charges, was invited back to his old post at the Opéra. He returned in triumph, remaining in power there until his retirement in 1958. And once more Balanchine left the Paris Opéra with a bad taste in his mouth.

Back in New York that fall, Balanchine staged Mozart's *Symphonie Concertante* for Ballet Society. The leading roles were danced by Tanaquil Le Clercq, Maria Tallchief, and Todd Bolender. It was a ballet that Balanchine had choreographed two years before for a program called *Adventure in Ballet*, presented at Carnegie Hall by the National Orchestral Society. He had choreographed it at that time for students of the School of American Ballet, with Bolender as guest artist, and its purpose was essentially educational—to show to the public, as well as to the student dancers, the relationship between a classical symphonic work and classical dance. In its restaging, it was not a great audience-pleaser, nor did it please most of the critics, who thought it followed the music too dutifully. There was nothing bravura about it. Tallchief, who thought it a beautiful work and quite difficult to dance well, later said of it, "I always wondered whether Balanchine had done it as a learning exercise because there were no furbelows or frills. It was like taking your medicine every day."

This was followed two weeks later by the premiere, on November 26, 1947, of a new ballet choreographed for Ballet Theatre, which had finally decided to recognize Balanchine's existence. The ballet was *Theme and Variations*, to the fourth movement of Tchaikovsky's Suite No. 3 in G Major for Orchestra, with Alicia Alonso and Igor Youskevitch as principal dancers. A pure dance ballet, like *Ballet Imperial*, it was intended, as Balanchine wrote, "to evoke that great period in classical dancing when Russian ballet flourished with the aid of Tchaikovsky's music." For setting there was a formal ballroom with pillars and crystal chandeliers and a formal garden in the background. Balanchine had problems with Youskevitch in this work. Youskevitch said he could only dance a ballet like this if he thought of himself as the prince in *Giselle* or *Swan Lake*. Balanchine wished he would not think—just do the steps. Alonso, always a splendid technician, seemed better than her best in this ballet, as if Balanchine had invented a new glamorous and radiant personality.

With critics and public alike, *Theme and Variations* made a big hit. The greatest classical ballet of our time, Walter Terry called it in his New York *Herald-Tribune* review. The reception pleased Lincoln Kirstein for Balanchine's sake, but he was jealous that the success came with another company, rather than their own, and for something less than Balanchine's best work, in his view. "Balanchine has had a vast critical success with his *Theme and Variations* to the 3rd suite of Tchaikovsky," he wrote to Stravinsky the day after Christmas that year. "In my opinion, and also that of Pavlik [Tchelitchev], it is not at all a first-class work, compared to the two Mozart concerti he did, but it appeals madly to the public, and I think now George has become recognized . . . after 15 years of work in this country."

About Ballet Society's future, he was not sanguine, though he was proud of the creative work it was commissioning and presenting. "Meanwhile we exist miserably enough," he wrote, "and every week there is a major crisis, each month a disaster. I have no gift to inspire confidence in people; they think I am a profligate *qui jette les galettes de son père*; and since this is what they think, they won't help."

The first work Ballet Society had commissioned was, in fact, by Stravinsky—*Orpheus*, which was well under way at the time of Kirstein's letter and was scheduled for its first performance in a few months. For Balanchine, the creation and preparation of this ballet was one of the happiest experiences of his life. He and Stravinsky had by then become close friends. Though they had respected each other since the days of *Le Chant du Rossignol*, the friendship had its real inception when they worked together on *Card Game* for the Stravinsky festival at the Met in 1937. As Russian émigrés, schooled in the subtle artistic ferment that was Paris after World War I, and now settled in America, the two men shared a common past as well as a similar outlook and aesthetic. For Balanchine, it was to be the most important personal relationship of his life. Throughout their friendship, it was always Igor Stravinsky, as the elder man (he was, after all, forty-two and Balanchine only twenty when they first met) and by far the more articulate and formally intellectual of the two, who played the dominant role. Balanchine always deferred to him. One of Balanchine's friends once observed, "The only time Balanchine loses that air of calm, complete authority he has is when he's with Stravinsky. Then he's like a boy with his father. The two can respect each other's opinions, be gay and playful together, work together—but they never forget who is the father and who the son." Balanchine would not have wished it any other way. Their friendship was aided by the respect in which each man held the other's vocation. For Balanchine, music was always the supreme art. For Stravinsky, classical dancing was, as he declared, "the perfect expression of the Apollonian principle," which since the midpoint of his life had been his guiding principle. He wrote of his "profound admiration for classical ballet, which, in its very essence, by the beauty of its *ordonnance* and the aristocratic austerity of its forms, so closely corresponds to my conception of art. For here, in classical dancing, I see the triumph of studied conception over vagueness, of the rule over the haphazard."

When Balanchine and Stravinsky got together, there was generally much merriment, ranging in expression from high wit to downright playfulness. ("It's a pleasure to be with Stravinsky," Balanchine once said to me, "because he's a happy man."); a good deal of matter-of-fact, detailed discussion of such technical aspects of music and the dance as they happened to be concerned with at the time; and very little theorizing about art. Both men shunned the romantic conception of the soulful artist creating his masterpieces out of agony and ecstasy. Rather, they prided themselves on being disciplined craftsmen, able to apply themselves to a job of work and produce it in good fashion and on time. They made their share of what the world acclaimed masterpieces, but they never admitted, when they were working on a ballet, that they thought of it as anything more than the task at hand. "If you set out deliberately to make a masterpiece, how will you ever get it finished?" Balanchine once said. From Stravinsky, Balanchine said, he learned the trait of being satisfied with what one had made, once it was done. Stravinsky used to say his own model for this attitude was God, who on the days that he created lovely flowers and trees and the birds of the heavens was satisfied, and who was also just as satisfied on the day he created crawling insects and slimy reptiles.

Orpheus was actually the first work that they collaborated on from beginning to end. Kirstein wrote that the *Orpheus* collaboration was one of the closest in ballet history. The choice of the Orpheus legend as subject was Balanchine's. Stravinsky liked the idea, and the formal letter commissioning the composition was sent by Lincoln Kirstein on May 7, 1946, enclosing a check for half the agreed fee of five thousand dollars. A few weeks later Balanchine went to Hollywood, where the Stravinskys now lived, to work out the conception and plan of the ballet. He arrived in time for Stravinsky's sixty-fourth birthday, bearing as a gift a choral acrostic he had composed on the name "Igor" to a Russian text that in translation went: "Name day and birthday! Guests, noise, and excitement! Get high on Grand Marnier! Don't forget a glass for me!" Stravinsky studied Balanchine's composition, then took a sheet of music paper and transcribed it, correcting the harmony. At the top he wrote, in English, "Birthday choral tune by George Balanchine harmonized by Igor Stravinsky Hollywood, Calif. June 18, 1946." Their collaboration was under way.

Every day Balanchine went to Stravinsky's house for lunch and work. The first thing Stravinsky asked Balanchine was how he wanted to approach the legend. "Why don't we do it like an opera?" Balanchine said. And that was the approach they took—but opera in the seventeenth- rather than the nineteenth-century manner, contemplative rather than melodramatic, not Verdi but Monteverdi as a model. (Stravinsky did, in fact, closely study Monteverdi's *Orfeo* score.) Consulting Ovid, they agreed on the main line of the action, dividing it into three scenes and twelve episodes. "There should not need to be a synopsis in the program," Balanchine said. "The movements and the music should express everything the audience needs to know."

Each contributed to the development of the plan. Stravinsky was the one who thought of the character of the Dark Angel, who accompanies Orpheus to Hades. Balanchine was the one who thought of using the singing head of Orpheus in the apotheosis, which Stravinsky expressed in a fugue for two horns. Before Balanchine left Hollywood that summer, they had agreed on the precise length as well as the exact nature of each episode. When Stravinsky asked Balanchine how much time should be allotted to the pas de deux for Orpheus and Eurydice, which is the emotional center of the ballet, Balanchine answered, "Oh, about two and a half minutes." For Stravinsky, this was too vague. "Don't say 'about,'" Stravinsky said crisply. "There is no such thing as 'about.' Is it two minutes, two minutes and fifteen seconds, two minutes and thirty seconds, or something in between? Give me the exact time, please, and I'll come as close to it as possible." It was a reproof Balanchine never forgot. He often cited it later as another important lesson Stravinsky taught him.

Stravinsky completed the score in the fall of 1947. Balanchine went over it with him during the Christmas holidays, which Balanchine and Maria Tallchief spent in Los Angeles. It was a noble score—poignant, lyrical, hieratic. The only forte passage came near the end of the ballet, for the violent action of the Bacchantes tearing Orpheus to pieces. Characteristic of the score's restraint was its treatment of the most emotional moment in the ballet—the moment when, having prevailed on Orpheus to remove his blindfold and turn his gaze on her, Eurydice falls dead. Nothing in the music had foreshadowed that tragedy, and its occurrence was marked only by a long measure of silence, as if recognizing, as Stravinsky said, "that certain things are beyond the power of human expression."

For Balanchine, the music that Stravinsky had written was all that he could have wished for, and more. The "and more" was essential. He counted on Stravinsky's producing music that would surprise him, and in turn he counted on being able to surprise Stravinsky when it came time to make the choreography. At one point during their plotting of the action the previous summer, Stravinsky came up with suggestions for dance movement. Balanchine replied—firmly, respectfully, cheerfully— "You compose the music. I will do the dancing."

For costumes and decor, the first choice of the *Orpheus* collaborators had been Tchelitchev. Long discussions were held. Tchelitchev expounded on his view of Orpheus as artist-scientist-magician and the Orpheus myth as symbolizing the power of the artist to create without the benefit of woman. This was hardly Balanchine's view of the myth, or of the artist; quite the contrary. At last, in the fall of 1947, Tchelitchev withdrew from the project, declaring that the idea was all wrong, that it was planned on too petty a scale for his talents and conceptions, and that it was hopeless to try to get Balanchine to think in mystical terms. More than ever, Tchelitchev said, he was confirmed in his decision never to work in the theatre again. Balanchine expressed regret, but he was probably relieved. Time was growing short, though, for selection of a designer. Kirstein suggested Isamu Noguchi, with whom he had previously worked, and whom he admired for the delicacy and rightness of the way he handled sculptural forms. Balanchine agreed. Particularly he appreciated the sense of space and airiness that Noguchi could create. The designs Noguchi evolved seemed absolutely right to Balanchine and Stravinsky, as well as to Kirstein. The setting was an archaic yet timeless world. The costumes, of embroidered wool, seemed to Kirstein suggestive of ritual tattoos. The props and other objects—the masks, bones, the lyre—were like sculptured carvings, imbued with ritual or magical import.

The premiere was scheduled for April 28, 1948, at City Center. Rehearsals began early in April, at which time Balanchine began choreographing. As was his custom, he did not try to plot out the actual steps until he had chosen his cast and assembled his dancers—Tallchief as Eurydice, Nicholas Magallanes as Orpheus, Francisco Moncion as the Dark Angel, Tanaquil Le Clercq as the Leader of the Bacchantes, and Herbert Bliss as Apollo. For this ballet, the palette of movement Balanchine had decided on was, for the most part, more like modern dance than classical ballet. It was part mime and gesture, part theatrical movement, as well as sequences of steps from the classical vocabulary. This

The Dark Angel (Francisco Moncion) seeks to console the bereaved Orpheus (Nicholas Magallanes).

style proved particularly advantageous for Magallanes and Moncion, both of whom were compelling as personalities but were not outstanding as classical ballet cavaliers.

As rehearsals went along, many wonders emerged in the choreography. The pas de deux for Orpheus and Eurydice, in which she twines herself about him beseechingly while he desperately strives to carry out the injunction that he not look at her, was a tour de force, yet so loving, so poignant, so infused with erotic urgency that the spectator would be scarcely aware of its choreographic virtuosity. Equally impressive, and perhaps even more unusual, was the pas de deux for the two men—Orpheus and the Dark Angel—which had a grave, supernatural tenderness. The dance of destruction Balanchine designed for Le Clercq was like a whiplash in its ferocity; it was one of the best roles of her life. Least effective, choreographically as well as musically, was the dance of the Furies in Hades. Balanchine was perfectly capable of portraying monsters and the monstrous, as he had shown in *Prodigal Son* and would shortly show in *Opus 34*, but for some reason he could never successfully do so to

Stravinsky music. The *Orpheus* Furies, with their chorus-line high kicks, were just not terrifying—not compared with the bald-pated, scurrying revelers in *Prodigal Son*. Similarly unconvincing were the passages Balanchine made for the underworld monsters of *Firebird*, when he did new choreography for that ballet the following year. The Balanchine-Stravinsky collaboration, in the course of its long, blessed history, would produce many extraordinary revelations, but a compelling vision of Hell would not be one of them.

From the start of the *Orpheus* rehearsals Stravinsky was present. Compact, dapper, authoritative, with his spectacles much of the time pushed up on his forehead like a racing-driver's goggles and only in interludes of repose being returned to their perch on his large nose, Stravinsky threw himself eagerly into all aspects of the ballet's final preparations. Together with Balanchine, he visited Noguchi's studio to inspect the decor, worked meticulously with the orchestra (which he would be conducting), and attended nearly all the dance rehearsals. When Balanchine told him he needed a few more measures of music for the pas de deux, Stravinsky simply composed them, without any fuss. The most troublesome section for the dancers proved to be the Bacchantes episode; Stravinsky spent some hours with Tanaquil Le Clercq and the other Bacchantes, helping Balanchine make the dancers understand and be comfortable with the complex rhythms. As usual, Stravinsky demanded precision. He could not tolerate musicians or dancers taking liberty with tempi for the sake of "interpretation." In rehearsal Maria Tallchief was putting her all into the death scene. Stravinsky turned to Balanchine and said, "How long is it going to take Maria to die? She must do it in five counts." That settled the matter. In performance, she knew she had better be dead and gone by the count of five because by count six the orchestra would be starting Orpheus' solo.

Rehearsals went smoothly—"ominously smoothly," to Kirstein's mind—except for financial problems. As backdrop for the journey between Hades and the world of the living, Balanchine had planned to employ a billowing white ceiling-to-floor China-silk curtain. Tchelitchev had invented something similar for *Errante* in 1933, and it had been enormously effective. But there was no money. The material alone would cost a thousand dollars, plus added costs for sewing, and the scenery shops were refusing to extend further credit. Two days before dress rehearsal it looked to Kirstein and the management as if they were going to have to take the regrettable step of asking Balanchine to alter his pas de

꒰ Orpheus. *Eurydice (Tallchief) twines about Orpheus (Magallanes), beseeching him to look at her.*

deux and forgo the effect he so wanted. While they were debating this, Balanchine, who had unobtrusively left the rehearsal hall, reappeared. In his hands was a thousand dollars in cash, which he handed over to the manager. He would never say where the money came from. All he would say was, "I didn't rob a bank."

The premiere April 28 was memorable. Edwin Denby was so overwhelmed that he stayed slumped in his seat during intermission, arousing solicitude among the ushers. Other critics were also much affected. Even John Martin was impressed. Shortly afterward in *The Nation*, B. H. Haggin wrote about *Orpheus* and the other recent Balanchine ballets that Ballet Society had presented. He said seeing them reinforced his conviction that Balanchine was "the greatest living creative artist."

The presentation of Balanchine's work was a prime reason for the existence of Ballet Society. The recognition was gratifying. Everything was fine, except that Kirstein's money was running out. The Society had about eight hundred subscribers, which was enough to cover about half the costs. How much longer it could go on was doubtful. At this point chance—that all-important agent of the classic plot—intervened. It so happened that Ballet Society's business agent, Frances Hawkins, had booked the Society into City Center, and she had persuaded a reluctant Kirstein to schedule three performances for the general public, in addition to the one for the subscribers. It was thus that it came to the attention of a man named Morton Baum. As chairman of the City Center's finance committee, Baum was in charge of the policy and operation of this theatre on West Fifty-fifth Street—the former Mecca Temple, which the city had taken over from a fraternal lodge for back taxes in 1941 and had converted into a center for popular-priced cultural events. Just to see what was going on around the place, Baum dropped into the City Center one evening when Ballet Society was performing. That night *Orpheus, Symphony in C,* and *Symphonie Concertante* were being performed. Baum was no ballet lover at that time—indeed, as a lawyer specializing in tax matters and a former alderman and assistant United States attorney, he was an eminently practical man—but that evening he quite lost his head. He went and found the house manager at the end of the evening, a man named Ben Ketcham. "Ben, who runs this? What is this all about?" Baum asked.

"Oh, it's an organization called Ballet Society. They rented the house for a couple of nights."

"Well, who runs it?"

"It's a fellow named Kirstein—Lincoln Kirstein—who runs it."

"Ben," said Baum earnestly, "I am in the presence of greatness."

When he later recalled his feelings of that night, a touch of wonder and surprise was apt to come over Baum's countenance, like a middle-aged man who should know better admitting to having fallen madly in love. He felt that he had to go right out and do something about it.

Baum's committee did not share this feeling. The City Center in those days sponsored the New York City Drama Company, which brought in some revenue, and the New York City Opera Company, which was a deficit operation, and the committee had no wish to upset the precarious balance by getting involved with a ballet company, which they knew could be a very costly toy. The committee member most vehemently opposed to the project was Gerald Warburg, Edward's brother. "You play around with Balanchine and Kirstein and you'll lose your shirt," he warned Baum. But Baum, using all his craft in support of his new passion, was able to win the committee over.

Then Baum went to talk to Kirstein, whom he had never met. A strange scene ensued. Kirstein, a pessimist even when things were going well, was in a mood of black despair. He could not raise any more money, and Ballet Society was on the verge of collapse. To Baum, Kirstein, too, seemed to be on the verge of collapse. Not waiting for Baum to state his business, but automatically assuming that it boded ill, Kirstein launched into a tirade. He raged against the whole ballet field—its managers, its politics, its repertoires, its audiences. At last, Baum managed to get in the question he had come to ask: "Mr. Kirstein, how would you like the idea of having Ballet Society become the New York City Ballet?"

Kirstein was flabbergasted. His astonishment was not so much over the novelty of the idea. Six months before, he had written to Stravinsky that there was much interest in Balanchine's idea for a permanent company in New York that would belong to the city and get civic support. What astonished Kirstein was the novelty of someone with power voluntarily coming to him with such a proposal, rather than he having to scheme, beg, argue, and contrive in order to achieve it. As he perceived that Baum really meant it and had not come to thwart him in some new way, he burst out, "If you do that for us, I will give you in three years the finest ballet company in America!" They shook hands on it. Then Kirstein rushed off to tell Balanchine the news, and Baum went back to his office to try to figure out how he was going to finance this new affair he had got himself into. That autumn of 1948, Ballet Society's performing group officially became the New York City Ballet, with Balanchine as artistic director and Kirstein as general director (unsalaried positions, both of them), and thus was born the first ballet company in the United States to be accorded the status of a public institution.

It was, to be sure, a public institution with a not very prepossessing home. The City Center was a monstrous dump—a barn prettied up with quasi-Oriental decorations. The acoustics were poor. The orchestra pit was grubby and narrow—like a men's lavatory, as Stravinsky commented when he conducted *Orpheus* there. The sight lines were not good for many of the holders of orchestra seats; to those in the first dozen rows, the dancers' legs appeared to be cut off at the ankles. The stage was small, and the backstage area was so cramped that the stagehands had to be fast on their feet to avoid the dancers' hurtling bodies as they made their spectacular exits into the wings. Nevertheless, for all the disadvantages, being taken on as a production company of the New York City Center of Music and Drama and having a home it could call its own was probably the decisive factor in the New York City Ballet's survival.

Kirstein, for his part, kept the promise he gave Baum. Within three years, the company was widely recognized not only as the finest ballet company in America but also as one of the most important in the world, with a repertoire and a style of dancing quite unlike any other.

Very early on, long before the general public became aware of the New York City Ballet, dancers and other ballet professionals sensed the potential of this new enterprise. Jerome Robbins, Janet Reed, Melissa Hayden, and Frank Hobi signed on during the first year, and the following year they were joined by Diana Adams, Hugh Laing, Nora Kaye, and André Eglevsky. Most stayed and flourished. Some, such as Nora Kaye and Hugh Laing, left after a season or two, having found Balanchine's company not the most congenial vehicle for their particular talents and personalities.

Of all those attracted to the company in the early years, the most important to its future was Jerome Robbins. During the New York City Ballet's first season, Robbins was so affected by a performance he attended that he wrote Balanchine a fan letter, expressing how much it would mean to him to become part of such a company and offering to serve in any capacity in which he could be used—as dancer, choreographer, handyman, whatever. Balanchine engaged him in the fall of 1948, and in 1949 made him associate artistic director.

Before joining the New York City Ballet, Robbins had made dances for a number of musicals, but he had choreographed only three ballets of substance. His first ballet—Fancy Free, presented by Ballet Theatre in 1944—had been a smash hit and had served as the basis for On the Town, the successful Broadway musical he made from it later that year. From the start of their association, Balanchine encouraged and fostered Robbins' development as a choreographer. During the making of The Guests, Robbins' first ballet after joining the New York City Ballet, Balanchine would come by the studio almost every day as a supportive gesture. "Sometimes," recalled Robbins, "he'd bring in some prop he'd found in a store that he thought might be of use to me. I was amazed. Here I was, just a young choreographer, and there was the great master of our age bringing in props to help me, as if he were some fourth assistant to the stage manager."

For the most part, it was Balanchine's style to be discreet with his assistance; he did not intervene or impose himself, or proffer advice un-

In 1950 Balanchine danced in a Glinka Mazurka at City Center. The occasion prompted this self-caricature.

less it was solicited. And such advice as he did give was apt to be laconic and allusive. When Robbins was choreographing *The Cage,* he asked Balanchine to come into the studio one day to look at what he had done so far. At that point, he had only the ending left to choreograph. He thought he was on the right track but couldn't be sure. Balanchine's comment, after viewing the run-through, was brief but exactly what Robbins needed to hear. "That's right," Balanchine said. "Keep it antiseptic."

Though Robbins inevitably learned much about his craft during the years he worked with Balanchine, fully as important as the technical opportunities were the spiritual and psychological benefits he derived from this association. "I used to wish I had lived in the Renaissance," Robbins once said to me, "until I realized that here I was, living in the same age with Balanchine, Stravinsky, Picasso." By his example as much as by anything he said, Balanchine helped Robbins relieve the tensions involved in the ambition to succeed. "He made me see that the work was more important than the success," Robbins told me, "that work in progress was what mattered most."

About a year after Robbins joined the company, Balanchine invited him to collaborate on a ballet. The work was *Jones Beach,* to a score by Juriaan Andriessen; the costumes were bathing suits donated by Jantzen. The choreographic collaboration was fluid and intimate. Sometimes one would do a minute or two of choreography, then the other would go on from there—or perhaps revise what had just been done; sometimes they would both work together. This was the first time Robbins had ever collaborated. He felt honored to be asked, though he also suspected that Balanchine might not have asked him if the music had been a score that was close to Balanchine's heart. In retrospect, he was convinced that the invitation to collaborate was yet another way in which Balanchine was then seeking to encourage and guide him. "Balanchine wanted to get me to choreograph more," he said. "He wanted to get me not to worry about making a masterpiece every time. 'Just keep making ballets,' he used to say, 'and every once in a while one will be a masterpiece.'"

During the New York City Ballet's formative years, its most crucial test, and the one that ultimately had much to do with establishing its reputation, was its first foreign engagement—six weeks at Covent Garden in London. This took place in the summer of 1950; the event was heralded as a semiofficial exchange for the visit the Sadler's Wells com-

∽ Ballet Imperial, *as performed by Britain's Royal Ballet.*

pany had made to the United States in 1949, during which time it had enjoyed an overwhelming triumph.

In the spring before the New York City Ballet's departure for England, Balanchine went to London to stage his first ballet for the Sadler's Wells company. The work was his *Ballet Imperial,* to Tchaikovsky's Second Piano Concerto, with new scenery and costumes by Eugene Berman. Balanchine had always felt very much at home in London, and he enjoyed being there once more. He found the British company a fine one to work with—intelligent, musical, well-disciplined. There were only two weeks of rehearsal before *Ballet Imperial*'s premiere on April 5, which was not much time to learn a complicated, technically demanding work in a style to which the company was unaccustomed.

In an interview with Barbara Newman some years later, Moira Shearer recalled the impression Balanchine made during rehearsal of *Ballet Imperial.* He arrived at the studio, she said, looking immaculate in a handsome suit, with a flower in his buttonhole, beautifully brushed hair, and polished shoes. "In the third movement, Michael (Somes) had to do a step three times, traveling diagonally backward and landing in arabesque from a double turn in the air. He did it one day and it was all right, but

Balanchine said, 'No, no, you don't understand it. This is how I would like it.' Whereupon he went to the corner, and in his suit and outdoor shoes, and with—I thought at the time—a great age, did the step with no warming-up. To me it was miraculous, because he did it very much better and more gracefully than this warmed-up dancer in the prime of his career."

Later during that session, Balanchine was unsatisfied with the way the rehearsal pianist was playing a particular passage. He tried, without success, to tell her what he wanted. "My dear, would you move over," he said at last, and taking a seat beside her, he played it the way it should go.

"By that time," recalled Shearer, "I was lost in admiration; that really gained respect in a way that nothing else could. This man knew exactly how it should be, and he could actually do it himself."

The first performance of *Ballet Imperial* at Covent Garden was received extremely well. There were seventeen curtain calls, including several for the choreographer. Nearly all the critics were favorably impressed. Richard Buckle wrote: "This is the highest form of ballet. Balanchine's ballet is a celebration of man's pride in his own humanity, the triumph of humanism in terms of the dance." Those who voiced reservations acknowledged the ballet's technical mastery but thought the work regrettably lacking in warmth. Cyril Beaumont expressed this viewpoint in the commentary he wrote for the magazine *Ballet*: "To sum up, *Ballet Imperial* seen in action arouses one's admiration for the ingenuity of its patterns, the extraordinary clarity and ample spacing of the figures, the skill with which music and movement are paralleled. But when the ballet is at an end, one is suddenly chilled. It is like a firework display which seemed so brilliant while it lasted, but of which the memory retains little or nothing, because emotion has not been present to preserve the impressions received. Will ballet-goers go to see *Ballet Imperial* time after time as they go to see *The Sleeping Beauty, Lac des Cygnes* or *Giselle*, always seeing some new element of beauty which they had not remarked before? I wonder."

Of the individual performances, the high points of the first night were Beryl Grey's solos and her dance with John Fifield and Kenneth MacMillan. Margot Fonteyn, in the leading part, did not shine with her usual luster. Many years afterward, looking back on her career, Fonteyn said, "I'm not physically equipped to be a good Balanchine dancer. I danced only one of his ballets, *Ballet Imperial*, and I danced it very badly."

Moira Shearer, who had the leading ballerina's part in the second cast, danced it more nearly to Balanchine's satisfaction. In preparation for her matinee performance, ten days after the premiere, he gave her special coaching one afternoon. She had noticed, when he was rehearsing Fonteyn, that he didn't want the ballerina dancing straight classicism—not straight up and down, as for *Swan Lake* or *Sleeping Beauty*. He wanted a diagonal angling of the body that would look dangerous, as if the dancer were taking risks and must surely fall. Fonteyn never achieved that look; apparently, she had decided not to take the risk. Watching her, Shearer had vowed that come what may, she would try to get it when she had the chance because that seemed to her the whole point to the part. When Balanchine coached her in their special session, he worked on that stylistic approach with her and also on a number of passages that were technically difficult and seemed to Shearer virtually impossible. Female dancers aren't usually asked to do double turns in the air, but there was one place, near the end of the ballet, where the ballerina was expected to do four in a row, with virtually no preparation. The turns didn't have to be high, but they had to look brilliant and astonishing. Shearer had never done anything like that before, but again she vowed, "Well, if I break both legs, never mind. I'll have a go." As she later told her interviewer, "I'm sure I reached a particular standard of technical dancing in *Ballet Imperial* that I never reached in anything else. He expected it, and you couldn't let that man down—you just couldn't."

The contract for the New York City Ballet's visit to England was signed the very next day after *Ballet Imperial*'s premiere, amid the euphoria that event had generated. David Webster, director of the Royal Opera House, said, as he handed the contract to the New York company's business manager, "Miss Hawkins, we shall be very glad to have the New York City Ballet at the Royal Opera House. But I also want you to know that London will make the company."

As events transpired, Webster's prophecy was borne out, even though the New York company's English sojourn was by no means all pure glory. The audiences at Covent Garden were often extremely enthusiastic in their reception of the American company and its ballets; the gallery, in particular, took the company to its heart, and at the end of the season subscribed for flowers to present to the dancers, a gesture the gallery had never before made for a visiting company. But the critics, by and large, were certainly not bowled over; some of them seemed personally affronted by Balanchine's whole approach to ballet.

The repertory that the company brought to England consisted of eighteen ballets, twelve of them by Balanchine: *Bourrée Fantasque, Concerto Barocco, Divertimento, Firebird, The Four Temperaments, Orpheus, Pas de Deux Romantique, Prodigal Son, Serenade, Symphonie Concertante, Symphony in C,* and *Jones Beach,* the ballet choreographed in collaboration with Robbins. The others consisted of Frederick Ashton's *Illuminations,* Lew Christensen's *Jinx,* Todd Bolender's *Mother Goose,* William Dollar's *The Duel,* and two ballets by Jerome Robbins—*The Guests* and *Age of Anxiety.* In addition, toward the close of the season, *The Witch,* a new ballet by the young British choreographer John Cranko, was given its first performance.

One of the main complaints to be heard, as the London season ran its course, was that there were far too many plotless ballets in this repertory. One or two might have been acceptable as examples of the genre, but there were nine such in all—and four of these were danced on a bare stage in only the simplest of costumes. Certainly, it was conceded, Balanchine's classicism, his interest in reasserting the dance element in ballet, was admirable and perhaps a necessary corrective; but wasn't he going much too far in this direction? Wasn't he taking all the poetry and all the romance out of ballet? This theme was much debated.

Of all Balanchine's ballets, the one that created the most furor, however, was not a storyless ballet, but his streamlined and cut version of *Firebird,* in which Maria Tallchief had scored perhaps the greatest success of her career when it was presented in New York the previous year. Balanchine's tampering with a beloved masterpiece, even though undertaken with the approval of Stravinsky, was felt to be close to sacrilege. The critic of *The Times* wrote, "*Firebird,* for which London had waited long, was also in last night's bill but alas! this is a poor emaciated creature. Mr. Balanchine's choreography is not Fokine's—where are the golden apples of yesteryear? Miss Maria Tallchief caught some of the glitter of the bird but none of her aloof, supernatural magic. The whole ballet was danced without the slightest trace of the atmosphere of Stravinsky's music against a décor containing motifs of smartness quite alien to a Russian fairyland. Perhaps this company is too immature for imaginative and romantic ballets."

Only Richard Buckle, of all the critics, approved unreservedly of *Firebird,* and the defense he penned for it in *The Observer,* in keeping with his role of being the *enfant terrible* of the ballet world, was more calculated to provoke than persuade. "One thing that is clear," he wrote, "about Balanchine's *Firebird*, which some of my matronly colleagues have been deploring, is that it is a great deal better than Fokine's. Fokine's had atmosphere, agreed, but so has Victoria Station. Balanchine's *Firebird* is an exciting ballet with dancing in it."

Next to *Firebird*, the ballet that got the roughest handling from the critics was *Illuminations*. This, at any rate, exonerates the critics of any charge of chauvinism, since *Illuminations* was the result of collaboration by three notable British talents—choreography by Ashton to music by Benjamin Britten (setting of the Rimbaud poems), with costumes and scenery by Cecil Beaton. "For what audience is this work intended?" wrote *The Dancing Times*. "It can only be comprehensible to those with the inclination to study the sordid existence, unhealthy mind and more frantic poems of a decadent nineteenth-century poet, Arthur Rimbaud."

The ballet that won the most widespread critical approval was the oldest ballet in the repertory. This was *Prodigal Son*, which by that time was twenty-one years old—a safe age. Even *The Dancing Times* (which had thought that Balanchine had failed to grasp the true nature of the music he had used for *Serenade*) praised this work, while reminding its readers, "At the time of its creation Balanchine was not hampered by the many theories which now impede his work."

In regard to the quality of the New York company's dancing, a typical analysis was that by Paul Holt in the *Daily Herald*: "These fresh young Americans bring no mystery or sentiment to their dancing. They are rugged, tough and gay. The men attack feats of grace as a sport and the girls make almost a miracle of their execution of the classical routine. That is the strangest thing about their visit. They are not so much interested in the folksy style. They are pure classicists absorbed by the perfection of the old Imperial Russian Ballet." The phrase most often quoted by way of summation was the one voiced by *The Times* in its first review after the company's premiere on July 10: "The American style may be said to be gracefully athletic rather than gracefully poetic." Despite the objections to *Firebird*, Maria Tallchief was highly praised as being "a magnificent dancer with a noble flashing style." Tanaquil Le Clercq, Melissa Hayden, Yvonne Mounsey, Patricia Wilde, and Janet Reed were all much admired as well. Francisco Moncion made a strong impression, by virtue of his dramatic abilities and commanding personality, but the male contingent, though satisfactory as partners, were generally deemed to be of less interest and ability than the female forces. As Clive Barnes aptly put it, "The world of Balanchine ballets, like the world of Shakespearian comedy, is dominated by beautiful women."

The company had its troubles also with the stage of Covent Garden, especially during the early portion of the engagement. Tallchief sprained an ankle in her first entrance in *Serenade,* and was out of action for a week. Melissa Hayden took so severe a fall in *The Duel* that she was knocked unconscious, and the curtain had to be lowered. In retrospect, Buckle humorously suggested that a memorial should be erected to all the gallant Americans who fell at Covent Garden. But these mishaps were generally viewed with sympathy.

The Covent Garden season had originally been planned to be of only five weeks' duration, but on the basis of the initial favorable audience reaction and box-office attendance, an extra week was scheduled. This turned out to be something of a mistake. Vacationers streamed out of London at the end of July. Attendance fell off considerably during August. The Covent Garden season concluded August 19. The New York City Ballet rested for a week, during which time Balanchine choreographed a new ballet, *Trumpet Concerto,* to music by Haydn, for the Sadler's Wells Theatre Ballet, and then set off on a hastily improvised three-week tour of the provinces. This tour, too, turned out to be rather a mistake, both from the point of view of the critical reception and of box-office receipts. When the finances were finally reckoned up, after the company had returned to New York toward the end of September, it was found that a total loss of $40,000 had been incurred, which was nearly twice the loss that had been anticipated.

Morton Baum was distressed by the size of the deficit. There was talk of cutting back on the fall season, or even canceling it altogether. Balanchine was exhausted, and not in a good frame of mind. The English visit had not been the total triumph he had hoped for. He and Maria Tallchief, after months of strained relations, were now deciding to separate, though they expected to be able to work together. With the City Center seeming to falter in its support, he talked of going to Italy for two years, to reorganize the La Scala ballet. "This would be a tragedy for me," wrote Lincoln Kirstein to Stravinsky.

But Baum found a way to finance the season after all, and it was immediately apparent, from the moment tickets went on sale, that the company had arrived. Even John Martin had now become a convert. Despite the various disappointments suffered, the London season had been crucial to the New York City Ballet's development. That visit *did* make the company, one way or another, as David Webster had foretold. For one thing, the attention the company had received abroad suddenly made the company worth noticing by those at home who had hitherto ignored it. Then, too, the applause and the criticism had tempered the company, stiffened its morale, and strengthened its sense of its own identity. Finally, and perhaps most fundamental of all, the English engagement had given the members of the company perhaps their first real opportunity to dance together for any extended period of time. The nine weeks in England was the longest season they had had so far. Up till then in New York it had not been financially possible to manage more than four weeks at a stretch.

Two years after this the New York City Ballet's position was consolidated for good when it made its second journey abroad—a five-month tour of Europe, starting in Barcelona and proceeding to Paris, Florence, Lausanne, Zurich, Paris again, The Hague, London, Edinburgh, and Berlin. Except for a mixed reception in London again, this tour was pretty much a procession of triumphs. The homage the company received at the conclusion of its three-week engagement at Barcelona's Teatro del Liceo exceeded anything that the young American dancers had dreamed of. While the applause went on and on, roses and laurel leaves rained down from the balconies and loges, baskets of flowers were brought in for the dancers until the stage resembled a garden, and a flight of doves went winging overhead about the theatre. The auditorium of the Central High School of Needle Trades had never been like that.

CHAPTER ELEVEN

God Creates, Woman Inspires, and Man Assembles

The first words that Tanaquil Le Clercq remembers hearing from her future husband, George Balanchine, were a reprimand. He told her that she was a naughty, saucy child, who was putting on gestures so mannered and affectedly pretty that he could not bear to look at her. Then he sent her out of the room. That was when she was twelve, and having just won a scholarship to the School of American Ballet, had begun taking classes there. For her part, on first impression, she thought the famous Mr. Balanchine something of an old fogy and a very dull teacher, and she could not see what was supposed to be so great about him. She was a high-spirited girl, with a quick wit and a quick tongue. She had long legs and a proud bearing; she was rather like a mettlesome young racehorse. Clearly she had the makings of a fine dancer.

Before long she formed a more favorable impression of her mentor, and under his tutelage, she soon began to show herself an accomplished technician. At the age of seventeen she danced her first professional solo role, the lead in the choleric section of *The Four Temperaments*. At twenty, when she appeared with the New York City Ballet in its important first engagement at Covent Garden, she attracted much favorable attention. She and Balanchine were married on December 31, 1952, not long after the annulment of his marriage with Maria Tallchief. It was his

An Irving Penn study for Vogue *of Tanaquil Le Clercq as Ariadne, with the three collaborators in the 1948 Ballet Society production of the ballet-cantata* The Triumph of Bacchus and Ariadne—Corrado Cagli, *the designer; Vittorio Rieti, the composer; and Balanchine.*

239

fourth marriage. Le Clercq was then twenty-three years old, and he forty-eight. Sheila Benson, who later became a film critic for the *Los Angeles Times*, was a student at the School of American Ballet when Tanaquil was there. "I remember vividly the morning seven years later when I read that Balanchine had married Tanaquil," she wrote. "A classmate called me and her sigh was unenvious. 'She married him for all of us,' she breathed. And so she did."

By the time of her marriage, Le Clercq had become recognized as uniquely gifted. With her vivacity, her unbelievably long, svelte legs and supple, sinuous figure, her cheeky wit, theatricality, and flawless sense of timing, she was a ballerina of rare versatility. In *Bourrée Fantasque* she showed her talent for comedy, proving, as one critic wrote, "that it was possible to be simultaneously beautiful and funny." The adagio of *Symphony in C* she danced with such elegance and musicality that those who saw her performance could scarcely bear to see anyone else dance it afterward. In *Orpheus* she was powerfully dramatic, in *Afternoon of a Faun* subtly but provocatively sexual, in *La Valse* delicate and touching, avid for the experience that would doom her. "What precocious sense of the transience of beauty and gaiety enabled her to dance this role with such infinite delicacy and penetration?" the critic Lillian Moore wrote of Le Clercq's performance in *La Valse*. "Fleet, fragile, touchingly young, incredibly lovely, she brought it a haunting quality which lifted it into the realm of poetry."

She was thought of as having a brighter future than any young dancer of her day, but that future abruptly came to an end in late October 1956 at the age of twenty-seven when, while the New York City Ballet was on tour in Copenhagen, she was felled by poliomyelitis. The doctors could do nothing to save her career. They barely saved her life.

Balanchine, a deeply mystical man, sometimes would later recall, with a kind of horrified awe, a ballet he made featuring Tanaquil when she was a girl of fifteen. It was a little ballet put on at the Waldorf-Astoria in 1944 for the benefit of the March of Dimes. *Resurgence,* it was called, and it was set to music from Mozart's Quintet in G Minor for strings. The scene represented a ballet classroom, where the young students were to be seen practicing their steps and leaps with eager devotion, obviously rejoicing in the virtuosity of their agile bodies. Suddenly there appeared among them a grotesque, black-clad monster—the evil Polio. He reached out his foul hand and touched one of the girls, and she fell paralyzed to the floor. The girl was Tanaquil. Balanchine danced the role of Polio. "It was an omen," he would later say, looking as if he blamed

Tanaquil Le Clercq in Metamorphoses, *and with Francisco Moncion in* La Valse.

himself for what, years later, came to pass. "It foretold the future." In this little ballet, Tanaquil was then placed in a wheelchair, where, as the others hovered about her in sorrow, she performed exquisite, pathetic variations to the music with her arms and upper body. For the climax, there was a shower of silver coins. Miraculously restored, she rose radiantly from her chair. The others hastened to fetch her ballet slippers, and in a burst of joy she danced gloriously across the floor and off the stage. "It was, alas, a balletic finale," said Balanchine later. "Nothing like that ending will happen in Tanny's real life."

In real life the doctors had to declare that she would never walk again but would always be paralyzed from the waist down. Balanchine, for a time, hoped for a miracle through prayers. He and his wife found it hard to accept the opinions of the medical specialists that nothing could be done to restore her body any further and that additional aid from then on would have to take the form of mechanical appliances for the handicapped. "They've got marvelous appliances now, those doctors, that will

Tanaquil Le Clercq and Jerome Robbins in Bourrée Fantasque.

breathe for you and eat for you and everything else," Balanchine said. "But that's not what a dancer like Tanny wants. She wants her own body back, or even any little bit of it that she can get back. She will work, she will do exercises endlessly. Tell Tanny to do this a hundred times—" he flexed his wrist—"and she will do it with pleasure. The others do not really understand exercises. They must do something—make a mat or weave a basket. But a dancer knows that to move is already an accomplishment, without making anything."

When she was first brought home to New York, she was, as may be imagined, in a despondent state of mind. She never mentioned ballet, and those around her carefully avoided the subject. This phase of acute distress passed. In time she was able to speak freely and without obvious pain about the subject, and in 1962, when *La Valse* was revived, she took pleasure in coaching Patricia McBride in the role she had originally created. In 1970 she accepted an invitation to teach ballet at the Dance Theatre of Harlem.

In New York the Balanchines lived in a spacious five-room apartment at Seventy-ninth Street and Broadway, just four blocks from the building where the school and ballet company then had their studios. The Balanchines also had a weekend house near Weston, Connecticut. The New York apartment, painted white, reflected Balanchine's own unclassifiable tastes, as well as, here and there, his handiwork, for he liked to do carpentry. An ornate French chandelier hung from the ceiling; over the fireplace was an early-nineteenth-century New England weather vane; and an Audubon eagle, lifesize, was enthroned on one of the walls. Dominating the living room were two grand pianos, and on one was an inscribed photograph of Stravinsky. The sofa and two chairs—ornately carved pieces covered in blue Italian silk—were mid-nineteenth-century American, by Belter. It was the kind of furniture one sees in the salons of prosperous mustached Westerners in cowboy films. As a lad, when Balanchine first began seeing movies, he used to think how wonderful it would be to have furniture just like that, and when he was furnishing his apartment, he was lucky enough to find these pieces in an antique shop specializing in the rental of theatrical props. It was a serene and sunny apartment. It was Balanchine's thought that since Tanaquil was now so confined, it was his duty to make the apartment like a fairy tale for her. On the broad wall of the sitting room was a great, gleaming brass pendulum clock. And on a wall of the kitchen—where Balanchine concocted his French sauces, his galantines, and his kulitch and pascha, the special treats he served at his annual Easter party—was another conspicuous timepiece, as big as a street clock. For a choreographer, as for a composer, time is of the essence. In his everyday life, Balanchine was noted for his punctuality.

His Russian Easter party was always the main festivity of the year. His Russian friends would gather at the apartment to dine right after midnight services. The next day another party would be held for Americans, non-Orthodox, and other friends. For these Easter celebrations he always prepared his most lavish board—roasts, ptarmigans, fish in aspic, specially prepared horseradish and garnishes, salade Olivier, and, of course, the traditional pascha and kulitch, which contain all the rich ingredients and exotic tastes one dreams of during Lent: sweet butter by the pound, mounds of sugar, vanilla beans, saffron, cardamom, pressed almonds, raisins. Invariably, this event occurred in the midst of a ballet season. For three days before Easter he was apt to be choreographing all day and cooking virtually the whole night through. On the day the kulitch was to be baked, he would have to keep phoning home from the studio during breaks in the rehearsal sessions to find out if the dough had risen. As soon as he got word it had, he would rush home to get it into the oven in proper shape.

No household help lived at the apartment. A maid came in to do the housecleaning. Most of the other chores—the shopping, the cooking, and all the rest—were done by Balanchine, and it was he who tended Tanaquil and ministered to her daily needs. He tried to be away from the apartment as little as possible, but there were tasks that took him out of town from time to time. While he was away, a friend or Tanaquil's mother stayed with her, or she often chose to remain alone in the apartment, kept company by Mourka, their white-and-ginger-colored cat, a pampered and much admired creature. Balanchine had trained this cat to perform brilliant jetés and *tours en l'air*; he used to say that at last he had a body worth choreographing for. He talked of presenting Mourka publicly, in a program titled—in parody of the revolutionary program he had presented as a youth in Russia—"The Evolution of Ballet: From Petipa to Petipaw." Once, at a party at his apartment during the Christmas season, Stravinsky asked to see Mourka perform. Guests present later said that was the only time they had ever seen Balanchine nervous before a performance. Mourka's amazing feats were subsequently featured in *Life* magazine, and he was also the subject of a charming book by Tanaquil Le Clercq, with photographs by Martha Swope, entitled, *Mourka: the Autobiography of a Cat.*

On free evenings, when Balanchine was at home, he and his wife might have friends over to the apartment. If there was a good science-fiction movie playing, they might drive out to a suburban drive-in; if not, they would stay home and watch television. On television, Balanchine's predilection was for westerns. "That's my bad taste, I suppose," he once remarked to me. "If you were to say to me, 'What's the best thing in America, artistically the best thing?' I would reply, 'Cowboys! Westerns!' The people are right for it, they know how to do what they're doing, and to me it all rings true. When I see on the screen that wonderful Nevada or Arizona space and horses galloping beautifully across it, I am instantly satisfied. I find no fault in it at all." With the ballets shown on television, he was much less satisfied. He, himself, had some fairly good experiences with a few ballet programs he had put on for the Canadian Broadcasting Company, but his efforts for the American companies so far had been disappointments to him in one way or another. His biggest disappointment was probably *Noah and the Flood,* a ballet-oratorio with music by Stravinsky, which CBS presented in 1962. He made some caustic obser-

༄ *In the Balanchine apartment, as Balanchine puts Mourka through his paces.*

vations to me about his experience with *Noah and the Flood* in an interview published in a book about television entitled *The Eighth Art*:

> *It all turned out the same frustrating way as I've been saying always happens on American television—exactly. No matter how promising something seems to be when you are first planning it, by the end the artistic considerations get all swallowed up. . . . Though I have learned not to hope for much from American television, still I had hopes for this production because the music was to be a specially commissioned work by Stravinsky and I thought that if they have been bold and cultivated enough to commission music by Stravinsky, maybe they'll have the taste to put it on in a way that does it justice, or at least not to mess it up. But, no. They take a work of art and re-arrange it to look commercial while at the same time giving the public a sickening and patronizing lecture about what an artistic experience they're having. The music that Stravinsky wrote was marvellous—one of his most wonderful pieces in orchestration, sound, conception, everything. But the music lasts less than a half-hour and the producers had sold the work to the network as a one-hour package. So they smothered the work by a whole goulash of other things they dumped into the package to fill it up.*

And he told me that he had frankly not been happy with his own choreography for that production. "I wanted to make choreography that was not too obtrusive—which did not interfere with the music. But the choreography that was seen on the screen was really just a rough draft—my first sketchy thoughts. I intended to make changes and improvements—but we got into the studio, the panic took over and then suddenly it became impossible to do what needed to be done."

On television the dance programs that gave him the most pleasure to watch were those of Fred Astaire, whom he admired exceedingly. He called Astaire the best male dancer of the day, and he said that an Astaire dance sequence always came off much better on television than a traditional ballet because the latter was conceived for the stage, not the screen, whereas from the start, when Astaire prepared a dance, he imagined how it would look with a frame around it, on the screen.

At the time his wife fell ill, Balanchine was absent from ballet for a full year—staying in Copenhagen during the months she was in the hospital there, and then going with her to Warm Springs, Georgia, where she underwent additional treatment. Rumors circulated that Balanchine was likely to retire from ballet altogether—that he did not have the heart to continue, and that even if he did, it might not be feasible. These rumors were dispelled when he rejoined his company in the fall of 1957 and, within the space of ten weeks, while at the same time supervising the preparation of the company's repertory, choreographed four major ballets, each in a markedly different style of dance. The ballets were *Square Dance, Agon, Gounod Symphony,* and *Stars and Stripes.*

The company, which had sagged noticeably in his absence, responded immediately to his presence, and the season that ensued was hailed as the most brilliant and distinguished that the New York City Ballet had ever presented. After that, no more talk was heard of his retiring. When a reporter subsequently asked him if he had ever thought of quitting, Balanchine looked at him in astonishment. "How can I quit?" he said. "I'm a choreographer. All I know how to do is make ballets. As long as I can move around enough to show my dancers what I want them to dance, I expect to go on making ballets. That's my job."

Opus 34, The Nutcracker, Western Symphony, Ivesiana, Pas de Dix, Allegro Brilliante, Divertimento No. 15, Square Dance, Agon, Stars and Stripes, Episodes, The Figure in the Carpet, Donizetti Variations, Monumentum Pro Gesualdo, Liebeslieder Walzer, A Midsummer Night's Dream, Bugaku, Movements for Piano and Orchestra—these ballets, and many others, came cascading from him, as happily and artfully as the play of Italian fountains, in the years after his company had become established. The sixth decade of his life, beginning in 1954, saw him choreographing more than thirty ballets, as well as staging three operas—for Hamburg, the Met, and for NBC—and supervising the mounting of various of his works by ballet companies throughout the world, from Winnipeg to Milan. It was the most prolific era of his whole career. Lotte Lenya, who was in the 1933 performance of *The Seven Deadly Sins* and also in the 1958 production (which turned out to be virtually a new work in its choreography, rather than a revival), commented after the later occasion, "It was breathtaking to work with him again after twenty-five years and find him so full of ideas and energy still. With other creative people I've known, the time always comes when you can say to yourself, a little sadly, 'Well, that's it—there'll be no more surprises.' But with Balanchine you can't say that. Who knows what he's still got up his sleeve!" Balanchine, himself, commented, when asked how it happened that he seemed to gain in vigor as he grew older, "That's nothing. Old people don't get tired—it's only the young who tire. Confusion exhausts them.

Balanchine as Drosselmeyer during a television performance of The Nutcracker.

I've got more energy now than when I was younger because I know exactly what I want to do."

What he wanted to do most, of course, was to keep his school and company going, which was no small task, and to continue to make ballets in which the dance predominated, exploring new possibilities in his old art all the time. The two objectives were inseparable in his mind, since he could not conceive of choreography except in the tangible, living terms of the bodies of the dancers who assembled on call before him at rehearsal time, "My dancers, you might say, *are* my choreography, at the moment of performance."

His most distinctive contribution to ballet, as had long been evident, was his bold assertion of the dance element. Other elements had held the limelight previously—the virtuosity of the individual ballerina, the costumes, the decor, the plot; sometimes the dancing got lost altogether. Balanchine was the first to make the choreography, in effect, the star of the show, evolving what has been called perhaps the purest kind of ballet, in which all the drama is in the dance itself—in the pattern of movement unfolding in intimate relationship with the music. These ballets of his were sometimes called "abstract," but he always considered this a misnomer, since he was not trying to present any abstractions and since he did not see how anything performed by living human beings could be called "abstract." He preferred to call them "plotless" ballets. Plotless or not, there was always drama in them, and an often surprising range of emotion, as well as a distinctive attitude or outlook. Many of these ballets showed up best when danced in practice clothes on a bare stage against a simple cyclorama. This practice was begun in 1951, and it proved to be a happy conjunction of the young company's need to save money with Balanchine's need to present his dancers and choreography without the distraction or competition of elaborate sets and costumes. "Our poverty is what saved us," he later said.

I once spent an hour with Frederick Ashton discussing Balanchine, whom Ashton declared to be undeniably one of the two greatest choreographers in the world. (He modestly refrained from naming the other.) But he said he feared for the future of the pure-dance ballets. Such ballets, he said, seemed to him much harder to maintain than ballets built on a narrative structure, and he believed they were bound to deteriorate once Balanchine was no longer present to keep them up. Whether this is so or not, it was never a concern I heard Balanchine voice. He was choreographing only for the present, and he was content to let the future take care of itself.

In addition to the pure-dance ballets, Balanchine would generally, each season, do any of a number of quite different kinds of ballets, depending on what he thought the repertory needed at the moment. In doing so, he likened himself to a chef, or a restaurant owner, who has the obligation to present his patrons with a varied menu, so that they will feel satisfied and well dined and will want to come back again. Among the long roster of ballets he made in his lifetime are to be found acknowledged masterworks in a wide range of categories: narrative ballets such as *Prodigal Son* and *Orpheus,* which are reckoned among the most powerful dramatic pieces in the contemporary ballet repertoire; romantic evocations of mood and atmosphere, like *Liebeslieder Walzer* or *Cotillon*; novelties on the order of *Western Symphony* and *Square Dance*; and strange visions of indefinable nightmare, such as *Ivesiana* and *Opus 34.* In all of these he sought to convey his ideas not in a literal way but in terms of dance metaphors. As Kirstein said, "He has no interest in any effect that is not danced." When he chose to do a ballet with a plot, he could tell a

story with masterly clarity and economy. He thought it should not be necessary to have to learn the language of pantomime in order to follow what was taking place on the stage, as did the St. Petersburg ballet-omanes in the old days, who used to attend regular classes in the subject. Nor should it be necessary to read an involved synopsis in the program. "The curtain should just go up, and if the spectators understand what's going on, it's good—if not, not," Balanchine said. In a narrative ballet, the relationships should be such as can be grasped on sight. He once compressed the essence of his years of consideration of this matter into a nutshell of wisdom he called Balanchine's Law, which went: "There are no sisters-in-law in ballet." Yet when, in 1962, he choreographed *A Midsummer Night's Dream,* he was able to make clear, with no apparent strain, that whole complex tangle of relationships, with all the humor, fantasy, romanticism, and suspense one could wish—and to do it all through dance conceptions, not through mime.

It was Balanchine who kept the classic tradition of ballet alive in the twentieth century. He carried out a revolt against the Fokine revolution-aries, but his revolution was not a counterrevolution. For if he kept clas-sic ballet alive, it was not through idolatry and archaeology, but through constant innovation, experiment, and discovery. Always Balanchine thought of ballet as a living art, not as a relic of the past to be wor-shipfully or academically preserved. The company's repertoire was not a museum; when Balanchine mounted such traditional works as *The Nut-cracker* and the second act of *Swan Lake* he freely restaged them to suit his company's personnel and his own preferences. Balanchine's classicism is a contemporary classicism—designed to be seen by twentieth-century eyes and make its effects on twentieth-century nerves. The classic vocab-ulary of steps is employed in a different way from Petipa: extensions are higher, movements may be faster and more staccato, combinations more complicated and intense, and executed with minimal obvious prepara-tion. Aside from the obvious fact of having jettisoned the plot and dis-pensed with the pantomime, Balanchine differed from Petipa's approach in such respects as his employment of several ballerinas in a work, danc-ing parts of equal importance, or in the importance given to the corps de ballet as an element of the total dance composition. In Petipa's ballets the corps danced very little but was mainly used for pictorial effects. In Balanchine's ballets the corps is expected to dance a great deal and per-form demanding feats of skill: a New York City Ballet corps member will swoop easily through a chain of steps that a Petipa ballerina would have

A moment from A Midsummer Night's Dream, *with Arthur Mitchell as Puck.*

thought impossible to do. The same thing has happened in nearly all fields of physical attainment: women now run marathons in faster time than the men's world record at the turn of the century. But despite the differences in technique, Balanchine shared with Petipa—and with the other great exponents of classicism, in all the arts, throughout the ages— a common outlook as to the relationship of his art to society, and to humanity. "The secrets of emotion Balanchine reveals," Denby wrote in a discussion of Balanchine's classicism, "are like those of Mozart, tender, joyous and true. He leaves the audience with a civilized happiness. His art is peaceful and exciting, as classic art has always been."

True, and it's well to remember the passion in Balanchine's works, even the most formal of them—as in Mozart and the other great classicists. That element is probably what distinguishes the classic artists who matter to us from those who don't. "A classical work is beautiful by virtue of its subjugated romanticism," André Gide once observed. Can one doubt the importance of the romantic element in Balanchine—in his life, as well as in his work?

Indeed, the romantic and the classical were intertwined. Considering some of his overtly romantic ballets, one might be tempted to reverse Gide and opine that a romantic work is beautiful by virtue of its subjugated classicism. Take as instance Liebeslieder Walzer, a romantic ballet that is one of Balanchine's loveliest and most perfect achievements. In that ballet, the "plot" is a line of action of increasing liberation from the mundane. In the first act the four couples in the ballroom take ever more freedom with the conventions of the ballroom waltz, while at the same time offering us fleeting glimpses of the heightened emotions they experience: exhilaration, adoration, jealousies, doubts, longings, fears of mortality—who knows exactly what those poignant gestures and glances signify? Yet how affecting they are. These dancers, in their elegant garb, are real people to us, and as the curtain comes down for the pause between the acts, it seems to us that Balanchine has taken them as far as they can go in their liberation.

But when the curtain comes up, we see that he can take them further. For now they are no longer human beings dancing in a ballroom, but dancers of a special sort—classical ballet dancers. The women no longer wear ballroom gowns and pumps but are dressed in long, semi-transparent tulle tutus and toe shoes. Now the women soar. The whole mood is transformed, going far beyond even the most heightened reality. During the making of this ballet, Balanchine, as was his habit, said little

Liebeslieder Walzer—*Violette Verdy with Conrad Ludlow (left) and Nicholas Magallanes.*

about his intent. Shortly after the first performance, I talked with him about it and commented on what seemed to me to be happening in this work. In reply, he said succinctly how he saw it. "In the first act, it's the real people that are dancing. In the second act, it's their souls."

In short, for Balanchine, the way to achieve the quintessence of romanticism was through the classical ballet vocabulary. What drama he makes of this paradox! And how revealing this ballet is of Balanchine's philosophy and values. How does an artist show a human being's soul? Well, for a start, if he is George Balanchine, he puts her in toe shoes. And it is also revealing that for the men no equivalent transformation is possible. Their clothes stay the same. Balanchine didn't really need to utter his famous statement "Ballet is woman," for nearly all his ballets said it, just as they also said that the only way a man can achieve or approach the liberation of his soul is by the homage and devotion he shows woman.

Very different in appearance from both his romantic and his classic ballets were Balanchine's ballets to contemporary music. In a line of

ballets that began with *The Four Temperaments* in 1946 and whose high points up till 1963 were *Ivesiana* in 1954, *Agon* in 1957, *Episodes* in 1959, and *Movements for Piano and Orchestra* in 1963, he boldly explored realms of movement not seen before in ballet and made them a part of the vocabulary that classic ballet could henceforth use. These works were quite different from each other in implicit content and spirit. *Agon* was pert and witty, a high-wire act, a contemporary comment on skill and danger, employing for effect in places a typically American kind of understatement, like that of the astronaut saying, as he emerged from the capsule after orbiting the world, "Boy, what a ride!" *Episodes,* to the music of Webern, seemed to be about alienation and depersonalization, not in explicit terms of any plot but in its very essence—in the way the dancers were manipulated, like so many manikins, as if devoid of all will. *Movements,* which, like *Agon,* had a Stravinsky score, was rarefied, remote, beyond good and evil, with an impersonal, godlike serenity. But each of these works was hailed, as it appeared, as a landmark, a breakthrough—one of those rare productions that affect the course of dance history. How advanced Balanchine's explorations were was revealed, whether the comparison was intentional or not, during the season of *Episodes'* premiere, at which time that work was danced in two parts, with the opening part choreographed and danced by Martha Graham and her company. The modern dance group, in handsome, ornate Elizabethan costumes, danced the story of the death of Mary, Queen of Scots; the classical ballet company went through its strange, elliptical paces in stark, black-and-white practice clothes. The critics wrote what a curious thing it was to see the two companies together this way and noted inevitably that it was the modern dancers who seemed old-fashioned, the classic ballet company who looked modern.

In regard to the Balanchine ballets in the novelty category—these lighter offerings, which were intended, as Balanchine might say, to fill a place similar in the repertory to that occupied by a baked Alaska in a chef's menu—they often took as their starting point some device or gimmick. In *Native Dancers* it was simply the conception of the females as fillies, the males as jockeys; in *Square Dance,* it was the perception of common musical forms in the country dances of today and the works of seventeenth-century classical composers; in *Western Symphony,* the amusement was in putting classical ballet steps to "Red River Valley" and "On Top of Old Smoky." Once I asked him if he really took seriously some ballet he was choreographing. I forget which ballet it was—*Native*

Episodes, with Allegra Kent and Bart Cook.

Dancers, perhaps, or *Square Dance*. "Oh, yes," he answered promptly. "You always have to be serious, even about your jokes—*especially* about your jokes." Even in these, the gimmick was almost always a dance conception, not one imported from the world of mime; and even in his novelties Balanchine would often work more deeply than he may have set out to do. In *Bugaku*, for instance, Balanchine went beyond the Japanese setting, costumes, and mannerisms, which are the superficial aspects of the ballet, and achieved in his choreography, through tempos as slow and alien as those of a deep-sea diver on the ocean bottom, a profound and powerful sense of a culture different from our own.

To some critics, all this seemed perhaps illicitly easy and facile. Balanchine's ability to work in many styles was a trait he shared with certain other contemporary artists—with Picasso and Stravinsky, for example. Perhaps the twentieth century has been the age of the great chameleon, of the quick-change artist. No matter how diverse they are, though, a common thread runs through all of Balanchine's works. They all bear his strong stamp; it would not be possible to mistake them for the work of anybody else.

In all of his ballets, whatever the genre, music was always the platform for him—or, better yet, the sustaining element in which he swam and sported. A friend who went backstage to congratulate Balanchine after the premiere, in 1952, of *Caracole*, a ballet to Mozart's *Divertimento No. 15*, found Balanchine off to one side, by himself, in a kind of rapture. "Oh, that Mozart—that music!" he kept saying, and paid no heed to his admirer's compliments on the wonders of his choreography.

Even when the score that Balanchine choreographed for was not a masterpiece, it was always treated by him with affection and appropriate respect. This was not the same as being solemn about it. Some of the intellectuals in the City Center audience—the ones who flocked reverently to the "twelve-tone nights," which after a time became a feature of every season, when all four ballets on the program would be danced to serial music and there would not be a single resolved cadence to be heard the whole evening long—were shocked when, in 1958, their admired Mr. Balanchine chose to do a ballet, *Stars and Stripes*, to the marches of John Philip Sousa. Boulez they would have been ready for, or Stockhausen—but *Sousa*! They decided finally that Balanchine must be spoofing, but he never said he was. His only comment was, "I like Sousa's music. It makes me feel good."

When Balanchine was engaged in making a ballet he would sometimes offer prayers to the composer if he ran into difficulties. "Let us pray to Gounod," he was heard saying to some of the company when he was choreographing *Gounod Symphony.* "He will help us." This brought smiles to the lips of some of those who heard him. They assumed he was being whimsical, but he was not. He meant it—not symbolically, either, but simply and literally. He was certain that the composers often heard his prayers and interceded to help him assemble the materials of his ballet in suitable style—"assemble," not "create." Creation is an act performed only by God, he believed.

Some critics have opined that Balanchine was actually too musical for his own good. They declared that what he did was closer to eurythmy than ballet, as they defined ballet. The most distinguished of the critics who took this line was Cyril Beaumont. Reviewing *Ballet Imperial* in 1950, Beaumont wrote, "The relation between music and choreography is almost automatic. It seems to me to be less creative choreography than the literal reproduction in terms of the dance of the rhythm, texture, and pattern of the music. It is a mathematical process rather than a creative one." Discussing *Symphony in C,* Beaumont commented, according to Anatole Chujoy, that Balanchine repeated whole sections of his choreography to conform with the music, and that this was a fault because it left the audience with the impression that the choreographer could not think of any other steps to put in that place. Aside from the fact that this was a curious observation to make in regard to a choreographer who had proved himself to be as facile as any who ever lived, it missed the intention completely. Balanchine often liked to show a dance motif or section twice, because he knew that audiences often failed to grasp what they were seeing the first time. His choreographic repeat frequently served a parallel function to that fulfilled by the musical repeat in the score. He knew that in dance, as in music—and in life, too—a repeat is not a repeat, in its effect. One cannot bathe twice in the same stream; the experience is different the second time. Actually, there are to be found in Balanchine's ballets numerous instances in which the music repeats and the choreography does not. The most obvious example is *Opus 34,* a nightmare ballet to the music of Arnold Schönberg. The ballet consisted of two parts. The score was played through twice. In the first part, the choreography was in Balanchine's characteristic modern, plotless style; the second part, to the same music, was a hallucinatory operating-room scene, and here the choreography was of a strange dance-mime character. Sometimes in his ballets Balanchine followed the music even more closely than those in the audience, including perhaps Cyril Beaumont, might have been aware of. In *Episodes,* for instance, there occurs an odd moment when the women are turned upside down and do entrechats with head down, feet in the air. When I asked him about this, Balanchine replied gravely, "Oh, I have to do that. That's where Webern inverts the theme. See, it's right here in the score." But one may be certain that Balanchine would not have choreographed it that way if the action had not, first and foremost, pleased him visually and been in accord with his palette of movement for that particular ballet. There are theme inversions in Bach's *Double Violin Concerto* but no upside-down entrechats to be found in the ballet Balanchine choreographed to that score. Similarly, in *Movements for Piano and Orchestra,* at the start Stravinsky exposed the sequence of notes in his tone row with great rapidity, and Balanchine deployed his dancers in the same way. Later in the piece, Stravinsky brought back the tone-row sequence, but this time in very leisurely fashion; Balanchine repeated his earlier choreographic deployment, but in the new leisurely tempo. Such turns and devices gave Balanchine pleasure. They can be considered, since so few people in the audience are ever aware of them, the private games of a choreographer. Yet it is quite likely that such subtle conjunctions of dance patterns to the musical patterns work in subliminal ways on even an uncomprehending audience to convey the overall effect characteristic of Balanchine ballets in all his genres—of appropriateness and harmony, of surprises that are seldom gratuitous, and of fulfilled expectations.

"I don't see how anyone can be a choreographer unless, like Balanchine, he is a musician first," Stravinsky wrote. Unfortunately, he added wryly, very few choreographers have been musicians. In Stravinsky's opinion, Balanchine's musicality enabled him to free himself from the obvious constrictions of the music, particularly the tyranny of the beat (which, Stravinsky said, trapped Nijinsky inextricably in his choreography for *Le Sacre du Printemps*), and to construct dance phrases that have a life of their own yet are always subtly linked with the music's essence and inner life. In a passage from *Themes and Episodes,* one of the books he wrote with Robert Craft, Stravinsky paid perhaps the ultimate tribute to Balanchine's musicality, expressing how much the choreographer revealed to the composer about his own music:

"To see Balanchine's choreography of the *Movements* is to hear the music with one's eyes; and this visual hearing has been a greater revelation to me, I think, than to anyone else. The choreography emphasizes relationships of which I had hardly been aware—in the same way—and the performance was like a tour of a building for which I had drawn the plans but never explored the result. Balanchine approached the music by identifying some of the more familiar marks of my style, and as I heard him fastening on my tiniest repeated rhythm or sustaining group, I knew he had joined the work to the corpus of my music, at the same time probably reducing the time lag of its general acceptability by as much as a decade. I owe him even more for another aspect of the revelation: his dramatic point is a love parable—in which ballet is it not?—but the coda had a suggestion of myth that reminded me of the ending of *Apollo*."

Stravinsky also wrote how astonished he was at a rehearsal he attended when at one point Balanchine asked the dancers to repeat a section without the music. "To my amazement they were able to count it by themselves, which is rather better than many orchestras. But are the *Movements* ballet music? Barbarous locution to a Balanchine! What he needs from me is not a *pas de deux* but a motor impulse."

"Oh Brave New World that has such dancers in it!" So wrote, in a most un-British burst of enthusiasm, the critic of the London *Times* after spending a season in New York, attending all the performances of the New York City Ballet. The London *Times'* reports are always unsigned, but the voice in this case was clearly that of Clive Barnes, then the liveliest and most knowledgeable of England's younger generation of critics. His visit to New York took place in the spring of 1962, a decade after the American company had been last seen in London, and he was impressed to see how much the company had developed since then—"beyond expectation if not recognition." The company's senior ballerinas—Diana Adams, Melissa Hayden, Jillana, Allegra Kent, Violette Verdy, and Patricia Wilde—had recently been joined, he said, by a remarkable influx of younger dancers, and he named as the most notable Patricia McBride, Suzanne Farrell, Gloria Govrin, Patricia Neary, Mimi Paul, and Suki Schorer. A splendid new generation was coming along. Perhaps the most significant change that had occurred in the past ten years was that the male members of the company— with such as Jacques d'Amboise, Edward Villella, and Arthur Mitchell leading the way—were now just as impressive in their dancing as the women, whereas a decade before they had been completely overshadowed. New York, he wrote, has become the dance capital of the world, and the effect of seeing the New York City Ballet performing there is "as exhilarating as horses at Epsom or Mozart in Salzburg."

In carrying on the New York City Ballet, Balanchine and Kirstein continued their remarkable collaboration. Their bond was not weakened by their early failures, and what is perhaps even more rare, it seemed even strong enough to survive success. Throughout the years, they always approached matters in a very different way. Kirstein could be moody and irascible. His rages were famous, as were his bouts of euphoria. Driven by the haunted energy of the insomniac, and perpetually bringing forth great plans for new projects, many of them quixotic, some of them inspired, Kirstein often exhibited the aggressiveness of a man who was innately shy, whereas Balanchine bore himself with the quiet ease of one who was supremely confident. Entering the company's studios when all was in chaos, Balanchine could calm matters simply by his untroubled presence. Kirstein, on the other hand, was apt to come in at a time when everything was going swimmingly, peer about him, and ask, with an agonized scowl, "Is anything wrong?" Nevertheless, there was seldom any divergence on matters of fundamental principle. Balanchine often publicly expressed his gratitude to Kirstein. He said that if it weren't for Kirstein, he not only might never have come to the United States but, for lack of a company, also might never have fashioned the ballets he had. When this was repeated to Kirstein, he glared as if he had been insulted, and snapped that it was nonsense—that such a talent as Balanchine's would have found a way of expressing itself, in a form not too different from the one it took, whether he had helped or not. Be that as it may, Kirstein throughout played his role—patron, advocate, interpreter, supporter, colleague—in an extraordinary way. As John Martin wrote, "The General Director [of a ballet company] usually hires the Artistic Director to carry out his policies; Kirstein, on the other hand, has hired himself, so to speak, to carry out Balanchine's policy."

Certainly, there was never any question about whose influence predominated in the New York City Ballet. The company reflected in such a multiplicity of ways the personality of George Balanchine that it seemed less an ensemble of skilled performers he had gathered and trained than a kind of emanation from him. "Nowhere else in the world," to quote Martin again, "is there a ballet company that is similarly the creation of a single mind." Every dancer in the company either had been trained by Balanchine from an early stage or had been retrained according to Balanchine's principles of dance technique. The values and stylistic standards that prevailed were those of Balanchine's neoclassicism—a mode that was grand and aristocratic in manner, but naturally so, without pomposity; full of invention yet lucid in quality; tearing no passion to tatters but, instead, enlivened by a constant play of subtle wit and irony and an unfeigned delight in the pleasures of the dance. And nearly all of the ballets in the repertory—three quarters, at least—had been choreographed by Balanchine himself.

In actuality, Balanchine bore the title of artistic director for only a few years. The adjective offended him, and the time came when he demoted himself, in title, to "ballet master." On the program he was thereafter listed as one of three ballet masters, along with Jerome Robbins and John Taras. Only through alphabetical precedence, presumably, did his name get listed first. It didn't matter. In his domain his power was absolute. He needed no grand title any more than Stalin needed to be anything but party secretary.

Money interested him even less than titles. For the first sixteen years of the New York City Ballet's existence, Balanchine took no salary. He was satisfied with the twelve to fifteen thousand dollars a year he averaged from royalties on his ballets, at $25 a performance. In 1964, at the insistence of the Ford Foundation, he finally went on salary. The foundation, which was considering awarding a multi-million-dollar grant to the company and the school, made this a condition of the grant. It made the Ford Foundation nervous to give huge sums to an operation run by a volunteer. So, along with his royalties, Balanchine was henceforth paid $10,000 a year as head of the company and $9,000 a year as chairman of the faculty of the school.

In its first year at the City Center, the New York City Ballet gave but twenty-four performances. By the 1960's it was giving, in an average year, a total of around a hundred and fifty performances, spread out over two or three seasons, in New York alone, plus whatever tours were made. In the course of a year's performances in New York, the New York City Ballet was being seen by a total audience of around three hundred thousand people. This, as even some devotees of the ballet may be surprised to realize, was at least five times as large an audience as Diaghilev's Ballets Russes commanded in the twenties. That company did not dare risk more than a couple of weeks a year in Paris, even in a small theatre, holding no more than eight hundred people; in Monte Carlo, the theatre's capacity was only four hundred.

In New York by 1963 almost as many people attended ballet during the course of a year as baseball—a piece of information often cited by ballet writers, though almost never by sports columnists. Nor was it New York alone that had taken to ballet. Still more significant was the fact that regional ballet companies were springing up all over the United States, supported by small-town bankers, shopkeepers, and others who not long before would have sneered at having anything to do with such a thing. Over a hundred such companies had come into existence by then. The dream that Balanchine and Kirstein discussed, in 1933, of seeing ballet take root in America as a living, flourishing art had become a reality.

As for Balanchine, during the 1950's he attained recognition and status on a new, grand scale. He had founded a school, a company, a style, a repertory—a range of achievements matched by few, if any, individuals in the history of ballet. He had become, without question, the dominant figure in ballet for the present era. His influence went far beyond that of his own company. In Germany, for example, where he had mounted some of his ballets and done some work with the ballet company of the Hamburg Opera, he was credited with having initiated a whole new interest in ballet. Throughout the world his ballets were being performed by nearly all the major and numerous lesser companies. In the United States, in addition to supervising his school, directing his company, and choreographing new ballets each season, he had become increasingly active in fostering ballet in general and improving its standards. He traveled about the country, advising the regional ballet companies; conducted annually a free seminar for the ballet teachers of America; sent small groups of his dancers here and there on lecture-demonstration tours; organized free ballet performances for underprivileged children; and contributed his experience and insight in a variety of other ways.

By now, the audience for his kind of ballet had grown considerably, and critics who, for many years after Balanchine began working in America, had been antipathetic to his efforts had become ardent advocates. The London *Times* critic noted, on his visit to New York, that Balanchine seemed to have trained his audience and his critics almost as carefully as he trained his dancers. When the New York State Theater was built at Lincoln Center, it was Balanchine's advice that was most heeded as to what the theatre should be like. "I did the house with Balanchine in mind," said the architect, Philip Johnson. "I have always wanted to design a theatre for him." And the New York City Ballet agreed to open the theatre formally on April 23, 1964, and to be the resident company.

Beyond the world of ballet now, fame in its various characteristic manifestations had come to Balanchine—a *Time* cover story, a *New Yorker* profile, features in *Life* and other magazines, an invitation to the White House.

Balanchine was actually Jacqueline Kennedy's first guest in the White House. It was January 25, 1961. The visit was informal, just the two of them in an upstairs living room. She was wearing a velvet suit and looked pale. She said she wanted to show her esteem for him and solicit his advice as to how she could help the arts. She offered him tea. "You don't have anything stronger?" Balanchine asked. He was charmed by her. When the press later sought his impression of her, he answered appreciatively, "She looks like a pussycat."

In April he took part with other notables in a panel in Washington on the subject: "If I Were President . . ." He said he would only want to be president if he could have Jacqueline Kennedy as first lady, and then, with her help, do what should be done to bring beauty into people's lives. Subsequently he wrote her a letter, urging her to take on the role of "spiritual savior" of America.

"I don't mean in a religious sense," he wrote, "but I mean to distinguish between material things and things of the spirit—art, beauty. No one else can take care of these things. You alone can—if you will.

"Your husband is necessarily busy with serious international problems and cannot be expected to worry too much about the nation's art and culture. But woman is always the inspiration. Man takes care of the material things and woman takes care of the soul. Woman is the world and man lives in it. Woman makes the earth into a home for man.

"Even in art, it is woman who inspires man. God creates, woman inspires, and man assembles.

"I firmly believe that woman is appointed by destiny to inspire and bring beauty to our existence. Woman herself is the reason for life to be beautiful, and men should be busy serving her. . . ."

It was a letter such as Don Quixote might have addressed to Dulcinea. Jacqueline Kennedy's reply was politely noncommittal.

Balanchine returned to expressing himself in ballets, not letters. As for the fame that had come to him, he refused to take it seriously. To a friend who showed him a flattering article, Balanchine commented, "Publicity overrates everything," and then, specifying to clinch his point, added, "Picasso's overrated. I'm overrated. Even Jack Benny's overrated."

THE MAKING OF AGON

A rehearsal in 1957, as Balanchine shows Stravinsky for the first time the choreography he has made for this ballet.

They begin with a discussion, in Russian, on tempi. "The pianist says he doesn't know how to play it," says Balanchine. "I don't either," replies Stravinsky.

As the dancers—Barbara Walczak, Todd Bolender, and Barbara Milberg—crouch downward for the ending of the coda to their pas de trois, Balanchine snaps his fingers and cries, "Now!"

Barbara Walczak and Barbara Milberg dance the gaillard. Stravinsky, who has by now shucked his jacket, claps out the rhythm. He says he thinks the last bars of their dance "beautiful but dangerous" because they must do complicated arm movements to a count of nine. "I'm afraid I don't know how long nine is," Stravinsky says. Balanchine subsequently simplified the ending.

The exuberant conclusion of the bransle double, with Melissa Hayden, Roy Tobias, and Jonathan Watts. "Horosha!" exclaims Stravinsky.

One of numerous forays to the piano. During this one, just before the adagio pas de deux, Stravinsky wants to be sure that the music here will be played in such a way as to bring out an echo of the music at the end of the preceding section.

Balanchine strikes a dynamic pose as he describes the quality of movement one part should have.

The adagio. In this section Balanchine seems to have succeeded in his aim of happily surprising Stravinsky, who claps when it is finished and says, "Wonderful! Wonderful!" It is the first time he has seen Arthur Mitchell. He asks his name and compliments him. Diana Adams is known to him, and he speaks of her admiringly to Balanchine. "She has legs like the Solingen scissors trademark," he says.

Stravinsky dances.

They discuss the ballet's conclusion. Stravinsky thinks the four young men should swing their arms in more controlled and precise fashion than they were doing; Balanchine agrees, and they go through that part again to everybody's satisfaction.

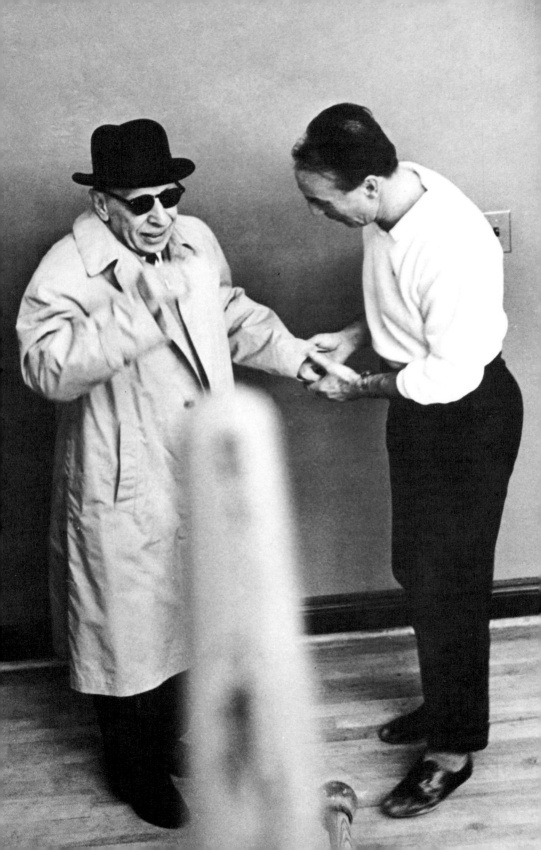

CHAPTER TWELVE

Come Back, Come Back, Come Back

G. M. Balanchivadze had left Russia at the age of twenty, a promising youth. As George Balanchine, he came back in 1962 at the age of fifty-eight, world-famous, at the head of a brilliant American ensemble, which was as much his creation as were the Balanchine ballets it performed.

On the basis of what was known of Russian taste in ballet, and of various advance indications and prior encounters with leading figures in the Russian ballet world, no great success was expected for Balanchine or his company. There had been, for instance, the interesting occasion in 1959, when the Bolshoi had made its first trip to the United States and was enjoying a spectacular triumph. Since the Bolshoi's schedule did not permit its members to attend a regular performance of the New York City Ballet, Balanchine arranged to put on a special rehearsal for the visitors while they were in New York. The event turned out to be something of a fiasco. The Russians were able to make little or nothing of what they saw the New York City Ballet do, and they looked as if they were pretty sure they would not like it even if they did understand it. Their faces registered bewilderment, pain, boredom, and stiff politeness.

The first ballet presented was *Agon,* as complex and sophisticated a piece of choreography as had ever been devised. "It was like giving *Finnegans Wake* to someone who has never gone beyond Galsworthy," commented one American witness of the Bolshoi troupe's baffled reaction both to the choreography and to Stravinsky's twelve-tone-technique score. The Russians were used to ballets that tell a tale or convey a

Respectful farewell.

273

readily understandable situation and, if possible, impart a moral. Nothing of that sort was to be found in *Agon*. Its entire orientation seemed to them incomprehensible. As his point of departure in the score, Stravinsky makes use of some seventeenth-century dance forms, and so does Balanchine when it suits him. At one point, a soloist goes through an elaborate, decorous saraband, but as an observer has noted, "It recalls a court dance as much as a Cubist still life recalls a pipe or guitar." A few introductory words by Balanchine about his intentions might have given some of the audience a clue to the way to look at the ballet, but Balanchine, sticking to his belief that if a ballet is any good, it does not require a program note or other explanation, told them only the title and the name of the composer. The Russians have a word that is similar in sound to *Agon* and means "fire"; throughout the ballet some of the Bolshoi members, who had misheard Balanchine's announcement, sat conscientiously trying to make some sort of fire dance out of the choreography. The title—*Agon*—is, in fact, the Greek word for "contest," but that knowledge would not have been of much help, either, to a spectator expecting to see a recognizable representation of some portion of "life." Within *Agon*'s self-contained cosmos, presented to the audience with an air of cool, ironic detachment, there do occur, in a mysteriously coherent pattern, the most amazing events—sometimes intensely exciting and charged with drama, sometimes sparklingly witty or lucidly nonsensical, sometimes, as in the pas de deux, suffused with eroticism—but the events are choreographic events; they could not happen in what we call the real world, though they seem inevitable in the world called *Agon*. Complex as *Agon* is, it had nevertheless delighted New York audiences and had received a great ovation at its premiere two years before. The New York audiences, of course, had been acquainted with Balanchine's way of organizing dance movement and Stravinsky's way of organizing sound, and they had also been prepared for *Agon* by all that had happened in art in the Western world during the past few decades—all the innovations and discoveries that had shaped the taste and outlook not just of sophisticates but of the broad public—to the point where surrealism, for example, far from shocking anybody, had become a comfortable cliché of popular advertisements. At that City Center rehearsal for the Bolshoi in 1959, one was reminded how little the Soviet Union had been touched by such influences.

After *Agon*, the New York City Ballet danced two other plotless Balanchine ballets—*Symphony in C* and *Serenade*. These were somewhat better received than *Agon,* no doubt partly because the nineteenth-century music sounded less strange, and partly because in these ballets Balanchine's choreography makes more use of familiar steps. Even so, no great enthusiasm was discernible. The quality of the dancing did not help matters. The members of the New York company were visibly nervous, and some of them danced as awkwardly as they ever had danced in their lives. When they began making obvious mistakes, Balanchine, who had been sitting in the first row, went up on the stage to work with them, as patiently as if this were a routine rehearsal. If he felt any chagrin at the company's performance, he showed no signs of it.

An odd scene took place when Balanchine met with the Bolshoi's chief choreographer, Leonid Lavrovsky, at an informal reception that was held in the City Center's balcony lobby after the rehearsal. There was a long table heaped with food and drink in the middle of the lobby, and there the Russian and American dancers animatedly swapped information about their trade, chattering in snatches of English, Russian, and French but communicating mainly by gesture—their hands swooping about in the air to describe steps and choreography in the manner of fighter pilots in a bull session showing what their planes had done. Off to one side, near a staircase, one of the New York City Ballet's ballerinas stood weeping, because she knew she had not performed well. At the opposite side, Balanchine and Lavrovsky were to be seen in the center of a small group, smiling and talking vivaciously. They had once been schoolmates at the Imperial Theatre School in St. Petersburg, and Lavrovsky had even been a member of Balanchine's Evenings of the Young Ballet ensemble, so this was a reunion for them. As movie and still cameras focused on them and flashbulbs popped, they embraced and kissed each other heartily on the cheek. From a distance it looked like a tableau symbolizing the end of the Cold War and the kind of understanding and mutual affection that cultural exchanges can bring. But what the two men were actually saying to each other, as those who understood Russian discovered on approaching the group, was that they had no use for each other's conception of art.

Lavrovsky, a chunky, shaggy-haired man given to blunt, forceful gestures, was heard saying as he beamed at Balanchine, "You know, in the Soviet Union work such as yours would be condemned as mere formalism, as inhuman."

To this, Balanchine—elegant, courteous, but fully as forceful—replied, "Well, I'm certainly not interested in using beautiful dance movement and gesture as merely a caption for some silly story."

Tolerantly, Lavrovsky said, "Ah, well, someday you'll come around to our way of doing things."

With equal assurance, Balanchine retorted, "What do you mean 'come around'? I went through all that and left it behind me long ago—thirty-five years ago, to be exact." This last, as both were fully aware, was a reference to the date when Balanchine had left the Soviet Union.

"Just one more, please!" a camerman called, whereupon the two men embraced again and once more kissed each other mightily on the cheek.

After that visit, there was little reason to expect that the New York City Ballet would ever be invited to perform in the Soviet Union, or that Balanchine would go if he were invited—or, unlikeliest of all, if these eventualities should come about, that the company would enjoy a great triumph there.

Two years after that, in the fall of 1961, another Russian troupe came to the United States. This was the Kirov Ballet Company, from Leningrad—the troupe that, under the name of the Maryinsky, had been the company into which, as a youth, Balanchine had graduated at the end of his school training. The members of the Kirov company attended numerous performances of the New York City Ballet and several class demonstrations. Though they did not like everything equally, they were much more receptive than the Bolshoi to the Balanchine ballets they saw. It was noticeable that they seemed more sophisticated in their tastes than the Bolshoi and expressed themselves more freely; they mingled more readily with the Americans and did not appear to be quite so compulsive about echoing the party line in their aesthetic judgments. This difference reflected to some extent, in Balanchine's opinion, the greater cosmopolitanism of Leningrad, in comparison to which Moscow has always been more rigid and provincial in outlook, but it was also a reflection of the fact that, during the two years that had elapsed between the two visits, the thaw that Khrushchev had initiated had been continuing in Russia's intellectual and cultural life. It was ceasing to be treason to be interested in Western art forms, and it was conceivable even to like some.

Following this, increased speculation was heard about the possibility of a Russian tour by the New York City Ballet. It began to seem vaguely possible, then expedient, and then, in the way many projects have of gaining momentum, an absolute must—a solution, somehow, to all the State Department's unsolved problems. The State Department was in favor of it; the impresario Hurok favored it, so he could have a quid pro quo to offer Russia in connection with his bargaining to bring the Bolshoi back to the United States for a second time; the press wanted it because it seemed like a great story. The public assumed that Balanchine would naturally be eager to go and that he must feel that his life was not really complete until he had revealed to his Russian compatriots what he had achieved, and gained their approval of it. Well, possibly. But if Balanchine did feel that way, under his guarded exterior, he certainly did not show it. Profoundly and strenuously anti-Communist in his politics and in his entire orientation, he kept saying that he would never go to Russia. At first, he asserted that the company also would not go. Later, as all the various intangible pressures increased, he could be heard to declare that the company might go, if the State Department wanted it to, but that it could go without him. By the spring of 1962, he was becoming less firm. By then it had begun to seem, as the Marxists might put it, an absolute historical necessity that the New York City Ballet be transported five thousand miles to the land of Lenin and dialectical materialism to show that Americans were just as capable as the Russians in the production of fantasy and enchantment. Once this assumption was granted, and the corollary assumption that all this was somehow relevant to the cementing of peace and amity between the two countries, then it was unthinkable that the New York company should go without Balanchine. That would have been a mortal insult. Balanchine was made to see that his duty as an American citizen was to go back to Russia, and he acquiesced.

An eight-week tour was planned. Preceding the Russian tour there would be a five-week tour of Europe. In negotiations with the State Department the company's administrators had insisted that this be part of the arrangement, in order to provide the company with as many weeks of work as possible. This was an abiding issue in the company's considerations: how to put together enough weeks of work every year to keep the dancers alive. The European tour went exceedingly well, though its beginning, which was at Hamburg, was disastrous. There, the singers, who had been picked up in Germany to perform *Liebeslieder Walzer* with the company, turned out to be incompetent. Hardly had the performance commenced when the audience began to laugh and to applaud sarcastically. The dancers, appalled, could not at first understand what was happening; then it became clear that it was the singing, not the ballet or the dancing, which was being ridiculed. After that, *Liebeslieder Walzer* was dropped for the rest of the tour.

In Hamburg also there occurred, the next day, a grave accident. Jacques d'Amboise and Victoria Simon were struck by a streetcar in front of the theatre. Both were seriously injured. D'Amboise was not able to dance again until the middle of the Russian engagement, about eight weeks later, and even then had not recovered his full strength.

Despite these setbacks the company, as a whole, looked magnificent during the European preliminaries to the Russian tour that was to be, whether Balanchine saw it that way or not, the main event. The London *Times* printed in September two reports on it from Zurich. A theme of the *Times'* reports, as well as those of other British reviewers who made the trip to the Continent to see the New York City Ballet in action, was what a shame it was, verging on the scandalous, that so many years had gone by without London's powers-that-be in the realm of ballet making the effort necessary to arrange for an appearance of the New York company there. Meanwhile the New York City Ballet was off to Russia. "The Russian ballet world will certainly be startled," wrote the *Times.* "One hopes it will also be enchanted, for America, and perhaps the western world, is sending what is probably its strongest cultural ambassador."

On the evening of October 6, 1962, the plane carrying Balanchine and the ninety other members of the New York City Ballet organization landed at Sheremetyevo Airport in Moscow. A host of dignitaries and officials were waiting to greet the party. There were speeches and an interview for Radio Moscow. "Welcome to Moscow, home of the classic ballet!" the interviewer said to Balanchine.

"I beg your pardon," replied Balanchine. "Russia is the home of romantic ballet. The home of classic ballet is now America."

Among the crowd present at the airport was Balanchine's brother, Andrei, who was now the leading Georgian composer and of high repute throughout the Soviet Union. It was their first meeting in forty-three years. The two embraced warmly. Balanchine was quite surprised to find that he was several inches taller than his brother. "He's short," Balanchine subsequently remarked, when asked by an acquaintance to describe what his brother was like. "He's a very short brother." The two men had not much chance to talk at the airport, but they spent much time together in succeeding days. They had never corresponded during their long separation, but each had been aware of the main facts of the other's life. Andrei was the only one of the immediate family left alive in Russia.

Their father had died in 1937 at the age of seventy-six, their mother, also at an advanced age, just a few years before this visit. Balanchine had been informed of these deaths at the time they had happened. He had kept in touch with his mother, and for years after his departure from Russia he had sent her food parcels from time to time, until the authorities put an end to all private exchanges between Russia and the outside world. Their sister, Tamara, was also dead. She was the one whom Balanchine had accompanied on the day she tried out for the Imperial Theatre School in St. Petersburg when, to his surprise and dismay, they had accepted him instead. Turned down by the school then, she had tried again the following year and had been admitted but was dropped at the end of her probationary year. After going to the Caucasus with her parents, she had become a painter and an architect and returned to Leningrad. She was killed during a German air raid in World War II. From his brother, Balanchine also learned the details of how his father had died, which he had not known. His father, it seemed, had developed gangrene in one leg and was told that an amputation was required in order to save his life. "What?" he answered, "I, Meliton Balanchivadze, stump about on one leg? Never!"

"But it's absolutely necessary. If you don't have an operation, you'll be dead within two days," his doctor said.

"So be it then," his father said lightly, with a shrug of his shoulders. "Death is a beautiful girl, who is going to come and take me in her arms. I look forward to the experience." Two days later he died. This account, as Balanchine heard it from his brother, made a deep impression on him, for it seemed so in keeping with his memories of his father's character.

The company was to open at the Bolshoi three days after their arrival in Moscow—the first American ballet company ever to appear on that stage. Then, for the bulk of their three-week Moscow engagement, they would shift over to the Palace of Congresses in the Kremlin, an immense theatre seating six thousand people, which is well over twice as many as the Bolshoi holds, and with a far larger stage. A new glass and concrete building, it is one of the few pieces of modern architecture to be seen in Moscow and makes a curious contrast with the dominant Slavic medieval style of the Kremlin buildings around it. During this time the company would have an interlude of one more performance at the Bolshoi in order to free the Palace of Congresses for the scheduled celebration of the 150th anniversary of Napoleon's retreat from Moscow, and the company's final performance of the engagement would also be given in the more glamorous Bolshoi. All seats for all the performances had been sold out in advance.

The repertory brought to Russia consisted of eighteen ballets, out of which five different programs were made up. Sixteen of the ballets were by Balanchine. The program for the opening night, October 9, was *Serenade*, Jerome Robbins' *Interplay*, *Agon*, and *Western Symphony*. In the audience that night were the foreign minister, the minister of culture, the American ambassador, and numerous other dignitaries and functionaries. It was a boiled-shirt, bureaucratic audience, and it responded bureaucratically—with politeness, tinged with puzzlement and suspicion. They might not have known much about art, the bureaucrats in that opening-night audience, but they knew, down to the least tittle, what they were supposed to like, and in ballet it was not this—not these stark or wispy bits of nothing, with no story and no scenery and, except for the last ballet, the simplest of costumes.

The critics next day expounded officially the response the audience had made manifest. To be sure, the company was recognized immediately as an extraordinarily brilliant ensemble, who had mastered to a point of virtuosity the classic technique. In *Izvestia* Aram Khachaturian wrote of "the impeccable classic technique of which the artists are in brilliant possession." And the Soviet choreographer Rostislav Zakharov wrote: "Their strict discipline, precision and deep sense of the musical rhythm, which is often very intricate, combined with a fine classic dance technique, produce a highly gratifying impression. George Balanchine, the company's artistic director, has managed to instill in the young dancers an exacting attitude toward their art." Also recognized from the first was Balanchine's remarkable choreographic abilities and ingenuity, but his conception of art was deplored. What a sad waste of talent and effort! "G. Balanchine in his creative practice adheres to the principle of plotlessness," wrote Khachaturian. "This principle is foreign to Soviet artists and spectators. Without an idea, without a subject, there cannot be true emotional art." One critic went so far as to call Balanchine a fanatic who had frivolously sacrificed ballet's great tradition to his own vision of the dance.

All this was just about what one might have predicted. What no one had expected, though, was what happened subsequently. In the huge Palace of Congresses, one began to be aware quite early in the engagement of a sense of growing interest on the part of the audience, a sort of deepened hush of concentration. Then spontaneous murmurs of appreciation began to be heard here and there which grew, one evening, into an outburst of enthusiasm. The breakthrough came quite suddenly. John Martin, who had accompanied the New York City Ballet's party to Russia, wrote back to *The New York Times* that the point where the tide of understanding turned was with the first presentation of the Bizet *Symphony in C.* "Though the program had opened with the *Raymonda Variations,* received in all but stony silence," he wrote, "the Bizet work brought forth not only applause throughout and repeated curtain calls at the end but also rhythmic cries of 'Bal-an-chine' until the choreographer was forced to come forward and bow his acknowledgment." Martin thought that a possible explanation for the audience reaction might have been that the frank titling of this ballet as a symphony eliminated all possibility of confusion as to whether or not it had a plot or subject to be puzzled over. Nearly all Russian critics who saw it agreed that *Symphony in C* was sheer joy—"a life-affirming" ballet, as Golovashenko hailed it, "a true festival of dancing . . . agile and light, diversified and wonderfully harmonious." Even Petipa, wrote one, could not have invented such a breathtaking display of classical choreography as Balanchine had done in this work.

After that night, whatever the critics might write—and they would always have their doubts and reservations and dutiful scruples—the spectators were unequivocal in their enthusiasm. Night after night excitement was sustained at a high pitch. Now nearly every ballet in the repertory went over well, including those that were supposed to be the most difficult and alien. *Agon* made a great impression whenever given. Undoubtedly the biggest surprise of all was the tumultuous favor that *Episodes* won from the time of its first presentation. In New York, as Martin recalled, this ballet, "perhaps the most puzzling avant-garde work in the repertory," had not always fared too well; many Balanchine fans in America found the style of dance, with its distortions and strange, impersonal manipulations, and Webern's twelve-tone music disconcerting and unpalatable. But here in Moscow there were storms of applause between each of the individual sections. Balanchine was particularly pleased that the Muscovites did not laugh during the brief "Five Pieces" section; in New York during that part, with its curious dramas compressed into just a few seconds of time, there were often nervous titters to be heard.

In discussing the New York City Ballet, the Russians noted, generally with approval, that the company had succeeded in abolishing the star system—the cult of personality. In practice, spectators soon developed their own favorites among the dancers. Probably the most admired were Allegra Kent, who, one critic said, had something of the flavor of Ulanova, and Edward Villella. The Russians did not have the opportunity to see Diana Adams and Jacques d'Amboise at their best, because of the effect of their injuries and disabilities. Arthur Mitchell won everybody's favor. As the one black member of the company, he was naturally the subject of special interest to the Russians, but beyond that, they much admired the way he moved and carried himself. Among the lesser soloists there was praise for Mimi Paul and Suki Schorer. The latter reminded the Russians of the Bolshoi's Ekaterina Maximova.

The greatest ovations nightly were always for the choreographer. They called for him until he appeared. Then they would often shout their thanks and gratitude: "*Spa-si-bo! Spa-si-bo!*" Balanchine seemed at first delighted, even euphoric, at the reception. Some of the members of the company remarked that they had never before seen him so ready to take a curtain call. But even then he was in a complicated state of emotions, a more complicated state than, perhaps, he himself realized. There was one evening when Balanchine stood in the wings at the end of the performance, making no move to go forward, while the applause for him went on and on. Francisco Moncion, who was nearby, said, "Mr. Balanchine, they're calling for you. Aren't you going to take a bow?"

Balanchine turned a haggard look on him and said, "Well, what if I were dead!" And he did not appear.

During his stay in Moscow, Balanchine did not go about the city much for pleasure. What he saw of Moscow, under the bleak October skies, he did not like: this was hardly surprising, for nobody who has been brought up in Leningrad finds Moscow appealing. He felt that he was not there for his own amusement or edification, but to fulfill a duty; so he put it, anyway. Whatever the American Embassy asked of him, he did. He gave interviews to the press and made whatever appearances were required, no matter how much time they took. Daily he conducted a company class, which many dancers and teachers from the Bolshoi attended. The Russians recorded some of these sessions on 16 millimeter film for future study. There was considerable amazement expressed by some of the Russian teachers, as they watched his company's classes, as to how he got human bodies to move in such complicated yet harmonious patterns. In the detailed technical analyses and appreciations made by the Russians,

Jacques d'Amboise and Diana Adams in one of the many surprising moments from Episodes.

the American dancers always rated the highest commendation for their clean-cut footwork; if they had any outstanding common fault, the Russians felt, it was that they did not work enough on developing the lyrical expressive use of their arms and shoulders. In return for Balanchine's efforts, the Bolshoi school put on a demonstration class for him and the company. It was conducted by Elizaveta Gerdt, now a woman of over seventy, who had been Balanchine's favorite ballerina when he was a boy, and the wife of his revered teacher, Andreyanov.

One evening, while in Moscow, Balanchine was excited to discover that a new ballet by the man who had been his first choreographic inspiration—Kasian Goleizovsky—was being performed. Goleizovsky, after languishing in obscurity for a long time, had in post-Stalinist years been reinstated. Balanchine went to see a rehearsal of the ballet— *Scriabiniana,* it was called—but was disappointed. It seemed to contain nothing new—just repetitions of ideas that forty years before had seemed daring. He had intended to call on Goleizovsky but after seeing this ballet could not bring himself to do so. If he met Goleizovsky, he would have to say he had seen his work, and he knew that he would not be able to bring himself to praise it, because he was incapable of feigning an enthusiasm he did not feel. In addition, he found himself reluctant to spoil his cherished memories of the magnificent young Goleizovsky by seeing him as he would look now. He left Moscow without calling on him.

Near the end of the company's engagement in Moscow the Cuban crisis erupted; the United States and the Soviet Union were suddenly at the brink of war over the Soviet missile emplacements in Cuba. On October 29, when the company was scheduled to give its closing performance in Moscow, the crisis was at its peak. The American Embassy issued a warning that demonstrations could be expected, and the company was rehearsed in the procedures that were to be taken if trouble broke out in the theatre. There were, in fact, demonstrations in the Bolshoi that night, but not of the sort that dancers would wish to fend off. That night the audience gave the New York City Ballet the greatest ovation, according to Bolshoi personnel, ever given at that theatre. It went on for twenty minutes and ceased only after Balanchine came forward and made a short speech, inviting those who wished to see more to follow the company to Leningrad. Outside the stage door a large crowd was gathered. Many had attended every one of the twenty-four performances given in Moscow. "Come back," they cried, as the company's bus started off for the hotel. "Come back, come back, come back!"

Members of the New York City Ballet taking their daily class while in Russia. This photograph was taken at a rehearsal hall in Leningrad—one that Balanchine himself had rehearsed in as a youth.

. . .

Early the first morning in Leningrad, Balanchine said eagerly to Nathalie Molostwoff, a Russian expatriate like himself, who was on the staff of the School of American Ballet and was one of his good friends, "Let's go see my old house!" Now he was in his hometown and for the first time seemed to find zest in looking about him. They went out to his old neighborhood and stood for a long time before the house. "It all looks much as I remember it," Balanchine said. "But I didn't need to come here to be reminded of it. I've always had a picture of it right here," he added, putting his finger to his forehead. They went around the corner in search of the neighborhood church, where he had been taken every Sunday when he was small. That was changed. The building still stood, but its cross had been taken down, and it was now a factory. As for the great Cathedral of Our Lady of Kazan, for which his father had written chorales and where he had seen his uncle consecrated, that had been converted into Leningrad's Anti-God Museum. Balanchine did not have the heart to go in and see what it was like. He did manage to find that morning a small church that was still in use, and he went in, made his devotions, and lit a candle to his patron saint. In each city in Russia where the company stayed Balanchine managed to find a church in which he could practice his faith.

In Leningrad, the New York City Ballet had no initial coolness to overcome. Here all was triumph, from the rise of the first curtain in the lovely Kirov Theatre—the old Maryinsky, where Balanchine, as a boy of ten, had made his first appearance on stage. This was the place, this gold-and-royal-blue jewel of a house, that always haunted his memory as *the* ideal theatre. Many of his former classmates were in the audience that first night to cheer for Balanchine and his company. "But," as Martin wrote, "there was more involved in the evening's success than nostalgia and sentiment." The ballets made their own impression on a sensitive and aware audience. In Leningrad, even the critics paid only a brief lip service to the official line about plotless ballets being of necessity cold and inferior. The intellectuals were by now very well aware of what Balanchine was driving at, and coming as this did just at a time when an aesthetic revolution was stirring against socialist realism in all the arts, they were hit very hard by it. One of the most important events of the whole Soviet tour was a meeting with Balanchine that the choreographers of Leningrad requested. They gathered around a table in a room next to the Ballet School's museum, a room in which Balanchine had once taken classes, and listened intently as he talked to them about the principles of his art. "Why should we do Shakespeare?" he said. "Shakespeare's already done Shakespeare." Some of the older choreographers seemed to be left in despair by Balanchine' words, but the younger ones listened eagerly and they requested another meeting with him, which was held two days later.

Another high point of the trip was a matinee to which the New York City Ballet had invited the artists of the city—dancers, theatrical people, painters, writers, students. At the end of that program, Konstantin Sergeyev, the Kirov's artistic director, led ten young ballerinas of the Kirov Ballet onto the stage, where they presented bouquets to each of the New York company's leading dancers and to Balanchine. Sergeyev made a gracious speech, proudly claiming Balanchine as a native of this city. Balanchine accepted the honors being bestowed, on behalf not of himself, he said, but of America and the city of New York.

By this time, the Russians—the Russian authorities, at any rate—seeing Balanchine's success in their country, were picturing him as a sort

Surrounded by the teachers of the ballet school in Leningrad.

of Prodigal Son. Not that penitence was expected from him, but perhaps there might be tears of joy and kinship and reconciliation, ending with Balanchine being picked up and tenderly wrapped in Father Russia's cloak. Stravinsky took part in just such an emotional reconciliation scene at the end of September during his return visit to his homeland, after nearly half a century of absence. But not Balanchine. Politely but adamantly Balanchine rejected the role of the Prodigal Son. In his frontier-style garb—with string ties and pearl-button vests—which he wore most of the time during the tour, he looked more like someone out of *Western Symphony*. Every time he was hailed as a great fellow Russian, whose achievements were part of the great Russian culture, he would always interrupt the speaker to demur and, in the old-fashioned Russian he had learned as a boy in St. Petersburg, would insist that he was not a Russian, he was an American. In a certain fundamental way, perhaps, he showed himself never more Russian than those times when, resisting the flattery of his admiring hosts, he proclaimed himself an American through and through. To resist proffered affection is not an American trait. Describing Balanchine's response to the admiration of the Russians, Lincoln Kirstein afterward recalled the coronation scene in Eisenstein's *Ivan the Terrible*. "Do you remember that scene?" he said to the friend with whom he was talking. "Ivan is on his throne. The nobles bow down before him; they heap gold upon him. And he sits there, implacable—he is absolutely implacable."

Here Balanchine was, having what most observers would call the greatest triumph of his life, but he insisted that it meant nothing to him, and that it was of no great moment to him to be back in the country of his birth. By now he had become so accustomed to concealing his feelings that perhaps he convinced himself that he was really feeling as little as he said. Yet those around him could see that he was visibly affected by what was happening, and he seemed to be suffering from an increasing strain of which the physical demands on his energy were only a part. He looked gaunt. And he began to have nightmares such as he had not had for years—nightmares that he had lost his passport, that he had been thrown into prison, that he was suffocating. In a postscript of a brief, careful letter to Tanaquil Le Clercq, who had stayed in New York, he signaled what it was like for him. "Remember the *Invasion of the Body Snatchers?*" he wrote. At last, he could stand the strain no more. So when the company ended its two-week stay in Leningrad, instead of going on to Kiev with it, he flew back to the United States for a week's respite.

Balanchine rejoined the company in time to go on with it to Georgia, where it would scarcely have dared show up without him. As the son of Georgia's honored composer, he was treated as a Georgian national hero. Crowds mobbed him wherever he went. There were endless toasts to be drunk, all—as is the Georgian custom—from a brimming full glass, and there were endless flowery speeches. The only moments that Balanchine was allowed to spend by himself were at his father's grave at Kutais. What the Georgians would have loved best, as they kept letting him know, would be to see him as the son of Georgia's great composer, now do a ballet to Georgian music—to the music, for instance, of his own brother. Resisting this politely was something of a problem. He could hardly come out and say that he did not care for his brother's music, but it was not possible for him to praise it.

There was one harrowing evening when he and Mrs. Molostwoff had dinner at Andrei Balanchivadze's home in Tbilisi. All evening she had enjoyed seeing the warm family feeling and comradeship between the two reunited brothers. Then Andrei suggested that he would like to play some of his recent compositions for his brother, and he put a record on the phonograph. During the next two hours Andrei played one record after another. Balanchine sat, with his head in his hands, looking down at the floor. Mrs. Molostwoff found the situation unbearable, and she found herself praying that Balanchine would say just one kind word to his brother about his music. But he said nothing and at last Andrei, passing the awkwardness off with a jest, stopped the phonograph. Afterward, Mrs. Molostwoff berated Balanchine for his silence.

"Would it have hurt you so much to make some small compliment about his music?" she said.

"I couldn't," Balanchine replied, looking remorseful and unhappy. "I just couldn't."

So, crowned with laurels, Balanchine and the New York City Ballet returned early in December to New York. He rested and convalesced, recovering his strength and health, while the company prepared its annual pre-Christmas performance of *The Nutcracker,* and then Balanchine settled down to choreograph two new works for the forthcoming spring season.

CHAPTER THIRTEEN

The Essential Tradition

In 1969 the School of American Ballet moved to spacious, handsome quarters at the new Juilliard School at Lincoln Center. For some thirteen years before that the school and the New York City Ballet had shared studios on the upper floor of a decrepit two-story building at Eighty-third Street and Broadway. Balanchine lived not far from Lincoln Center and he would go back and forth between his apartment and the school or theatre several times a day. As he walked briskly along Broadway, he was continually greeted—by dancers in the company, young students of the school, ballet mothers on their way to pick up their children after class, by other performers involved with Lincoln Center, and by members of the public who happened to recognize him. He responded with courtly bows left and right as he walked along. The neighborhood around Lincoln Center was something of a melange; within a few blocks were discount stores, a car rental agency, delicatessens, coffee shops, laundromats. The scene was one that might well perplex a visiting balletomane of another era—Degas, say, or Théophile Gautier, or Czar Alexander III, or Louis XIV—but once inside Balanchine's studios, watching a class or a rehearsal in progress in one of the large practice rooms, the visitor would have felt himself quite at home. Degas' painter's eye would have been as fascinated by what went on here as it was by the compositions it caught at the Paris Opéra ballet three quarters of a century before. In their essential quality, ballet studios have changed less than most things in the three hundred years since the basic principles of ballet technique were worked out at the court of Louis XIV.

∿ Company class.

291

To see Balanchine in this environment was to be reminded how much tradition meant to him and how much a part of tradition he was, for all his contemporaneity and his innovations—to see him take his place in a line of ballet masters extending back in time through Petipa, and Didelot before him, to Noverre and Lully. He did, in fact, believe that he was anointed by apostolic succession to carry on and extend this tradition. One discerned Balanchine's traditionalism most clearly, perhaps, in his attitude toward his school, for the curriculum he established was much like the one he went through as a boy in St. Petersburg. That, in turn, though it stressed accelerated tempos and bravura movements, was much like the system of training that Didelot had brought from France to Russia a hundred years before. Some of the teachers Balanchine employed— such as Felia Doubrovska, Pierre Vladimirov, Anatole Oboukhoff, and Alexandra Danilova—were themselves a living link to the past.

Balanchine himself conducted a daily class for the company, as well as an occasional class for advanced students. I remember the first time I saw him teach. It was around 1960, in the old studios on Broadway. It was an advanced class of about twenty pupils, including several on this occasion who were leading dancers of the New York City Ballet. For the space of an hour and a half Balanchine worked his class intensively through the fundamental positions and steps that are the vocabulary of ballet; he walked about the room from one dancer to another, correcting this one's stance in the fourth position, and that one's arabesque, and tossed off piquant comments to the group as he moved about. He was good-humored, agreeable, yet demanding. Stopping before Diana Adams, he sought to get her to increase the turnout of hips, legs, and feet that is the curiously satisfying basis of ballet technique. "Push the heel forward— more, still more! Open the hips!" he told her. Then, assuming a natural position, with toes pointed forward, he said to the group as a whole, "Anybody can stand like this. But when you force it, like this—" and he forced his toes and hips outward—"then you feel you've done something." With a smile, he told a small, very young-looking brunette in the second row, "Don't ask why it must be like this. Don't analyze. Just do it." He moved on to développé à la seconde—a sidewise unfolding and extending of the leg that, he said, must be as elegantly continuous as the movement of an elephant's trunk, and he illustrated this with a gesture of the arm that at once made it uncannily both a leg and a trunk. Then the dancers went on to leaps, and he reminded them of how the upflung arms pull the body into the air, of the composition they must make in space at

Teaching company class in the early 1960's. Among those distinguishable in this photo are Patricia Wilde, Maria Tallchief, Kay Mazzo, Suzanne Farrell, Melissa Hayden, and Jacques d'Amboise.

the top of their leap, and of the crucial importance of coming down softly. He had them line up and go separately across the room in a sequence combining a gliding step, a leap, an intermediate step, and another leap. When Violette Verdy had done this, he called her back and had her try it again, telling her that she must push forward on the glide, not rest on it. Miss Verdy, who was dressed in a bright-blue sweater and black tights, with her golden hair in a shining topknot, nodded eagerly as she listened. As she went through it again, Balanchine cried at the start of her second leap, "Stay up in the air!" and, incredibly, she seemed to obey this impossible command, hovering momentarily in space like a hummingbird. There were gasps of appreciation from the other dancers. Balanchine nodded, the faintest trace of a smile on his lips. "Tha . . . at's right," he said. "You're getting it."

CHAPTER FOURTEEN

What's the Matter with Now?

ONDAY, AUGUST 21, 1973: It's noon and quite hot. A breeze that can be seen though not felt stirs the tops of the eucalyptuses and pines that rim the Greek Theatre in Griffith Park in Los Angeles, where the New York City Ballet is on tour. Fortunately, it's not very smoggy today, not yet. It's possible to take a deep breath without choking, and one can actually discern the blue of the sky above the milky haze. Up on the stage George Balanchine is conducting company class. In these classes, it is his practice to concentrate on some particular aspect for a large part of the hour-and-a-half session. Today he seems to be working his dancers mostly on assemblés—vertical jumps, done sometimes from a stationary position, sometimes after a glissade, a pas de bourrée, or other small step. Balanchine is stressing that the two legs must come together in the air with the toes pointed and must be absolutely together for the landing, in the fifth position. The landing must be at the identical spot on which the dancer began. Before takeoff and on landing the knees must bend in a demi-plié. A strong demi-plié on landing is actually the most crucial part of the jump. It's not how high you go that gives the illusion of height and ease, he reminds them, for Nijinsky's elevation was actually only a few inches higher than that of a run-of-the-mill performer. What's important is how you land. While what he is imparting is essentially what he learned at the Imperial Theatre School, he has, he says, speeded up the process. He likes to say that he has taken

Balanchine (right) and Jerome Robbins, as two beggars in the finale of the premiere performance of Pulcinella at the 1972 Stravinsky Festival.

295

the cholesterol out of it. The accent, in his nasal twang, falls on the last syllable—"cho-les-ter-rol." He also says that in his teaching he is more demanding than were his Russian teachers, that he stuffs his dancers with more technique—force-feeds them like a Strasbourg goose. I've told him the two metaphors seem contradictory, or at least hard to digest, but he denies that. Anyway, he declares the result is what counts: in the one case, *paté de fois gras truffée de Strasbourg*; in the other, the Balanchine style of dance.

On the stage this morning, being put through their paces, are such leading dancers as Jacques d'Amboise, Patricia McBride, Kay Mazzo, John Clifford, Peter Martins, Karin von Aroldingen, Sara Leland, Anthony Blum, Jean-Pierre Bonnefous, and Helgi Tomasson. D'Amboise moves cautiously through the sequences that the others behind and around him are doing full out. He has been out for a couple of months with a torn cartilage in his right knee, for which he has had an operation. Ballet dancers are vulnerable. The profession is risky, and brutal on the body. Violette Verdy and Gelsey Kirkland are also out with injuries at the moment. D'Amboise looks dark under the eyes. As he essays his leaps, his face wears a questioning, introspective look, as if he is monitoring his body—his body which is his instrument and his livelihood, and which throughout his professional life he has entrusted to Balanchine for the accomplishment of whatever Balanchine has seen fit to ask of him. D'Amboise is thirty-nine years old, has been one of the world's most dazzling male dancers since he was seventeen, and may well be wondering at this moment if he will ever again do a virtuoso role.

Also onstage are numerous lesser-known soloists and members of the corps de ballet. When the company made its second trip to Russia (in 1972), many Russian ballet teachers and dancers flocked to the studios to watch Balanchine teach. They expressed surprise at finding principal dancers, soloists, and corps-de-ballet members all taking class together. In the Russian companies the classes are segregated, for it is assumed that the corps members neither need to practice technique as difficult as the soloists', nor are capable of doing so. Balanchine's expectations for his corps are much higher; the corps gets more challenging and varied assignments in the New York City Ballet than in most other companies. On any given night, in fact, several dancers who are nominally corps-de-ballet members may be seen dancing solo parts, and often to great acclaim.

Rehearsal follows class, after a short break. By this time a number of spectators have filtered into the Greek Theatre and are scattered about the seats of the orchestra section. Some of them are probably friends of company members; others may simply be visitors to the park who noticed an open gate and wandered in. Onstage, under Balanchine's calm, merciless gaze, the performers work through the ballets they will present this evening and the two following evenings: *Swan Lake, An Evening's Waltzes,* and *Tchaikovsky Suite No. 3.* The stage is concrete, very hard on the feet, and the dancers are unhappy about that. Balanchine sympathizes. He offers to simplify, for safety reasons, a terrifying leaping turn that Helgi Tomasson has to make in the Tchaikovsky, ending on one knee with upflung arm. Tomasson is a quiet, slim, black-haired young man who was brought up in Iceland. He joined the company in 1970, one of a trio of newcomers who in recent years have strengthened the company's male contingent, the other two being Peter Martins, from the Royal Danish Ballet, and Jean-Pierre Bonnefous, from the Paris Opéra Ballet. Tomasson is rather small in build, but he has a beautiful line. His technique is clear and pure, perhaps the purest of any male now dancing. For some reason or other, he is not a great crowd pleaser. Perhaps his dancing is too pure—or perhaps too impersonal. He is a dancer's dancer. He thanks Balanchine for his consideration but says he'd prefer not to have the step changed; he'd like to do it the way it's supposed to go.

Balanchine is wearing gray slacks, a blue sport shirt with turned-up cuffs, and sandals. On his right wrist is a turquoise bracelet. In the early sixties, at the time of the company's first trip to Russia, Balanchine looked at times almost cadaverous. His face was gaunt, his body as spare as any of his dancers. But he is plumper now, with even the suggestion of a belly. His posture and movements are still elegant, though, and still vital. Now that his cheeks have filled out, his aquiline nose no longer seems so prominent. His face is without wrinkles still. His eyes are penetrating, his eyebrows haughty. He has looked out at the world in just that way all his life; there's a photograph of him at the age of four that is quite frightening in the implacable authority of the child's gaze.

TUESDAY: The company's having a good time this afternoon. They're at Falcon Studios—a low, rambling, wooden building on Hollywood Boulevard near Western Avenue. This is where they work most of the time during their Los Angeles stay; they rehearse at the Greek Theatre only on the days when they are scheduled to present a new program. They have just finished class and are working on *Pulcinella.* This ballet is not on the Los Angeles programs but is scheduled to be performed three times at Wolf Trap Farm Park, outside Washington, D.C., where the company will begin a short engagement next week. Balanchine and Jerome Robbins collaborated on *Pulcinella*. They put it together in a great rush for the Stravinsky Festival the previous summer, that extraordinary occasion in commemoration of what would have been Stravinsky's ninetieth birthday, when the New York City Ballet staged thirty Stravinsky ballets in eight days, twenty-one of them brand new. Now Balanchine is going through it with the ensemble, smoothing out rough patches and putting in new choreography here and there as the fancy strikes him.

Pulcinella is a mime ballet, with broad comedic action; it's part *commedia dell'arte*, part pure Marx Brothers, with lots of visual gags and buffoonery. The plot line is a takeoff on the Faust legend—a compact with the devil made by a clown. Balanchine is in high spirits this afternoon. He is all over the place. He leaps, he twirls, he staggers like a drunk, bows like a courtier, sighs like a love-struck girl. He is acting out and dancing all the parts. His characterizations are always vivid, pungent. His movements are broad, zestful, extravagant, yet always elegant. All great comics have been elegant—Chaplin, Keaton, Harpo Marx, Zero Mostel, even Jackie Gleason—and Balanchine seems fully aware of what the elegant line does for the buffoonish point. For Carol Sumner, Pulcinella's girlfriend, he mimes tender femininity. For Edward Villella, the Pulcinella, he does a vomiting sequence, staggering around holding his belly. For a quintet of musicians, he choreographs a new variation, having them saw away at their imaginary instruments until they are playing so low they are only inches off the ground. None of them gets down as low as he does, so none of them is quite as funny on their first try; they lack his extravagance. A moment later he is being a solemn constable, and then a gross wench. The wenches are played by a couple of men in the company who will wear monstrous padded bosoms and be partnered by the constables. Balanchine sketches out a miniature romantic passage for them, culminating in a sauté and an airy lift. "Now you get a chance to be Margot Fonteyn," he tells the men, as their constable partners hoist them.

There aren't many ballets like this in the company's repertory, consisting as it does mostly of plotless works, and the company seems to be finding this one an agreeable change. They joke and laugh as they work and applaud some of Balanchine's characterizations. None of them, it is apparent, is as free and easy in the mime gestures as Balanchine, in part

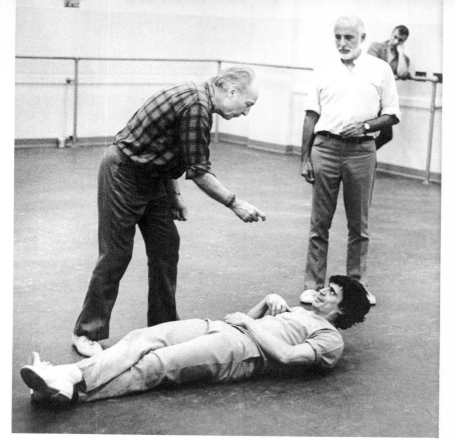

As Robbins watches, Balanchine shows how the Devil will resurrect Pulcinella (Villella) from his coffin in the opening scene.

perhaps because he has given them so little opportunity in the past to develop this sort of talent. Seeing how happily, and how expressively, he mimes when the work calls for it, one can't help wonder that he has indulged this side of himself so little in the more than two hundred ballets he has choreographed in his life.

Now he wants to show Carol Sumner how she should unveil as Pulcinella's bride. He hurries to the side of the studio and comes back with an orange towel, which he drapes over his head for the veil. His gesture as he then lifts it off is proud—the gesture of a woman who knows she is beautiful. "It's like you say, 'Look! Here I am!'" The joke here is that Pulcinella will not be entranced but disappointed; he had hoped to find some wonderful new creature under the veil, but it turns out to be just his familiar mistress. Carol Sumner is, in fact, beautiful, but she doesn't unveil as confidently as Balanchine. For one instant, as this man nearly seventy years old lifts an orange towel from his head, we have the illusion that we are being shown a great beauty and are privileged.

Carol Sumner is still in the process of mastering the role, for it was set originally on Violette Verdy. Miss Sumner says something to Balanchine and he replies cheerfully, "Don't worry. I change my mind all the time. If I didn't, I'd still be doing the things people did a hundred years ago."

Villella has a split leap to do at one point. Balanchine talks to him about it. Villella nods. Facing each other, smiling slightly, both of them go up in the air together like a dancer and his mirror image. "That's better," says Balanchine.

Periodically he has the group run through what they have worked up so far. As he watches, he takes a characteristic stance, hands at his front pockets, eyes intent—like a gunfighter about to execute a fast draw. From time to time he consults with Rosemary Dunleavy, the assistant ballet mistress, as to how certain parts went in last year's production. The choreography is preserved mostly in the muscles and nerves of the dancers, rather than on paper or film. Sitting on a chair by the piano, however, is the company's official notator, or choreologist as he is titled, a man named Jurg Lanzrein, who is jotting down symbols on a large pad as he takes note of this or that bit of action. Eventually he will have a written record of the ballet in the notation method known as the Benesh system. In the three years he has been with the company, he has notated twenty-two ballets. In the future, presumably, someone familiar with that notation system should then be able to reconstruct those ballets quite successfully from his notations alone. So far, though, when some outside company says it would like to mount a Balanchine ballet, the work is likely to be transmitted not through Benesh notation but by someone like Rosemary Dunleavy or the ballet master John Taras or some other company member with a retentive memory who knows all the steps of all the dancers in that ballet by heart, who will fly to Paris or Copenhagen or wherever it may be, to teach the ballet to those who will have to dance it.

All during the rehearsal today, problems have been arising with the accompanist—some confusion as to the cuing of entrances and episodes. It turns out that the marked copy of the score, the one on which cues were penciled in when the ballet was being choreographed, had been left behind through some oversight, so they are having to work with an unmarked copy. Here would be a classic opportunity for Balanchine to throw a temper tantrum, if he were a person of such a temperament. But

Balanchine and Violette Verdy rehearse the exquisite refinements of a kick in the behind.

Balanchine and Robbins show the men in the cast the flat-footed hoofing sequence in the finale.

he is not. He simply goes over to the piano, saying, "Let's mark everything again." With the assistance of Rosemary Dunleavy and suggestions from some of the dancers, he goes rapidly through the whole score with the accompanist, putting down those cryptic cues—"boys' lifts," "attitude," "wheelbarrow," "split leaps"—that will be convenient points of reference during rehearsals. This takes about fifteen minutes. That's precious rehearsal time. There are only a limited number of minutes available—one hundred twenty all told—to devote to *Pulcinella* before they get to Wolf Trap, and Balanchine is responsible for every one of those minutes, for making sure that what has to be done gets done. Watching the way he is working at improving *Pulcinella* at this session, and the way he has responded to this unanticipated interruption, I am reminded how fortunate is his nature—that he is someone who always does the best he can under the circumstances and then never frets over what he may have failed to do. If a ballet he has done proves imperfect, he will improve it when he finds the time, as he is doing now with *Pulcinella*. If it still fails to satisfy, he will drop it from the repertory without a qualm and make something new to take its place. Only someone who is prolific can operate with that kind of assurance.

I also find myself recognizing another trait of his, which I feel I had not sufficiently appreciated in the past—his organizational ability. The way he manages the complex logistics of his enterprises—the making of a ballet, the running of a company and a school—makes me think he could probably run a corporation, if he was of a mind. Everyone pays homage to his artistry, few have recognized his practicality.

It's time to resume at the section where he left off to mark the score. A clap of the hand is followed by the quiet but authoritative, "Aa . . . aa . . . aaand one!" Dancers and pianist come in unhesitatingly on the beat, with no need for preliminary explanation or palaver. Balanchine's "Aa . . . aa . . . aaand" is the great mobilizer to action, to beauty, the rouser of somnolent bodies, the whip for the trained lions.

At a little after two there's a short break. Some of the dancers are free to leave now. As Carol Sumner departs, Balanchine says to her, "Be prepared to dance this—in Wolf Trap." She raises her eyebrows. "Violette is still limping. In her foot—and I think," Balanchine says, putting his hand over his heart, "here as well."

During the break Balanchine relaxes in a director's chair near the piano, and Villella sits on the floor near him. Balanchine comments on the vitality of the music. I say to him, "Didn't you work out some choreography for *Pulcinella* when you were still a student in Russia, maybe fifty years ago?"

"More than fifty, probably. How old was I when I first saw this score? Maybe seventeen." As Villella listens with some fascination, Balanchine recalls that as soon as he came across this Stravinsky score he began trying to make dances for parts of it, just to see what might be done. That was possibly around 1921, the year Balanchine graduated from ballet school, though it may have been a couple of years later, when he was working with his Young Ballet. "We didn't have much music to dance to then—Minkus, Fritz Kreisler, like that. I set one of the Ravel waltzes around that time, I remember. And I composed music myself for some pas de deux." He laughs. "One of them was a *ro-man-za*." He drawls the word, a touch of self-mockery. "I was lazy, so I had Gusev dance and I played the piano." The Gusev he mentions went on to a distinguished career as a dancer, choreographer, and teacher with both the Bolshoi Ballet and the Kirov. The girl who danced that pas de deux with him was the brilliant Olga Mungalova. "Another of our group of young people liked to write poetry," Balanchine goes on, "and he wrote some lyrics for my *ro-man-za.*"

"Who was that?" I ask.

"Mravinsky. He's now music director of the Leningrad Philharmonic."

The break is ending. The moment of reminiscence is over. Back to work they go on the musicians' sequence. New steps, new bits of business emerge. The musicians are in a semi-circle around Villella. Balanchine provides them with a variation that requires some of them to turn around and back toward the audience. "I want to show Berman's behind," says Balanchine playfully. "I mean the backs of Berman's costumes. Because they're so fantastic. So you do like this—like a model." They proceed to model, carrying themselves as if clad in the most resplendent garb. The effect is quite an amazing illusion, for what they are actually wearing at the moment is a mishmash of practice attire. One young man wears cut-off jeans, another orange bathing trunks, another a striped rugby shirt. Villella has on black tights and a black Syracuse University T-shirt. His comic vomiting section, as the music gulps and burbles, ends this section.

The section is now quite firmly set. Balanchine declares himself satisfied. There are still three minutes left, though, so there will be one more run-through of this section. "I've learned how to cheat the union," Balanchine remarks to me. He is referring to the dancers' union, the American Guild of Musical Artists.

"How?" I ask.

"I do everything before."

"Before what?"

"Before it is too late."

WEDNESDAY: Melissa Hayden is at rehearsal this afternoon. She is working on *Cortège Hongrois,* the ballet that Balanchine fabricated to some of Glazunov's *Raymonda* music especially as a farewell present for her, a public homage. She is fifty years old and is retiring from the company after dancing with it for twenty-two years, much of that time as the leading ballerina, though the company, with its aversion to the star system, would never say so. Her final performance as a company member is scheduled for September 1, at Wolf Trap. *Cortège Hongrois* seems to me an unsuitable present. Romantic schmaltz in the Russian-ballerina vein has never been her forte. She has been marvelous in dramatic roles—in *Medea* or *The Cage,* for instance—or in parts that require keen wit, such

Edward Villella.

as her *Stars and Stripes* or *Agon* roles. I have been told that Balanchine was heard to say as he was choreographing *Cortège Hongrois*, "Wait till Millie goes. I'll change everything around for Pat McBride, and it will look wonderful." A cruel remark, if it was made, but Melissa Hayden, an indomitable force in her own right, is equal to coping with all the ambiguity of the occasion. She is going to treat this ballet as if it did in fact show her off like a precious jewel. She is going to wear a look of triumph even when she finds the choreography awkward or uncongenial. She will carry it off, and at every performance she gives of it till her publicized final appearance audiences will cheer and weep.

Partnering her at this rehearsal is Peter Martins, the tall, blond, handsome Dane. Balanchine is half sitting on a low red table in front of the mirror. Beside him sits young John Clifford, wearing white pants and sneakers. The *danseur noble* part in *Cortège* that Martins is learning is one that Clifford knows. The part was set originally last May on Jacques d'Amboise, who got hurt after two performances. Clifford, as the quickest study in the company, stepped into the breach, but Martins, being bigger and more noble-looking than Clifford, is considered preferable for the part. Martins will dance it with Miss Hayden tomorrow night if he can learn the part in time. If not, Clifford can always fill in again. Meanwhile Clifford is being helpful. Eager and energetic, he keeps bouncing out on the floor to show Martins how this or that step goes, and he makes himself available to Balanchine for consultation. Balanchine goes out onto the floor, too, from time to time, but he doesn't look as spry and exuberant as he did yesterday. He is limping somewhat, and his face looks rather haggard. He hurt his knee during rehearsal yesterday, the same knee that originally suffered a torn cartilage in 1927 and was operated on then. On and off ever since, the knee has been bothersome. Today I see him push at it with both hands every so often, and wince.

After the rehearsal session ends, I see Balanchine and Clifford talking together at one side of the studio. I join them and learn that Clifford is trying to get Balanchine's appraisal of two ballets Clifford has choreographed, using a young Los Angeles ballet troupe and showing them to Balanchine here at the studios just before the beginning of today's rehearsal. Clifford, who is twenty-six, aspires to distinction as a choreographer; the New York City Ballet has performed six ballets he had made in the past five years. Clifford is not having much success in getting Balanchine to talk, but he persists.

"Well, what about the Bach in general?" he asks. One of the two ballets is called *Bachiana* and makes use of three pieces by Bach—an arioso, a preludium, and the "Sleepers Awake" aria. Balanchine sniffs. "First of all," he says at last, "I don't like the music—the Ormandy transcription."

Clifford asks him how he liked the fugue part.

Balanchine says, "I don't know. You still have to learn to be more polyphonic."

"Visually?"

"Yes, visually."

After several more questions that produce only shrugs or cryptic responses, Clifford asks, "Well, what about the other piece—the Mayuzumi?"

"Awful!" replies Balanchine. "The music is awful."

"But I thought you liked Mayuzumi." In 1963 Balanchine had used Mayuzumi's music for his ballet, *Bugaku.*

"He used to be all right. Now he's *passé.*" With a sniff and a wave of the hand, Balanchine dismisses Mayuzumi.

Clifford persists. "Well, did you like anything you saw? If you would tell me what things you like, I would know when I am doing right."

Balanchine shrugs, says nothing. Clifford waits. Eventually, Balanchine says, "Well, the steps aren't bad."

"To the Bach?"

"To the Mayuzumi. Only the music is so awful. Why don't you find some other music to go with those steps you've made?"

Clifford looks baffled. The suggestion must seem particularly odd, coming as it does from the choreographer who, more than any other, derives his inspiration from the music. "Do you mean it?" Clifford asks.

"Yes, why not?"

"Well, I don't know," says Clifford. "Like what?"

"Something pretty," says Balanchine. "You do that." He starts to go.

Clifford, still hoping for guidance, tries to prolong the conversation. "Well, what do you think of Hovhaness?"

"Who?"

"Hovhaness."

"Awful!" says Balanchine. With a courteous nod, he says good-bye.

"I'm ready to dance *Cortège* if you need me," Clifford calls after him.

He seems no whit downcast by Balanchine's unresponsiveness and lack of enthusiasm. I know from conversations I've had with Clifford that he reveres Balanchine and his work. It's evident that he would dearly love more guidance from the Master, perhaps even a smidgen of praise. But it's also evident that he knows how rare praise from Balanchine is and has adapted himself to surviving without it—as have all the others in the company. He has told me that Balanchine has only once complimented him on his choreography. The compliment was worded, "You are just like Jerry Robbins—you both have the same faults."

I leave the studio with Balanchine and Melissa Hayden. I am driving them back to their hotel—the Montecito, a residential hotel on Franklin Avenue in Hollywood. Balanchine is in the front seat, Miss Hayden in back. As we drive west along Hollywood Boulevard, the two of them talk about Clifford—not about his choreography but about his amazing facility as a dancer. "He can learn a part just by watching somebody dance it once," says Miss Hayden.

"He knows all the girls' parts as well as the boys'," Balanchine says to me. "He'd be as happy to fill in for Melissa as for Peter."

Balanchine and I have planned to have a talk this evening. We meet backstage at the Greek Theatre shortly before performance time. Balanchine has not been assigned a backstage room of his own, so we are using Allegra Kent's dressing room; she is off tonight. Wearing a blue blazer and a red patterned shirt, Balanchine sits in the chair before the makeup table, and I take a chair nearby. The mirror reflects his profile as we talk.

I have said that I would be interested in his appraisal of what has happened to him in the past decade. He replies, "It's all in the programs," as if he had had no life except what his company has danced. "Basically, it's a continuation of what I've always done," he adds, "except that as I go on, I analyze better, eliminate what's not so necessary. I'm not trying to do things that are original or great. I've never thought like that. What I'm doing is entertainment—en-ter-tain-ment." He lingers on the word for emphasis. "I was brought up in the theatre—an Italian style theatre—with the philosophy that when the public pays money, you have to entertain them. So along with the more complicated things I do, like the ballets to late-Stravinsky music, I always do easier things. That's for the public's sake. For us, for our dancers, there's really no such thing as music that's too difficult. Some music just takes a little more time to work out, that's all."

The backstage public-address system pages some dancer. Balanchine gets up and switches off the speaker over the door. When he has resumed his seat, he talks about his dancers' abilities—how they are better now than dancers used to be, faster, more skillful. At last the company draws its talent almost exclusively from the school and no longer holds auditions for outsiders. And as we talk Balanchine concedes that the New York City Ballet company is finally beginning to look the way he has always wanted a company to look. Because he has known most of his dancers since they were children in the school, working with them is now easier. They know instinctively what he wants; it has been bred into them.

I remark that it must be pleasant for him to be surrounded by so many people who now regard him as something of a father. He replies, with a smile, "They call me 'Mother,'" and adds, gravely, "'Mother' is better than 'Father.'" His muse is female; Terpsichore is his White Goddess.

I ask him if it is possible to tell at an early age whether a child is going to be a great ballerina. I have the romantic notion of a ballet master's taking in at a glance some twelve-year-old at the barre and proclaiming, "That girl will be another Ulanova!"

Balanchine tells me it doesn't work that way. A child may look promising at twelve but terrible at eighteen because as she grows up her body configuration may change. "She may end up with short legs and an enormous body," he says, uttering his vision of the ultimate feminine horror. He adds a theory of heredity I have heard from him before: "In that case, I am certain that the child's mother is short, the father tall, because I believe you inherit your legs from your mother, your body from your father."

There is a distant burst of applause, then, faintly, the strains of music. *Swan Lake* must be beginning onstage. A moment later someone knocks at the door. A couple of young girls put their head in. "Allegra?" inquires one. Balanchine looks under his chair, then in the washbasin, then in a drawer. "Not here," he says. Giggling, the girls retire.

On December 16, 1963, the Ford Foundation announced an unprecedented grant for ballet totaling $7,756,750, nearly all of it to ballet enterprises associated with Balanchine. A few months later, the New York City Ballet inaugurated the State Theater at Lincoln Center, an edifice that was probably the first theatre in history to be designed especially to satisfy the wishes and needs of a choreographer. With those two events Balanchine and the New York City Ballet entered a new era. Jean Cocteau declared in *The Blood of a Poet*, "When you smash a statue, you run the risk of becoming one yourself." For many years Balanchine and his company had been the avante-garde; now they became, in effect, the establishment. From then on the company would be dancing under quite different conditions from those of its impoverished earlier years, before quite different audiences, and would be subject to quite different expectations. Some of Balanchine's devotees, particularly among the intellectuals, were uneasy about the new status and they assumed, because in the modern tradition the artist's role is that of rebel and outsider, that Balanchine too must be feeling twinges. Not so. He took it all as his birthright, though long delayed. What, after all, could be more establishment than the atmosphere in which he had spent his formative years—the Imperial Theatre School, supported by the largesse of the czar of all the Russias? That was hardly a school for the training of outsiders or rebels.

Now, in Allegra Kent's dressing room, he makes it clear how little he shares the nostalgia that one sometimes hears early adherents of the New York City Ballet express for the old City Center on Fifty-fifth Street, where the New York City Ballet was born in 1948 and passed through the perils, travails, and triumphs of the succeeding years. "City Center was like a nest that Baum provided for us when we needed it. But you don't stay in your nest forever. It was like being in high school. The time comes when you move on to the university. We made do there, we improvised, we did the best we could. But the stage was only forty-five feet, we had no wing space, we had no place to put scenery. The State Theater is a *real* theatre. It's big, it's beautiful. The stage is ample, we have room for lots of scenery. It's what I always had in mind. I knew we'd have a theatre like that someday, and so during the time we were at City Center I staged everything so it would also look good on the big stage I expected us eventually to get. I didn't know *how* we were going to get it, but somehow I knew we would."

Of all the buildings in Lincoln Center, he continues, his State Theater is by far the most satisfying—aside, perhaps, from the acoustics. Lincoln Center as a whole looks, he says, rather like an airport—particularly Philharmonic Hall. The Metropolitan Opera seems to him inconsiderately placed for the dowagers and their consorts who are its patrons, because they have to walk so far from their limousines; in a more gracious age sedan chairs would have been provided. He doesn't pay much attention to the business transacted at the meetings of the Lincoln Center Council. Don't the various Lincoln Center constituents have common interests and concerns? I inquire. About all they have in common, he says, is "the *chauffage centrale,*"—the central heating system.

We go on to talk about the consequences of the Ford grant. At the time the grant was announced, a great howl arose from the rest of the dance world—from Martha Graham, Agnes de Mille, Helen Tamiris, Lucia Chase, and the others. As Clive Barnes later wrote in *The New York Times*, "Anyone would have imagined that City Ballet had stolen the money rather than been given it." The grant would create a monopoly, they protested, and all dance companies and schools except those approved by Balanchine would wither away. In actuality, things have worked out very differently; the Ford Foundation grant in fact constituted a breakthrough, benefiting the whole realm of dance. Other foundations, which had previously restricted their grants to scholars or researchers, got the idea that it was legitimate to sponsor performing-arts institutions. Dance in the United States is flourishing now as never before. Surveys show that the number of dance performances has increased more than five hundred percent in just the last ten years, that the total dance audience has increased over six hundred percent, and that the country is now blessed with a diversity of companies and styles such as it never knew before.

As for the New York City Ballet, by 1971–72 it had grown to an enterprise with an annual budget of close to five million dollars. Its deficit had grown commensurately, despite the fact that the company played in New York to houses averaging about eighty-five percent of capacity—for that is the reality of a ballet company, of nearly all the performing-arts institutions. The more they prosper, the more they lose. None can be expected to subsist on box-office receipts alone; almost all require sizable subsidies, whether from foundation grants, federal and state assistance, or private contributions. Before contributions the New York City Ballet deficit for that year was around $1.5 million. As ballet companies go, this can be considered a smallish deficit, compared to the scale of the company's operations. The company earned sixty-eight percent of its total expenses at the box office that year. According to economic studies of the performing arts that have been made, this is an unusually high proportion of costs to earn at the box office. Most major ballet companies in the world don't expect to earn much more than half of their expenses at best. Some earn much less.

In the 1971–72 year the New York City Ballet presented two hundred and thirty performances, which were attended by an estimated total audience of well over half a million people. This was far more performances than the Bolshoi or the Royal Ballet gave. In all, the company performed thirty-five weeks: twenty-three weeks at its New York City home, the

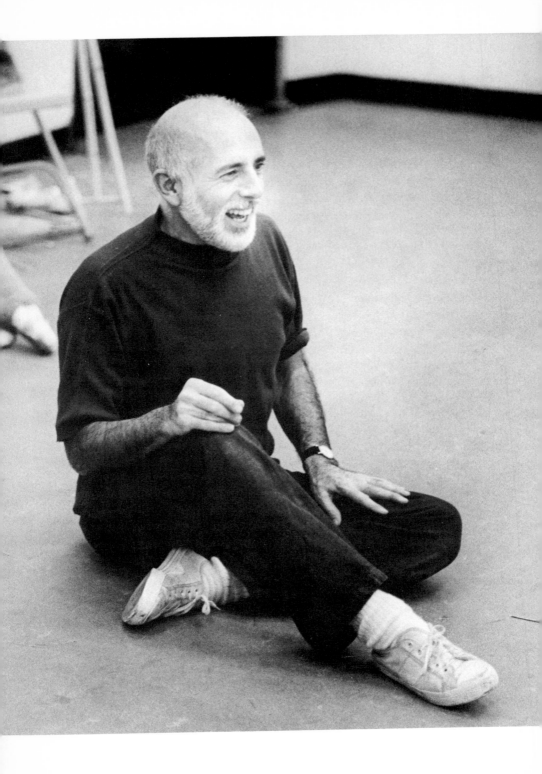

State Theater; four weeks at the Saratoga Performing Arts Festival in upstate New York, which has been the company's summer home since 1966; a week at Ravinia; a week at Wolf Trap Farm Park; a week at Munich, during the Olympic Games; four weeks in the Soviet Union; and a week in Poland.

Comparatively little of all this performing activity actually was the consequence of Ford Foundation assistance. As Balanchine now reminds me, that grant—much of which was spread out over ten years—was mostly for education. "Now we can give more than twice as many scholarships as before," he says. "We help those students who are poor to finish their high-school education while studying ballet. A lot of that money was for other ballet schools throughout the country, and we send out representatives to look at what they're doing, and advise. I go myself, sometimes." Shaking a finger at me, he says, "I personally added to Ford. You see, education for education's sake means nothing. After dancers have learned what they can learn, they have to have ballets to dance. So I give anybody in America who asks, small schools, big schools, whatever—I give them my ballets free. The critics accuse me of taking Ford's millions, but they never mention this thing I do. No one else gives their ballets free. If I wanted to charge for the rights to my ballets, I could be a millionaire."

Balanchine seems to be still smarting over the protests and criticism that the Ford grant engendered. Nevertheless, he is manifestly gratified by what has happened to his ballet school in recent years, with the Ford Foundation's help. The School of American Ballet has unquestionably become the national academy for classical ballet. Its new quarters at Juilliard are elegant. The faculty is distinguished. And the school need no longer accept any but the most promising of applicants, who come now from all over the country. It places its graduates in every major company in North America and Europe except the Royal Ballet, which is limited only to British subjects. "Our company can't any longer absorb all the good dancers coming out of the school," Balanchine tells me. "They keep coming and coming. So the other companies take them. Six or seven girls were just taken on by the Geneva ballet. So our American dancers are now influencing Europe."

Whenever possible, he tells me, he likes to include parts in the company's ballets for children from the school. He has never forgotten what an enchantment and a revelation it was for him when, at the age of ten,

Jerome Robbins.

he appeared in his first performance at the Maryinsky. So in recent years, in addition to *The Nutcracker,* he has provided roles for many children from the school in such ballets as *A Midsummer Night's Dream, Harlequinade, Don Quixote,* and *Choral Variations on Bach's "Von Himmel Hoch"*; and Jerome Robbins has also choreographed for children, using fifty-four girls from the school in his *Circus Polka* for the Stravinsky Festival. "The children are becoming part of our lives now," Balanchine says.

There is another knock at the door, and Edward Bigelow, the company's assistant manager, comes in. He is wearing a black Mao jacket. "Do you want me to remind you to call Ira Gershwin?" he asks.

Balanchine has been on friendly terms with Ira Gershwin at least since 1937 when both were working on the movie *The Goldwyn Follies.* More recently, Gershwin and Balanchine were associated on *Who Cares?* a ballet to Gershwin songs that Balanchine choreographed in 1970. To Bigelow's question, Balanchine replies, "Well, his letter asked me to call at six. It's after nine now, he may be in bed. Better I do it tomorrow."

As Bigelow leaves, I hear the music beginning for the second ballet on the program—the Prokofiev music that Jerome Robbins has used for *An Evening's Waltzes.* Lilting, yet somber, it is music that leaves one uneasy, and Robbins' choreography, which comes to my mind as I hear the orchestra in the distance, well matches its ambiguities.

I don't remember what moved Balanchine to do so—whether it was something I said or what—but he has begun talking about his view of himself and his role, talking as seriously as I have heard him talk. He is both a mystic and a fatalist. "I am only a servant, that's all," he says, his hands spread open, like a supplicant's. "I am a waiter—for God. We are all servants of God, or destiny, whatever you wish to call it. I am not so proud, and I am not so great—I'm nothing but what He has wanted me to be. He has said to me, 'You are going to teach and serve and make them dance,' and I know that nothing anybody on earth could do could prevent me from doing what He wants me to do. And as soon as He says, '*Fini*. That's enough for you'"—Balanchine whistles, as one would when summoning a dog—"then I will go." He nods, regarding me. His face, expressionless except for the searching intensity of the eyes, is like the face on an icon. "It's like with Stravinsky. They—the heavenly hosts—said to him, 'It's beautiful what you've done. You've left a fantastic amount of things. That's all we want you to do—you can't do any more than that.' And they took him away."

He goes on to talk about the spiritual assistance he gets from composers in heaven with whom he is in touch when he makes a ballet. They help only those who really like their work, he says, and they can't be fooled—they know very well the difference between those who fake admiration and those who are sincere in it.

But what does their help consist of? I ask. How is it manifested?

"Well, often we prepare a big ballet, by Tchaikovsky, say," he replies. "We have just a short time, and not enough money. The day comes, it's six o'clock. The dancers don't know their parts, some are sick, the orchestra hasn't had enough rehearsal time, the costumes look terrible, we haven't had a chance to plan the lighting. And then it's time for the ballet to go on—and all of a sudden everything looks wonderful. That's *his* doing." He points to the heavens, "Tchaikovsky's."

I respond that in my experience just about every theatrical production has run a similar course, but Balanchine is not to be swayed by such skepticism. He knows what he knows.

As we talk, and particularly as we talk about composers, Stravinsky's name is often on his lips. Balanchine tells me that he has recently been reading a new book containing letters written by Petipa to Tchaikovsky, detailing how many variations he will need in the new ballet they are doing, and specifying just how long the music for the variations should be—in one instance, forty-five seconds. "It reminds me of when I would work with Stravinsky—like on *Orpheus* or *Danses Concertantes*—and we would talk in much the same way. 'How long do you think such and such a variation ought to be?' he would ask me. 'A minute and five seconds,' I would say. 'I think a minute and six, maybe,' he would answer. And he was only half-joking. For Stravinsky one second was an enormous difference."

With pleasure, Balanchine recalls Stravinsky's wry humor. "I was staying with him when we were working on *Orpheus*. He had written something—*Scènes de Ballet*—that Billy Rose had commissioned him to do for the show *Seven Lively Arts*. Dolin and Markova were to dance it. The pas de deux was beautiful. The melody was played by a trumpet—a beautiful silver sound, like something you might hear in the woods. But dancers, ballerinas—they really don't believe anything sounds as beautiful as a violin. That's what they really love to dance to—all that heartthrob, you know. So the morning after the first performance a telegram arrives from Dolin, saying, 'Ballet great success but if you would allow violin to play pas de deux instead of trumpet it would be a triumph.' Stravinsky immediately writes a telegram in reply: 'Satisfied with great success.'"

Along with Stravinsky's wit, he recalls Stravinsky's gaiety. "He is like a child, so lighthearted, so funny, so playful. He loved games. He had childlike enthusiasms. It's always such a pleasure to be with him." About half the time when Balanchine is talking about Stravinsky he uses the present tense, as if Stravinsky were still among us. When I remark on this, Balanchine responds, "But he *is* still here. Absolutely! He's in this room right now. And the whole Stravinsky Festival, he was with us all the time, flying around in the air and loving every minute."

Of that occasion the British critic Richard Buckle wrote in the London *Sunday Times,* "There has never been anything like this festival before in the history of ballet." New York City, with its muggers, mobs, and derelicts, he wrote, was like a glimpse of hell, but to climb the steps to the golden promenade of the State Theater that week in June of 1972 when Balanchine and his company paid homage to the whole range of Igor Stravinsky's music was like entering heaven, night after night. The festival cost $347,000, but box-office receipts, contributions, and various economies made up eventually for about $300,000 of the outlay. The logistics of preparing all the works while carrying on the normal spring season repertory were, in Lincoln Kirstein's words, "like a miniature Normandy invasion." So many ballets were being prepared simultaneously that sometimes the choreographers had to rehearse them with different dancers than those who would be performing them on the stage. Then those dancers would somehow find the time to teach the roles to those who would eventually perform. No other company beside the New York City Ballet could have put on such a festival; no other company would have even thought of trying. And in the life of that company it was a high water mark, a conjunction of dedication and achievement such as may happen once in a lifetime. Those who participated recollect the experience with awe, as a time when they outdid themselves, submitting to a larger vision. For all the strain and effort, it was a happy week—not a commemoration for the dead Stravinsky, but a celebration of the living spirit. On opening night Balanchine told the audience that Stravinsky had merely "taken leave of absence" and was with them now. "I spoke to him on the telephone, and he said, 'George, it's all yours.'" And on the last night of that week, when Balanchine and Kirstein came before the curtains and invited the audience to join them in a toast to Stravinsky, the two of them seemed assured—and so perhaps were some of the audience by then—that somewhere the composer must be lifting a glass in response.

For a few years preceding the festival, some critics had taken to asserting that Balanchine was all through. He had unquestionably done great things in his lifetime, they said, but it had become painfully apparent that he had now lost his creative powers and was foisting trivialities and pale imitations of himself on the public. Such Balanchine ballets as *PAMTGG*—a costly attempt at a pop ballet, done in 1971 to a setting of the commercial jingle "Pan Am Makes the Going Great"—they declared an intolerable embarrassment, a waste of everybody's time, spirit, and money, and a prime example of the sad decline of a former master who didn't know when to quit. Meanwhile Jerome Robbins had returned to the company as a ballet master in 1969, after having devoted himself mostly to musical comedy and theatre for more than a decade, and he was turning out some remarkable ballets: *Dances at a Gathering, In the Night, The Goldberg Variations, Watermill,* and *An Evening's Waltzes.* These Robbins ballets, said the critics who disparaged Balanchine, were the only worthwhile new works now being offered by the New York City Ballet. But that judgment—that Balanchine was all through—was effectively laid to rest by what Balanchine did for the Stravinsky Festival.

In addition to his collaborative effort on *Pulcinella*, Balanchine choreographed seven ballets: *Symphony in Three Movements, Violin Concerto, Danses Concertantes, Divertimento from "Le Baiser de la Fée," Scherzo a la Russe, Duo Concertant,* and *Choral Variations on Bach's "Von Himmel Hoch."* Of the other twelve new ballets presented, Jerome Robbins did four, John Taras three, Todd Bolender two, and one each was done by John Clifford, Richard Tanner, and Lorca Massine (Frederick Ashton and Antony Tudor were also invited to participate, but declined.) At least three of the ballets Balanchine choreographed—*Violin Concerto, Symphony in Three Movements,* and *Duo Concertant*—have been hailed as masterworks, extending a degree further the possibilities of the art of dance. And the *Danses Concertantes,* the *Divertimento,* and the *Choral Variations* are also each in their way works of extraordinary beauty. The assurance and facility with which Balanchine worked as he was choreographing these ballets, along with participating in all the myriad decisions involved in putting on the festival, amazed even those who had long been associated with him. It is probable that the weeks in which Balanchine was preparing his Stravinsky Festival ballets were the most intensely creative period of his life.

As we talk, I seek now to elicit from Balanchine what his preferences are among his ballets. It is a futile attempt, as I had suspected it would

Violin Concerto—with Kay Mazzo (upper left), Karin von Aroldingen and Jean-Pierre Bonnefous (upper right and lower left), and Kay Mazzo and Peter Martins (lower right).

be. The only ballet he mentions in response is *Violin Concerto,* and what he says about it is that it is "well done," meaning technically it is a satisfactory accomplishment. He used the same music for *Balustrade* in 1941. Increasingly these days Balanchine resists giving his ballets any title other than the one the composer gave the music. "What is *Balustrade?*" he says now. "Stravinsky never wrote *Balustrade;* he wrote *Violin Concerto.* The ballet should be announced as what it is. Then the musicians can come, the young people who love music and who want to hear the composition—they'll know what they're getting. They don't have to look at the ballet if it bores them, they can just listen to the music. And that's fine with me, that's wonderful. For just a dollar and seventy-five cents they can go upstairs and close their eyes and hear a marvelous concert—of music nobody else is playing."

If it is futile to try to learn Balanchine's preferences among his works, it is even more futile to question him about the future, particularly in regard to the preservation of his works. He denies any interest in that. He says he doesn't want his work preserved. "For whom?" he asks me. "For people to see that I don't even know what they're like, that aren't even born yet? And are my ballets going to be danced by dancers I don't know, that I haven't trained? Those won't really be my ballets. The choreography, the steps—those don't mean a thing. Steps are made by a person. It's the person dancing the steps—that's what choreography is, not the steps by themselves."

"But for later on—" I start to say.

Balanchine interrupts. "I'm not interested in later on. I don't have any later on. We all live in the same time forever. There is no future and there is no past. So always I say when people talk to me about the future, 'What's the matter with Now? Now is when it is good, Now is when it is beautiful, Now there are all these wonderful dances to be seen that I have worked like mad on. So public come in, fill the theatre—Now.'"

I persist. Isn't he at least interested in the ballet company continuing into the future, to live on after him?

"For myself, I don't care," he answers. "If my friends and the young people who are coming on in the company want to continue, that's fine with me. I hope they'll be able to do it. But to me, personally, it will mean nothing."

"You're not interested in leaving some monument behind?"

Portrait study by Martha Swope of Suzanne Farrell and Balanchine when **Don Quixote** *was being prepared in 1965.*

Balanchine as Don Quixote, Suzanne Farrell as Dulcinea, in a performance of Don Quixote.

"Absolutely not."

The question of a successor to Balanchine in the New York City Ballet is one that is much speculated on in the world of ballet. It is a question that will never be faced within the company as long as he is there. As much a factor as his fatalism is his vitality and will. Once, during a conversation, I bluntly put the question to him—"What will happen to the company after you go?" He replied, "Who's going? I'm a Georgian, I will probably live to a hundred thirty-five." And he says to me now what he has often said in the past—that as long as he can move around and show people what he wants them to do he will continue to make ballets, but if it gets to the point where he has to sit down he will have to stop, because he can't envisage making ballets that way.

"It's all in the programs." In 1969 he obtained a Mexican divorce from Tanaquil Le Clercq, after sixteen years of marriage. It is no secret that for several years before that he had been preoccupied with the young ballerina Suzanne Farrell, a preoccupation amounting to an obsession, and that, despite the forty years' difference in their ages, he hoped to marry her. But she married a young man in the company named Paul Mejia at just about the time that Balanchine was getting his divorce, and in May of that year she and Mejia left the New York City Ballet because, she told the press, after their marriage Balanchine would not give her husband the roles he expected and deserved. In a sense, Balanchine's cryptic remark to me is true. It *is* all in the programs—the adoration of the aging choreographer for the young ballerina, his idealization of her, his despair over her. It's in the ballets he made for her in the eight years after she joined the company, at the age of sixteen—ballets like *Meditation, Variations,* the "Diamonds" section of *Jewels, Metastaseis and Pithoprakta,* and of course, most explicitly, *Don Quixote,* in which Balanchine himself at times performed the role of the romantic, deluded knight to her Dulcinea. And life without her, after she left, is also in the programs, in the quite different looking ballets that he made as he gave up his obsession with choreographing for that one body and spread his attention once more over the other dancers in the company.

Since his divorce, Balanchine has lived in an apartment on West Sixty-seventh Street. It was originally two small apartments, whose walls Balanchine had torn out to provide him with a thirty-five-by-twenty-foot living room. He lives by himself. He tells me he now prefers it that way. "The time comes when you just want to be alone," he says. "At the end of the day now I am tired. I don't want to have to think about anybody else. I come home at night and throw everything off, all my clothes. Dancers are like that, their bodies need a rest." He has no piano in his apartment and, he says, "no trace of ballet." His piano, his music, and his pertinent materials are all in the office he maintains in the State Theater building. He used to like to watch westerns on TV for relaxation, but his TV set is broken, and he finds it no loss because westerns aren't what they used to be—they've gone psychological and significant. His reading these days consists mostly of popular science, like Fred Hoyle's *Frontiers of Astronomy,* and the Bible.

"How much do you read the Bible?"

"Always. Slowly. It tells you everything, the wars, the prophesies. It's very interesting, the Bible. It's entertaining."

FRIDAY: Most of the company members are assembled at the Falcon Studios this afternoon. Robert Irving, the conductor of the company's orchestra, is present, sitting near the piano; in front of him is the red table, on which scores are stacked. He has a pocket metronome in one hand, and as the piano plays he conducts with the other, using a yellow pencil for a baton. A plump, florid, sandy-haired man, he is wearing a short-sleeved green shirt, tan pants, and sneakers with no socks. His glasses are halfway down his nose. This session is devoted to getting the tempi set for fifteen ballets that will be filmed in two Berlin studios over a six-week period, beginning in mid-September. For various reasons— mostly, I presume, to do with money—the music will be recorded ahead of time in Vienna and tape will be sent to Berlin for use in the filming. So it is essential that Balanchine and Irving agree on all the tempi today. Frequent consultations occur between the two men, as they go quickly through bits of one ballet after another. The piano plays for each tempo change, and those dancers who would be dancing that part of the ballet go into action on the studio floor, enabling Balanchine to judge whether the tempo is suitable. Sometimes he decides just by watching, sometimes he dances along with the others. His knee doesn't seem to be troubling him today, and he is once more in good spirits. It's of interest to me to see what little sections get chosen as tempo proving grounds, and I find it rather poignant to have these moments suddenly materializing and then disappearing before my eyes: the swooning falls of the second movement of *Symphony in C,* which no one has ever danced as expressively as Tanaquil Le Clercq; the passage in the elegy section of *Serenade,* which Balanchine once told me is like the destiny that each man carries through life; the sinuously bouncy portion of Stars and Stripes that Balanchine says now has to be danced like a shag. "It should be dirty," he says, and he and Irving agree on a perfect dirty tempo for it. After making each decision, they check the score to see what tempo marking the composer or arranger had specified. It is seldom the same as theirs. The biggest discrepancy shows up in Serenade's elegy. Balanchine and Irving prefer it at sixty-nine. "What does Tchaikovsky say?" Balanchine asks.

"Ninety-six," says Irving, after looking at the score.

"It must be a misprint," says Balanchine.

Eventually they settle for doing it even a shade more slowly—at sixty-six.

In this way in two hours they run through snippets of Symphony in C, Stars and Stripes, Serenade, La Valse, Pulcinella, Episodes, Violin Concerto, Concerto Barocco, Divertimento from "Le Baiser de la Fée," Agon, Tarantella, Valse Fantaisie, Tchaikovsky Pas de Deux, Liebeslieder Walzer, and Duo Concertant. It is as if one is watching a show called "Highlights of the New York City Ballet." For some members of the company, I reflect, it must be like having their whole life flash before their eyes.

By three o'clock the job is done. Balanchine goes off to keep an appointment with Ira Gershwin, and everybody else in the company departs except the accompanist and two dancers—Patricia McBride and Helgi Tomasson. For the next hour they rehearse the pas de deux they will be dancing tonight in Balanchine's Donizetti Variations. They work quietly, purposefully, with mutual courtesy and consideration. Their attention is on what to an observer may seem small, practical details—on a handhold during an arabesque, on whether a glissade should end one way, or with the two of them a few inches closer together. Watching them at work I am reminded of a story I have been told about Pierre Vladimirov, who was Nijinsky's successor as premier danseur at the Maryinsky. Sometimes after a performance the czar would send his carriage to the stage door for Vladimirov. The balletomanes would unhitch the horses and pull the carriage through the streets, such was the adulation he was accorded. Yet it was his habit at the end of a performance—after the applause and the cheers, and before going out to face his admirers—to change into practice tights and spend twenty minutes working at the barre. He did that, he said, "to cleanse himself"—to remind himself, after the abandon of the performance, of the essential discipline on which it was all based. As Miss McBride and Tomasson work alone in that studio, I sense in them the same simplicity of dedication. Balan-

Patricia McBride and Helgi Tomasson in the Divertimento *from "Le Baiser de la Fée."*

chine is present, too, in the only way that matters to him—in the bodies of these dancers. The question that I have asked him—"What will happen to the New York City Ballet after you go?"—seems to me no longer a question worth asking. It will go on—in some manner that we can't guess and that Balanchine can't guess, either, and wouldn't presume to try.

CHAPTER FIFTEEN

At Seventy

alanchine's seventieth birthday—January 22, 1974—was for him an ordinary working day. Habitually, he would rise before six A.M., even if he had gone out after a performance the night before, for he required little sleep. He would make himself a pot of tea, perhaps play a hand of Russian solitaire as he gathered his thoughts, and then do some ironing—the look and smell of a freshly ironed shirt always gave him pleasure. For all his sophistication, he was, as Gold and Fizdale have written, "Olympian in his simplicity." By seven he was ready to attack the business of the day, his first action being to phone his longtime personal assistant Barbara Horgan at home and go over the day's schedule with her. On this particular day, he taught company class as usual, rehearsed Karin von Aroldingen and John Clifford in the new work he was choreographing, an avant-garde duet to *musique concrète* called *Variations pour une Porte et un Soupir*, tinkered with some passages in *Don Quixote*, which nine years after its premiere he was still trying to shape to his satisfaction, made some arrangements concerning ballets of his that the Paris Opéra Ballet would perform in March at its Stravinsky Festival, experimented with the mock-up that had been made of the enormous black silk skirt, the size of the full stage, which von Aroldingen would wear in the new ballet and, in between these sessions, transacted with the company manager and staff whatever business required his consultation and decision, which could be anything from ticket prices to publicity plans to union negotiation issues to ideas for improving the acoustics of the State Theater.

In the wings.

329

Turning seventy was, to his mind, nothing to make a fuss over. He preferred, in general, not to have his birthday celebrated, or even noted, though occasionally friends insisted on making a small party for him and he did not care to disappoint them by resisting. But his nature was to ignore such commemorations. He had devoted his life and art to resisting the passage of time, or rather to shaping time so as to give the illusion of its not passing. All real ballets, W. H. Auden once wrote, take place in Eden, a world of pure being where there is no memory and no anticipation, and the joy of being alive is manifested through an eternal present. Auden may well have got that thought from his friend George Balanchine, who lived with it. Ballet masters traditionally have been a long-lived race. Vestris lived to eighty-two, Noverre to eighty-three, Didelot to seventy, Blasis to eighty, Bournonville to seventy-four, and Petipa to ninety-two, after retiring at age eighty-five. With such precedent to consider, Balanchine may not have been completely whimsical when he would turn aside questions as to who might succeed him by responding that it was too soon to ask, since he fully intended to live and work to one hundred thirty-five—or at least one hundred. He had two longevity advantages, after all, that not even Petipa had enjoyed—namely Georgian ancestry and modern sanitation.

As he went into the eighth decade of his life, he looked in fine shape. His face was without wrinkles, and he still moved with youthful zest. Indeed, one of the jokes the company enjoyed during the making of *Coppélia* later that spring was watching Balanchine, in high spirits, showing Shaun O'Brien, the ballet's comic but sinister Dr. Coppélius, how an old man would walk.

Though the New York City Ballet had grown to ninety dancers, he still ran it as if it were a family. When he returned from a trip to Europe, like a good father he brought back presents, often perfume for the ballerinas—L'Origan for Karin von Aroldingen, Via Lanvin for Patricia Neary, Caline for Colleen Neary, Narcisse Noir for Carol Sumner. They were convinced that he knew exactly which perfume was right for each of them. And he would say that for him this was a practical kind of gift; he was able to tell as soon as he entered the State Theater's elevator which of his ballerinas had already arrived. He liked being able to keep track.

The relationship between Balanchine and his dancers was intimate, intricate, subtle, and pervasive. From morning, when they took class from him, till evening, when they saw him standing in the wings, watching, he was a constant presence. And when he wasn't physically present, he was seldom absent from their awareness. When they looked at themselves in the mirror, it was through his eyes they tried to look. Dancers used to joke that after he was gone, if that day ever came, they would put a life-size placard of him in the wings to remind them that wherever he might be, he probably still had his eye on them. It didn't matter how great a success they might have with critics or audiences, if they suspected they had not come up to Balanchine's standards. Only he really perceived what they were doing in performance, they believed, and only his judgment mattered. It was said, in the school as well as in the company, that Balanchine could tell from seeing just one demi-plié everything he needed to know about a dancer's future.

In her book *Winter Season,* Toni Bentley, a corps de ballet member, wrote, "A lover once said to me, 'If I could have even half the power over you that this Balanchine has . . .'

"Most women," she continued, "have two important men in their lives—their father and their lover. We have three. Mr. Balanchine is our leader, our president, our mother, our father, our friend, our guide, our mentor, our destiny."

Balanchine could be merciless in his expectations and his judgments, and he seldom praised even the most fabulous of his dancers. Yet he valued them for what they were and, even more, for what they might be. He loved dancers as a breed, even with all his awareness of the breed's faults and inadequacies. Sometimes, frustrated by the limitations of the human organism, he would expostulate, in mock despair, "Even a cat has a better body!" But then he would take comfort in not having to choreograph for centipedes—all those legs to have to make steps for! He often said he had been put on earth to make dancers work as they should, to make them extend themselves to the limit. "A dancer is like a musical instrument," he told an interviewer. "It must be played with a full-bodied tone—and pitilessly."

Sometimes he compared dancers to horses who, he said, were lazy by nature and would never race if you didn't put a rider on them to make them race. He was that rider. But he was also perfectly well aware that his standard of work, his idea of laziness, was not that of the ordinary human being; he knew very well how hard dancers worked compared with most other mortals. He was always quick to defend dancers against slights by outsiders. To hear people utter the commonplace remark that dancers have no brains annoyed him exceedingly. "That's not true!" he would say indignantly. Sniffing his dry sniff, he would name one after another of his dancers and talk about how intelligent they were. All his life it was his dancers with whom he identified, not with the famous, rich, or fashionable. In 1934, at the very first gala given to celebrate the establishment of the American Ballet Company, he gave up the place set for him among dignitaries and celebrities and went to one of the tables set for the lowly dancers. In Barcelona, during the New York City Ballet's first tour of Europe, he raised a fuss when he learned that dancers would not be allowed to sit in box seats. "My dancers will sit where they want," he declared. "They are good enough to sit anywhere." Jean Rosenthal, the designer who lit the ballets in the early years of the New York City Ballet, told me this story. She said that in ten years of working with Balanchine this was the only time she ever saw him really angry.

When Jerome Robbins first joined the New York City Ballet in 1948, he was appalled, he has told me, by the company's apparent lack of discipline. "I had to hush the dancers. Balanchine, though, seemed able to concentrate and work serenely in the midst of any hubbub. I asked him why he wasn't more strict. He said that when he had been in a ballet company as a young man, there had always been a harsh taskmaster over him and the others, like a jail warden. He had hated that, and he didn't want to be one himself now that he was in authority."

To a surprising extent Balanchine ruled without rules. He was a dictator but not a disciplinarian. His commands generally were put in the form of suggestions. "I think maybe it's better if you do like this—" The only discipline he valued was the self-discipline that came from the desire to achieve. Most performing-arts organizations enunciate codes of company regulations, specifying required conduct and penalties for such infractions as missing rehearsal, being later than the established check-in time for performance, not wearing proper costume, etc., etc. Balanchine did not put much stock in such codes. "If someone doesn't come early enough to the theatre and warm up properly," he said when the subject was once raised, "she won't dance well. And I'll know it. And after a while, she'll want to go somewhere else."

Unlike the directors of other major companies, he did not sign his dancers to exclusive year-long contracts. He was liberal with leaves of absence. If an opportunity arose for a lucrative engagement elsewhere, he readily granted permission even if it sometimes meant having to recast a scheduled ballet. He knew he was not paying the principals what many of them could get at other companies or in special appearances. When they worked with him, he wanted their participation to be wholehearted, not merely the fulfillment of a legal agreement. Part of his motivation in regard to granting requested leaves, some suspected, may also have been that he never wanted to admit that he needed anybody, not even the greatest in the world—not Farrell, not Nureyev, not Makarova, not Baryshnikov, not Tallchief, not anyone.

What he was after from his dancers could not be obtained by fiat, he knew. He asked the impossible, and the impossible could not be commanded. Those who wanted to try to achieve it were those he wanted to have stay. Those others, no matter how talented, were free to leave, as were also those who had other ambitions—whether of money or stardom or a more time-honored repertory or a less rarified ambience—than could be satisfied at the New York City Ballet.

"It's like the Pope represents Christ. I represent Terpsichore, goddess of the dance," he once told a reporter, and he probably meant it, though one could never be certain how seriously he intended such utterances to be taken. Dancers enlisting in his company were expected to take on faith that he knew what was best for them and for the art of ballet. In short, all he asked of them was their souls—freely given. Some found this the most diabolical of demands, and intolerable to sustain. Others found it the way to their artistic salvation.

He never tried to hold on to anyone who was not totally committed. A talented ballerina told Balanchine she was thinking of leaving the company. "Go in peace!" was his reply. She went in tears to Lincoln Kirstein, hurt that Balanchine hadn't tried to persuade her to stay. How could he be so cruel and unfeeling?

Within the New York City Ballet, there was only one form of punishment that mattered. That was for Balanchine to lose interest in a dancer, withdraw his attention from him or her—in effect, leave the dancer in limbo. Once he had made a judgment, he could be implacable. A dancer whom he had stopped casting wanted to know why. He told her she was simply not interesting to look at. What should she do to become more interesting? she asked. His reply was, "Suffer!"

Early in his career, Peter Martins underwent the experience of being relegated to Balanchine's limbo. The experience was so painful that he came very close to leaving the company. This was in 1970, when Martins was twenty-three. In the Royal Danish Ballet he had become a principal at the age of twenty—the youngest to attain that status, except for Erik Bruhn. That same summer (1967) Martins had come to Balanchine's attention when, after Jacques d'Amboise had suffered an injury, he was recruited on two days' notice to dance *Apollo* with the New York City Ballet at the Edinburgh Festival. Three years later, after several further guest appearances, he joined the company as a principal dancer. It was a time of personal as well as professional decision in his life, for it marked the end of his marriage to the dancer Lise La Cour, and he was leaving behind his two-year-old son, Nilas.

He made the move with high hopes. In Denmark he had felt isolated, stifled. Although young, he was already becoming dissatisfied with his profession—not with dancing, but with ballet and where ballet seemed to be heading. "There was never anybody around who I thought knew more than I did," Martins recalled, in a conversation I had with him. "That bothered me, and the reason it bothered me was that I knew that I didn't know nearly enough. Then I met Balanchine." Working with Balanchine on *Apollo* in Edinburgh had been a revelation for him. "I fell in love with this man," Martins has written in his autobiography *Far from Denmark*. "He was so wonderfully natural. His approach, his attitude to his craft. This was an enormously great man. One eye on him and I knew what dancing was all about. He radiated knowledge and authority. He was never condescending, and he never pretended to know more than he did, yet maybe there wasn't much he didn't know."

Yet for his first year with the New York City Ballet, things went badly. One of his problems was company class. Nothing in his experience had prepared him for classes such as Balanchine gave. On one day Balanchine might start with only a ten-minute barre and then as the first step in the center demand a double tour en l'air to grand plié. On the next day he might start with a twenty-five minute barre then go on to half an hour of pas de bourrée's. In class, Balanchine would frequently ridicule Martins and give devastating imitations of him, as one who was stiff, prissy, and formal. Martins began to avoid Balanchine's class and instead to take Stanley Williams' men's class at the school and another class elsewhere.

After a while, Balanchine began taking parts away from him. "That was difficult for me to understand, because you don't take someone like me out," Martins has said. "Once you get a role in Denmark, you have it, you own it. That's your role till you die, till you can't crawl any more, unless you become pathetic."

Hurt, unappreciated, and unloved, Martins came to the conclusion that there was no future for him in the company. With the encouragement of Erik Bruhn, who years before had done an unhappy stint with

◆ *Peter Martins and Kay Mazzo in* Duo Concertant.

Balanchine and the New York City Ballet, he entered secretly into negotiations with American Ballet Theatre. ABT agreed to all his demands, and a lunch was arranged with the company's director, Lucia Chase, to sign the contract. But when it came time to sign, he found he couldn't do it. "I couldn't risk the loss of working with Balanchine," he wrote in *Far from Denmark,* "and from this minidrama I discovered that my commitment was deep and irrevocable, and the task was to live with it, and to make it work."

Some time afterward, he went to Balanchine to try to clarify his situation: why wasn't he being used?

Balanchine answered, "You see, dear, you don't seem to be interested. I never see you anywhere, not in class, maybe in O'Neals' restaurant. When people show interest, I use them. If they don't, I leave them alone. And you don't show interest."

To Martins, this was a shocker. He hadn't realized the impression he was giving—of being someone who was cool, distant, bored, resistant—for he did not feel that way. He thought of himself as someone seething with passion. He told Balanchine he was prepared to change. Balanchine, in turn, said if Martins would show he was serious and determined and prepared to listen and to learn, there would be ample opportunities for him. This conversation was the turning point of Martins' career with the New York City Ballet. The atmosphere improved immediately. Balanchine began saying hello instead of ignoring him when they passed in the hall. Martins began regularly taking Balanchine's company class and trying not to hold back for fear of looking less than correct or perfect. He began to take chances and let himself go, which was just what Balanchine sought from his dancers.

In the 1972 Stravinsky Festival, Balanchine for the first time choreographed on Martins, using him in two new ballets, both masterpieces— *Violin Concerto* and *Duo Concertant.* These ballets, critics have written, were a breakthrough for Martins, revealing him as a dancer with a special flavor and character.

An allegation that has been frequently made was that Balanchine's dancers were expected to suppress their personalities. Most of those who have danced for Balanchine would deny this. Their experience was that he encouraged and cherished true differences in personality, but he discouraged stage mannerisms that were not true to their natures—particularly the fake glamour of the old-fashioned prima ballerina. His intuition, his message, was that a dancer expresses personality most truly not by gesture or acting or facial expressions but by the way the dancer dances.

By the time of the Stravinsky Festival, Peter Martins had come to his own understanding of this. "Balanchine had brought me to discover how I could vary, extend, and increase the range of the way I danced," he wrote. "And what he made me give up was any fear of looking inadequate or awkward. It was this very lack of fear, the willingness to try anything, that he seemed to like in me. What he was urging me to, what he was allowing me to discover, was my own way of moving. It was my true personal manner, a frame for further exploration (a way of existing on stage that was the sum of my physique, training, character, philosophy, temperament). I was becoming less rigid by becoming more particular, and he had pushed me to this. I had found a way of behaving more fully on stage. More of myself was implicated in the performance. I was altered as a dancer, for there was simply more of me, imaginatively."

The ballet that Balanchine was rehearsing on his seventieth birthday, *Variations pour une Porte et un Soupir,* had its premiere on February 17, 1974. It was a novelty that aspired to the status of a provocation. The

〜Variations pour une Porte et un Soupir—*with John Clifford and Karin von Aroldingen.*

best description of it is the one given by Lincoln Kirstein in *Thirty Years*, his personal chronicle of the New York City Ballet's history:

"The French composer Pierre Henri, experimenting with 'non-musical' sonorities, used an amplified creaking door swinging on un-greased hinges paired against the breathing of a body in love, anxiety, or agony. The stage was draped in the enormous skirts of a dancer drenched in blackness, menace, or death as she struggled to come to some sort of companionship—erotic, maternal, mortal (?), with a gray-skinned bi-ped, insectile, infantile, neuter but not exactly inhuman. One might read tokens and metaphors of drowning, frustration, suffocation. The theatrical scale was gigantic; the light-struck flood of black silk rippled and ballooned in an orgy of peristaltic motion. Fatally, the duet, hero-ically, performed by Karin von Aroldingen and John Clifford, assumed something of the aroma of a high-grade nightclub number. Technical arrangements were no easier for stage crew than for dancers. The action of the silk drapery had to be synchronized with music and the metrical play of the choreography. The effect was by no means unimpressive, although the enormous yardage tended to smother much personal anguish in the *pas de deux*."

At the end of the performance, the night of the premiere, loud boos were to be heard from the audience. The dancers were upset but Balanchine looked satisfied, as did Lincoln Kirstein, who came backstage with a smile on his face to congratulate Clifford and von Aroldingen. Clifford said he feared it hadn't gone over very well, for he had heard booing. Kirstein replied, "That was me. I was the one who started the booing. We could use a controversy."

For Kirstein, *Variations pour une Porte et un Soupir* offered an opportunity to reflect on the nature of repertory and, in particular, Balanchine's didactic, intuitive, innovative, and assured approach to repertory. "It's time wasted to lament the brief life of *Une Porte et un Soupir*," he wrote in *Thirty Years*. "It will not be revived; perhaps it doesn't deserve revival." And he went on to observe: "'Failures' often pave the way for later 'successes.' Ballets that have lived longest are not those which were first warmly welcomed. Part of the craft of repertory is judgment which prods an audience by stubborn insistence or by long experience of laws of fluctuation in public acceptance.

"Increasingly, owing to Balanchine's instruction, our public has become participant with our company. At least a determining section of it has begun to feel it has a right, even an obligation, to respond by love or hate. This warmth, pro or con, is ultimately passionately supportive. Certainly we wouldn't want it any other way, nor will Balanchine stop his whimsical, reckless, capricious or knowing adventures into the dubious realm of alternatives."

The New York City Ballet has been scolded by some critics for its policy of constantly introducing new works, only about a third of which survive for more than three seasons. Balanchine maintained this policy not merely because of the challenge and stimulation it afforded him, though that was probably part of it. He was convinced it was absolutely necessary. By now, the New York City Ballet had amassed a huge, varied subscription audience, on whom it depended and to whom it was obligated. The company enthralled the audience but was also in thrall to it, and could not safely ignore its needs. This audience, Balanchine believed, was voracious in its appetite for new works. From early on, he had encouraged and titillated this appetite, and he did not think he could safely put the audience on a restricted diet now. And most of the burden fell of necessity on him—the sorcerer with insufficient apprentices. It was not merely ego and selfishness that dictated that three-fourths of the ballets performed in any given season were his. Outside choreographers did not prosper when they tried to work with this company's style. Robbins was often masterful but could not be expected to choreograph with Balanchine's facility. And the other in-house choreographers—such as John Taras, Jacques d'Amboise, John Clifford, and Peter Martins—had only intermittent success in producing ballets that could hold an audience's attention for repeated viewings.

Because the audience was so broad and varied—loyal at its core but also restive, and with the potential for fickleness all audiences share—Balanchine believed that the new works he offered had to be varied in character. That was one of the main elements Balanchine considered when planning a season. He had also to be cognizant of political considerations, institutional strategies, and financial needs and constraints. In addition, in choosing to do a particular ballet, he almost always did so with the needs of his ensemble in mind—sometimes it would be to show off or develop a certain ballerina, or to do something special for the corps, or even to make an opportunity for the children at the school to perform. And always, whatever he chose to do, he had to challenge and please himself at the same time as he was satisfying and surprising his audience.

The spring of 1974 provided a good example of Balanchine's feeling for the needs of repertory. The ballet Balanchine set to work on immediately after *Une Porte et un Soupir* was, in its way, more surprising as a choice, more controversial even than the avant-garde electronic number—at least to some of Balanchine's devotees. It was *Coppélia,* and the surprise was engendered by Balanchine reaching back into standard nineteenth-century ballet repertory and producing a lavish story ballet. About once in every decade, it seemed, he did something like that, and it always seemed to call for some explanation when he did so, since one of the fundamental principles he and Kirstein had agreed on from the very start of their collaboration was: no revivals. Balanchine's own reasons, or rather explanations, for choosing to do *Coppélia* at this time were various. He felt he needed to do something special, he said, for the Saratoga Springs audience. The company could use another evening-long ballet. Also, he wanted a new ballet that would make liberal use of children from the school. And, as he explained, "I thought if all the children in the ballet brought their brothers and sisters and parents—already we would have one audience." He thought highly of Delibes as the first great ballet composer, and of the music for this ballet in particular. And finally, when he thought over all the possibilities of what he might do at this time, this choice, he said, seemed "the least harmful."

He invited Alexandra Danilova to collaborate with him on staging the ballet. In the 1930's and 40's she had been the West's reigning Swanilda. For the company, seeing Balanchine and Danilova work together was a special treat. She could recall innumerable details from the Petipa version she had danced in at the Maryinsky, and Balanchine took pride in her photographic memory. Her mastery of pantomime was also a revelation to the American dancers, especially the speeded-up version she and Balanchine decided to adopt for the contemporary audience. Both were highly theatrical, these two septuagenarians, as they acted out all the parts for the company. Both also behaved as models of deportment, treating each other with great courtesy and appreciation. Despite their having been lovers in years past, they maintained a certain easy formality, based on the imperial hierarchy of the company. When Danilova spoke of her collaborator to a company member, it was always "Mr. Balanchine"— never "George."

The choreography they did was a combination of old and new, the principal new material being the dances Balanchine made for the third act. Balanchine also brought to the ballet a different tone from the one it had developed in productions elsewhere in the last few decades. It had become too realistic, too cozy, too rustic—a kind of genre piece. As Clive Barnes wrote in *The New York Times,* "What Balanchine has done is to restore it to a kind of fairyland. This is not a realistic peasant ballet—from beginning to end it is a fantasy, largely for children and with children. Because Balanchine has seen this as a children's ballet (if I understand his mind right), he understands the child's need for horror. Coppélius is made into a serious Hoffmanesque character, full of Gothic creepy horror. The setting, with its oblique angles and odd lines, suggests a children's Dr. Caligari. . . ."

"Ballet is unnatural," Balanchine used to say. It is also undeniably a strange and absurd preoccupation for human beings to devote themselves to—as strange and absurd and unnatural, at least, as chess or mathematics or baseball or many other of civilization's pursuits, and it is also, when one thinks about it, undeniably sinister in the use it makes of human beings as the plastic material of the choreographer. Yet ballet, this most artificial of art forms, can also be, when shaped by a master, a technique for transcendence, for "lifting the clay into the clouds," as someone has written. In Balanchine's *Coppélia* these paradoxical insights were incorporated in the basic metaphor—the parallel between the comic, sinister maker of lifelike dolls and the ballet master who creates ballerinas. "Coppélius is not a buffoon, and Swanilda is not a zany," wrote Arlene Croce in *The New Yorker*. "He's a misanthrope, a tyrant, believably a genius who can create dolls everyone thinks are alive. . . . Balanchine's Coppélius is kin to other Balanchine artist-heroes—not only Drosselmeyer but Don Quixote and Orpheus and the Poet of *La Sonnambula*. When he raises Swanilda-Coppélia onto her pointes and she remains locked there, upright or jackknifed over them, he's the strangest of all alchemists, seeking to transform his beloved twice over: doll into woman, woman into ballerina. Swanilda must become as totally manipulatable, totally perfectible, as a Balanchine ballerina. She must be a work of art, and then burst out of her mold."

Among the audiences at Saratoga Springs that summer, there was no spectator more intent than Suzanne Farrell. She and her husband, Paul Mejia, owned an island in the Adirondacks, and one day they drove to Saratoga Springs for a performance. It was the first time she had seen the New York City Ballet in some years, and she yearned to be part of it again. This was *her* company. Those were *her* ballets, many of them—conceived for her and lovingly fashioned by the greatest master of the age to show her off to best advantage. At last she decided to write to Balanchine. Her letter very simply asked if there wasn't some way she could once more be part of this endeavor. Balanchine's response, essentially, was: why not? Let's go to work.

No question was raised by Farrell this time on behalf of Mejia. She knew that there was no use trying—that Balanchine might accept her but would not tolerate Mejia's presence. Mejia, after a period of free lance dance engagements, eventually became codirector, with Maria Tallchief, of the Chicago City Ballet.

Five years had passed since Farrell's departure. By now, Balanchine had recovered from his infatuation, though the wound had been deep and painful and had taken time to heal. Still, Balanchine was a survivor, a believer in the simple motto he uttered to Clive Barnes, who saw him one day crossing Lincoln Center's plaza with his arm around a young woman. "Life goes on," Balanchine said, as they passed.

He did not intend to marry again. He was too old for that, he said. But by now he had formed a strong attachment to Karin von Aroldingen that

Karin von Aroldingen and Sean Lavery in Vienna Waltzes.

was to be the most important relationship in his life from then on. It was different from the kind of relationship he had had with any other woman—less romantic, but far more comfortable, and based on a deep friendship and loyalty that grew with the years.

Born in Germany, Karin von Aroldingen had first seen the New York City Ballet in Berlin in 1956, when she was fifteen, and had become enamored of the company. She became a soloist with the Frankfurt Ballet, where in 1960 she danced the part of Anna in *The Seven Deadly Sins.* Lotte Lenya sang the Anna role in that production and talked much to her about Balanchine. When Balanchine went to Hamburg in February 1962 to stage *Eugen Onegin* for the Hamburg Opera, von Aroldingen went to that city, with an introduction from Lenya, to audition for him. Balanchine told her she was terrible, and he would never take her in the New York City Ballet. Twenty-one years old then, large, rawboned, athletic but not stylish, she looked to him more like a Valkyrie than a ballerina.

Nevertheless, something about her had impressed Balanchine—perhaps it was her willpower, her undeniable determination. A few weeks later, after his return to the United States, he asked the company's general manager Betty Cage to write to her and offer her a position in the corps de ballet. She accepted and joined the company a few months later. In 1965, she married a New York real-estate broker named Morton Gewirtz. Their daughter, Margo, was born a year later. Determined to interrupt her dance career as little as humanly possible, von Aroldingen danced through the entire spring season, until she was in the sixth month of her pregnancy. She followed the company to Saratoga Springs to take classes into her eighth month. A month after her daughter was born, she was back onstage in time for the start of the winter season. Balanchine, who was notorious for objecting to his dancers becoming mothers, could not help but admire her sense of timing, as well as her dedication. He became the infant's godfather. In the years that followed, Balanchine became virtually a member of the Gewirtz family. He acquired a condominium in Southampton, Long Island, near to one that they owned, and spent much of his free time with them there or in New York City. They became the closest thing to a family of his own that he had experienced since he was a small child.

Suzanne Farrell's return to the stage with the New York City Ballet took place one evening in late January 1975. She danced the adagio movement of the Bizet *Symphony in C,* with Peter Martins. There had been no advance announcement or publicity. As the audience recognized her, there was a tremendous burst of applause, then silent, rapt absorption. At the end of the adagio, to the cheers of the audience, she took four calls. There was no doubt that she was home, and welcome.

The return of Farrell brought a lift to the company's spirits. She challenged the standards and the limits of possibility in a way that no other female dancer did. At the same time, her return caused some tremors among the leading ballerinas, those who had felt ignored at the time of Balanchine's preoccupation with Farrell in the late sixties or who had carried the flag for the company in the difficult days after her departure. They were a devout sisterhood, these ballerinas of Balanchine, but they were also human. One of those who was troubled was Kay Mazzo, a young woman of a tenderhearted and not very competitive nature, who had devotedly done what she could to fill in when Farrell left. Quickly, she had had to learn most of the Farrell parts in the repertory, and this had been difficult, because Balanchine had never allowed anyone to understudy Farrell. So enraptured had he been with the way she looked and moved, he could not bear, when she was in the company, to think of anyone else performing her roles. Now, after Farrell's return, the Farrell roles that Mazzo had danced were given back to Farrell. It was inevitable, but still Mazzo felt hurt.

Another who felt unease was Patricia McBride, normally so steady and reliable a personality as to have won from Kirstein the testimonial of being the company's bellwether, the one who in good times and bad kept the whole ensemble in focus. She had become the company's leading ballerina and, with her delightful performance in Coppélia, was now being hailed as America's ranking ballerina.

One day she found that Farrell had been assigned the "The Man I Love" number in Who Cares?, a part made on McBride that she had come to assume was exclusively hers. She went to Balanchine to complain—an unusual step, for all her life Balanchine had been for her the father whose wishes were never questioned and who always knew what was best. Her complaint touched a nerve. Angrily, Balanchine turned on McBride. "You're awful, dear! Awful! I'm the only choreographer who choreographs special things for each of his ballerinas, not just for one." And he walked off, leaving McBride in tears. As it turned out, she needn't have fretted about losing her roles to Farrell, particularly not this one. Farrell danced "The Man I Love" only a couple of times in New York, and nowhere near as engagingly as McBride.

For many months in 1974 and early 1975, Balanchine concerned himself with preparing a Ravel Festival, which was presented in the late spring, beginning May 14 and running through to May 31. This caught people by surprise. "Why Ravel?" they asked. "Why not Ravel?" Balanchine answered. It did seem a strange choice, as Nancy Reynolds noted in Repertory in Review, "particularly since Balanchine had never shown a special affinity for Ravel's music as support for his ballets." In forty years he had done only La Valse and two productions of the opera L'Enfant et les Sortiléges.

Other incentives presumably were at work—such as using the festival format as a box-office draw in the spring, when box office tended to sag. Political motives seemed also to be present. The festival was made the occasion for honoring France as well as Ravel. Madame Giscard d'Estaing, wife of the president of France, attended the opening night. In a statement from the stage inaugurating the festival, Balanchine offered a testimonial to France's contribution to ballet as well as to his own health and longevity. "La Belle France gave us La Danse. But another thing, one absolutely important thing—why I am still alive—it's because of the wine."

From France, in return, Balanchine was awarded the Legion of Honor, presented at the opening gala by the French ambassador. A week later, Balanchine collected another award, the Distinguished Service Award from the National Institute of Arts and Letters. The accompanying citation read: "He has transfigured the human body and made of its energies hundreds of works of art that seem to reveal answers to questions no one has yet asked."

Sixteen new ballets were choreographed for the Ravel Festival, seven of them by Balanchine. Of these only one seemed a work of major distinction. That was *Le Tombeau de Couperin*. One other work—*Tzigane*—was notable because of the extraordinary solo danced by Farrell. In regard to the festival as a whole, Reynolds summed it up in a sentence: "The magic was missing."

One of the aspects of his company in which Balanchine took great pride was the orchestra. He used to brag about it as the best ballet orchestra in the world. During the fall of the following year, that orchestra placed him in a quandary. The negotiations for the musicians' contract became very difficult. The orchestra wanted a pay scale that would eventually give them parity with the Metropolitan Opera orchestra. They threatened to strike if their demands were not met. Balanchine was puzzled. To the conductor Hugo Fiorato, he said, "Tell me, Hugo, why do the musicians want so much money?"

The conductor replied, "Well, they have families to support. They think they're entitled to a decent living. Nowadays a garbageman makes more than a member of the orchestra. Why should a garbageman get more than a musician?"

Balanchine looked at him as if the answer were obvious. "Because garbage stinks," he said.

On December 13, 1976, in the middle of *The Nutcracker* run, the New York City Ballet's orchestra went out on strike. Most of the winter season had to be canceled before the strike was settled, causing a revenue loss of about a million dollars. When the strike was finally settled, the audience at the first performance booed the orchestra, and for the rest of the abbreviated season the conductor did not risk signaling for the customary round of applause for the orchestra before the evening's final ballet. In *Thirty Years*, Lincoln Kirstein wrote, "The worst thing that ever happened to the New York City Ballet was the musicians' strike of 1976."

* * *

At this period of his life, Balanchine seemed to be in an expansive mood as a choreographer, oriented toward lavish spectacles—costumed, decorated, using broad effects, popular forms, and all the resources that could be mustered. Or, to put it more accurately, he had come to the conclusion that the company needed more such productions. That being so, he would get himself in the mood, just as he expected to be able to summon his muse on union time. In the spring of 1976, before the musicians' strike, he produced his biggest spectacle to date, using seventy-seven dancers, in *Union Jack*—a ballet perversely commemorating the bicentennial of the American Revolution by paying a shamelessly affectionate tribute to America's ancestor and former foe.

Union Jack was Scottish regiments, marches, parades, tattoos, the music hall, the Royal Navy in fond caricature. It was yet another of those Balanchine works, like *Stars and Stripes* or *Western Symphony*, in which Balanchine extended the boundaries of what could be accommodated in classical ballet—in this case the elements, devices, and spirit of British folk culture, popular entertainment, and mass pageantry. Some of that he had made use of fifty years before when he choreographed *The Triumph of Neptune* for Diaghilev's Ballets Russes.

The big ballet to which Balanchine turned his attention after the musicians' strike was settled was *Vienna Waltzes*, to music of Johann Strauss the Younger, Franz Lehar, and Richard Strauss. Premiered on June 23, 1977, it was an instant success with the public and became for some years the company's single most popular ballet, selling out the house every time it was scheduled. A smash hit, and calculatedly so—yet it was also more than that. It was, in fact, the history and essence of Vienna, as incarnated in the waltz, down to the vision of that society's impending disintegration manifested in the music of *Der Rosenkavalier*. The doomed charm of that music, with its edge of hysteria, had never before been so acutely captured in dance.

The largest potential audience of all, of course, was the television audience, and Balanchine now reached out for that, too—taking the company that summer after the Saratoga Springs season to Nashville to tape two programs for the *Dance in America* series for the Public Broadcasting System. His past experiences with television had been so unhappy that he had vowed to have nothing more to do with it, but a number of factors operated to change his mind now. He liked and trusted

෨ Vienna Waltzes.

the two director-producers he would be working with, Merrill Brockway and Emile Ardolino, both of them tactful, courteous personalities who were sensitive to music and the dance and who knew the New York City Ballet repertory intimately. Unlike previous television directors he had worked with, Brockway and Ardolino made it clear they would welcome his active collaboration from start to finish in the preparation of the programs and would respect his judgments. Ample rehearsal and taping time had been promised, and an excellent facility had been provided— the sound stage of the Grand Ole Opry, for which *Dance in America* had built a special floor for the dancers. So satisfied was Balanchine with the working arrangements and the results that he agreed to take the company back to Nashville for further programs on two subsequent occasions. Ultimately *Dance in America* presented six programs of Balanchine choreography. Each of these programs was seen by several million people.

By the autumn of 1977, Balanchine's interest in lavish spectacles had run its course—for the time being. He never followed one line for long. On his return from Nashville, he set to work on two very different ballets. One—to music from Verdi's *Don Carlos*—was *Ballo della Regina*; it was essentially a display piece, spotlighting the bravura talents of Merrill Ashley, who had just been made a principal dancer. The other was *Kammermusik No. 2*, to music of Hindemith. This ballet, which had its premiere January 26, 1978, was projected, like some new space vehicle, along the trajectory that had previously been explored by such works as *Agon, Episodes*, and *Violin Concerto*. *Kammermusik No. 2* was one of the most ingenious and technically accomplished ballets Balanchine had made, and one of his least ingratiating. Kirstein thought it Balanchine's most extreme exercise. Though he found it fascinating, he also found it "slightly repellent, inhuman, desperate, insistent, harshly deliberate; even cruel."

For Balanchine, these two ballets were—each in its own way—just as much a necessity as a smash hit such as *Vienna Waltzes*. They were just as important to the fulfillment of his own needs as a choreographer, to the needs of his dancers and their repertory, and—whether the audience knew it or not at the time—to the audience's needs as well.

⁓ Kammermusik No. 2, *with Karin von Aroldingen and Sean Lavery.*

CHAPTER SIXTEEN

An Appetite for Renewal

On March 15, 1978, Balanchine suffered a heart attack. He was at home, and the attack was a mild one. He phoned Barbara Horgan and Edward Bigelow, who took him to his cardiologist's office, where a cardiogram confirmed the infarction, and then they drove him to New York University Hospital. The attack came, in some ways, as a relief to his mind. He had been suffering extreme fatigue, with occasional dizzy spells, and had felt generally miserable. He had gone to a number of specialists and taken numerous tests to try to discover what ailed him. Not knowing had been frustrating for him. On the way to the hospital, Horgan remembers, he acted quite jolly, as if now that he knew what he had to deal with, he'd soon take care of it.

For two weeks he was hospitalized, then he rested at his apartment for much of April. His cardiologist, who was medically conservative, urged him to greatly reduce his activity, henceforth enjoy lots of bed rest, and take serious measures toward retirement. Balanchine did not appreciate this advice, or intend to heed it, particularly since he was now feeling better than he had for quite some time.

In September, he became a patient of Edith J. Langner, an internist and general physician. Though a variety of specialists had treated him for one thing or another over the years, up to then he had not had a general physician, concerned with his overall health and well-being. Dr. Langner had treated Horgan, Farrell, and other members of the company, who recommended her. She was young, alert, progressive, sympathetic. Balanchine liked and respected her. She knew that retirement was not

Rehearsing Baryshnikov in Prodigal Son.

351

acceptable to Balanchine, nor was she interested in advocating it. She did think he might benefit from some adjustment of his daily regimen, and particularly from watching his diet. Dr. Langner was concerned about his consumption of rich foods, sweets, and alcohol, all of which he loved. His notion of a delicious, simple sandwich, for instance, was to take an untoasted half of a Thomas' English muffin, apply about a quarter-inch layer of sweet butter, spread over that a mound of first-rate caviar, then cover with the other half of the muffin. That was the kind of thing Dr. Langner thought he should cut down on, and she talked seriously to him about the merits of the low-cholesterol Pritikin Diet for heart patients.

One day Balanchine told her a story—one of his favorite Stravinsky anecdotes. Late in life, Stravinsky suffered from a condition that resulted in the production of too many red blood cells. It was a serious affliction, and his doctor had forbidden him to drink alcoholic beverages. One evening Stravinsky arrived in New York and Balanchine joined him at the Pierre Hotel. "Come," said Stravinsky, "we'll have a celebration. We'll have caviar and champagne, and maybe a little Scotch to start off with." Balanchine responded, "But you can't do that. You know your doctor has said you mustn't drink." "That's true," Stravinsky said. "I guess I'd better call him." So he put in a call to his doctor at home, and when the doctor came on the line, he said, in a childlike voice, "Doctor, Mr. Balanchine is here with me. And we're so happy to see each other we want to celebrate. Can't I please drink some champagne?" The doctor said, "No! Absolutely not!" In the same tiny, begging voice, Stravinsky said, "Oh, but, doctor, my good friend Balanchine is here, and we don't see each other so much." The doctor replied, "That doesn't matter. You know it's absolutely not good for you." "Please, doctor," Stravinsky said, "just one bottle of champagne and—" "Oh, to hell with it!" the doctor said in exasperation. "I wash my hands of you." Putting down the phone, Stravinsky said to Balanchine, with an angelic smile, "The doctor says okay."

Dr. Langner got the message, which by now had become fairly evident to her—that there was a limit to what Balanchine would allow in the way of altering or moderating his life activities and habits. At any given moment, what he wanted to do now was what mattered most to him. Possible future consequences did not much concern him.

About three weeks before his heart attack, Balanchine had been interviewed by a reporter, who had asked if there was any chance of Mikhail

Baryshnikov ever joining the New York City Ballet. Balanchine acknowledged Baryshnikov's abilities. "He's talented—he points his feet well," was the way he generally expressed his praise for this world-acclaimed star. But, said Balanchine to the reporter, "What would he do in our company? We have nothing for him, and no partner; they're all too tall. Besides, the public would scream if he wasn't doing those jumps and lifts all the time."

Whether Balanchine was aware of it or not, Baryshnikov was at that very time coming to the conclusion, after much deliberation, that the time had come for him to leave American Ballet Theatre and make a change that would further his development as an artist. He was not content to go on being a superstar—the greatest male dancer in the world, brilliantly repeating what he had already mastered. He had reached his peak. There seemed to him only one way to go beyond it, and that was to work with Balanchine and have the experience of being a member of Balanchine's company. Describing his mood at that time, he later told reporters, "At first I thought 'I will kill myself if he doesn't ask me.' Slowly I realized that I would never forgive myself if I did not try. I am thirty, with a few years left. If he said, 'You are not right in some way physically,' I would go through a terrible depression, but I could stand it."

Impelling him was another motivation as well. To make this move would be to justify his defection from the Soviet Union—justify it to the world and, more important, to himself, by demonstrating that it was not greed for fame and material wealth that had led him to act as he had. In his mind, as well as in the view of many of his Russian colleagues who had seen the New York City Ballet on its 1962 and 1972 Soviet tours, it was that company that was the true heir of Russian ballet, not the Kirov or the Bolshoi. In that sense, for him to leave Russia and join the New York City Ballet was not to go into exile but rather to find at last his true spiritual home.

Through Jerome Robbins, who had choreographed *Other Dances* for him and Makarova at American Ballet Theatre, and through others, including his friend Peter Martins, Baryshnikov sent out signals. Early one morning in April, he got a call from Balanchine, who said, "I think we ought to talk. Come to my place. We can talk in Russian." Baryshnikov went to Balanchine's apartment, still uncertain whether Balanchine would be interested in him, and at best assuming that lengthy negotiations would have to take place. But over a cup of tea, and within half an hour, everything was settled. Baryshnikov would join the New York City Ballet that coming summer as a regular member, at regular pay for a principal. (This was then around seven hundred fifty dollars a week. At American Ballet Theatre he earned from three thousand to five thousand dollars a performance.) But he would be free to make lucrative guest appearances outside of New York, just as other members of the company were under the company's standard contract. He would dance the regular repertory and receive the regular billing. None of this was laboriously spelled out; much of it was simply understood. There were no demands or counteroffers. As Baryshnikov later said to me, when recalling this occasion, "I knew the rules of the game."

Baryshnikov made the announcement to the press on April 26. He was ebullient and exultant. "I am entering the ideal future of Maryinsky Ballet," he declared. "Two hundred years ahead, but here it is! And now I will find my new face." He spoke of what a privilege it would be to work for Balanchine. "I would love to be the instrument in his wonderful hands." Taking cognizance of those who warned him about Balanchine's known aversion to stars and who foresaw problems in the relationship, whether of temperament or artistry, Baryshnikov said, "I never called myself a star. I'm a dancer." And he added, "It's like a marriage. I feel as if I'm in a church, and in church you do not think of divorce. Some people here are skeptical, but my Russian friends will understand at once and rejoice. There Balanchine is an incredible symbol of uncompromised creative genius."

Reporters who sought Balanchine's reaction to all this got a much more matter-of-fact response, in keeping with Balanchine's characteristic posture, so low-key as to be provocative. He told the press that he didn't expect the addition of Baryshnikov to affect the company. "Nothing changes in the company," he said. "Why should it? It's just an additional member—a very good dancer coming in. We have so much to do and so many people sick, it's good to have someone healthy."

Wrote Clive Barnes in the *New York Post* of all this upheaval: "It is no great deal. Just imagine President Carter declaring he was a Republican."

Baryshnikov's last performance with American Ballet Theatre was May 18, and he began rehearsal with the New York City Ballet not long afterward. He went with the company to Saratoga Springs at the end of June, and there he made his debut July 8, dancing Franz in *Coppélia*. The debut took place at a Saturday matinee, sponsored in part by the local McDonald's hamburger outlets. No advance announcement of Baryshnikov's appearance had been made to the press. As John Corry wrote in

↬ *Working with Baryshnikov on* Orpheus.

The New York Times, "It is possible that Mr. Baryshnikov might have made his debut less conspicuously; it is difficult, however, to see how."

At Saratoga that summer, Baryshnikov learned and danced in a number of ballets, including *Rubies, Stars and Stripes,* and *Afternoon of a Faun.* Balanchine spent time coaching him, and Baryshnikov felt that Balanchine was encouraging and enthusiastic about what he was doing. Baryshnikov saw quite a bit of Balanchine outside of the theatre as well. Balanchine would invite him to meals he had cooked, and sometimes, after going fishing early in the morning at a local stream, Baryshnikov would stop off at the little cottage in the country that Balanchine shared with Edward Bigelow, and they would sit out under a large oak in the front yard and talk. The two men seemed quickly to develop a genuine fondness and interest in each other. They exchanged reminiscences about Russia, they talked about food, women, America, the world—not a great deal about ballet, though occasionally about what music was danceable and what wasn't. Balanchine could not help but respond positively to Baryshnikov's open, sunny nature, his ardent curiosity, and the seriousness of his commitment. For his part, Baryshnikov was fascinated by Balanchine's personality—particularly by a combination of simplicity and sophistication such as he had never encountered. He told his friend, the critic Gennady Smakov, who had also left the Soviet Union and settled in the United States, "He's marvelous. In his judgments there's something wise and childlike at the same time. 'You dress girls up in nice costumes, teach them to dance, and, you know, it works out very nicely sometimes.' He lives in the most remarkable way, very ascetically—no excess furniture, nothing superfluous, not even a record player. And, at the same time, he's such a Russian Grand Seigneur, aesthete, and gourmet. It's as if all the culture he has stored up inside him is enough and there is nothing he needs from outside."

After Saratoga, Baryshnikov accompanied the New York City Ballet to Copenhagen, on the company's first visit to Denmark. Among his memories of that visit is one of exploring Copenhagen with Balanchine in the latter's quest for the perfect herring. He made his New York debut with the company on November 18 at the gala opening of the winter season, dancing *Rubies,* with Patricia McBride as his partner. In the course of the next year he would appear in twenty-two roles. One of the reasons he gave for his defection, when he left the Soviet Union in 1974, was that in the Soviet system there were too few opportunities to dance; with so few ballets in the repertory and so many dancers, he had danced only three or four times a month. That would certainly not be a complaint with the New York City Ballet; to the contrary, that year he would find himself often working to the point of exhaustion. And he would encounter frustrations, as well as satisfactions.

Meanwhile, Balanchine was having problems with his health once more. In September, he started experiencing great fatigue again. Then angina attacks began, which grew worse as the winter came on. He was able to go to Washington in December for ceremonies at the White House, when President Carter presented him and four other artists with the first Kennedy Center Awards, but he had an alarming attack in Union Station as he was about to leave Washington. Pale and shaking, he sat down in the station and took some nitroglycerin that he carried with him. Frightened, Barbara Horgan, who accompanied him, asked, "Shall I get a policeman?" He replied, "What for? I haven't committed a crime." In a while the attack passed and the color came back into his face. On the train he administered one of his favorite all-purpose remedies—a double shot (or "hooker," as he called it) of scotch, with a beer chaser, and got through the rest of the journey.

In January, he made a trip to Europe and spent some time in Zurich working with Patricia Neary, his former ballerina, who had just become director of the Zurich Ballet and was about to mount the first European production of *A Midsummer Night's Dream*. On his return he took a series of stress tests at New York University Hospital. He was told that the extent of the arterial restrictions that were causing his angina pains could only be determined by an angiogram, and that, depending on what the angiogram showed, heart bypass surgery might need to be considered. These findings frightened him. Lincoln Kirstein had had bypass surgery in 1975 and made an excellent recovery, but still Balanchine was terrified by the thought of such an operation and was almost as afraid of the angiogram test, which itself carried some mortal risk. He vowed to cure what ailed him in his own way, without resorting to such extreme measures, as he had cured other ailments in his life.

But things got worse rather than better. He dragged through the springtime, doing what he could to fulfill his duties—teaching company class occasionally, attending rehearsals and performances when he could, coaching Baryshnikov in some of his new roles when he had the strength. He had not choreographed a ballet since *Kammermusik No. 2*, in January 1978, and as it turned out, he would not be able to make another for his company till May of 1980, when he choreographed *Ballade*. Those two years were the longest unproductive period of his adult life. During this time the only choreography he undertook was to fulfill a commitment he had made to the New York City Opera for a ballet that would share a double bill with Purcell's *Dido and Aeneas*. The ballet he chose to do was *Le Bourgeois Gentilhomme,* with music by Richard Strauss, a subject he had tackled on two previous occasions, in 1932 and 1944. Rehearsals started in February, with the premiere scheduled for April 8. Because of Balanchine's poor health, he asked Robbins to collaborate on it with him, and he also asked Martins to choreograph one of the dances. For his principals he had Rudolf Nureyev as Cléonte, Patricia McBride as Lucile, Jean-Pierre Bonnefous as M. Jourdain, with students of the School of American Ballet as the corps.

The engagement of Nureyev to work with Balanchine occasioned surprise and curiosity. A famous story had circulated for years concerning the first meeting of the two men in 1961, right after Nureyev's defection from the Soviet Union. Nureyev came to Balanchine saying how much he would love to dance with his company. Balanchine asked what he wanted to dance. *Giselle*, said Nureyev, and the full-length *Swan Lake*. "We don't have those ballets," said Balanchine, "and we never will. If that's what you want to dance, you should go somewhere else. And maybe someday when you get tired of playing the prince, we can talk again." The anecdote is generally taken to exemplify the total incompatibility between the two men. In actuality, though the artistic paths each took greatly diverged, Balanchine and Nureyev took pleasure in each other's company when they met. Though in the minds of most ballet observers, Nureyev, with his flamboyant personality, would seem to be the antithesis of "the Balanchine dancer," Nureyev has cherished those Balanchine ballets—*Agon, Apollo, Prodigal Son*, and *Theme and Variations*—he has had the opportunity to dance with the Royal Ballet and other companies. His British biographer John Percival has written, "If I could only ever see Nureyev again in one role, I should be tempted to make that role Apollo."

Despite Balanchine's health problems, those associated with the preparation of *Le Bourgeois Gentilhomme* that spring remember it as a happy experience, with lots of laughter. The only indication of Nureyev's superstar status was that he kept his own valet-masseur-factotum on hand. Toward Balanchine he was attentive, respectful, solicitous. He brought imagination and high spirits to his comic part, which consisted in large measure of numerous disguises and many changes of costume he adopted throughout the ballet to fool M. Jourdain. The ballet was not a success with audience or critics. Arlene Croce thought the production a pretentious embarrassment. All of Nureyev's disguises as Cléonte related, in her mind, "to the quick-change artist that Nureyev has become, hopping from company to company, from role to role." It did not seem to her that there was any evidence of a successful collaboration between the star and the choreographers.

The New York City Ballet's spring season opened with a gala on May 1—a program that featured Baryshnikov dancing *Apollo* for the first time with the New York City Ballet. *Apollo* had been out of the New York City Ballet repertory since 1972. There were rumors that Balanchine had made changes in it.

Few were prepared, though, for the extent of those changes when the curtain went up that evening. Balanchine had cut the prologue and Apollo's first solo. He had altered the ending, cutting out the apotheosis of Apollo and the Muses ascending the staircase to await the chariot that would take them to Parnassus. The ballet now ended with the famous sunburst image of Apollo with the three Muses in arabesque. For years Balanchine had been pruning away at the set; now he had stripped it of everything except the stool on which Apollo sits to judge the Muses. In excising virtually all of the narrative element in the ballet, he had eliminated much of what many of those who cared deeply for the work had taken to be its central meaning. With the beginning gone, the ballet no longer dealt with the theme of the unformed Apollo discovering his powers and learning to give them mature expression. With the ascent toward Parnassus cut, the ending no longer conveyed that sense of the tragic which Stravinsky had said he sought to express in his music. Putting the sunburst image at the end transformed that image from a casual, passing miracle into something static and insistent, albeit still wondrous—making it, in the words of Robert Garis, into "a kind of Apollo-logo."

The changes distressed many of Balanchine's most devoted admirers. "Ugly," was the word Garis used in an article in *Ballet Review*—a "depredation." How could Balanchine have done this to his most hallowed work—the ballet he had characterized as the turning point of his creative life? To the cries of anguish and disapproval, Balanchine retorted, "I don't have to explain why I change things. I can do with my ballets whatever I like. They are mine. . . . I made them, and I can change them if I want to."

True enough, but still—why? And how could he, the most musical of choreographers, have taken the liberty of cutting the music—*Stravinsky's* music, no less? Subsequently, Balanchine did offer a number of explanations. Some of them seemed defensive and impatient, some were quite unexpected. In an interview by John Gruen for *Dance Magazine,* Balanchine advanced the suggestion that the chief reason the ballet had originally been done with a prologue was to enhance the royalties of composer and librettist, for royalties were greater for a ballet in two parts than in one. The original decor and costumes, when the ballet was made for Diaghilev, had been ugly and pointless, Balanchine said, and over the years he had been gradually altering and eliminating much of that. Recently he had looked at the birth scene and decided it was not interesting, so he had cut it out. As for the staircase that he had excised at the end, it had not been in the original version anyway but had been something he had substituted for the mountains that had been in that version, when there had also been a chariot. The staircase, too, looked silly to him now. "So I changed. I know that people were screaming and saying, 'Oh, he's changed it! It was so beautiful. *Why* did he have to change it?' But I know why I changed it. I took out all the garbage—that's why."

Summing up, he said, "Look, *Apollo* only becomes interesting when the dancing starts—that's what it's about . . . that's what *all* my ballets are about! Dancing isn't about anything except dancing—everything else is boring."

As for the historically-minded—and even among critics who reviewed the revised version favorably, a note of nostalgia and historical loss was sounded—Balanchine declared that what they were yearning for was neither possible nor desirable. There is no such thing as accurate historical preservation of a ballet; it changes with every cast change. Paintings can be preserved; ballets can't be and shouldn't be. If present-day critics and audiences could actually see *Apollo* as it was performed in 1928, "they would laugh their heads off at how it used to be."

Throughout the years Balanchine's partisans had defended his willingness to take liberties with classics of the bygone era—other choreographers' classics; now they were appalled when he took the same free hand with his own classics. In actuality, he had constantly tinkered with his ballets (those he had not discarded) all his working life, sometimes making drastic alterations; in many instances, critics and audiences had not even noticed. He had an appetite for renewal. That was what made him the choreographer he was.

I suspect that the very fact that *Apollo* had by now become so sanctified—even his own company was dancing it reverently—was what bothered and challenged him most. He *had* to change it—or change himself. In the following year, the fall of 1980, he changed it once more, restoring Apollo's first solo but not the prologue. That remained the authorized version for the rest of his life.

An intriguing sidelight to all this is the question of what, if anything, it reveals about the Balanchine-Stravinsky relationship. Was there a dark side to their relationship that Balanchine never acknowledged, perhaps never even consciously recognized? Robert Garis, in his *Ballet Review* article "Balanchine—Stravinsky: Facts and Problems," argues that the working relationship was not the total harmony it had always been said to be.

"I am arguing, then," Garis writes, "that there had developed a quiet disagreement through the years between Balanchine and Stravinsky about the relationship between music and dance, if only in the fact that

Stravinsky thought it correct, and more fruitful, for the music to come first as a kind of assignment to the choreographer, and that Balanchine had got into the habit instead of hunting up his own music and doing what he wanted with it. And I am arguing, too, that this disagreement brought with it another quiet disagreement, about the nature and dimension of Balanchine's talent. Stravinsky calls him a 'master,' meaning surely to praise him highly. I think Balanchine knew he was something more than what Stravinsky meant."

To be great as a choreographer was presumably not the equal of being great as a composer. Stravinsky took that for granted, and Balanchine always seemed to as well. It was only late in Stravinsky's life, Garis thinks, that Stravinsky came to a true recognition of Balanchine's genius, not merely mastery. That was when he saw Balanchine's choreography for *Movements*. The revelation drew from Stravinsky a tribute on a different order from anything he had hitherto expressed.

Much of Garis' article is admittedly speculative, using as evidence Balanchine's puzzling treatment of a number of Stravinsky ballets. His argument cannot be verified, but as a speculation it is intriguing and seems to me psychologically credible.

The revision of *Apollo* was just about the last ballet effort Balanchine was able to make that spring of 1979, for his angina was increasing in severity. By the end of May it was so bad that he could not walk or even get up and brush his teeth without acute pain. At last, after a severe attack experienced while he was at his Southampton condominium, he decided he could no longer put off having the angiogram. His doctors believed he made that decision in the nick of time. Five days after the angiogram, on June 17, he underwent triple bypass surgery. The operation was deemed successful, but it put him out of action for the rest of the summer.

Just before Balanchine had gone into the hospital in June, Baryshnikov had come to him with some news and a dilemma. Lucia Chase was planning to resign as artistic director of American Ballet Theatre, and the position was being offered to Baryshnikov. What did Mr. Balanchine think he should do? Predictably, Balanchine said, "You must do what you think is best for you," but added that, in view of the terms and guarantees being offered, he did not see how Baryshnikov could say no. Uncertain, Baryshnikov sought advice from others he respected. One was Peter Martins, his closest friend in the company. Martins' advice was not to take it. He didn't want the company to lose him, and he didn't want to lose the friendly rivalry that had developed between them. For Baryshnikov's own sake, he thought he should stick it out with the New York City Ballet, despite the difficulties and disappointments he was encountering. "Let them find another director," he said. "I'm sure they have a long list."

Baryshnikov replied, "They do. You're on that list, too," adding with a grin, "but a lot farther down than I am."

"Look, Misha," said Martins. "You finish what you have to do here. If you stay another year or two, you will find you have solved your problems, and you will leave feeling a lot better than if you leave now. Let them take somebody else. In two years whoever they have taken will have fallen apart, and if you still want the job then, it will be there for you."

At the time Baryshnikov joined the New York City Ballet, there were those who thought they perceived a grand plan, with Baryshnikov being moved into a position of contention as a successor to Balanchine. If there was such a plan, Balanchine did not acknowledge it, nor did Baryshnikov feel he had been let in on it. Martins clearly seemed to him the one most favored. On one occasion, Martins sounded him out as to whether he had such aspirations. Baryshnikov replied to him, "How could I ever expect to run New York City Ballet? I don't even know *Barocco*."

And to me Baryshnikov later said, when we discussed that topic, "That's a choreographer's company—and I'm not a choreographer."

While Baryshnikov was in the company, Balanchine did encourage him to try his hand at choreographing, as he encouraged others. Specifically, he suggested a Tchaikovsky work. Baryshnikov told Balanchine he didn't know whether he could do it. "There's no problem," Balanchine replied. "If you can't think of anything else, just take one of my ballets and do the reverse." But Baryshnikov did not take him up on the suggestion. He had more than enough to do, trying to master the style, learn the repertory, and overcome the constant aches in his muscles, tendons, knees, and back. And he didn't want to risk a failure.

Finally, in mid-June, at just about the time of Balanchine's operation, Baryshnikov made his decision, announcing it publicly on June 27. He would take the position of artistic director at American Ballet Theatre, but he would not start on it till September 1980. That would give him

⟿ *Baryshnikov as the cockney Pearly King in* Union Jack.

one more year to dance with the New York City Ballet. He went on with the company to Saratoga Springs in July, to London in September, and then to Washington for the company's engagement at Kennedy Center. During that engagement, on October 15, the company announced that because of continuing injuries, Baryshnikov had decided to resign at once. The role of the Poet in *La Sonnambula* in Washington was the last part he danced with the New York City Ballet.

He had begun to fear that if he continued he would do his body irreparable damage. It seemed to him that he was losing his flexibility and becoming stockier and more muscular. During his fifteen months with the New York City Ballet he had stayed away from Balanchine's classes, except for a couple of sessions, because the quick, jerky, small movements were different from what his body had been trained to do. But just such movements were built into the Balanchine choreography, and Baryshnikov was increasingly concerned that he was jeopardizing what he was best at—his exquisite legato, his miraculous ballon, his theatrical presence—while becoming less confident that he would ever excel, by his standards of achievement, at this other style of ballet.

Thus ended a sincere and courageous experiment. It was a rare thing to see someone at the top of his profession willing to risk his precious reputation as he had done—in effect becoming an apprentice again—to enlarge his scope. His biggest disappointment during this experience, he told me, was that the critics didn't seem to perceive what he was trying to do. "Balanchine would tell me, 'Don't read the critics—I never do.' But of course he did." Things might have worked out better if he had had a partner with whom he was compatible; for some reason he and Patricia McBride did not hit it off well or show each other off to advantage. It might have helped if he had been a few inches taller and could have had Suzanne Farrell as a partner. Most of all it would have helped if he had been twenty when he joined the company, instead of thirty. And certainly it was unfortunate that Balanchine was ill during most of his tenure and never had the opportunity to make a ballet for him as Baryshnikov must surely have hoped when he spoke of putting himself as "an instrument in his wonderful hands." Some months after leaving Balanchine's company, after the immediate hurts and disappointments had passed, Baryshnikov summed up for his biographer Gennady Smakov: "I'll never regret that I worked with him. He is a great man and a great choreographer. And I think he deflated certain of my fantasies about myself while helping me to acquire greater confidence in my field."

There's a story about another star's experience with Balanchine that I've long puzzled over. The star was Erik Bruhn, who was in the fifties the ranking male ballet artist of the Western world, the consummate and quintessential *danseur noble*. Bruhn was a member of the New York City Ballet during the winter 1959–60 season and again during the winter 1963–64 season. Like Baryshnikov, Bruhn was at the height of his fame when he joined the New York City Ballet, and he was about the same age, thirty-one, during his first season with the company. Both times he was extremely unhappy. He has said that it was like a death for him. He believed that Balanchine disliked him and sought to destroy him. During his second stint with the company, he developed terrible stomach pains, which he was convinced at the time were brought on by Balanchine's treatment of him but which turned out to be a perforated ulcer.

The story that has puzzled me is one I first encountered in an interview with Bruhn published in John Gruen's *The Private World of Ballet;* it is substantially repeated in the biography of Bruhn that Gruen wrote. It tells of his experience with *Apollo*—remarkable how many anecdotes that ballet has engendered! Apollo was the one major ballet role that Bruhn had not danced in his life. He longed to do it, and Balanchine had promised him he would when he signed on for the 1963 season. Here is what happened, as Bruhn tells it in the Gruen biography:

> To be taught Apollo by Balanchine himself was, of course, the most exciting thing I could think of. He told me that he would work with me alone on a certain Sunday—that the three girls in the ballet would not be present, and that he would demonstrate all their variations himself. Well, to be with Balanchine alone was something incredible. It was the one and only time that Balanchine and I had a real rapport. During the session he said, "You are the Apollo!" I remember his coming into the studio with a very bad cold, looking as though he were falling apart. But in the three or four hours that we worked together, he was transformed. It was as though he had just invented the ballet all over again, and the years seemed to drop off him. What was so fantastic was that he danced every part himself, including all the Muses. He and I danced the pas de deux and it was glorious. After working for hours he said, "You've learned the part. You know it!" And that was quite true, because he was such an incredible teacher.
>
> Anyway, this was Sunday. Monday would be a dark night. On Tuesday I looked at the call-board and saw that Balanchine had scheduled me

to dance in Apollo *that night,* without *a rehearsal! I was shocked. I went to the company manager and said that I couldn't possibly dance in the work. I was told that Balanchine said I knew the ballet. I thought it must be a joke. Finally I told the manager to tell Mr. Balanchine that I would dance Apollo that night on the condition that Balanchine himself would dance with me onstage—exactly the way he had in the rehearsal room. I was not about to go on that stage and see those three girls for the first time without having rehearsed with them. Well, Balanchine refused to give me that rehearsal and I didn't get to dance the ballet. It was another instance of what I was going through with the company, and it was the worst thing that happened between me and Balanchine. And, of course, to this day I have not danced Apollo.*

Many things troubled me about that story. Did it really happen this way? If so, why did Balanchine do it? And what does it tell us about Balanchine's nature? If he was indeed willing to put on a production of *Apollo* without adequate rehearsal, did this mean that Balanchine didn't care about that ballet? But, as was well known, it was a ballet that had always been special to him and that he always hovered over in rehearsal. I had seen that when I watched him preparing the 1958 revival with Jacques d'Amboise. Was Balanchine's action, then, a devious act of malice against Bruhn? Had he intended to undermine or publicly humiliate Bruhn—a noted perfectionist—by scheduling him to go before the public under conditions in which he could not possibly perform up to his standards, in the one role that mattered most to him and would be sure to attract the critics' attention? Bruhn doesn't say so directly, but in the context of what he has said elsewhere in the book about the destructiveness of Balanchine's relationship with him that is the implication the story leaves.

I spoke with a number of people about this story. One was Betty Cage, who was company manager at the time. She didn't remember the episode. If it did happen, she could only conjecture that there must have been some emergency and that Balanchine honestly believed that Bruhn was ready to dance it creditably. It was true that the relationship between Balanchine and Bruhn had not gone well. "Balanchine always had this lingering problem with stars, you know," she said. Still, it seemed to her utterly out of character that Balanchine's scheduling of Bruhn in this cherished role would have been motivated by a desire to embarrass him.

I also asked Maria Tallchief for her memories and comments. She would have been the one scheduled to dance Terpsichore in that performance. She, too, found it hard to credit that it could have happened as described. "In the first place, unless somebody was injured, you don't put somebody into the role the next day. These things are done weeks ahead of time. . . . I remember looking in at a rehearsal when George was rehearsing Erik in *Apollo*. I had on a blue sweater and George looked up and said, 'I've never seen you in blue before.' No, it could not have been true—unless somebody was injured. It's just possible that Jacques hurt his foot—and George might have said, 'Erik can do it,' because Erik was an incredible partner." In her view, Balanchine would have had no ulterior motive. "Balanchine admired Erik," she said.

Finally one day, when I was talking with Peter Martins about Balanchine, I asked what he made of the story. Martins replied, "That story has been amplified to such a terrific degree that it has become a classic. 'How could Balanchine ask a great dancer to go on stage without a rehearsal?' Look, it's happened in my own life at least fifteen times. You just go out and do it."

"The unstated motivation implied in the book," I said, "was that Balanchine was putting him out there to humiliate him."

"That was not beyond Balanchine. He's humiliated me many times," Martins conceded. But much more likely in this case, he thought, was that Balanchine was putting Bruhn to the test. "Balanchine was no fool. He liked to challenge dancers. He liked to put them in tough situations to see how they function. Our life is full of emergencies, and a dancer has to be able to produce—just like that. And I'm sure Balanchine tested Erik just as he tested everyone else. I'm sure he thought, 'Okay, he's a great dancer, he's a wonderful partner. Let's see how he functions under pressure.' I'm sure that's the way he did with Erik. 'Come on! Just go on stage! An arabesque is an arabesque. You hold her. What's the big deal? Just do it!'"

Martins decided to illustrate his point with a story out of his own experience. "Look, I remember Balanchine at seven o'clock a few years ago—Misha [Baryshnikov] and I were going to have dinner at eight o'clock at a restaurant on the East Side. I was still in the theatre working on some music with a pianist for a ballet I was about to do. The first ballet on the program that night was *Donizetti Variations*, starting at eight. The person cast was Helgi Tomasson. At seven o'clock somebody knocked on the door of the music room. It was Balanchine looking for Misha. Helgi had called in to say his back was so bad he couldn't move.

Misha, who had done the ballet, had been called at home but wasn't there. Balanchine looked at me and said, 'You do.' I said, 'I don't know this ballet. It's one of the ballets I've never done in my life.' He said, 'I know you don't know, but I will teach it to you.' I said, 'When?' He said, 'Now.'

"I said, 'Look, Mr. B., it's ten after seven. To teach me will take at least an hour. Plus there's makeup to put on. And what would I wear?'

"'You wear *Bournonville* costume—no problem. Makeup takes you five minutes. I'll teach you right now.'

"'Mr. B., this is ridiculous.'

"'You can do.'

"So I thought a minute, and I thought all right, I can do it. 'Mr. B.,' I said, 'I'll make a deal with you. I'll do it under one condition.' He stiffened—he must have thought I was going to blackmail him. 'I'll do it under the condition you give me a chance to do another performance of it—the *Donizetti*.' He had never let me do it before.

"'Oh, really?'

"'Yes, that's all. If I can come in on one hour's notice, then give me another performance of it.'

"'Absolutely, dear,' he said, 'You'll be able to do it as much as you want.' He was relieved. He took me downstairs and taught me the ballet. Kay Mazzo was there onstage warming up. He taught me without her, and then in the last two minutes she and I went over a couple of things. I knew Kay Mazzo, I knew how she danced. I didn't have to partner her in practice. I just needed to know the steps she would be doing—and Balanchine had done them for me. Then I ran off and put on my makeup. And I did it. After the performance, Balanchine came up to me and said, 'Thank you very much,' and he walked away."

Baryshnikov was waiting at the restaurant, having been phoned there by Martins' dresser and told that Martins would be an hour late. When Martins arrived at the restaurant, he told Baryshnikov what had happened. Baryshnikov said, "Thank God I wasn't home!"

The point Martins was making with this story was not only that filling in at short notice was not such a big deal, but also that Balanchine valued dancers who were willing to take chances—provided, of course, they had the technique to justify it. He was interested in process, in becoming, more than in perfection. For him perfection, as a state of achievement, was admirable—but then what? His interest was in dancers who tried to go beyond themselves or who were willing to try what was asked of them even if they had doubts and even if it went counter to their image of themselves. Balanchine's appreciation for risk-taking was one of the reasons Suzanne Farrell's dancing so pleased him. She never danced a role exactly the same way twice. It was also why Balanchine was said not to mind when dancers fell down, provided that it happened when they were putting out their utmost energy. They were just fulfilling the maxim he often uttered in company class when demanding ever more effort: "It's better to die a hero than live a coward."

After Martins had concluded his story I had one question left to ask him. "Did you get a chance to do the *Donizetti* again?"

He laughed, and said, "Never." About a year after this episode he went to Balanchine and said, "Remember your promise?"

"Promise? What promise?"

"The *Donizetti*—"

"I remember," said Balanchine in a dry voice, putting his finger along his nose. "We'll see. One day . . . " For some reason that he never bothered to explain to Martins, he just didn't want him in that ballet. And Martins, no longer all that eager to do it, never asked again.

Because of his operation, Balanchine missed the 1979 summer season at Saratoga Springs; it was the first time he had missed a season. He was in the hospital nearly a month and then went to his Southampton place to recuperate. The New York City Ballet was scheduled to go to London in early September for a three-week engagement. It would be the company's first appearance in London since 1965, and Balanchine had no intention of missing this trip. By then, he was feeling quite lively—better than he had felt in quite some time—even though he still had a number of troublesome afflictions. Occasional problems with dizziness and his sense of balance persisted, and cataracts on both eyes were dimming his vision; in due time there would have to be operations to remove the cataracts and provide new lenses for him.

Still, those who saw him in London thought he had made a remarkable recovery. On opening day of the company's engagement Arlene Croce observed him strolling among the crowds near Covent Garden looking serene. Niels-Jørgen Kaiser, the director of Tivoli, who had come over from Denmark to see the company perform and do an interview with Balanchine for Radio Denmark, went out to supper with him one day, and he was struck by Balanchine's vigor. They went to a seafood restaurant on Swallow Street. Balanchine would not take a taxi, preferring to walk. Kaiser had trouble keeping up with him, Balanchine walked so briskly. "I'm like an old automobile," Balanchine told Kaiser. "They've given me a new engine. Soon they'll give me a couple new headlamps. And then I'll be just as good as new."

The London season was immensely popular with the public, all performances selling out except for one Wednesday matinee, but less of a triumph with the British critics who, as before, objected to the company's high-energy style of ballet. "The corps de ballet was a ballet master's nightmare with hands and arms all over the place," wrote one critic of *Symphony in C*. And G.B.L. Wilson wrote in *Dance News*, "In Mr. Balanchine's work so often the arms and hands seem overstretched and straining for something—which at first sight offends us. . . . Similarly our hips must always be level—to be otherwise is an affront to sensibility. And when we see one of Mr. Balanchine's girls raise her leg vertically and raise her hip to get it there, a shiver of horror runs through the audience (so many of whom are students, teachers and dancers)." Balanchine had always been fond of London, but he told the critic Alexander Bland of *The Observer* that it was probably a good thing that he had not been permitted years ago to get a work permit and settle in England, as he had once hoped to do, because he really wasn't dignified enough for a country where "if you are awake it is already vulgar." Bland was not amused. "Though technically fastidious," Bland wrote, "he certainly lacks the regulator of good taste, which is one of Britain's hallmarks."

Back in New York that fall, Balanchine was full of plans and eager to get back into action. He had a couple of new ballets he wanted to do for the spring, and he wanted to restage for the New York City Ballet two ballets he had done under other auspices—the *Walpurgisnacht Ballet* from Gounod's *Faust*, which he had made for the Paris Opéra in 1975, and *Le Bourgeois Gentilhomme*, which he wanted to try yet again, this time using Peter Martins, Suzanne Farrell, and Frank Ohman in the lead roles, with Heather Watts and Victor Castelli dancing the divertissement. He had also started planning a Tchaikovsky festival for the spring of 1981, and was thinking about what music to choreograph himself and what to assign to others. Tchaikovsky had called him on the phone, he said, and told him not to put it off too long. As always, he could not enjoy the luxury of simply being a choreographer. He was essentially the company's impresario and managing director as well as its teacher, ballet master, and artistic director.

One of the matters that occupied his attention was the improvement of acoustics at the State Theater, a cause he felt strongly about. The project had got its practical start a few years before at a dinner party at the apartment of Leslie R. Samuels and his wife, Fan Fox. There Balanchine got into conversation with the acoustical specialist Cyril M. Harris, and between them they roughed out what needed to be done and how it could be accomplished. Later that evening Balanchine summarized the conversation for his host and said how urgent he thought it was. Samuels responded, "Count me in for a million!" Ultimately he—or more precisely he and his wife's foundation, the Fan Fox and Leslie R. Samuels Foundation—got counted in for not $1 million but $4 million out of the $4.5 million the project ended up costing. Actual work would not commence till 1981. In the meantime much detailed planning had to be done, including planning for how to carry on the work with the minimum disruption of the performing schedules of the New York City Ballet and the New York City Opera.

The two new ballets Balanchine choreographed were presented in the spring of 1980. On May 9, the premiere of *Ballade* took place, to music by Fauré. It featured Merrill Ashley, partnered by Ib Andersen—a new soloist from the Royal Danish Ballet—and a corps of ten women. Croce described it as "a small, perfect vanity case of a ballet, the kind of exquisite miniature Balanchine fashions from time to time when he wants to make a fuss over one of his ballerinas." In *Ballo della Regina*, two years before, he had shown off Ashley's brilliant allegro capabilities, her extraordinary technical facility. Now he had made a ballet that was intended to demonstrate that there was a great deal more to her than that—to show a lyrical side to her, and to reveal her as a personality as well as a technician. The ballet's function was to show this to the audience, but before that its function was to show it to Ashley herself and convince her that this, too, was within the realm of her nature and possibilities. In that sense, it was a teaching ballet, as so many of Balanchine's ballets have been, from *Serenade* on.

Balanchine once said to me, "I always hear people talking about my importance as a choreographer. I think my real importance has been as a teacher." At the time he said that, I had difficulty accepting it or grasping what he meant. Gradually I think I came to understand what he was getting at, and to see the large sense in which he was using the word "teacher." Of course he taught in his company classes, in a way no other artistic director did. There he was tremendous—fierce, funny, obsessive, inhumanly patient, with gnomic utterances and apt, farfetched metaphors for every occasion. That teaching was quintessential. For he had to develop his dancers to new levels of proficiency in order for them to be able to execute choreography that he was not even able to conceive until they had attained those levels. Beyond the classroom studio, he also taught them various lessons in ballets he made. His choreography was often his most potent teaching instrument. One lesson was the kind he gave Ashley in *Ballade*: not to think of herself as limited or typed. Many years previously he had done something similar for Maria Tallchief, then famed as America's most brilliant bravura dancer. To bring out her latent lyricism, he choreographed *Scotch Symphony* and his version of *Swan Lake* for her. For Mimi Paul he once did the exact opposite. He made for her a pas de deux full of jumps—the *Valse Fantaisie* section of *Glinkiana*—because she was convinced she was not a jumper. In her early years Suzanne Farrell had difficulty with bourrées. So in *Don Quixote* in each act he set her a different problem in bourrée. Many choreographers routinely choreograph to a dancer's strengths. "Show me what you can do here!" they might say, "Good, let's keep that." But I know of no other who so thoughtfully choreographed to a dancer's weaknesses.

In a real sense, the audience became part of this pedagogical process and provided the supportive environment that enabled it to flourish. The audience had to learn to be patient, to appreciate what was happening when they saw dancers from whom they expected one kind of perfection or achievement striving to achieve something quite different—and to take positive pleasure in such explorations and adventures. So Balanchine throughout all those years taught his audience as well.

If one accepts Balanchine's description of himself as a teacher, his lifelong aversion to stars becomes more understandable. A star doesn't learn; a star shines. A star doesn't want a part, but a vehicle. Makarova's complaint that Balanchine preferred someone he could mold rather than a dancer of her consummate talents was true, but she couldn't understand why. The explanation does not lie in his having the nature of a Svengali, as some have claimed. There was something of that in him, certainly, but he was motivated at least as much by curiosity: what could this person become? Developing promising young dancers to their limits and beyond was his satisfaction and stimulation. It was this that constantly renewed him.

The new ballet that Balanchine created next, after *Ballade*, was also a romantic work but in almost every way—tone, treatment, subject, style, and attitude—quite different from *Ballade*. It was given its premiere June

19. Many found it an astonishment. In this ballet, Balanchine for the first time in his life worked with music by Schumann. He put the composer's name into the title—*Robert Schumann's "Davidsbündlertänze"*—thereby focusing attention, as the ballet itself did, on the composer as well as the composition. In an interview with Balanchine before the premiere, *The New York Times* critic Anna Kisselgoff wondered whether the public might be put off by such a mouthful of a title. Balanchine replied magisterially, "If you can't pronounce it, don't come."

The ballet dealt with the life of Schumann, the inner and fantasy life as much as the historical life, in relation to his wife, Clara. It was not a narrative or a biography, but a meditation on Schumann's life—or, more precisely, a meditation by Balanchine on the meditation Schumann himself had expressed in the suite of eighteen piano pieces he called the *Davidsbündlertänze*. Before a Gothic backdrop, designed by Rouben Ter-Arutunian in the style of Caspar David Friedrich, four couples danced these pieces, as performed by an onstage pianist. The couples were Karin von Aroldingen and Adam Lüders, Ib Andersen and Kay Mazzo, Suzanne Farrell and Jacques d'Amboise, and Peter Martins and Heather Watts.

A constant play of emotions permeated the ballet, with mercurial changes from euphoria to despair or from assertiveness to doubt, and sometimes several emotions troublingly intermingled. The style of dance employed seemed novel for Balanchine. "Compared to almost any other piece of Balanchine choreography, even compared to *Meditation,*" Croce wrote, "the ballet has almost no intricacy or sweep of phrase. Instead, we see dancing used as an extension of a dramatic situation: steps are repeated over and over or protracted into poses or connected not by other steps but by walks, runs, hesitant gestures, glances. The lack of density and the free look of the timing make us feel we're witnessing a series of short, probing conversations."

Intensely dramatic as the ballet was, its drama was not tied to biographical narrative or plot. The most overt programmatic moment was the appearance onstage during Lüders' nightmare solo of the Philistine forces of society that drove Schumann to madness and attempted suicide—represented by five menacing figures in tall top hats and black cloaks, armed with great quill pens like lances. (The quill pens might have been a reference on Balanchine's part to some of his own wars with the scribes.) Originally, Balanchine had planned to wash these Philistines away in a great flood, but that proved technically impractical so he

just had them recede from sight. "I always like to get rid of those dark people who don't understand anything," he told Kisselgoff.

Many in the audience were greatly affected by the ballet, moved to the point of tears, without knowing quite why. Many interpretations were put forward. One of the most thoughtful was by Richard Poirier in an essay on Balanchine, titled "An American Genius," in *The New Republic*. The thematic meanings of the ballet, he wrote, for him have to do with the idea in life and in dance of "support"—dramas of sexual, psychological, social support emerging out of the way Balanchine has treated the act of dance support in the ballet. "With an intensity at once very poignant and very beautiful, we are shown versions of the problem, or is it the delight? the opportunity? of physically and psychologically holding up our partner or would-be partner, and of being held up or supported in return. Of course this is a kind of meaning inherent in any dance, but once again, and after its glorious renditions in the Stravinsky Festival's *Violin Concerto* and *Duo Concertant*, it is revealed as a central generative force in Balanchine's imagination of himself, of his art, and of a composer who infused classical forms with intense personal emotion. The psychological ambiguities and mysteries that for Balanchine are inherent in dancing, especially in partnering, have found in Schumann's life and music analogies that are unusually direct and vivid. That is why the ballet seems so emotionally charged, even, to some viewers, overwrought."

In 1976 the orchestra had struck for six weeks, and that was bad. In the winter of 1980, the dancers voted to strike, and that was worse. For Balanchine, this was the greatest outrage of his experience. It was heresy, insurrection, anarchy. He took it as a personal repudiation. How could the family he had created and nurtured do this to him? How could the instruments of his art now balk and refuse to serve that art? He spoke of taking his ballets and going elsewhere. Princess Grace of Monaco had asked him to help her start a company. Perhaps he would go there. As for the dancers, they were nothing but ingrates, upstarts, materialists. Why should a sixteen-year-old corps member be able to demand four hundred dollars a week? Why should they expect to have nice apartments and live comfortably and secure at that age? When he was a dancer and choreographer for Diaghilev he had to pawn his pants because he earned so little. Why should they expect to have it easier?

∿ *Heather Watts and Peter Martins in* Robert Schumann's "Davidsbündlertänze."

In their meetings, the company members, hearing of these rumblings from Olympus, went through their own anguish. There were those who believed they should put up with anything rather than hurt Balanchine, particularly at this time of his life and in his state of health. Others argued that it was time for them to grow up and become adults—it was time to stop acting as if New York City Ballet were a family and to recognize that it was an institution. And that meant learning how to cultivate appropriate hostility toward management. But did that include Mr. Balanchine? Was Balanchine management? Or was he one of them? Or was he a law unto himself? Their debates, when they contemplated the awesome image of the one who had created their cosmos, grew metaphysical and theological. Their union leaders—representatives of the American Guild of Musical Artists—kept reminding them that the issue was money.

The strike vote had been taken at a meeting attended by less than half of the hundred or so company members. The vote had been twenty-six to eighteen. On December 23, Balanchine let it be known that he would like to meet with the entire company after company class. It would be the first time he had talked with all of them together in three years. In her book *Winter Season,* Toni Bentley has described the scene. Balanchine walked in calmly, and quietly called them to gather around him. All sat on the floor at his feet, except for Peter Martins and a few senior men, who remained standing at the back. Balanchine spoke for about ten minutes, in a tone that Bentley characterized as "simple and friendly." He said that he and Lincoln Kirstein were the heads and rulers of the company, and they had made their final offer, but they were not willing to allow the future of the New York City Ballet to be decided by such a small number of votes. If seventy dancers were to vote to strike, that would be different. "Fine, okay, I will be happy," he said. "We will go elsewhere and make a new company in a day. This is the fifth company, and we will make the sixth. We have always done so. You can go to John Clifford, Canada, Ballet Theatre, Europe—fine. I want a vote for myself, and I don't give a damn if it's illegal. Yes or no from a hundred and five!"

Bentley has written that at this point she and the others were terrified that he was going to ask them right then and there to raise their hands in front of him to decide whether or not to end the New York City Ballet. Nobody would have dared speak out or vote no. But he didn't do that. He just said there would be a box and he wanted to know what they all thought. With that, he left. A week later the dancers voted to accept a management offer that differed very little from the one they had rejected six or seven weeks previously. Essentially, it provided a three-year agreement, with wage increases of 41 percent over that period: starting corps de ballet salaries would increase from $300 to $400 a week over three years; those with at least four years in the company would receive from $500 to $575; soloists' wages would increase from $580 to $650; principals' wages would continue to be set through individual negotiation.

It had been a traumatic episode. What it had revealed was that the New York City Ballet could no longer be run as Balanchine's family. It had grown too big and had become too complex an organization, and he was no longer able to attend to it all as he had up until just a few years before. The chief way in which he had maintained close contact with his dancers had been his daily company class, but for the past three years, because of his poor health and frequent absence, he had been able to teach class only intermittently. Many of the new company members hardly knew him. Like many others, Toni Bentley was sad about the changed spirit and nostalgic for the old days.

For the first time Balanchine was beginning to admit to intimates that he might not live forever. That summer, he surprised Niels-Jørgen Kaiser, when they had lunch together at the end of the Tchaikovsky Festival, by declaring in quite a matter-of-fact tone that he didn't have time to waste on unnecessary things these days because he had only two more years to live.

Death was a thread running through the Tchaikovsky Festival. Whereas the 1972 Stravinsky Festival had been a celebration, this one had more of the quality of a memento mori—a mood that was especially accented by the Balanchine ballets that opened and closed the festival. It opened with Suzanne Farrell, in a solemn black tutu, dancing the Preghiera of *Mozartiana*. It closed with Balanchine's treatment of the *Adagio Lamentoso* movement of the *Pathetique*, in which prostrate monks in black suggest the heavings of a giant heart beating its last and which ends with a small boy blowing out a single candle on a darkened stage. Tchaikovsky, of course, had brooded much on death and finally did end his unhappy life by suicide; melancholy shadows even his lightest music. Even if Balanchine had been in a sanguine frame of mind, he, with his sensitivity to music, would have needed to include some representation of Tchaikovsky's despair in his choreography. The other two Balanchine ballets in the festival certainly were more buoyant, especially the *Garland*

Waltz, with its delightful use of sixteen children from the school. Still, to many it seemed that Balanchine was uttering a valedictory note in his ballets on this occasion. Wrote the British critic Clement Crisp, after Balanchine's death, "I felt that Balanchine the creator said his farewell to us at the end of the 1981 Tchaikovsky Festival."

Working on the Tchaikovsky Adagio Lamentoso.

CHAPTER SEVENTEEN

The Last Year

n 1982 Russian Easter fell on April 18. For several days before, Balanchine cooked and prepared for his traditional party. Friends had been concerned that the effort would overstrain him, but he wanted to do it and insisted he felt up to it. As a concession to their concerns he agreed not to go through the laborious process of making kulitch but to purchase it at Babka, a shop whose kulitch came close to meeting his exacting standards, but he made pascha and all the other customary dishes and laid in a stock of his favorite champagne—which had also been the czar's—Roederer Cristal. The party usually began around one A.M. after the services, which Balanchine and the others would attend. That night the weather was rainy and blustery. At the church of Our Lady of the Sign on Park Avenue at Ninety-second Street, the worshipers with their lit candles could not make the usual procession around the open courtyard; they had to shuffle along the staircase. As they were proceeding, Balanchine's candle went out. The person standing beside him sought to relight it. Three times he relit it, and each time it went out immediately. "Leave it," Balanchine finally said. "It's not supposed to be lit." Some bystanders thought Balanchine looked ominous as he spoke.

A few days after Easter, Balanchine went to Dr. Seymour Solomon, of Montefiore Hospital, for a complete neurological examination. Dr. Solomon specialized in gerontological neurology. He and his department were unusual in that they assumed that old people can continue to thrive and that many impairments suffered by the aged are treatable, not neces-

With Peter Martins.

381

sarily inevitable. Still, the chief complaint voiced by the seventy-eight-year-old Balanchine was a new one to Dr. Solomon. In the subsequent consultation report he sent to Dr. Langner, Dr. Solomon wrote: "In recent weeks he noted difficulty pirouetting to the right when standing on his left foot. Pirouetting to the right when standing on the right foot, his balance was relatively unimpaired." In a postscript Dr. Solomon proposed that in future discussions of subtle truncal ataxia in the medical literature this symptom should be known as "Balanchine's Sign."

Though the neurological examination produced few discernible findings and no reliable diagnosis, Balanchine was suffering. At times he felt as if a factory were operating in his head. He could no longer play the piano, for he said if he touched only one note, he found the din intolerable. Even when there were no external noises, there was a constant roaring in his ears. His vision was fuzzy, for the cataract operation in his right eye had not been wholly successful, and he still had a cataract on his other eye, as well as glaucoma. He was having difficulty reading, or even watching television, and when he stood in the wings for a performance the dancers were blurred and shadowy. He kept asking why the lighting was so dim. Most distressing to him was how tottery he had become. "Do you realize what it means to a choreographer to lose his sense of balance?" he said to his Danish friend Niels-Jørgen Kaiser when they met that summer. Afraid of falling, he was embarrassed to be seen using a cane, so he carried an umbrella even in fine weather. He was distressed also by the way he looked now—no longer slim and erect but, to his mind, puffy and ugly. To look like that seemed to him not merely a misfortune but morally reprehensible. That was the way ordinary people looked, not ballet dancers or ballet masters.

In Dr. Langner's mind, the real decline in his physical condition became noticeable near the end of April 1982, and after that his deterioration became increasingly evident. Yet he was capable of pulling himself together for an occasion. When there were meetings or interviews, he would stage the circumstances carefully to conceal his weaknesses. He would seat himself firmly on the sofa in his office at the State Theater, an elbow on the side bolster as an inconspicuous prop, and answer questions in a confident voice, sometimes guessing at what had been asked. In June, during the Stravinsky Centennial, he was interviewed in his office by Alan Kriegsman of *The Washington Post*. Kriegsman had heard that Balanchine was seriously ailing, and he was surprised at how vigorous and alert Balanchine seemed. Kriegsman himself had recently suffered a heart

Last minute adjustments of the scenery at dress rehearsal of Noah and the Flood.

attack and was fearfully considering an angiogram and possible coronary bypass operation. Balanchine urged him not to put off the operation, if one was indicated. "You'll feel wonderful after the operation," Balanchine said enthusiastically. "You'll be jumping around like a boy."

For at least two years, Balanchine had been planning a festival celebrating the hundredth anniversary of Igor Stravinsky's birth, and he had scheduled it for the week of June 10 to 18. He was aware that even if he were still at the top of his powers, this commemoration was not likely to be the extraordinary creative efflorescence the 1972 Stravinsky Festival had been. By now most of Stravinsky's best music had been choreographed, and new ballets might have to be set to less than top-drawer Stravinsky. Still, Balanchine believed that a festival dedicated to the range of Stravinsky's output would be a joy—a tribute to his great friend, a present for himself as well as the public, a reminder to the world of the long, intimate relationship between the composer and the New York City Ballet. No other company in the world had put into dance so many of Stravinsky's compositions. No other orchestra had even played so many. During the Centennial week fifty-five Stravinsky works were performed, eleven of them new ballets. His supervision of the centennial turned out to be the last ballet activity of Balanchine's career. He could not have wanted a more fitting end.

For the Centennial, Balanchine choreographed only two small works himself—*Elégie* and *Tango*. In collaboration with Jacques d'Amboise he restaged *Noah and the Flood*, and with the assistance of John Taras and Vera Zorina he staged a presentation of the cantata *Perséphone*. But he was no longer able to summon at will his powers of attention and concentrate them into that laser beam of certainty that had always characterized his way of working. During *Noah and the Flood* he became confused and was content to let d'Amboise finish it. He seemed much more his old self, though, when choreographing *Tango*. He was constantly out of his chair to show the dancers what he wanted done, including the lifts. Solicitously, they kept urging him to take it easy. By now he and his leading dancers knew each other so well he could communicate a whole chain of steps by a gesture or a phrase, and they could tell just by the way he sniffed how well they had done it. For *Tango* he had cast the twenty-year-old Christopher d'Amboise as partner for the forty-year-old Karin von Aroldingen. The pairing, suggested to him no doubt by the brash, ironic sultriness of the music, intrigued and amused him. He asked Jacques d'Amboise to attend rehearsals, not to help him out, but to learn Christopher's part. Said Balanchine, "Father will understudy son." It was a wry jest. Mortality was in the air. The father, hobbled and stiff from injuries and the ravages of time, was no longer capable of breezing through the part for the son that the fading choreographer was still capable of conceiving.

He had planned one additional work for the Centennial but had not been able to get to it. That was Stravinsky's *Variations for Orchestra*, which he had choreographed for an ensemble in 1966, but which he wanted to do over again as a solo for Suzanne Farrell. As the festival drew to a close, he found himself occasionally feeling well enough to work and arranged for rehearsals with Farrell. In these sessions, he made a new ballet to that music, changing everything except the running steps and grand jeté of the first eight measures and the walkover at the end. This, his last piece of choreography, was presented on July 2. Balanchine admitted to being satisfied. "The first time I did it, I didn't have it right," he said to Farrell. "Now it's exactly what the music calls for."

Two evenings after that premiere, the season ended. At the insistence

∽ *Suzanne Farrell in* **Variations for Orchestra.**

of the audience and the company, Balanchine took the final curtain call. He succeeded in disguising his instability by holding on to the curtain, not obviously but artfully, with the hand that was behind his back as he bowed, as if playing the role of someone gracious enough to appear but not vain enough to linger.

As usual, he accompanied the New York City Ballet to Saratoga later that month for its summer residency, but he was not well enough to go to the theatre. He remained the entire time at the cottage in the countryside he shared with Edward Bigelow. There Orville H. Schell, the corporation lawyer who was chairman of the board of the New York City Ballet, called on him one day. On Schell's mind was the troublesome succession issue. He hoped on this visit to resolve it. From all he had seen and learned in the past few years, Peter Martins was the one best suited and best prepared to run the company capably. It was evident to Schell that Balanchine had been testing Martins, and that Martins had passed those tests. Increasingly, Balanchine had relied on Martins—to teach company class, to choreograph, to assist with casting and repertory—but still Balanchine would make no formal designation or pronouncement. When pressed, he often asserted he didn't care what would happen to his company, or to his ballets, after he died. He may well have meant it, at least in part. All his life he had resisted being dictated to by the past, and he was equally resistant to suggestions that he now dictate to the future. That morning at Saratoga, Schell and Balanchine chatted amiably on many matters, but Schell, experienced as he was at asking tough questions, could not bring himself to pose bluntly the one he wanted Balanchine to answer. And Balanchine volunteered nothing.

In late August, Balanchine's eye doctor operated to remove the cataract on his left eye and implant a lens. The operation, it was hoped, would remedy some of his balance problems as well as improve his eyesight. For several weeks thereafter he had to remain cooped up in his New York apartment, growing so restless that he decided to reward himself with a trip to Washington when the New York City Ballet went there in early October. A few days before that trip, feeling much improved, he took part in an audition for the planned revival of *On Your Toes*, and he strongly urged the producers to engage Makarova for the Russian ballerina part, and Valentina Kozlova as her understudy and alternate.

The train trip to Washington on October 2 went well, with Balanchine lively, talkative, and cheerful all the way, but on arrival he suddenly became ill, with nausea and high fever. He was hospitalized at George Washington Hospital for ten days with what was diagnosed as viral influenza. There he was given another series of neurological tests. On his return to New York, he was again confined to his apartment though not bedridden. In the weeks that followed, he suffered several quite frightening falls. One of them came when he slipped on a scatter rug while hastening to answer the phone. All his life he had been accustomed to moving rapidly—as a lad, recalled Danilova, he could catch mice with his hand as deftly as a cat could pounce—and he could not always remember now to move with caution. The phone call had been from his eye doctor wanting to know how his lens implant was doing; the answer, as the doctor learned to his horror, was that it had been doing all right until he had fallen just now. Early in November, he fell again; this time the fall caused hairline fractures of four ribs and his left wrist. He decided to have himself admitted to Roosevelt Hospital for observation. There he spent the last five months of his life.

At the hospital, it was apparent from the start that there was little that could be done for him of a medical nature beyond giving him vitamin injections and sedatives when he needed them to sleep. His physicians could offer no hope for recovery. He was suffering from a progressive deterioration of the brain and nerve centers. Tests had conclusively established that it was not Alzheimer's Disease, but the exact cause of his affliction remained a mystery. It was not until some time after Balanchine's death that a pathologist's autopsy was able to conclude with certainty that the disease was a rare, little-known infection called Creutzfeldt-Jakob Disease—caused by a virus that may incubate in the brain and spinal cord for twenty years or more before symptoms appear. Only in recent years has the disease been identified. As yet no cure has been found. In the United States only about two hundred cases a year are recorded; the doctors could not guess how Balanchine had incurred it. Characteristically, patients die within a year after the first symptoms show themselves. In Balanchine's case, it took nearly five years.

At first, after being admitted, Balanchine tried to run the company from his hospital bed. He was constantly on the phone to staff members, and he got annoyed, as he always had, when he phoned the office on a Saturday and got no answer. He had never been able to accept Saturday as a holiday. Gradually the calls decreased, as increasingly his consciousness was taken over by the effort it took to stay alive.

At first also, he kept saying that in Switzerland or somewhere else in Europe there must be clinics that would cure him—some place like the clinic near Mont Blanc where he had recovered from tuberculosis as a young man. Barbara Horgan and his doctors investigated that possibility; there were clinics available, but none that realistically offered any better prospect of a cure, and none that made sense for him. There he would be isolated. Here, at Roosevelt Hospital, four blocks from the State Theater, those who loved or revered him—those many whose lives he had shaped or affected or touched—had easy access to him. They weren't ready to part from him; they needed time to come to terms with that. To many of his younger dancers, he was a god who had existed from the beginning of time. They couldn't imagine what their lives would be like without him. For whom would they dance? And the older dancers and associates also had built their lives around him. Even in his dying, he had to pay heed to the needs of those who had served him. In January, a few of those closest to him in the company gathered at his bedside to celebrate his birthday. "That was nice, they made a party for you," Dr. Langner said to him on her visit the next day. With his characteristic clarity and forthrightness, he replied, "It wasn't for me. It was for them."

Among the many who visited him was the composer Morton Gould.

On one visit, early in December, he brought with him a tape of a section of music he had composed for the ballet *The Birds of America*. Balanchine listened and said it was nice. They talked about the ballet a little. Then Balanchine, who was under sedation, fell asleep. He might have fallen asleep even without sedation. By then *The Birds of America* had been in gestation for nearly forty years and had been endlessly discussed. As generations of writers had yearned to write "The Great American Novel," so Lincoln Kirstein had yearned from early on to produce "The Great American Ballet." This was to be it. It was to be a heroic, three-act spectacle with the naturalist John James Audubon, posited as the lost son of Louis XVI and Marie Antoinette, as its emblematic central figure. Somehow or other the Audubon-Dauphin character was also to be Johnny Appleseed as well as Buffalo Bill, and any number of American themes, settings, and legends were to be figured forth. By the third act, the westward march of American civilization would have reached the Golden Gate and the twentieth century; the legendary characters of this act would be such as Fred Astaire, James Cagney, Ginger Rogers, and Buster Keaton. Kirstein had written a scenario for this ballet; so, at one time or another, had Louis Bromfield, Glenway Wescott, and even Céline. Karinska had sketched some of the costumes. Rouben Ter-Arutunian had designed sets. Balanchine had speculated on dance possibilities and whom he might cast. His first choice for Pocohontas, naturally, had been Maria Tallchief. To mount this ballet would have cost, according to a 1976 estimate, around a million dollars. By this time— 1982—it would cost a third again as much. Yet it had not been abandoned. There had been a session on it just the previous spring. At that time Balanchine had proposed assigning sections to various company choreographers rather than doing it all himself. In truth, he had probably long ceased to be excited by this project. The ideas and symbolic themes had never meant as much to him as they had to Kirstein. His was not a mind that feasted on abstractions.

Over the years, the spectacle he had been more interested in putting on, if he had the means, was *The Sleeping Beauty*. But he would not do it, as he put it, "bargain basement." He would put it on only if he could produce it on a scale comparable to *The Sleeping Beauty* whose enchantment he would never forget, the one he had appeared in as a boy in St. Petersburg, where the company had numbered some two hundred dancers and the stage had been grand enough for the most spectacular effects. Such effects—cascading fountains, grand formal gardens, a sumptuous palace, a forest that overgrows the palace before the audience's eyes, a lake across which the Lilac Fairy's boat could sail—could not be obtained at the State Theater, whose backstage space was relatively restricted. With Ronald Bates, the company's stage manager and lighting director, Balanchine had explored the possibility of achieving the desired effects with lighting projections, but those did not make him happy. He was nostalgic, I suspect, not only for the nineteenth-century fantasy but for the nineteenth-century stage machinery as well. He enjoyed recalling that at the Maryinsky, when they put on a ballet like *The Corsair,* which called for storm-tossed seas, the authorities could request a detachment of the czar's guards, whose assignment would be to lie down under the ocean drop cloth and heave as needed. So why couldn't a great country like America be able to match the czar in the effects department?

Balanchine's interest in mounting *The Sleeping Beauty* came and went over the years, stimulated from time to time by the emergence of a dancer whom he yearned to show off in the Princess Aurora role. The human material he had to work with was always what moved him most. In the early 1960's, when he was infatuated with Suzanne Farrell as dancer-muse-woman, he kept picturing her in this ballet and kept saying he was determined to do it for her; during his frustrated courtship of Farrell, recalled one who was present at many of their conversations, he dangled the role before her like a diamond pendant. More recently, his interest in staging *The Sleeping Beauty,* dormant after Farrell left the company, had revived with the emergence of sixteen-year-old Darcy Kistler as the youngest principal dancer in the company's history.

The Birds of America and *The Sleeping Beauty*—these were the two grandest projects he left unconsummated. Over the course of his long career, inevitably there were other projects that excited him but, for one reason or another, never came into being. Sometimes he had to give them up because of circumstances he could not control—for example, when the authorities at the Soviet State Theatre turned down his request to stage *Le Sacre du Printemps* in 1923, or when the death of George Gershwin in 1937 put an end to plans the two of them had been making for an original ballet for Goldwyn's *Follies,* or when the orchestral strike of 1976 forced him to abandon the revival of *The Seven Deadly Sins* he was happily working on with Bette Midler. Sometimes he gave a project up because he found it would cost more than it was worth; he was always acutely cost-conscious. Sometimes he simply lost his enthusiasm; this was most likely to happen when he commissioned music that didn't satisfy him. I remember him animatedly telling me around 1960 about a fantastic ballet he envisaged that he called *The Upside-Down Ballroom.* I have no idea what happened with that; he never mentioned it again. One ballet he was keen to make at one time was *Salome,* with Suzanne Farrell in the title role. He consulted Stravinsky as to suitable music and settled on Alban Berg's "Lulu Suite." At the time, Stravinsky and Robert Craft jested wickedly about Balanchine's motives in regard to his choice of subject. They surmised, wrote Craft in his diary, that his incentive was the awareness that a modern-day Salome would retain none of her veils. That project died when Farrell married in 1969 and left the company. Balanchine revived it in 1977, after her return. A set was designed and actually built for *Salome,* but the project once more had to be shelved because of budget problems. After that season, what with Balanchine's declining health and other commitments, it was never again considered.

By and large, those projects that had failed to materialize went unmourned by him. "If only . . . " had never been part of his vocabulary. If he had really burned to do any of these ballets, one had the sense (at least after he had his own company) he would eventually have found some way to do them. As he lay dying, he had few unfulfilled dreams. He had accomplished his ambitions—and that may have been because his ambitions always came out of the present and the materials at hand, rather than vague, grandiose aspirations for the future.

And how much he did accomplish! In the history of dance, has there been a more prolific choreographer? By coincidence, the exact inventory of his choreographic output in his lifetime came along just then, at the very end of his life, in a large, handsome volume entitled *Choreography by George Balanchine: A Catalogue of Works.* Wrote Kirstein in his preface, "A printed listing of the works of George Balanchine may be set alongside the Koechel catalogue of Mozart: the works of choreographer and composer share many qualities." Among the four hundred twenty-five items listed are more than two hundred ballets, five films, twenty-three musical comedies and revues, six stagings for choral works, ten plays for which Balanchine arranged movement sequences, fifty-nine operas for which he choreographed the dances, and any number of occasion pieces for the most disparate of occasions—from a fox-trot in Petrograd in 1921 in honor of the treaty reinstating Anglo-Soviet trade relations, to a polio ballet for the March of Dimes, to a cotillion promenade for some five hundred couples for the Negro Debutante Ball at the 369th Armory in Harlem in 1953. In addition to the works listed, with pertinent production details for each, the volume's appendices documented much other relevant information as to the range of Balanchine's activities and influence. Six full pages were required to list all the companies in the world performing his ballets. So scrupulous and comprehensive an inventory had never been undertaken before, in regard to the work of any other choreographer. The catalogue's preparation required the use of more than three hundred researchers in thirteen countries over a four-year period. It was fortunate that research on the project began when it did, before Balanchine's memory grew unreliable, for he was able to cooperate in its presentation, answering questions and verifying details. The first copy off the press was brought to Balanchine by Nancy Lassalle, one of those who had been most involved in the preparation of the work, on December 24. He kept it by his bedside. "There it is," he told visitors, "the Bible."

From time to time Peter Martins had been visiting Balanchine at the hospital, sometimes just to talk, sometimes with company problems that needed resolving. He made one such visit one day in mid-January. The account I give here is as Martins related it to me a few months later. On this occasion, when he sought Balanchine's advice as to how Balanchine would handle a particular problem that had arisen, Balanchine refused to tell him. "No, dear," said Balanchine. "It's not a matter of what I would do. It's what you would do. What works for me may not work for you. You do your way."

"I understand your point, Mr. B., but given the circumstances that you're here, and it's your company, what would you like done?"

To this Balanchine replied, according to Martins, "Look, you're going to be doing it for a long time, and you'll make millions of mistakes—just like I did in the beginning. There's only one witness to all my mistakes—that's Lincoln—and he didn't tell. You have to accept the mistakes you're going to make. Make them, and forget them. And one thing more—don't ask anybody else what they would do. Just do yourself what you think is right."

Martins sought one thing more on that occasion—Balanchine's official blessing as successor. It was a time of turmoil, distress, and uncertainty, for him and for the company. Martins knew he had powerful support on the board of the New York City Ballet, as well as among the dancers and staff, but still he felt insecure. It was not enough to be the heir apparent; he craved the assurance of being the heir designate. Balanchine would not give him that assurance. "Look," Balanchine said, "nobody is going to hand it to you. You're going to have to take it, you're going to have to fight for it. Not a single person is going to give it to you." It was clear to Martins that the unspoken end to that last sentence was, "including me," and he pursued the matter no further. This was his last visit to the hospital. He felt that by then he and Balanchine had said to each other all that needed to be said, or could be said.

In the weeks that followed, Balanchine became weaker and less co-herent, and more and more confused. He had difficulty recognizing peo-ple he had known for years, and often addressed American friends in Russian. Increasingly, speech became difficult. Nightmares assailed him, but also he must have heard music in his head and seen visions of splen-dor still. A visitor one day saw him asleep with his arms over his head in a perfect port de bras couronne. In February, Maria Tallchief, in town for the School of American Ballet reunion, went to the hospital to spend some time with him. As she came into the room, she saw that his fingers were moving. Looking up at her, he said, "I'm making steps." Around that same time the young principal dancer Joseph Duell, visiting one afternoon between rehearsals, found Balanchine in a weak and dazed state. Duell talked to him a few minutes with no response, until he hap-pened to mention that he had been thinking about the importance of the fifth position, whereupon a fog seemed to lift from Balanchine's mind and he gave a lucid explanation of just what it is about the fifth position that makes it significant in the anatomy of classic dance. Another day, Jacques d'Amboise and Karin von Aroldingen were in the room when Balanchine, who had been lying silent, said, "I'm going to make a Vi-valdi Chorale for you. I've been thinking about it. Will you dance?"

"Of course," said d'Amboise.

"I mean—now."

So d'Amboise and von Aroldingen improvised some steps—a waltz for lack of anything better—in the small room for a few moments, until, too distressed to continue, they stopped and tried to hide their feelings with some light remark to the nurse who was watching them.

The most attentive and most important visitor for him throughout the months he lay dying was Karin von Aroldingen. Even when he was at a low ebb, he would respond to the sound of her footsteps approaching in the corridor. "Karin!" he would say, and his face would light up. And when he was no longer capable of articulate speech, she would sit by him for hours, stroking his head and crooning to him, as to a child.

In mid-March, the board of the New York City Ballet met to face up to the painful recognition that Balanchine would never return and to deal with the consequences of that situation. Among board members, there was a reluctance to appoint a successor while Balanchine still lived, but a new season was coming up in six weeks, and the company could not continue to be run by committee. There was consensus that Martins was the obvious choice to run the company, but there was also much concern that Robbins not be alienated or offended. Balanchine had always recognized the importance of Robbins to the New York City Ballet. He had been content to discommode himself, if necessary, to meet Robbins' needs as a choreographer; he would give Robbins first choice of dancers, first choice of rehearsal time and studios—and Balanchine, with a shrug, would accommodate himself to what was left. Robbins was touchy, hypersensitive, often difficult, insecure, yet his artistic contributions to the company were second only to Balanchine's. For years before the emergence of Martins, Robbins had been spoken of in the press as Balanchine's likely heir; to some, he seemed reminiscent of Prince Edward, growing old as he waited to ascend the throne. Now he was sixty-four. Those who knew Robbins were aware that he did not find day-to-day administration or supervision congenial to his temperament. So they thought they knew that he didn't really want the job of artistic director, but there was some belief among them that through seniority and talent he had earned the right to have the position offered to him. Unlike many other companies, the nature of the New York City Ballet was that it needed a constant supply of first-rate new ballets. As a choreographer, Martins had promise, but, with only seventeen ballets under his belt, he was still an apprentice, whereas Robbins was a world-renowned master. If the company was to thrive, it needed not only the ballets Robbins had already made in its repertory but also the prospect of new Robbins ballets. It needed these more than ever now if the company was not just to become a Balanchine museum, which was the last thing in the world Balanchine himself would have wanted.

The board resolved its dilemma by naming both men ballet masters in chief. Martins was to be responsible for day-to-day artistic decision-making. Robbins was to be available as artistic adviser and given a free hand to do his own ballets—to be, in effect, "a prince with his own territory within the company," as one reporter put it. A delicate, complicated resolution, it remained to be seen how it would work out.

Balanchine never learned this news. By the time of the announcement, he was no longer in touch with such realities or concerns. The spring season opened April 26. Four days later, at 4:00 A.M. Saturday, April 30, Balanchine died, carried off at last by pneumonia. It was a good day to die, his priest, Reverend Adrian Oullette said, being the day on which the church celebrated the resurrection of Lazarus. The New York City Ballet went ahead with the two performances scheduled for that day, without alteration of the program. Before the matinee, Kirstein spoke to the audience. "I don't have to tell you that Mr. B. is with Mozart and Tchaikovsky and Stravinsky," he said. "I do want to tell you how much he valued this audience, which is like a big family that has kept us going for fifty years and will keep us going for another fifty. The one thing he didn't want was that there be an interruption. So there will be none. Think of yourselves as the marvelous, supportive, cohesive family who understands the family that's about to perform now." It was a weekend when Balanchine's live presence—in the ballets he had conceived, in the dancers he had trained, in the style he had developed, in the standards he had established—was widely evident. In addition to the performances being given by his company at the State Theater, the students of the School of American Ballet were presenting *Valse Fantaisie* and *Western Symphony* in their annual workshop performances at the Juilliard Theatre, the American Ballet Theatre was rehearsing their revived version of *Symphonie Concertante* to present on Monday, the opening night of their season at the Metropolitan Opera House, and *On Your Toes* was playing on Broadway.

At the funeral services, nearly thirteen hundred mourners crowded the Cathedral of Our Lady of the Sign, a small church without seats, planned to accommodate nowhere near that number. The service was long, and the air was heavy with grief and the scent of incense, flowers, and burning candles. Among those present were six generations of dancers, from schoolchildren to ballerinas who had danced for the czar. But there were also many who were not dancers or members of the dance world, but simply people who had had the experience of seeing Balanchine's ballets and treasuring them. And there were also those who knew him personally, in some capacity other than ballet master, whose lives had been affected simply by the nature of his being and the way he lived his life.

In the memorials and tributes, the sense of loss seemed to go far beyond the specialized world of dance. Some of the most telling tributes appeared in literary journals or newspapers and magazines of general circulation. Of these, one of the most eloquent was that written by the pianists Arthur Gold and Robert Fizdale, his friends for many years, in

The New York Review of Books. They wrote: "George Balanchine liked to say, quoting Mayakovsky, 'I am not a man, but a cloud in trousers.' And now the luminous cloud has floated off, leaving us with a loss far deeper than the grave. Balanchine spoke for all of us. Diffident as he was in private life, in his ballets he shared his daydreams, his joys, his troubled loves, his fears, his instinct for elegance and order, and his passion for youth with those who admired his work. He has been a poet for poets, a musician for musicians, and a dramatist for anyone who wishes to understand the human heart. Reality for him was the stage and he gave us stylized visions that seem truer than life. . . . "

In his lifetime, Balanchine was frequently compared with Picasso and Stravinsky as one of the three preeminent geniuses of the age. He was the last of those giants. In some ways he had to accomplish even more than they did in order to give his genius the opportunity to flourish. They did not need to found a company and a school, and to supervise large organizations, in order to realize their visions. When Picasso and Stravinsky began their careers, they were working in art forms that had long been accorded public recognition and critical stature. But when Balanchine started, his art—choreography—had not yet won such standing, either with artists or with the public. He figured very largely in the importance that the art form has now achieved.

The comparison with those two renowned modern artists should be taken only so far. Balanchine's art, to my mind, was more genial than that of Stravinsky, his talent more ready to be put to whatever occasion or services were required, and his temperament more naive. In this—as well as in his facility—he was closer to Mozart. And among painters, Picasso seems not quite right in character as the essential comparison— similar in facility, certainly, and in his abilities in a variety of styles; but more aggressively modern in spirit than the choreographer, more insistently motivated by the need to shock. As Susan Sontag wrote, Balanchine, though he had absorbed naturally all the lessons of modernism, was "free of all the superstitions of modernity." Rather than Picasso, a truer comparison, perhaps, would be with Matisse, whose works seem predominantly motivated, as do Balanchine's, by the desire to give pleasure.

After Balanchine's heart attack in 1978, he made a will. His estate did not consist of much in the way of property. He left his apartment on West Sixty-seventh Street to Karin von Aroldingen. He also left her his Mercedes, but by the time the will was filed the Mercedes had been stolen. To Barbara Horgan, whom he named as executor, he left his interest in the condominium at Southampton and the balance in his savings account; the balance in his checking accounts he left to Tanaquil Le Clercq, as well as royalties from the book he had co-authored. To his brother, Andrei, he left two gold watches that Lincoln Kirstein had given him.

That was the extent of the material property. The rest of the will consisted of a listing of his ballets. These were his riches; these had been his life. The title, rights, and royalties to these ballets he left severally to eighteen people—dancers mainly—who had been associated with his companies. The greatest bequest of rights was made to Tanaquil Le Clercq, for whose financial security he was most concerned.

In the wording of the will, he created some possible future problems for the New York City Ballet—problems that would not have arisen had he willed title to the ballets to the company and merely the royalty rights to the individuals. The possibility exists that these new owners, or their heirs, could seek to interfere at any time they choose with the company's artistic policies or withdraw their ballets if they choose. It is not known if Balanchine considered that possibility at the time he drew up the will in 1978 and did not let it deter him, or if he was consciously expressing in his will his belief in human beings more even than in the institution to which he had dedicated so much of his life. Later on, he did become sufficiently concerned to consult with his attorney about modifying the will to make certain the New York City Ballet would be able to continue performing his ballets without challenge after his death. But the revisions the attorney drafted were never formalized.

He was buried in a small, old cemetery in Sag Harbor, Long Island. It was a town he had come to know only recently but found charming. He had left no instructions as to what he wished done with his body. As death approached, this was naturally a question that those close to him had to think about. Stravinsky had been buried in Venice. So had Diaghilev. Some thought that was where Balanchine's body belonged. But he disliked Venice. Others thought of Monte Carlo, of which Balanchine had had fond memories, or of Paris, or London, or Zurich. But no place in Europe contained the proper soil to hold the remains of the greatest master of movement in history. If his remains belonged anywhere, it was in the United States. He was, as he often proudly declared, with that aristocratic lift of his head and in that low, courteous, decisive voice that never lost its Russian accent, an American.

A Chronological List of Balanchine's Ballets*

1920– 1924 As a youth, before leaving Russia at the age of twenty, Balanchine choreographed numerous works, including *La Nuit,* to music by Anton Rubinstein; *Poem,* to music by Fibich; *Waltz and Adagio* and *Extase,* to compositions of his own; *Enigma,* to Arensky's music; *Marche Funèbre* by Chopin; a dance to one of Ravel's *Valses Nobles et Sentimentales;* and dances to the music of Scriabin, Glazunov, Mussorgsky, Kreisler, Sibelius, Brahms, Cui, and other composers. In addition he choreographed a mimed action to Alexander Blok's poem *The Twelve* and a pantomime ballet to the Cocteau-Milhaud *Le Boeuf sur le Toit;* and he did dances for the Maly Opera's production of *Coq d'Or* and for theatrical productions of Shaw's *Caesar and Cleopatra,* and Toller's *The Broken Brow.* His duets were generally danced by himself, with Alexandra Danilova as partner, or with Lydia Ivanova, Tamara Geva, or Olga Mungalova. In the larger works they were joined by, among others, Vera Kostrovitskaya, Nina Stukolkina, Leonid Lavrovsky, Pyotr Gusev, Nicholas Efimov, and Mikhail Mikhailov.

1925 **LE CHANT DU ROSSIGNOL**
MUSIC: *Igor Stravinsky.* DECOR AND COSTUMES: *Henri Matisse.*
PREMIERE: *June 17, 1925, Gaîté Lyrique Théâtre, Paris, by Les Ballets Russes de Diaghilev.*
CAST: *Alicia Markova, Lydia Sokolova, Serge Grigoriev, Nicolas Kremnev, George Balanchine, et al.*

BARABAU
MUSIC: *Vittorio Rieti.* DECOR: *Maurice Utrillo.* LIBRETTO: *Vittorio Rieti.*
PREMIERE: *December 11, 1925, The Coliseum, London, by Les Ballets Russes de Diaghilev.*
CAST: *Léon Woizikowsky, Serge Lifar, Alice Nikitina, Alexandra Danilova, Tamara Geva, et al.*

1926 **ROMEO AND JULIET ENTR'ACTE**
MUSIC: *Constant Lambert.* PAINTING: *Max Ernst and Joan Miró.*
PREMIERE: *May 4, 1926, Opéra de Monte Carlo, by Les Ballets Russes de Diaghilev.*
CAST: *Tamara Karsavina, Serge Lifar, et al.*

---

* For the most comprehensive and detailed information on Balanchine's output throughout his life, the reader is referred to *Choreography by George Balanchine: A Catalogue of Works.* Published in 1983 by The Eakins Press Foundation, New York, this handsome 407-page book is an invaluable work of scholarship.

NOTE: *The choreography for the two-part Romeo and Juliet was by Bronislava Nijinska. Balanchine's choreography for the entr'acte was without music, with the curtain partially lowered so that only the performers' legs were visible.*

LA PASTORALE
MUSIC: *Georges Auric.* DECOR AND COSTUMES: *Pedro Pruna.* LIBRETTO: *Boris Kochno.*
PREMIERE: *May 29, 1926, Théâtre Sarah Bernhardt, Paris, by Les Ballets Russes de Diaghilev.*
CAST: *Felia Doubrovska, Alexandra Danilova, Serge Lifar, Léon Woizikowsky, Tamara Geva, et al.*

JACK IN THE BOX
MUSIC: *Erik Satie.* DECOR AND COSTUMES: *André Derain.*
PREMIERE: *June 8, 1926, Théâtre Sarah Bernhardt, Paris, by Les Ballets Russes de Diaghilev.*
CAST: *Alexandra Danilova, Lubov Tchernicheva, Felia Doubrovska, Stanislas Idzikovsky, et al.*

THE TRIUMPH OF NEPTUNE
MUSIC: *Lord Berners.* DECOR: *Prince A. Shervashidze.*
PREMIERE: *December 3, 1926, Lyceum, London, by Les Ballets Russes de Diaghilev.*
CAST: *Alexandra Danilova, Lubov Tchernicheva, Lydia Sokolova, Serge Lifar, George Balanchine, Constantin Tcherkas, et al.*

1927 **LA CHATTE**
MUSIC: *Henri Sauguet.* ARCHITECTURAL AND SCULPTURAL CONSTRUCTIONS: *Gabo and Pevsner.* LIBRETTO: *Sobeka (Boris Kochno), based on a fable by Aesop.*
PREMIERE: *April 30, 1927, Opéra de Monte Carlo, by Les Ballets Russes de Diaghilev.*
CAST: *Serge Lifar, Olga Spessivtseva, et al.*

1928 **APOLLO (originally APOLLON MUSAGÈTE)**
MUSIC: *Igor Stravinsky.* DECOR AND COSTUMES: *André Bauchant. (In 1929, Gabrielle Chanel designed new costumes.)*
PREMIERE: *June 12, 1928, Théâtre Sarah Bernhardt, Paris, by Les Ballets Russes de Diaghilev.*
CAST: *Serge Lifar, Lubov Tchernicheva, Felia Doubrovska, Alice Nikitina, Sophie Orlova, et al. (Alexandra Danilova alternated with Nikitina as Terpsichore.)*

THE GODS GO A-BEGGING
MUSIC: *George Frederick Handel, arranged by Sir Thomas Beecham.* DECOR: *Léon Bakst, originally used for Daphnis et Chloé.* LIBRETTO: *Sobeka (Boris Kochno).*
PREMIERE: *July 16, 1928, His Majesty's Theatre, London, by Les Ballets Russes de Diaghilev.*
CAST: *Alexandra Danilova, Lubov Tchernicheva, Felia Doubrovska, Léon Woizikowsky, Constantin Tcherkas, et al.*

1929 **LE BAL**
MUSIC: *Vittorio Rieti.* DECOR: *Giorgio de Chirico.* LIBRETTO: *Boris Kochno.*
PREMIERE: *May 7, 1929, Opéra de Monte Carlo, by Les Ballets Russes de Diaghilev.*
CAST: *Alexandra Danilova, Felia Doubrovska, Eugenia Lipkowska, Anton Dolin, André Bobrov, Léon Woizikowsky, George Balanchine, Serge Lifar, et al.*

PRODIGAL SON (or LE FILS PRODIGUE)
MUSIC: *Serge Prokofiev.* DECOR AND COSTUMES: *Georges Rouault.* LIBRETTO: *Boris Kochno.*

PREMIERE: *May 20, 1929, Théâtre Sarah Bernhardt, Paris, by Les Ballets Russes de Diaghilev.*
CAST: *Serge Lifar, Léon Woizikowsky, Anton Dolin, Felia Doubrovska, Mikhael Fedorov, Eleanora Marra, Nathalie Branitzka, et al.*

1930   AUBADE
MUSIC: *Francis Poulenc.* DECOR AND COSTUMES: *Angeles Ortiz.*
PREMIERE: *January 21, 1930, Théâtre des Champs-Élysées, Paris, by Les Ballets Russes.*
CAST: *Vera Nemtchinova, Alexis Dolinoff, et al.*

1931   JOSEF-LEGENDE
MUSIC: *Richard Strauss.* DECOR AND COSTUMES: *Kjeld Abell.*
PREMIERE: *January 18, 1931, The Royal Theatre, Copenhagen, by the Royal Danish Ballet.*
CAST: *Ulla Poulsen, Børge Ralov, et al.*

1932   LA CONCURRENCE
MUSIC: *Georges Auric.* CURTAIN, DECOR, AND COSTUMES: *André Derain.* LIBRETTO: *André Derain.*
PREMIERE: *April 12, 1932, Opéra de Monte Carlo, by the Ballets Russes de Monte Carlo.*
CAST: *Léon Woizikowsky, Tamara Toumanova, Metek Borovsky, Yurek Shabelevsky, et al.*

COTILLON
MUSIC: *Emmanuel Chabrier.* DECOR AND COSTUMES: *Christian Bérard.* LIBRETTO: *Boris Kochno.*
PREMIERE: *April 12, 1932, Opéra de Monte Carlo, by the Ballets Russes de Monte Carlo.*
CAST: *Tamara Toumanova, David Lichine, Léon Woizikowsky, et al.*

LE BOURGEOIS GENTILHOMME
MUSIC: *Richard Strauss.* DECOR: *Alexandre Benois.*
PREMIERE: *May 3, 1932, Opéra de Monte Carlo, by the Ballet Russes de Monte Carlo.*
CAST: *Tamara Toumanova, David Lichine, et al.*

SUITES DE DANSE
MUSIC: *Mikhail Glinka.*
PREMIERE: *May 5, 1932, Opéra de Monte Carlo, by the Ballets Russes de Monte Carlo.*
CAST: *Eleanora Marra, Léon Woizikowsky, Nina Verchinina, Lena Kirsova, David Lichine, Metek Borovsky, Yurek Shabelevsky, Valentina Blinova, Tamara Toumanova, Tatiana Riabouchinska, et al.*

1933   SONGES
MUSIC: *Darius Milhaud.* DECOR AND COSTUMES: *André Derain.* LIBRETTO: *André Derain.*
PREMIERE: *June 7, 1933, Théâtre des Champs-Élysées, Paris, by Les Ballets 1933.*
CAST: *Tamara Toumanova, Roman Jasinsky, et al.*

MOZARTIANA
MUSIC: *Mozart-Tchaikovsky (Suite No. 4).* DECOR AND COSTUMES: *Christian Bérard.*
PREMIERE: *June 7, 1933, Théâtre des Champs-Élysées, Paris, by Les Ballets 1933.*
CAST: *Tamara Toumanova, Roman Jasinsky, et al.*

THE SEVEN DEADLY SINS (LES SEPT PÉCHÉS CAPITAUX)
(ballet-cantata)
MUSIC: *Kurt Weill*. DECOR: *Caspar Neher*. LIBRETTO: *Bertolt Brecht*.
PREMIERE: *June 7, 1933, Théâtre des Champs-Élysées, Paris, by Les Ballets 1933*.
CAST: *Tilly Losch, Lotte Lenya, et al.*

ERRANTE
MUSIC: *Franz Schubert, transcribed by Franz Liszt, orchestrated by Charles Koechlin*.
DECOR AND COSTUMES: *Pavel Tchelitchev*. LIBRETTO: *George Balanchine and Pavel Tchelitchev*.
PREMIERE: *June 10, 1933, Théâtre des Champs-Élysées, Paris, by Les Ballets 1933*.
CAST: *Tilly Losch, Roman Jasinsky, et al.*

FASTES
MUSIC: *Henri Sauguet*. DECOR AND COSTUMES: *André Derain*.
PREMIERE: *June 10, 1933, Théâtre des Champs-Élysées, Paris, by Les Ballets 1933*.
CAST: *Tamara Toumanova, Roman Jasinsky, et al.*

LES VALSES DE BEETHOVEN
MUSIC: *Ludwig von Beethoven*. DECOR AND COSTUMES: *Emilio Terry*.
PREMIERE: *June 10, 1933, Théâtre des Champs-Élysées, Paris, by Les Ballets 1933*.
CAST: *Tilly Losch, Diana Gould, Roman Jasinsky, et al.*

1934 ### ALMA MATER
MUSIC: *Kay Swift, arranged by Morton Gould*. DECOR: *Eugene Dunkel*. COSTUMES: *John Held, Jr.* LIBRETTO: *Edward M. M. Warburg*.
PREMIERE: *December 6, 1934, Hartford, Connecticut, by Producing Company of the School of American Ballet. Presented by the American Ballet, March 1, 1935, at the Adelphi Theatre, New York*.
CAST: *Leda Anchutina, Ruthanna Boris, Gisella Caccialanza, Kathryn Mullowny, Heidi Vosseler, William Dollar, Charles Laskey, Eugene Loring, et al.*

1935 ### REMINISCENCE
MUSIC: *Benjamin Godard, orchestrated by Henry Brand*. DECOR AND COSTUMES: *Serge Soudeikine*.
PREMIERE: *March 1, 1935, Adelphi Theatre, New York, by the American Ballet*.
CAST: *Leda Anchutina, Ruthanna Boris, Gisella Caccialanza, Elena de Rivas, Holly Howard, Annabelle Lyon, Elise Reiman, William Dollar, Paul Haakon, et al.*

SERENADE
MUSIC: *Pyotr Tchaikovsky*. DECOR: *Gaston Longchamp*. COSTUMES: *Jean Lurçat*.
PREMIERE: *March 1, 1935, Adelphi Theatre, New York, by the American Ballet*.
CAST: *Leda Ancthutina, Ruthanna Boris, Gisella Caccialanza, Kathryn Mullowny, William Dollar, Charles Laskey, et al.*

DREAMS
MUSIC: *George Antheil*. DECOR AND COSTUMES: *André Derain*. LIBRETTO: *André Derain*.
PREMIERE: *March 5, 1935, Adelphi Theatre, New York, by the American Ballet*.
CAST: *Leda Anchutina, Ruthanna Boris, Paul Haakon, Gisella Caccialanza, William Dollar, Holly Howard, Charles Laskey, et al.*

TRANSCENDENCE
MUSIC: *Franz Liszt, orchestrated by George Antheil*. DECOR: *Gaston Longchamp*. COSTUMES: *Franklin Watkins*. LIBRETTO: *Lincoln Kirstein*.
PREMIERE: *March 5, 1935, Adelphi Theatre, New York, by the American Ballet*.
CAST: *Elise Reiman, William Dollar, Charles Laskey, et al.*

1936 MAGIC

MUSIC: *Wolfgang Amadeus Mozart.* DECOR AND COSTUMES: *Pavel Tchelitchev.*
PREMIERE: *February 14, 1936, Avery Memorial Theatre, Hartford, Connecticut, by the American Ballet.*
CAST: *Felia Doubrovska, Lew Christensen, et al.*

THE BAT

MUSIC: *Johann Strauss* (*Overture to* Die Fledermaus). COSTUMES: *Keith Martin.*
LIBRETTO: *Lincoln Kirstein.*
PREMIERE: *May 20, 1936, Metropolitan Opera House, New York, by the American Ballet.*
CAST: *Leda Anchutina, Rabana Hasburgh, Annabelle Lyon, Lew Christensen, Charles Laskey, et al.*

ORPHEUS AND EURYDICE

MUSIC: *Christoph Willibald Gluck.* DECOR AND COSTUMES: *Pavel Tchelitchev.*
PREMIERE: *May 22, 1936, Metropolitan Opera House, New York, by the American Ballet.*
CAST: *Lew Christensen, Daphne Vane, William Dollar, et al.*

1937 LE BAISER DE LA FÉE

MUSIC: *Igor Stravinsky* (*"inspired by the music of Tchaikovsky"*). COSTUMES: *Alice Halicka.* LIBRETTO: *Igor Stravinsky* (*based on "The Virgin of the Lake"*).
PREMIERE: *April 27, 1937, Metropolitan Opera House, New York, by the American Ballet.*
CAST: *Kathryn Mullowny, Rabana Hasburgh, Gisella Caccialanza, Leda Anchutina, William Dollar, Annabelle Lyon, et al.*

CARD GAME (or CARD PARTY)

MUSIC: *Igor Stravinsky.* DECOR AND COSTUMES: *Irene Sharaff.* LIBRETTO: *Igor Stravinsky and M. Malaieff.*
PREMIERE: *April 27, 1937, Metropolitan Opera House, New York, by the American Ballet.*
CAST: *William Dollar, Lew Christensen, Annabelle Lyon, Charles Laskey, Leda Anchutina, et al.*

1941 BALUSTRADE

MUSIC: *Igor Stravinsky* (*Concerto for Violin and Orchestra*). DECOR AND COSTUMES: *Pavel Tchelitchev.*
PREMIERE: *January 22, 1941, Fifty-first Street Theatre, New York, by Original Ballet Russe.*
CAST: *Tamara Toumanova, Paul Petroff, Roman Jasinsky, et al.*

CONCERTO BAROCCO

MUSIC: *Johann Sebastian Bach* (*Double Violin Concerto in D Minor*). DECOR AND COSTUMES: *Eugene Berman.*
PREMIERE: *May 29, 1941, Hunter College Playhouse, New York, by the American Ballet Caravan.*
CAST: *Marie-Jeanne, Mary Jane Shea, William Dollar, et al.*

BALLET IMPERIAL

MUSIC: *Pyotr Tchaikovsky* (*Piano Concerto No. 2 in G Major*). DECOR AND COSTUMES: *Mstislav Doboujinsky.*
PREMIERE: *May 29, 1941, Hunter College Playhouse, New York, by the American Ballet Caravan.*

CAST: Marie-Jeanne, Gisella Caccialanza, William Dollar, Nicholas Magallanes, Fred Danieli, et al.

DIVERTIMENTO
MUSIC: Gioacchino Rossini, orchestrated by Benjamin Britten. DECOR AND COSTUMES: André Derain (from Songes).
PREMIERE: June 27, 1941, Teatro Municipal, Rio de Janiero, by the American Ballet Caravan.
CAST: Todd Bolender, Marie-Jeanne, Gisella Caccialanza, John Kriza, Olga Suárez, Fred Danieli, Marjorie Moore, et al.

FANTASIA BRASILEIRA
MUSIC: Francisco Mignone. DECOR AND COSTUMES: Erico Bianco.
PREMIERE: August 27, 1941, Teatro Municipal, Santiago de Chile, by the American Ballet Caravan.
CAST: Olga Suárez, Fred Danieli, Nicholas Magallanes, et al.

1942 ### PAS DE TROIS FOR PIANO AND TWO DANCERS
MUSIC: Theodore Chanler. COSTUMES: Pavel Tchelitchev.
PREMIERE: May 10, 1942, Alvin Theatre, New York, "Music at Work" benefit program for Russian War Relief.
CAST: Mary Ellen Moylan, Nicholas Magallanes.

CONCERTO
MUSIC: Wolfgang Amadeus Mozart (Concerto for Violin and Orchestra in A Major). DECOR AND COSTUMES: Pavel Tchelitchev.
PREMIERE: August 7, 1942, Teatro Colón, Buenos Aires, Argentina, by the Ballet of the Teatro Colón.
CAST: Maria Ruanova, Yurek Shabelevsky, Metek Borovsky, et al.

1944 ### DANSES CONCERTANTES
MUSIC: Igor Stravinsky. DECOR AND COSTUMES: Eugene Berman.
PREMIERE: September 10, 1944, New York City Center, by the Ballet Russe de Monte Carlo.
CAST: Alexandra Danilova, Frederic Franklin, Maria Tallchief, Nicholas Magallanes, Mary Ellen Moylan, et al.

WALTZ ACADEMY
MUSIC: Vittorio Rieti. COSTUMES: Alvin Colt. DECOR: Oliver Smith.
PREMIERE: Oct. 11, 1944, Metropolitan Opera House, New York, by Ballet Theatre.
CAST: Nana Gollner, Nora Kaye, Janet Reed, John Kriza, Diana Adams, Paul Petroff, et al.

1945 ### PAS DE DEUX
MUSIC: Pyotr Tchaikovsky (Sleeping Beauty entr'acte).
PREMIERE: March 14, 1945, New York City Center, by the Ballet Russe de Monte Carlo.
CAST: Alexandra Danilova, Frederic Franklin.

1946 ### NIGHT SHADOW (LA SONNAMBULA)
MUSIC: Vittorio Rieti (arranged from music of Bellini). DECOR AND COSTUMES: Dorothea Tanning.
PREMIERE: February 27, 1946, New York City Center, by the Ballet Russe de Monte Carlo.
CAST: Alexandra Danilova, Nicholas Magallanes, Maria Tallchief, Ruthanna Boris, Leon Danielian, Marie-Jeanne, et al.

RAYMONDA (*choreographed with Alexandra Danilova*)
MUSIC: *Alexander Glazunov.* DECOR AND COSTUMES: *Alexandre Benois.*
PREMIERE: *March 12, 1946, New York City Center, by the Ballet Russe de Monte Carlo.*
CAST: *Alexandra Danilova, Nicholas Magallanes, Nikita Talin, Leon Danielian, Julia Horvath, Pauline Goddard, Yvonne Chouteau, Herbert Bliss, Marie-Jeanne, Maria Tallchief, Gertrude Tyven, Patricia Wilde, et al.*

THE FOUR TEMPERAMENTS
MUSIC: *Paul Hindemith.* DECOR AND COSTUMES: *Kurt Seligmann.* LIGHTING: *Jean Rosenthal.*
PREMIERE: *November 20, 1946, Central High School of Needle Trades, New York, by Ballet Society.*
CAST: *Gisella Caccialanza, Georgia Hiden, Rita Karlin, Tanaquil Le Clercq, Mary Ellen Moylan,, Elise Reiman, Beatrice Tompkins, Todd Bolender, Lew Christensen, Fred Danieli, William Dollar, José Martinez, Francisco Moncion, et al.*

THE SPELLBOUND CHILD
MUSIC: *Maurice Ravel* (L'Enfant et les Sortilèges). DECOR AND COSTUMES: *Aline Bernstein.* LIGHTING: *Jean Rosenthal.* POEM: *Colette.*
PREMIERE: *November 20, 1946, Central High School of Needle Trades, New York, by Ballet Society.*
CAST: *Gisella Caccialanza, Ruth Gilbert, Georgia Hiden, Tanaquil Le Clercq, Elise Reiman, Beatrice Tompkins, Paul d'Amboise, William Dollar, et al.*

1947   DIVERTIMENTO
MUSIC: *Alexei Haieff.* LIGHTING: *Jean Rosenthal.*
PREMIERE: *January 13, 1947, Hunter College Playhouse, New York, by Ballet Society.*
CAST: *Gisella Caccialanza, Tanaquil Le Clercq, Mary Ellen Moylan, Elise Reiman, Beatrice Tompkins, Todd Bolender, Lew Christensen, Fred Danieli, Francisco Moncion, John Taras.*

RENARD
MUSIC: *Igor Stravinsky.* DECOR AND COSTUMES: *Esteban Francés.* LIBRETTO: *Igor Stravinsky.* LIGHTING: *Jean Rosenthal.*
PREMIERE: *January 13, 1947, Hunter College Playhouse, New York, by Ballet Society.*
CAST: *Todd Bolender, Lew Christensen, Fred Danieli, John Taras.*

SYMPHONY IN C (*originally* LE PALAIS DE CRISTAL)
MUSIC: *Georges Bizet.* DECOR AND COSTUMES: *Léonor Fini.*
PREMIERE: *July 28, 1947, Paris Opéra, by the Ballet de l'Opéra.*
CAST: *Lycette Darsonval, Tamara Toumanova, Micheline Bardin, Madeleine Lafon, Alexandre Kalioujny, Roger Ritz, Michel Renault, Max Bozzoni, et al.*
FIRST NEW YORK PERFORMANCE: *March 22, 1948, as Symphony in C, without decor.*
CAST: *Maria Tallchief, Tanaquil Le Clercq, Nicholas Magallanes, Francisco Moncion, Gisella Caccialanza, Herbert Bliss, Elise Reiman, Todd Bolender, et al.*

SYMPHONIE CONCERTANTE
MUSIC: *Wolfgang Amadeus Mozart* (Symphonie Concertante in E Flat, K. 364).
DECOR AND COSTUMES: *James Stewart Morcom.* LIGHTING: *Jean Rosenthal.*
PREMIERE: *November 12, 1947, New York City Center, by Ballet Society.*
CAST: *Maria Tallchief, Tanaquil Le Clercq, Todd Bolender, et al.*

THEME AND VARIATIONS
MUSIC: *Pyotr Tchaikovsky* (Final Movement, Suite No. 3 for Orchestra). DECOR AND COSTUMES: *Woodman Thompson.*

PREMIERE: *November 26, 1947, New York City Center, by Ballet Theatre.*
CAST: *Alicia Alonso, Igor Youskevitch, et al.*

1948 **THE TRIUMPH OF BACCHUS AND ARIADNE (ballet-cantata)**
MUSIC: *Vittorio Rieti.* DECOR AND COSTUMES: *Corrado Cagli.*
PREMIERE: *February 9, 1948, New York City Center, by Ballet Society.*
CAST: *Lew Christensen, Nicholas Magallanes, Tanaquil Le Clercq, Herbert Bliss, Marie-Jeanne, Charles Laskey, Francisco Moncion, Claudia Hall, Pat McBride, et al.*

ÉLÉGIE
MUSIC: *Igor Stravinsky (Élégie-Elegy for solo viola).*
PREMIERE: *April 28, 1948, New York City Center, by Ballet Society.*
CAST: *Tanaquil Le Clercq, Pat McBride.*

ORPHEUS
MUSIC: *Igor Stravinsky.* DECOR AND COSTUMES: *Isamu Noguchi.* LIGHTING: *Jean Rosenthal.*
PREMIERE: *April 28, 1948, New York City Center, by Ballet Society.*
CAST: *Nicholas Magallanes, Francisco Moncion, Maria Tallchief, Herbert Bliss, Tanaquil Le Clercq, et al.*

PAS DE TROIS CLASSIQUE
MUSIC: *Ludwig Minkus (Paquita).* COSTUMES: *Pierre Balmain.*
PREMIERE: *August 9, 1948, Royal Opera House, Covent Garden, London, by the Grand Ballet of the Marquis de Cuevas.*
CAST: *Rosella Hightower, Marjorie Tallchief, André Eglevsky.*

1949 **THE FIREBIRD**
MUSIC: *Igor Stravinsky.* DECOR AND COSTUMES: *Marc Chagall.* LIGHTING: *Jean Rosenthal.*
PREMIERE: *November 27, 1949, New York City Center, by the New York City Ballet.*
CAST: *Maria Tallchief, Francisco Moncion, Pat McBride, Edward Bigelow, Beatrice Tompkins, et al.*

BOURRÉE FANTASQUE
MUSIC: *Emmanuel Chabrier.* DECOR AND COSTUMES: *Karinska.*
PREMIERE: *December 1, 1949, New York City Center, by the New York City Ballet.*
CAST: *Tanaquil Le Clercq, Maria Tallchief, Janet Reed, Jerome Robbins, Nicholas Magallanes, Herbert Bliss, et al.*

1950 **PAS DE DEUX ROMANTIQUE**
MUSIC: *Carl Maria von Weber.* COSTUMES: *Robert Stevenson.*
PREMIERE: *March 3, 1950, New York City Center, by the New York City Ballet.*
CAST: *Janet Reed, Herbert Bliss.*

JONES BEACH (choreographed with Jerome Robbins)
MUSIC: *Jurriaan Andriessen.* COSTUMES: *Swimsuits by Jantzen.*
PREMIERE: *March 9, 1950, New York City Center, by the New York City Ballet.*
CAST: *Maria Tallchief, Melissa Hayden, Tanaquil Le Clercq, Jerome Robbins, Nicholas Magallanes, Frank Hobi, William Dollar, Roy Tobias, et al.*

TRUMPET CONCERTO
MUSIC: *Franz Joseph Haydn.* DECOR AND COSTUMES: *Vivienne Kernot.*
PREMIERE: *September 14, 1950, Manchester, England, by the Sadler's Wells Theatre Ballet.*
CAST: *Svetlana Beriosova, David Poole, David Blair, Elaine Fifield, Pirmin Trecu, Maryon Lane, et al.*

MAZURKA

MUSIC: *Mikhail Glinka* (A Life for the Tsar). LIGHTING: *Jean Rosenthal.*
PREMIERE: *November 30, 1950, New York City Center, by the New York City Ballet.*
CAST: *Janet Reed, Yurek Lazowski, Vida Brown, George Balanchine, Barbara Walczak, Harold Lang, Dorothy Dushok, Frank Hobi.*

SYLVIA: PAS DE DEUX

MUSIC: *Léo Delibes.* COSTUMES: *Karinska.*
PREMIERE: *December 1, 1950, New York City Center, by the New York City Ballet.*
CAST: *Maria Tallchief, Nicholas Magallanes.*

1951   PAS DE TROIS

MUSIC: *Ludwig Minkus.* COSTUMES: *Karinska.* LIGHTING: *Jean Rosenthal.*
PREMIERE: *February 18, 1951, New York City Center, by the New York City Ballet.*
CAST: *Maria Tallchief, Nora Kaye, André Eglevsky.*

LA VALSE

MUSIC: *Maurice Ravel* (Valses Nobles et Sentimentales, *and* La Valse). COSTUMES: *Karinska.*
PREMIERE: *February 20, 1951, New York City Center, by the New York City Ballet.*
CAST: *Diana Adams, Tanaquil Le Clercq, Yvonne Mounsey, Patricia Wilde, Herbert Bliss, Frank Hobi, Nicholas Magallanes, Francisco Moncion, Michael Maule, Vida Brown, Edwina Fontaine, Jillana, et al.*

CAPRICCIO BRILLANT

MUSIC: *Felix Mendelssohn.* COSTUMES: *Karinska.* LIGHTING: *Jean Rosenthal.*
PREMIERE: *June 7, 1951, New York City Center, by the New York City Ballet.*
CAST: *Maria Tallchief, André Eglevsky, et al.*

À LA FRANÇAIX

MUSIC: *Jean Françaix* (Serenade for Small Orchestra). DECOR: *Raoul Dufy.* LIGHTING: *Jean Rosenthal.*
PREMIERE: *September 11, 1951, New York City Center, by the New York City Ballet.*
CAST: *Maria Tallchief, André Eglevsky, Janet Reed, Frank Hobi, Roy Tobias.*

TYL ULENSPIEGEL

MUSIC: *Richard Strauss.* DECOR AND COSTUMES: *Esteban Francés.* LIGHTING: *Jean Rosenthal.*
PREMIERE: *November 14, 1951, New York City Center, by the New York City Ballet.*
CAST: *Alberta Grant, Susan Kovnat, Jerome Robbins, Ruth Sobotka, Brooks Jackson, Frank Hobi, Beatrice Tompkins, Tomi Worthham, et al.*

SWAN LAKE (ACT TWO)

MUSIC: *Pyotr Tchaikovsky.* DECOR AND COSTUMES: *Cecil Beaton.* LIGHTING: *Jean Rosenthal.*
PREMIERE: *November 20, 1951, New York City Center, by the New York City Ballet.*
CAST: *Maria Tallchief, André Eglevsky, Frank Hobi, Patricia Wilde, Yvonne Mounsey, Edward Bigelow, et al.*

1952   CARACOLE

MUSIC: *Wolfgang Amadeus Mozart* (Divertimento No. 15). COSTUMES: *Christian Bérard* (from Mozartiana). LIGHTING: *Jean Rosenthal.*
PREMIERE: *February 19, 1952, New York City Center, by the New York City Ballet.*
CAST: *Diana Adams, Melissa Hayden, Tanaquil Le Clercq, Maria Tallchief, Patricia Wilde, André Eglevsky, Jerome Robbins, Nicholas Magallanes, et al.*

BAYOU
MUSIC: *Virgil Thomson* (Acadian Songs and Dances). DECOR AND COSTUMES: *Dorothea Tanning.* LIGHTING: *Jean Rosenthal.*
PREMIERE: *February 21, 1952, New York City Center, by the New York City Ballet.*
CAST: *Francisco Moncion, Doris Breckenridge, Melissa Hayden, Hugh Laing, Diana Adams, Herbert Bliss, et al.*

SCOTCH SYMPHONY
MUSIC: *Felix Mendelssohn* (Symphony No. 3). DECOR: *Horace Armistead.* COSTUMES: *Karinska, David Ffolkes.* LIGHTING: *Jean Rosenthal.*
PREMIERE: *November 11, 1952, New York City Center, by the New York City Ballet.*
CAST: *Maria Tallchief, André Eglevsky, Patricia Wilde, et al.*

METAMORPHOSES
MUSIC: *Paul Hindemith* (Symphonic Metamorphoses on Themes of Carl Maria von Weber). COSTUMES: *Karinska.* DECOR: *Jean Rosenthal.*
PREMIERE: *November 25, 1952, New York City Center, by the New York City Ballet.*
CAST: *Tanaquil Le Clercq, Nicholas Magallanes, Todd Bolender, et al.*

HARLEQUINADE PAS DE DEUX
MUSIC: *Riccardo Drigo.* COSTUMES: *Karinska.* LIGHTING: *Jean Rosenthal.*
PREMIERE: *December 16, 1952, New York City Center, by the New York City Ballet.*
CAST: *Maria Tallchief, André Eglevsky.*

CONCERTINO
MUSIC: *Jean Françaix.* COSTUMES: *Karinska.* LIGHTING: *Jean Rosenthal.*
PREMIERE: *December 30, 1952, New York City Center, by the New York City Ballet.*
CAST: *André Eglevsky, Diana Adams, Tanaquil Le Clercq.*

1953 ## VALSE FANTAISIE
MUSIC: *Mikhail Glinka.* COSTUMES: *Karinska.* LIGHTING: *Jean Rosenthal.*
PREMIERE: *January 6, 1953, New York City Center, by the New York City Ballet.*
CAST: *Tanaquil Le Clercq, Melissa Hayden, Diana Adams, Nicholas Magallanes.*

1954 ## OPUS 34
MUSIC: *Arnold Schönberg.* DECOR AND LIGHTING: *Jean Rosenthal.* COSTUMES: *Esteban Francés.*
PREMIERE: *January 19, 1954, New York City Center, by the New York City Ballet.*
CAST: *Tanaquil Le Clercq, Herbert Bliss, Diana Adams, Patricia Wilde, Nicholas Magallanes, Francisco Moncion, et al.*

THE NUTCRACKER
MUSIC: *Pyotr Tchaikovsky.* DECOR: *Horace Armistead.* COSTUMES: *Karinska.* LIGHTING: *Jean Rosenthal.*
PREMIERE: *February 2, 1954, New York City Center, by the New York City Ballet.*
CAST: *Maria Tallchief, Nicholas Magallanes, Roy Tobias, Francisco Moncion, George Li, Robert Barnett, Janet Reed, Tanaquil Le Clercq, Yvonne Mounsey, Herbert Bliss, et al.*

WESTERN SYMPHONY
MUSIC: *Hershy Kay.* LIGHTING: *Jean Rosenthal. First presented without decor and danced in practice clothes. The following year costumes by Karinska and decor by John Boyt were added.*
PREMIERE: *September 7, 1954, New York City Center, by the New York City Ballet.*
CAST: *Diana Adams, Herbert Bliss, Janet Reed, Nicholas Magallanes, Patricia Wilde, Jacques d'Amboise, Tanaquil Le Clercq, André Eglevsky, et al.*

IVESIANA
MUSIC: *Charles Ives.* LIGHTING: *Jean Rosenthal.*
PREMIERE: *September 14, 1954, New York City Center, by the New York City Ballet.*
CAST: *Janet Reed, Francisco Moncion, Patricia Wilde, Jacques d'Amboise, Allegra Kent, Tanaquil Le Clercq, Todd Bolender, Diana Adams, Herbert Bliss, et al.*

1955 ## ROMA
MUSIC: *Georges Bizet.* DECOR AND COSTUMES: *Eugene Berman.* LIGHTING: *Jean Rosenthal.*
PREMIERE: *February 23, 1955, New York City Center, by the New York City Ballet.*
CAST: *Tanaquil Le Clercq, André Eglevsky, Barbara Milberg, Barbara Walczak, Roy Tobias, John Mandia, et al.*

PAS DE TROIS II
MUSIC: *Mikhail Glinka* (Russlan and Ludmila). COSTUMES: *Karinska.* LIGHTING: *Jean Rosenthal.*
PREMIERE: *March 1, 1955, New York City Center, by the New York City Ballet.*
CAST: *Melissa Hayden, Patricia Wilde, André Eglevsky.*

PAS DE DIX
MUSIC: *Alexander Glazunov* (from Raymonda). COSTUMES: *Esteban Francés.* LIGHTING: *Jean Rosenthal.*
PREMIERE: *November 9, 1955, New York City Center, by the New York City Ballet.*
CAST: *Maria Tallchief, André Eglevsky, Barbara Fallis, Constance Garfield, Jane Mason, Barbara Walczak, Shaun O'Brien, Roy Tobias, Roland Vazquez, Jonathan Watts.*

JEUX D'ENFANTS (choreographed with Barbara Milberg and Francisco Moncion)
MUSIC: *Georges Bizet.* DECOR AND COSTUMES: *Esteban Francés.* LIGHTING: *Jean Rosenthal.*
PREMIERE: *November 22, 1955, New York City Center, by the New York City Ballet.*
CAST: *Melissa Hayden, Roy Tobias, Barbara Walczak, Robert Barnett, Barbara Fallis, Jonathan Watts, Ann Crowell, Eugene Tanner, Una Kai, Walter Georgov, Roland Vasquez, et al.*

1956 ## ALLEGRO BRILLANTE
MUSIC: *Pyotr Tchaikovsky* (Opus 75, Third Piano Concerto). COSTUMES: *Karinska.* LIGHTING: *Jean Rosenthal.*
PREMIERE: *March 1, 1956, New York City Center, by the New York City Ballet.*
CAST: *Maria Tallchief, Nicholas Magallanes, Carolyn George, Barbara Fallis, Barbara Milberg, Barbara Walczak, Arthur Mitchell, Richard Rapp, Jonathan Watts, Roland Vasquez.*

DIVERTIMENTO NO. 15
MUSIC: *Wolfgang Amadeus Mozart.* DECOR: *James Stewart Morcom.* COSTUMES: *Karinska.* LIGHTING: *Jean Rosenthal.*
PREMIERE: *May 31, 1956, American Shakespeare Festival Theatre, Stratford, Connecticut, by the New York City Ballet.*
CAST: *Diana Adams, Tanaquil Le Clercq, Patricia Wilde, Melissa Hayden, Allegra Kent, Herbert Bliss, Nicholas Magallanes, Francisco Moncion, et al.*
FIRST NEW YORK PERFORMANCE: *December 19, 1956, New York City Center.*

A MUSICAL JOKE
MUSIC: *Wolfgang Amadeus Mozart.* COSTUMES: *Karinska.* LIGHTING: *Jean Rosenthal.*

PREMIERE: *May 31, 1956, American Shakespeare Festival Theatre, Stratford, Connecticut, by the New York City Ballet.*
CAST: *Diana Adams, Tanaquil Le Clercq, Patricia Wilde, Herbert Bliss, Nicholas Magallanes, Francisco Moncion.*

1957 SQUARE DANCE
MUSIC: *Antonio Vivaldi and Arcangelo Corelli.* LIGHTING: *Nananne Porcher.*
PREMIERE: *November 21, 1957, New York City Center, by the New York City Ballet.*
CAST: *Patricia Wilde, Nicholas Magallanes, et al.*

AGON
MUSIC: *Igor Stravinsky.* LIGHTING: *Nananne Porcher.*
PREMIERE: *December 1, 1957, New York City Center, by the New York City Ballet.*
CAST: *Diana Adams, Melissa Hayden, Arthur Mitchell, Todd Bolender, Roy Tobias, Jonathan Watts, et al.*

1958 GOUNOD SYMPHONY
MUSIC: *Charles Gounod.* DECOR: *Horace Armistead* (designed for Lilac Garden).
COSTUMES: *Karinska.* LIGHTING: *Nananne Porcher.*
PREMIERE: *January 8, 1958, New York City Center, by the New York City Ballet.*
CAST: *Maria Tallchief, Jacques d'Amboise, et al.*

STARS AND STRIPES
MUSIC: *John Philip Sousa, arranged by Hershy Kay.* DECOR: *David Hays.* COSTUMES: *Karinska.* LIGHTING: *Nananne Porcher.*
PREMIERE: *January 17, 1958, New York City Center, by the New York City Ballet.*
CAST: *Allegra Kent, Melissa Hayden, Robert Barnett, Diana Adams, Jacques d'Amboise, et al.*

WALTZ-SCHERZO
MUSIC: *Pyotr Tchaikovsky.* COSTUMES: *Karinska.* LIGHTING: *Nananne Porcher.*
PREMIERE: *September 9, 1958, New York City Center, by the New York City Ballet.*
CAST: *Patricia Wilde, André Eglevsky.*

SEVEN DEADLY SINS
MUSIC: *Kurt Weill.* DECOR, COSTUMES, AND LIGHTING: *Rouben Ter-Arutinian.* LIBRETTO: *Bertolt Brecht* (translated by W. H. Auden and Chester Kallman).
PREMIERE: *December 4, 1958, New York City Center, by the New York City Ballet.*
CAST: *Allegra Kent, et al., with Lotte Lenya singing the role of Anna.*

1959 NATIVE DANCERS
MUSIC: *Vittorio Rieti* (Symphony No. 5). DECOR AND LIGHTING: *David Hays.* COSTUMES: *Peter Larkin.*
PREMIERE: *January 14, 1959, New York City Center, by the New York City Ballet.*
CAST: *Patricia Wilde, Jacques d'Amboise, et al.*

EPISODES
MUSIC: *Anton Webern. Choreographed with Martha Graham, who choreographed and danced in the first half of the work. The Balanchine section, later presented independently, was then called* Episodes, Part II. DECOR AND LIGHTING: *David Hays.*
PREMIERE: *May 14, 1959, New York City Center, by the New York City Ballet.*
CAST (in the Balanchine section): *Violette Verdy, Jonathan Watts, Diana Adams, Jacques d'Amboise, Allegra Kent, Nicholas Magallanes, Melissa Hayden, Francisco Moncion, Paul Taylor, et al.*

1960 PANAMERICA
MUSIC: *Section II, Luis Escobar,* Preludios para Percusion; *Section IV, Carlos*

Chavez, Sinfonia No. 5 for String Orchestra; Section VIII, Julian Orbon, Danzas Sinfonicas. DECOR AND LIGHTING: David Hays. COSTUMES: Esteban Francés and Karinska.

PREMIERE: January 20, 1960, New York City Center, by the New York City Ballet.

CAST: Patricia Wilde, Erik Bruhn, Diana Adams, Nicholas Magallanes, Francisco Moncion, Maria Tallchief, Arthur Mitchell, Conrad Ludlow, Edward Villella, et al.

PAS DE DEUX (SWAN LAKE)

MUSIC: Pyotr Tchaikovsky. COSTUMES: Karinska. LIGHTING: Jack Owen Brown.

PREMIERE: March 29, 1960, New York City Center, by the New York City Ballet.

CAST: Violette Verdy, Conrad Ludlow.

THE FIGURE IN THE CARPET

MUSIC: George Frederick Handel. DECOR, COSTUMES, AND LIGHTING: Esteban Francés.

PREMIERE: April 13, 1960, New York City Center, by the New York City Ballet.

CAST: Violette Verdy, Edward Villella, Judith Green, Francisco Moncion, Francia Russell, Patricia McBride, Nicholas Magallanes, Mary Hinkson, Arthur Mitchell, Diana Adams, Melissa Hayden, Jacques d'Amboise, et al.

MONUMENTUM PRO GESUALDO

MUSIC: Igor Stravinsky (Three madrigals by Gesualdo di Venosa recomposed for instruments). DECOR: David Hays.

PREMIERE: November 16, 1960, New York City Center, by the New York City Ballet.

CAST: Diana Adams, Conrad Ludlow, et al.

VARIATIONS FROM DON SEBASTIAN (DONIZETTI VARIATIONS)

MUSIC: Gaetano Donizetti. DECOR AND LIGHTING: David Hays. COSTUMES: Karinska and Esteban Francés.

PREMIERE: November 16, 1960, New York City Center, by the New York City Ballet.

CAST: Melissa Hayden, Jonathan Watts, et al.

LIEBESLIEDER WALZER

MUSIC: Johannes Brahms (Liebeslieder Walzer, Opus 52, Opus 65). DECOR AND LIGHTING: David Hays. COSTUMES: Karinska.

PREMIERE: November 22, 1960, New York City Center, by the New York City Ballet.

CAST: Diana Adams, Bill Carter, Melissa Hayden, Conrad Ludlow, Jillana, Nicholas Magallanes, Violette Verdy, Jonathan Watts.

JAZZ CONCERT: RAGTIME

MUSIC: Igor Stravinsky (Ragtime for Eleven Instruments). COSTUMES: Karinska. LIGHTING: David Hays.

PREMIERE: December 7, 1960, New York City Center, by the New York City Ballet.

CAST: Diana Adams, Bill Carter.

1961 ### MODERN JAZZ: VARIANTS

MUSIC: Gunther Schuller. DECOR AND COSTUMES: David Hays.

PREMIERE: January 4, 1961, New York City Center, by the New York City Ballet.

CAST: Diana Adams, Melissa Hayden, John Jones, Arthur Mitchell, et al.

ELECTRONICS

MUSIC: Electronic score by Remi Gassmann and Oskar Sala. DECOR AND LIGHTING: David Hays.

PREMIERE: March 22, 1961, New York City Center, by the New York City Ballet.

CAST: Diana Adams, Jacques d'Amboise, Violette Verdy, Edward Villella, et al.

VALSES ET VARIATIONS (RAYMONDA VARIATIONS)

MUSIC: Alexander Glazunov (Raymonda). COSTUMES: Karinska. DECOR: Horace Armistead (backdrop for Lilac Garden). LIGHTING: David Hays.

PREMIERE: *December 7, 1961, New York City Center, by the New York City Ballet.*
CAST: *Patricia Wilde, Victoria Simon, Suki Schorer, Gloria Govrin, Carol Sumner, Patricia Neary, Jacques d'Amboise, et al.*

1962   A MIDSUMMER NIGHT'S DREAM
MUSIC: *Felix Mendelssohn.* DECOR AND LIGHTING: *David Hays.* COSTUMES: *Karinska.*
PREMIERE: *January 17, 1962, New York City Center, by the New York City Ballet.*
CAST: *Melissa Hayden, Edward Villella, Arthur Mitchell, Jillana, Patricia McBride, Nicholas Magallanes, Bill Carter, Roland Vasquez, Gloria Govrin, Suki Schorer, Francisco Moncion, Violette Verdy, Conrad Ludlow, et al.*

NOAH AND THE FLOOD (*a ballet-oratorio for television*)
MUSIC: *Igor Stravinsky. Text chosen and arranged by Robert Craft.* DECOR AND COSTUMES: *Rouben Ter-Arutunian.*
PREMIERE: *June 14, 1962, on the CBS Television Network.*
CAST: *Edward Villella, Jacques d'Amboise, Jillana, et al. Narrated by Laurence Harvey.*

1963   BUGAKU
MUSIC: *Toshiro Mayuzumi.* DECOR AND LIGHTING: *David Hays.* COSTUMES: *Karinska.*
PREMIERE: *March 20, 1963, New York City Center, by the New York City Ballet.*
CAST: *Allegra Kent, Edward Villella, et al.*

MOVEMENTS FOR PIANO AND ORCHESTRA
MUSIC: *Igor Stravinsky.* LIGHTING: *Peter Harvey.*
PREMIERE: *April 9, 1963, New York City Center, by the New York City Ballet.*
CAST: *Suzanne Farrell, Jacques d'Amboise, et al.*

MEDITATION
MUSIC: *Pyotr Tchaikovsky ("Meditation" from* Souvenir d'un Lieu Cher, *Opus 42, No. 1, orchestrated by Alexander Glazounov).* COSTUMES: *Karinska.*
PREMIERE: *December 10, 1963, New York City Center, by the New York City Ballet.*
CAST: *Suzanne Farrell, Jacques d'Amboise.*

1964   TARANTELLA
MUSIC: *Louis Gottschalk (reconstructed and orchestrated by Hershy Kay).* COSTUMES: *Karinska.*
PREMIERE: *January 7, 1964, New York City Center, by the New York City Ballet.*
CAST: *Patricia McBride, Edward Villella.*

CLARINADE
MUSIC: *Morton Gould (Derivations for Clarinet and Jazz Band). Clarinet Solo by Benny Goodman.*
PREMIERE: *April 29, 1964, New York State Theater, by the New York City Ballet.*
CAST: *Gloria Govrin, Arthur Mitchell, Suzanne Farrell, Anthony Blum, et al.*

1965   PAS DE DEUX AND DIVERTISSEMENT
MUSIC: *Léo Delibes (from* Sylvia, La Source, *and* Naïla). COSTUMES: *Karinska.*
LIGHTING: *David Hays.*
PREMIERE: *January 14, 1965, New York State Theater, by the New York City Ballet.*
CAST: *Melissa Hayden, André Prokovsky, Suki Schorer, et al.*

HARLEQUINADE
MUSIC: *Riccardo Drigo* (Les Millions d'Arlequin). DECOR, COSTUMES, AND LIGHTING: *Rouben Ter-Arutunian.*

PREMIERE: *February 4, 1965, New York State Theater, by the New York City Ballet, with children from the School of American Ballet.*
CAST: *Patricia McBride, Edward Villella, Suki Schorer, Deni Lamont, Gloria Govrin, Carol Sumner, Michael Arshansky, et al.*

DON QUIXOTE
MUSIC: *Nicolas Nabokov.* DECOR, COSTUMES, AND LIGHTING: *Esteban Francés.*
PREMIERE: *May 28, 1965, New York State Theater, by the New York City Ballet, with children from the School of American Ballet.*
CAST: *Suzanne Farrell, Richard Rapp, Deni Lamont, Nicholas Magallanes, Jillana, Francisco Moncion, Patricia Neary, Conrad Ludlow, Kent Stowell, Suki Schorer, John Prinz, Sara Leland, Kay Mazzo, Carol Sumner, Frank Ohman, Robert Rodham, Earle Sieveling, Gloria Govrin, Arthur Mitchell, Patricia McBride, Marnee Morris, Mimi Paul, Anthony Blum, et al.*

1966 **VARIATIONS**
MUSIC: *Igor Stravinsky (Variations in Memory of Aldous Huxley, 1965).* LIGHTING: *Ronald Bates.*
PREMIERE: *March 31, 1966, New York State Theater, by the New York City Ballet.*
CAST: *Suzanne Farrell, et al.*

BRAHMS-SCHOENBERG QUARTET
MUSIC: *Johannes Brahms (Quartet No. 1, Opus 25, G Minor, orchestrated by Arnold Schönberg).* DECOR: *Peter Harvey.* COSTUMES: *Karinska.* LIGHTING: *Ronald Bates.*
PREMIERE: *April 21, 1966, New York State Theater, by the New York City Ballet.*
CAST: *Melissa Hayden, André Prokovsky, Gloria Govrin, Patricia McBride, Conrad Ludlow, Allegra Kent, Edward Villella, Suzanne Farrell, Jacques d'Amboise, et al.*

RAGTIME *(new choreography)*
MUSIC: *Igor Stravinsky (Ragtime for Eleven Instruments).*
PREMIERE: *July 15, 1966, Philharmonic Hall, New York.*
CAST: *Suzanne Farrell, Arthur Mitchell.*

1967 **TROIS VALSE ROMANTIQUES**
MUSIC: *Emmanuel Chabrier (orchestrated by Felix Mottl).* COSTUMES: *Karinska.*
LIGHTING: *Ronald Bates.*
PREMIERE: *April 6, 1967, New York State Theater, by the New York City Ballet.*
CAST: *Melissa Hayden, Arthur Mitchell, Gloria Govrin, Marnee Morris, Frank Ohman, Kent Stowell, et al.*

JEWELS
MUSIC: *"Emeralds"—Gabriel Fauré* (Pelleas et Melisande, Shylock); *"Rubies"—Igor Stravinsky (Capriccio for Piano and Orchestra); "Diamonds"—Pyotr Tchaikovsky (Symphony No. 3 in D Major).* DECOR: *Peter Harvey.* COSTUMES: *Karinska.*
LIGHTING: *Ronald Bates.*
PREMIERE: *April 13, 1967, New York State Theater, by the New York City Ballet.*
CAST: *Violette Verdy, Conrad Ludlow, Mimi Paul, Francisco Moncion, Patricia McBride, Sara Leland, Suki Schorer, John Prinz, Edward Villella, Suzanne Farrell, Jacques d'Amboise, et al.*

GLINKIANA *(Second Movement later became Valse Fantaisie)*
MUSIC: *Mikhail Glinka.* DECOR, COSTUMES, AND LIGHTING: *Esteban Francés.*
PREMIERE: *November 23, 1967, New York State Theater, by the New York City Ballet.*
CAST: *Violette Verdy, Paul Mejia, Mimi Paul, John Clifford, Melissa Hayden, Patricia McBride, Edward Villella, et al.*

1968   **METASTASEIS AND PITHOPRAKTA**
MUSIC: *Iannis Xenakis.* LIGHTING: *Ronald Bates.*
PREMIERE: *January 18, 1968, New York State Theater, by the New York City Ballet.*
CAST: *Suzanne Farrell, Arthur Mitchell, et al.*

REQUIEM CANTICLES (in memory of Martin Luther King, Jr.)
MUSIC: *Igor Stravinsky.* COSTUMES: *Rouben Ter-Arutunian.* LIGHTING: *Ronald Bates.*
FIRST AND ONLY PERFORMANCE: *May 2, 1968, New York State Theater, by the New York City Ballet.*
CAST: *Suzanne Farrell, Arthur Mitchell, et al.*

SLAUGHTER ON TENTH AVENUE (new version of sequence from 1936 musical comedy On Your Toes)
MUSIC: *Richard Rodgers (orchestrated by Hershy Kay).* DECOR AND LIGHTING: *Jo Mielziner.* COSTUMES: *Irene Sharaff.*
PREMIERE: *May 2, 1968, New York State Theater, by the New York City Ballet.*
CAST: *Suzanne Farrell, Arthur Mitchell, Michael Steele, Earle Sieveling, et al.*

LA SOURCE
MUSIC: *Léo Delibes* (La Source). COSTUMES: *Karinska.* LIGHTING: *Ronald Bates.*
PREMIERE: *November 23, 1968, New York State Theater, by the New York City Ballet.*
CAST: *Violette Verdy, John Prinz.*

1969   **VALSE FANTAISIE (formerly Part II of Glinkiana)**
MUSIC: *Mikhail Glinka.* DECOR, COSTUMES, AND LIGHTING: *Esteban Francés.*
PREMIERE: *June 1, 1969, New York State Theater, by the New York City Ballet.*
CAST: *Suki Schorer, John Prinz, et al.*

1970   **WHO CARES?**
MUSIC: *George Gershwin (orchestrated by Hershy Kay).* COSTUMES: *Karinska.*
LIGHTING: *Ronald Bates.*
PREMIERE: *February 5, 1970, New York State Theater, by the New York City Ballet.*
CAST: *Patricia McBride, Karin von Aroldingen, Marnee Morris, Jacques d'Amboise, et al.*

SUITE NO. 3 (includes the 1947 work Theme and Variation)
MUSIC: *Pyotr Tchaikovsky (Suite No. 3 in G Minor, Opus 55).* DECOR AND COSTUMES: *Nicolas Benois.* LIGHTING: *Ronald Bates.*
PREMIERE: *December 3, 1970, New York State Theater, by the New York City Ballet.*
CAST: *Karin von Aroldingen, Anthony Blum, Kay Mazzo, Conrad Ludlow, Marnee Morris, John Clifford, Gelsey Kirkland, Edward Villella.*

1971   **CONCERTO FOR JAZZ BAND AND ORCHESTRA (choreographed with Arthur Mitchell)**
MUSIC: *Rolf Liebermann.* LIGHTING: *Ronald Bates.*
FIRST AND ONLY PERFORMANCE: *April 27, 1971, New York State Theater, by the New York City Ballet and the Dance Theatre of Harlem.*

PAMTGG
MUSIC: *Roger Kellaway (based on themes by Stan Applebaum and Sid Woloshin).*
DECOR AND LIGHTING: *Jo Mielziner.* COSTUMES: *Irene Sharaff.*
PREMIERE: *June 17, 1971, New York State Theater, by the New York City Ballet.*
CAST: *Karin von Aroldingen, Sara Leland, Victor Castelli, Kay Mazzo, Frank Ohman, John Clifford, et al.*

1972 SONATA

MUSIC: *Igor Stravinsky (Scherzo from Sonata in F-Sharp Minor).*
PREMIERE: *June 18, 1972 (Stravinsky Festival), New York State Theater, by the New York City Ballet.*
CAST: *Sara Leland, John Clifford.*

SYMPHONY IN THREE MOVEMENTS

MUSIC: *Igor Stravinsky.* LIGHTING: *Ronald Bates.*
PREMIERE: *June 18, 1972 (Stravinsky Festival), New York State Theater, by the New York City Ballet.*
CAST: *Linda Yourth, Helgi Tomasson, Robert Weiss, Sara Leland, Edward Villella, Marnee Morris, et al.*

VIOLIN CONCERTO

MUSIC: *Igor Stravinsky.* LIGHTING: *Ronald Bates.*
PREMIERE: *June 18, 1972 (Stravinsky Festival), New York State Theater, by the New York City Ballet.*
CAST: *Kay Mazzo, Peter Martins, Karin von Aroldingen, Jean-Pierre Bonnefous, et al.*

DANSES CONCERTANTES (new choreography)

MUSIC: *Igor Stravinsky.* DECOR AND COSTUMES: *Eugene Berman (from the 1944 production).*
PREMIERE: *June 20, 1972 (Stravinsky Festival), New York State Theater, by the New York City Ballet.*
CAST: *Linda Yourth, John Clifford, et al.*

DIVERTIMENTO FROM "LE BAISER DE LA FÉE"

MUSIC: *Igor Stravinsky.* COSTUMES: *Eugene Berman (from Roma).*
PREMIERE: *June 21, 1972 (Stravinsky Festival), New York State Theater, by the New York City Ballet.*
CAST: *Patricia McBride, Helgi Tomasson, Carol Sumner, Bettijane Sills, et al.*

SCHERZO À LA RUSSE

MUSIC: *Igor Stravinsky.* COSTUMES: *Karinska.* LIGHTING: *Ronald Bates.*
PREMIERE: *June 21, 1972 (Stravinsky Festival), New York State Theater, by the New York City Ballet.*
CAST: *Kay Mazzo, Karin von Aroldingen, et al.*

DUO CONCERTANT

MUSIC: *Igor Stravinsky.* LIGHTING: *Ronald Bates.*
PREMIERE: *June 22, 1972 (Stravinsky Festival), New York State Theater, by the New York City Ballet.*
CAST: *Kay Mazzo, Peter Martins.*

PULCINELLA (choreographed with Jerome Robbins)

MUSIC: *Igor Stravinsky.* DECOR AND COSTUMES: *Eugene Berman.* LIGHTING: *Ronald Bates.*
PREMIERE: *June 23, 1972 (Stravinsky Festival), New York State Theater, by the New York City Ballet.*
CAST: *Violette Verdy, Edward Villella, Jerome Robbins, George Balanchine, Michael Arshansky, Francisco Moncion, Shaun O'Brien, Deni Lamont, Robert Weiss, et al.*

CHORAL VARIATIONS ON BACH'S "VON HIMMEL HOCH"

MUSIC: *Igor Stravinsky.* DECOR: *Rouben Ter-Arutunian.* LIGHTING: *Ronald Bates.*
PREMIERE: *June 25, 1972 (Stravinsky Festival), New York State Theater, by the New York City Ballet, with children from the School of American Ballet.*

CAST: *Melissa Hayden, Violette Verdy, Karin von Aroldingen, Sara Leland, Anthony Blum, Peter Martins, et al.*

1973 CORTÈGE HONGROIS

MUSIC: *Alexander Glazunov (last act of* Raymonda). DECOR AND COSTUMES: *Rouben Ter-Arutunian.* LIGHTING: *Ronald Bates.*

PREMIERE: *May 17, 1973, New York State Theater, by the New York City Ballet.*

CAST: *Melissa Hayden, Jacques d'Amboise, Karin von Aroldingen, Jean-Pierre Bonnefous, Colleen Neary, Merrill Ashley, et al.*

1974 VARIATIONS POUR UNE PORTE ET UN SOUPIR

MUSIC: *Pierre Henry.* DECOR AND COSTUMES: *Rouben Ter-Arutunian.* LIGHTING: *Ronald Bates.*

PREMIERE: *January 17, 1974, New York State Theater, by the New York City Ballet.*

CAST: *Karin von Aroldingen, John Clifford.*

COPPÉLIA (choreographed with Alexandra Danilova, after Marius Petipa)

MUSIC: *Léo Delibes.* LIBRETTO: *Charles Nuittier, after E. T. A. Hoffman's Der Sandmann.* DECOR AND COSTUMES: *Rouben Ter-Arutunian.* LIGHTING: *Ronald Bates.*

PREMIERE: *July 17, 1974, Saratoga Performing Arts Center, Saratoga Springs, New York, by the New York City Ballet.*

CAST: *Patricia McBride, Helgi Tomasson, Shaun O'Brien, Michael Arshansky, Marnee Morris, Merrill Ashley, Christine Redpath, Susan Hendl, Colleen Neary, Robert Weiss, et al.*

1975 SONATINE

MUSIC: *Maurice Ravel.* LIGHTING: *Ronald Bates.*

PREMIERE: *May 15, 1975 (Ravel Festival), New York State Theater, by the New York City Ballet.*

CAST: *Violette Verdy, Jean-Pierre Bonnefous.*

L'ENFANT ET LES SORTILÈGES (revised choreography)

MUSIC: *Maurice Ravel.* LIBRETTO: *Colette (translated by Catherine Wolff).* DECOR AND COSTUMES: *Kermit Love (Supervising Designer, David Mitchell).* LIGHTING: *Ronald Bates.*

PREMIERE: *May 15, 1975 (Ravel Festival), New York State Theater, by the New York City Ballet.*

CAST: *Paul Offenkranz, Marnee Morris, Christine Redpath, Jean-Pierre Frohlich, Tracy Bennett, Colleen Neary, Stephanie Saland, et al.*

SHÉHÉRAZADE

MUSIC: *Maurice Ravel.* LIGHTING: *Ronald Bates.*

PREMIERE: *May 22, 1975 (Ravel Festival), New York State Theater, by the New York City Ballet.*

CAST: *Kay Mazzo, Edward Villella, et al.*

LE TOMBEAU DE COUPERIN

MUSIC: *Maurice Ravel.* LIGHTING: *Ronald Bates.*

PREMIERE: *May 29, 1975 (Ravel Festival), New York State Theater, by the New York City Ballet.*

CAST: *Judith Fugate, Jean-Pierre Frohlich, Wilhelmina Frankfurt, Victor Castelli, Muriel Aasen, Francis Sackett, Susan Hendl, David Richardson, Marjorie Spohn, Hermes Condé, Delia Peters, Richard Hoskinson, Susan Pilarre, Richard Dryden, Carol Sumner, Laurence Matthews.*

PAVANE

MUSIC: *Maurice Ravel* (Pavane pour une Infante Défunte). LIGHTING: *Ronald Bates.*

PREMIERE: *May 29, 1975 (Ravel Festival), New York State Theater, by the New York City Ballet.*

CAST: *Patricia McBride.*

TZIGANE

MUSIC: *Maurice Ravel.* COSTUMES: *Joe Eula and Stanley Simmons.* LIGHTING: *Ronald Bates.*

PREMIERE: *May 29, 1975 (Ravel Festival), New York State Theater, by the New York City Ballet.*

CAST: *Suzanne Farrell, Peter Martins, et al.*

GASPARD DE LA NUIT

MUSIC: *Maurice Ravel.* DECOR AND COSTUMES: *Bernard Daydé.* LIGHTING: *Bernard Daydé, with Ronald Bates.*

PREMIERE: *May 29, 1975 (Ravel Festival), New York State Theater, by the New York City Ballet.*

CAST: *Colleen Neary, Victor Castelli, Karin von Aroldingen, Nolan T'Sani, Sara Leland, Robert Weiss, et al.*

RAPSODIE ESPAGNOLE

MUSIC: *Maurice Ravel.* COSTUMES: *Michael Avedon.* LIGHTING: *Ronald Bates.*

PREMIERE: *May 29, 1975 (Ravel Festival), New York State Theater, by the New York City Ballet.*

CAST: *Karin von Aroldingen, Peter Schaufuss, Nolan T'Sani, et al.*

WALPURGISNACHT BALLET

MUSIC: *Charles Gounod (Act III, Scene I of* Faust).

PREMIERE: *June 3, 1975, Théâtre National de l'Opéra, by the Paris Opéra Ballet.*

CAST: *Claudette Scouarnee, Sylvie Clavier, Jean-Paul Gravier, Joysane Consoli, Janine Guiton, et al.*

FIRST NEW YORK PERFORMANCE: *May 15, 1980, New York State Theater, by the New York City Ballet.*

CAST: *Suzanne Farrell, Adam Lüders, Heather Watts, Stephanie Saland, Judith Fugate, et al.*

THE STEADFAST TIN SOLDIER

MUSIC: *Georges Bizet (from* Jeux d'Enfants). DECOR AND COSTUMES: *David Mitchell.* LIGHTING: *Ronald Bates.*

PREMIERE: *July 30, 1975, Saratoga Performing Arts Center, Saratoga Springs, New York, by the New York City Ballet.*

CAST: *Patricia McBride, Peter Schaufuss.*

1976   CHACONNE

MUSIC: *Christoph Willibald Gluck (ballet music from* Orfeo ed Euridice). COSTUMES: *Karinska (the ballet was danced in practice clothes at the premiere, with costumes added later).* LIGHTING: *Ronald Bates.*

PREMIERE: *January 22, 1976, New York State Theater, by the New York City Ballet. (The choreography was a somewhat altered version of the ballet included in Balanchine's staging of the opera for the Hamburg State Opera in 1963.)*

CAST: *Suzanne Farrell, Peter Martins, Renée Estopinal, Wilhelmina Frankfurt, Jay Jolley, Susan Hendl, Jean-Pierre Frohlich, Elise Flagg, Bonita Borne, Elyse Borne,*

Laura Flagg, Nichol Hlinka, Susan Pilarre, Marjorie Spohn, Tracy Bennett, Gerard Ebitz, et al.

UNION JACK

MUSIC: Hershy Kay (adapted from traditional British sources). DECOR AND COSTUMES: Rouben Ter-Arutunian. Scottish costumes by Sheldon M. Kasman. LIGHTING: Ronald Bates.
PREMIERE: May 13, 1976, New York State Theater, by the New York City Ballet.
CAST: Helgi Tomasson, Jacques d'Amboise, Sara Leland, Kay Mazzo, Karin von Aroldingen, Suzanne Farrell, Jean-Pierre Bonnefous, Patricia McBride, Victor Castelli, Bart Cook, et al.

1977   ÉTUDE FOR PIANO

MUSIC: Alexander Scriabin (Étude in C-sharp minor, Opus 8, No. 1). COSTUMES: Christina Giannini.
PREMIERE: June 4, 1977, Spoleto Festival U.S.A., Charleston, South Carolina.
CAST: Patricia McBride, Jean-Pierre Bonnefous.

VIENNA WALTZES

MUSIC: "Tales from the Vienna Woods," "Voices of Spring," and "Explosion Polka," by Johann Strauss the Younger; "Gold and Silver Waltz," by Franz Lehár; "Waltzes from Der Rosenkavalier," by Richard Strauss. DECOR: Rouben Ter-Arutunian. COSTUMES: Karinska. LIGHTING: Ronald Bates.
PREMIERE: June 23, 1977, New York State Theater, by the New York City Ballet.
CAST: Karin von Aroldingen, Sean Lavery, Patricia McBride, Helgi Tomasson, Sara Leland, Bart Cook, Kay Mazzo, Peter Martins, Suzanne Farrell, Jorge Donn, et al.

1978   BALLO DELLA REGINA

MUSIC: Giuseppe Verdi (ballet music from Act III, Don Carlos). COSTUMES: Ben Benson. LIGHTING: Ronald Bates.
PREMIERE: January 12, 1978, New York State Theater, by the New York City Ballet.
CAST: Merrill Ashley, Robert Weiss, Debra Austin, Bonita Borne, Stephanie Saland, Sheryl Ware, et al.

KAMMERMUSIK NO. 2

MUSIC: Paul Hindemith. COSTUMES: Ben Benson. LIGHTING: Ronald Bates.
PREMIERE: January 26, 1978, New York State Theater, by the New York City Ballet.
CAST: Karin von Aroldingen, Colleen Neary, Sean Lavery, Adam Lüders, et al.

TRICOLORE

CHOREOGRAPHY: Though the ballet was conceived and supervised by Balanchine, the choreography was assigned to others—Peter Martins, Jean-Pierre Bonnefous, and Jerome Robbins—because of Balanchine's ill health.
MUSIC: Georges Auric (commissioned by the New York City Ballet). DECOR AND COSTUMES: Rouben Ter-Arutunian. LIGHTING: Ronald Bates.
PREMIERE: May 18, 1978, New York State Theater, by the New York City Ballet.
CAST: Colleen Neary, Adam Lüders, Merrill Ashley, Sean Lavery, Karin von Aroldingen, Nina Fedorova, et al.

1979   LE BOURGEOIS GENTILHOMME (new choreography, with Jerome Robbins)

MUSIC: Richard Strauss. DECOR AND COSTUMES: Rouben Ter-Arutunian. LIGHTING: Gilbert Helmsley, Jr.
PREMIERE: April 8, 1979, New York State Theater, by the New York City Opera, with corps de ballet of students from the School of American Ballet.
CAST: Patricia McBride, Jean-Pierre Bonnefous, Rudolf Nureyev, Darla Hoover, Michael Puleo, et al.

1980 BALLADE

MUSIC: *Gabriel Fauré (Ballade for piano and orchestra, Opus 19).* DECOR AND COSTUMES: *Rouben Ter-Arutunian (from* Tricolore). LIGHTING: *Ronald Bates.*
PREMIERE: *May 8, 1980, New York State Theater, by the New York City Ballet.*
CAST: *Merrill Ashley, Ib Andersen, et al.*

ROBERT SCHUMANN'S "DAVIDSBÜNDLERTÄNZE"

MUSIC: *Robert Schumann (Opus 6).* DECOR AND COSTUMES: *Rouben Ter-Arutunian.* LIGHTING: *Ronald Bates.*
PREMIERE: *June 19, 1980, New York State Theater, by the New York City Ballet.*
CAST: *Karin von Aroldingen, Adam Lüders, Suzanne Farrell, Jacques d'Amboise, Heather Watts, Peter Martins, Kay Mazzo, Ib Andersen.*

1981 MOZARTIANA (new choreography)

MUSIC: *Mozart-Tchaikovsky (Suite No. 4).* DECOR: *Philip Johnson and John Burgee. The scenery for this and all other ballets in the Tchaikovsky Festival was a unit set in the spirit of an ice palace, created from thirty-six hundred pieces of clear plastic tubing, whose arrangement could be varied for the individual ballet.* COSTUMES: *Rouben Ter-Arutunian.* LIGHTING: *Ronald Bates.*
PREMIERE: *June 4, 1981 (Tchaikovsky Festival), New York State Theater, by the New York City Ballet.*
CAST: *Suzanne Farrell, Christopher d'Amboise, Ib Andersen, et al.*

GARLAND DANCE

MUSIC: *Pyotr Tchaikovsky (from* The Sleeping Beauty, *Act I).* COSTUMES: *Karinska and Rouben Ter-Arutunian.* DECOR: *Philip Johnson and John Burgee.* LIGHTING: *Ronald Bates.*
PREMIERE: *June 9, 1981 (Tchaikovsky Festival), New York State Theater, by the New York City Ballet.*
CAST: *Students of the School of American Ballet.*
NOTE: *The Garland Dance was one of five short works presented under the title of* Tempo di Valse.

HUNGARIAN GYPSY AIRS

MUSIC: *Sophie Menter, orchestrated by Pyotr Tchaikovsky.* DECOR: *Philip Johnson and John Burgee.* COSTUMES: *Ben Benson.* LIGHTING: *Ronald Bates.*
PREMIERE: *June 13, 1981 (Tchaikovsky Festival), New York State Theater, by the New York City Ballet.*
CAST: *Karin von Aroldingen, Adam Lüders, et al.*

ADAGIO LAMENTOSO

MUSIC: *Pyotr Tchaikovsky (Symphony No. 6, Fourth Movement).* DECOR: *Philip Johnson and John Burgee.* COSTUMES: *Rouben Ter-Arutunian.* LIGHTING: *Ronald Bates.*
PREMIERE: *June 14, 1981 (Tchaikovsky Festival), New York State Theater, by the New York City Ballet.*
CAST: *Karin von Aroldingen, Judith Fugate, Stephanie Saland, et al.*
NOTE: *Balanchine's choreography was to the concluding movement of Symphony No. 6—Pathetique, the final work of the festival. The first movement was omitted, the second was choreographed by Jerome Robbins, and the third was played by the orchestra with the curtain lowered.*

1982 TANGO

MUSIC: *Igor Stravinsky.* DECOR: *Philip Johnson and John Burgee. Throughout the Stravinsky Centennial Celebration the basic set designed for the Tchaikovsky Festival was used in various arrangements.* LIGHTING: *Ronald Bates.*

PREMIERE: *June 10, 1982 (Stravinsky Centennial Celebration), New York State Theater, by the New York City Ballet.*
CAST: *Karin von Aroldingen, Christopher d'Amboise.*

NOAH AND THE FLOOD (revised staging, with Jacques d'Amboise)
MUSIC: *Igor Stravinsky.* DECOR AND COSTUMES: *Rouben Ter-Arutunian.* LIGHTING: *Ronald Bates.*
PREMIERE: *June 11, 1982 (Stravinsky Centennial Celebration), New York State Theater, by the New York City Ballet, with students from the School of American Ballet.*
CAST: *Adam Lüders, Nina Fedorova, Bruce Padgett, Francisco Moncion, Delia Peters, et al. Narrated by John Houseman. Other voices: Robert Brubaker, Barry Carl, John Lankston, and members of the New York City Opera Chorus.*

ÉLÉGIE (new choreography)
MUSIC: *Igor Stravinsky (Élégie-Elegy for solo viola).* DECOR: *Philip Johnson and John Burgee.* LIGHTING: *Ronald Bates.*
PREMIERE: *June 13, 1982 (Stravinsky Centennial Celebration), New York State Theater, by the New York City Ballet.*
CAST: *Suzanne Farrell.*

PERSÉPHONE (choreographed with John Taras and Vera Zorina)
MUSIC: *Igor Stravinsky (Mélodrame in three scenes for tenor, narrator, mixed chorus, children's choir, and orchestra).* TEXT: *André Gide. Production designed by Kermit Love.*
PREMIERE: *June 18, 1982 (Stravinsky Centennial Celebration), New York State Theater, by the New York City Ballet, with members of the New York City Opera Chorus and the American Boychoir.*
CAST: *Karin von Aroldingen, Mel Tomlinson, Gen Horiuchi, et al. Vera Zorina performed the spoken role of Perséphone, and the tenor Joseph Evans sang the role of Eumolpus the Eleusinian Priest.*

VARIATIONS FOR ORCHESTRA (new choreography)
MUSIC: *Igor Stravinsky (Variations in Memory of Aldous Huxley).* LIGHTING: *Ronald Bates.*
PREMIERE: *July 2, 1982, New York State Theater, by the New York City Ballet.*
CAST: *Suzanne Farrell.*

Operas with Choreography by Balanchine

NOTE: *In the listings below, unless otherwise stated, the dancers at the Opéra de Monte Carlo from 1925-1929 were members of Diaghilev's Ballets Russes, and those present during the 1932 season were members of the Ballet Russe de Monte Carlo; the dancers at the Metropolitan Opera from 1935-1938 were members of the American Ballet; the dancers at New York City Opera from 1948-1949 were members of the New York City Ballet. Where no principal dancers' names are given, the choreography was for the resident ensemble.*

LE COQ D'OR, by Nicolai Rimsky-Korsakov
PREMIERES: *Sepember 15, 1923, Maly Opera Theatre, Petrograd; February 4, 1937, Metropolitan Opera, New York (entire production staged by Balanchine).*

CARMEN, by Georges Bizet
PREMIERES: *January 25, 1925, Opéra de Monte Carlo; March 24, 1932, Opéra de Monte Carlo; December 27, 1935, Metropolitan Opera, New York, with Ruthanna Boris, Anatole Vilzak, Betty Eisner, Lew Christensen, Madeline Leweck, et al.; October 10, 1948, New York City Opera, City Center, New York, with Maria Tallchief, Francisco Moncion, et al.*

THAÏS, by Jules Massenet
PREMIERE: *January 27, 1925, Opéra de Monte Carlo.*

MANON, by Jules Massenet
PREMIERES: *February 5, 1925, Opéra de Monte Carlo, with Alexandra Danilova, Thadée Slavinsky, et al.; February 28, 1932, Opéra de Monte Carlo, with Valentina Blinova, Léon Woizikowsky, et al.; January 10, 1936, Metropolitan Opera, New York.*

LE HULLA, by Marcel Samuel-Rousseau
PREMIERE: *February 12, 1925, Opéra de Monte Carlo, with Vera Nemtchinova, et al.*

LE DÉMON, by Anton Rubinstein
PREMIERE: *February 14, 1925, Opéra de Monte Carlo, with Lubov Tchernicheva, Léon Woizikowsky, et al.*

FAY-YEN-FAH, by Joseph Redding
PREMIERES: *February 26, 1925, Opéra de Monte Carlo, with Vera Nemtchinova, Nicolas Kremnev, et al.; March 8, 1932, Opéra de Monte Carlo, with Tamara Toumanova, Marian Ladré, et al.*

FAUST, by Charles Gounod
PREMIERES: *March 5, 1925, Opéra de Monte Carlo; February 13, 1932, Opéra de Monte Carlo; December 19, 1935, Metropolitan Opera, New York; June 26, 1945, Ópera Nacional, Mexico City; June 3, 1975, Théâtre National de l'Opéra, Paris.*

HERODIADE, by Jules Massenet
PREMIERE: *March 7, 1925, Opéra de Monte Carlo, with Lubov Tchernicheva, George Balanchine, Thadée Slavinsky, et al.*

UN DÉBUT, by Philippe Bellenot
PREMIERE: *March 21, 1925, Opéra de Monte Carlo.*

L'ENFANT ET LES SORTILÈGES, by Maurice Ravel
PREMIERES: *March 21, 1925, Opéra de Monte Carlo, with Alexandra Danilova, Constantin Tcherkas, Alicia Markova, et al.; November 20, 1946, Ballet Society, New York, with Elise Reiman, Tanaquil Le Clercq, William Dollar, et al.; May 15, 1975, the New York City Ballet, New York State Theater, with Marnee Morris, Christine Redpath, Jean-Pierre Frohlich, et al.; May 25, 1981, television production for Dance in America, PBS, by the New York City Ballet, with Karin von Aroldingen, et al.*

BORIS GODUNOV, by Modest Mussorgsky
PREMIERES: *February 9, 1926, Opéra de Monte Carlo; April 20, 1953, Teatro alla Scala, Milan; December 16, 1974, Metropolitan Opera, New York.*

JUDITH, by Arthur Honegger
PREMIERE: *February 13, 1926, Opéra de Monte Carlo.*

LA RONDINE, by Giacomo Puccini
PREMIERES: *February 20, 1926, Opéra de Monte Carlo, with Lydia Sokolova, Léon Woizikow-*

sky, et al.; January 17, 1936, Metropolitan Opera, New York, with Kyra Blank, Daphne Vane, Douglas Coudy, et al.

LAKMÉ, by Léo Delibes
PREMIERES: *March 2, 1926, Opéra de Monte Carlo, with Lubov Tchernicheva, et al.; February 9, 1932, Opéra de Monte Carlo, with Eleanora Marra, et al.; December 23, 1935, Metropolitan Opera, New York, with Kathryn Mullowny, Betty Eisner, Nora Koreff (Kaye), Yvonne Patterson, Mary Sale, Elise Reiman, Lew Christensen, Douglas Coudy, Holly Howard, Charles Laskey, et al.*

JEANNE D'ARC, by Charles Gounod
PREMIERE: *March 28, 1926, Opéra de Monte Carlo.*

SAMSON ET DALILA, by Camille Saint-Saëns
PREMIERES: *January 27, 1927, Opéra de Monte Carlo, with Lubov Tchernicheva, et al.; February 11, 1932, Opéra de Monte Carlo, with Eleanora Marra, et al.; December 26, 1936, Metropolitan Opera, New York, with Daphne Vane, et al.; July 3, 1945, Ópera Nacional, Mexico City.*

LA TRAVIATA, by Giuseppe Verdi
PREMIERES: *February 8, 1927, Opéra de Monte Carlo, with Vera Petrova, Nicolas Efimov, et al.; March 3, 1932, Opéra de Monte Carlo, with Tatiana Lipkovska, Metek Borovsky, et al.; December 16, 1935, Metropolitan Opera, New York, with Anatole Vilzak, Gisella Caccialanza, Ruthanna Boris, et al.; October 17, 1948, New York City Opera, City Center, New York, with Marie-Jeanne, Herbert Bliss, et al.*

TURANDOT, by Giacomo Puccini
PREMIERES: *February 22, 1927, Opéra de Monte Carlo, with Lubov Tchernicheva, Alexandra Danilova, Stanislas Idzikowsky, Léon Woizikowsky, George Balanchine, et al.; February 21, 1932, Opéra de Monte Carlo, with Valentina Blinova, Tamara Toumanova, Léon Woizikowsky, Marian Ladré, Roland Guérard, et al.*

LA DAMNATION DE FAUST, by Hector Berlioz
PREMIERE: *February 26, 1927, Opéra de Monte Carlo.*

IVAN LE TERRIBLE, by Raoul Gunsbourg
PREMIERE: *March 3, 1927, Opéra de Monte Carlo, with Lydia Sokolova, Léon Woizikowsky, et al.*

OBÉRON, by Carl Maria von Weber
PREMIERE: *March 26, 1927, Opéra de Monte Carlo.*

MIREILLE, by Charles Gounod
PREMIERE: *January 28, 1928, Opéra de Monte Carlo, with Henriette Maikerska, Nicholas Kremnev, et al.*

DIE MEISTERSINGER VON NURNBERG, by Richard Wagner
PREMIERES: *February 5, 1928, Opéra de Monte Carlo, with Dora Vadimova, Henriette Maikerska, Nicholas Efimov, Constantin Tcherkas; February 3, 1936, Metropolitan Opera, New York.*

VENISE, by Raoul Gunsbourg
PREMIERE: *February 23, 1928, Opéra de Monte Carlo, with Alexandra Danilova, Léon Woizikowsky, et al.*

SIOR TODÉRO BRONTOLON, by Gian Francesco Maliepiero
PREMIERE: *March 8, 1928, Opéra de Monte Carlo.*

UN BALLO IN MASCHERA, by Giuseppe Verdi
PREMIERE: *March 10, 1928, Opéra de Monte Carlo.*

DON GIOVANNI, by Wolfgang Amadeus Mozart
PREMIERE: *March 17, 1928, Opéra de Monte Carlo.*

LA FILLE D'ABDOUBARAHAH, by Sanvel
PREMIERE: *March 20, 1928, Opéra de Monte Carlo, with Felia Doubrovska, Nicolas Efimov, Nicolas Kremnev, Michael Fedorov, Jean Yazvinsky, et al.*

ROMÉO ET JULIETTE, by Charles Gounod
PREMIERE: *January 24, 1929, Opéra de Monte Carlo.*

LA GIOCONDA, by Amilcare Ponchielli
PREMIERES: *January 26, 1929, Opéra de Monte Carlo, with Vera Petrova, Nicholas Efimov, Felia Doubrovska, Mezeslav Borovsky, Alexandra Danilova, Léon Woizikowsky, Lubov Tchernicheva, Constantin Tcherkas, et al.; February 18, 1937, Metropolitan Opera, New York, with Mona Montes, Leda Anchutina, Elise Reiman, Rabana Hasburgh, Anatole Vilzak, Gisella Caccialanza, Holly Howard, Kathryn Mullowny, et al.*

RIGOLETTO, by Giuseppe Verdi
PREMIERES: *February 28, 1929, Opéra de Monte Carlo; February 23, 1932, Opéra de Monte Carlo; December 28, 1935, Metropolitan Opera, New York.*

LA FEMME NUE, by Henri Février
PREMIERE: *March 23, 1929, Opéra de Monte Carlo, with Alexandra Danilova, Eugenia Lipkovska, Henriette Maikerska, et al.*

MARTHA, by Friedrich von Flotow
PREMIERE: *March 27, 1929, Opéra de Monte Carlo, with Vera Petrova, Eugenia Lipkovska, Léon Woizikowsky, et al.*

DIE VERSCHWORENEN, by Franz Schubert
PREMIERE: *April 1, 1929, Opéra de Monte Carlo, with Felia Doubrovska, Vera Petrova, Eugenia Lipkovska, et al.*

TANNHAÜSER, by Richard Wagner
PREMIERES: *January 21, 1932, Opéra de Monte Carlo, with Valentina Blinova, Léon Woizikowsky, et al.; December 26, 1935, Metropolitan Opera, New York, with Anatole Vilzak, Rabana Hasburgh, Annia Breyman, Kathryn Mullowny, Helen Stuart, Heidi Vosseler, Charles Laskey.*

LE PROPHÈTE, by Giacomo Meyerbeer
PREMIERE: *January 26, 1932, Opéra de Monte Carlo, with Eleanora Marra, Léon Woizikowsky, Valentina Blinova, Valentin Froman, et al.*

EINE NACHT IN VENEDIG, by Johann Strauss the Younger
PREMIERE: *February 2, 1932, Opéra de Monte Carlo, with Valentina Blinova, Léon Woizikowsky, et al.*

AIDA, by Giuseppe Verdi
PREMIERE: *March 19, 1932, Opéra de Monte Carlo; December 20, 1935, Metropolitan Opera, New York, with William Dollar, et al.; June 8, 1945, Ópera Nacional, Mexico City (choreo-*

graphed with William Dollar); October 28, 1948, New York City Opera, City Center, New York, with Maria Tallchief, Nicholas Magallanes, et al.

LA PERICHOLE, by Jacques Offenbach
PREMIERE: *March 31, 1932, Opéra de Monte Carlo.*

MIGNON, by Ambroise Thomas
PREMIERE: *January 4, 1936, Metropolitan Opera, New York, with William Dollar, et al.*

LA JUIVE, by Jacques Halévy
PREMIERE: *January 11, 1936, Metropolitan Opera, New York, with Gisella Caccialanza, William Dollar, Anatole Vilzak, Annabelle Lyon, Ruthanna Boris, Charles Laskey, Lew Christensen, Douglas Coudy, Kathryn Mullowny, Daphne Vane, Audrey Guerard, et al.*

THE BARTERED BRIDE, by Bedřich Smetana
PREMIERE: *May 15, 1936, Metropolitan Opera, New York, with Ruthanna Boris, William Dollar, Helen Leitch, Anatole Vilzak, Rabana Hasburgh, Gisella Caccialanza, Kyra Blank, Leda Anchutina, et al.*

LUCIA DI LAMMERMOOR, by Gaetano Donizetti
PREMIERE: *May 20, 1936, Metropolitan Opera, New York.*

ORPHEUS AND EURYDICE, by Christoph Willibald Gluck
PREMIERES: *May 22, 1936, Metropolitan Opera, New York, with Lew Christensen, Daphne Vane, William Dollar, et al. (entire production conceived in collaboration with Tchelitchev and staged by Balanchine); November 16, 1963, Hamburgische Staatsoper, Hamburg, with Christa Kempf, Heinz Clauss, Angèle Albrecht, et al. (entire production directed by Balanchine); November 22, 1975, Chicago Lyric Opera, danced by Chicago Lyric Opera Ballet.*

CAPONSACCHI, by Richard Hageman
PREMIERE: *February 4, 1937, Metropolitan Opera, New York, with Kyra Blank, Rabana Hasburgh, Joseph Levinoff, Elise Reiman, Charles Laskey, Heidi Vosseler, Leda Anchutina, William Dollar, Kathryn Mullowny, Daphne Vane, Lew Christensen, Douglas Coudy, et al.*

MAROUF, by Henri Rabaud
PREMIERES: *May 21, 1937, Metropolitan Opera, New York, with Ruthanna Boris, Rabana Hasburgh, Eugene Loring, et al.; August 7, 1942, Opera of the Teatro Colón, Buenos Aires, with Leticia de la Vega, Yurek Shabelevsky, et al.*

THE FAIR AT SOROCHINSK, by Modest Mussorgsky
PREMIERE: *November 3, 1942, New Opera Company, New York, with Gisella Caccialanza, William Dollar, et al.*

THE MARRIAGE OF FIGARO, by Wolfgang Amadeus Mozart
PREMIERE: *October 14, 1948, New York City Opera, City Center, New York.*

EUGEN ONEGIN, by Pyotr Ilyitch Tchaikovsky
PREMIERES: *November 7, 1948, New York City Opera, City Center, New York; February 27, 1962, Hamburgische Staatsoper, Hamburg (entire production directed by Balanchine).*

TROUBLED ISLAND, by William Grant Still
PREMIERE: *March 31, 1949, New York City Opera, City Center, New York, danced by the company of Jean-Léon Destiné.*

THE RAKE'S PROGRESS, by Igor Stravinsky
PREMIERE: *February 14, 1953, Metropolitan Opera, New York (entire production staged by Balanchine).*

LA FAVORITA, by Gaetano Donizetti
PREMIERE: *April 16, 1953, Teatro alla Scala, Milan, with Olga Amati, Giulio Perugini, Vera Colombo, Gilda Maiocchi, Mario Pistoni.*

ADRIANA LECOUVREUR, by Francesco Cilea
PREMIERE: *May 7, 1953, Teatro alla Scala, Milan, with Walter Marconi, Mario Pistoni, Tilde Baroni, Gilda Maiocchi, Carla Calzati, Nuccy Muti, Maria Bazzolo, et al.*

AMAHL AND THE NIGHT VISITORS, by Gian Carlo Menotti
PREMIERE: *May 9, 1953, Teatro della Pergola, Florence, with Raimonda Orselli, Alberto Moro.*

THE MAGIC FLUTE, by Wolfgang Amadeus Mozart—production made for television
PREMIERE: *January 15, 1956, NBC Opera Theatre (entire production staged by Balanchine).*

RUSLAN AND LUDMILLA, by Mikhail Glinka
PREMIERE: *March 30, 1969, Hamburgische Staatsoper, Hamburg (entire production staged by Balanchine).*

PRINCE IGOR, by Alexander Borodin
PREMIERE: *February 23, 1973, Deutsche Oper, Berlin, danced by Ballet der Deutschen Oper.*

THE RELUCTANT KING, by Emmanuel Chabrier
PREMIERE: *November 19, 1976, Juilliard American Opera Center, New York, danced by students of School of American Ballet.*

Musicals with Choreography by Balanchine

WAKE UP AND DREAM
PREMIERE: *March 29, 1929, London.* PRINCIPAL DANCER: *Tilly Losch.*

COCHRAN'S 1930 REVUE
PREMIERE: *June 1930, London.* PRINCIPAL DANCERS: *Serge Lifar, Alice Nikitina, Nicholas Efimov.*

SIR OSWALD STOLL'S VARIETY SHOWS
PREMIERE: *February 16, 1931, London.* PRINCIPAL DANCERS: *Doris Sonne, Hedley Briggs, Natasha Gregorova, Maria Gaya.*

COCHRAN'S 1931 REVUE
PREMIERE: *March 19, 1931, London.*

ORPHÉE AUX ENFERS
MUSIC: *Jacques Offenbach.* PREMIERE: *December 24, 1932, Théâtre Mogador, Paris.* CAST: *Felia Doubrovska, Anatole Vilzak, Irina Baronova, et al.*

ZIEGFELD FOLLIES, 1936
NEW YORK PREMIERE: *January 30, 1936.*

ON YOUR TOES
NEW YORK PREMIERE: *April 11, 1936.* PRINCIPAL DANCERS: *Tamara Geva, Ray Bolger.*

BABES IN ARMS
NEW YORK PREMIERE: *April 14, 1937.* PRINCIPAL DANCER: *Duke McHale.*

I MARRIED AN ANGEL
NEW YORK PREMIERE: *May 11, 1938.* PRINCIPAL DANCER: *Zorina.*

THE BOYS FROM SYRACUSE
NEW YORK PREMIERE: *November 23, 1938.* PRINCIPAL DANCERS: *George Church, Betty Bruce.*

KEEP OFF THE GRASS
NEW YORK PREMIERE: *May 23, 1940.* PRINCIPAL DANCERS: *Ray Bolger, José Limón, Daphne Vane, Betty Bruce.*

LOUISIANA PURCHASE
NEW YORK PREMIERE: *May 28, 1940.* PRINCIPAL DANCERS: *Charles Laskey, Zorina.*

CABIN IN THE SKY (*entire production directed by George Balanchine*)
NEW YORK PREMIERE: *October 25, 1940.* PRINCIPAL DANCERS: *Katherine Dunham and troupe.*

LADY COMES ACROSS
NEW YORK PREMIERE: *January 9, 1942.* PRINCIPAL DANCERS: *Eugenia Delarova, Lubova Rostova, Marc Platt.*

ROSALINDA (Die Fledermaus)
NEW YORK PREMIERE: *October 28, 1942.* PRINCIPAL DANCERS: *José Limón, Mary Ellen Moylan.*

THE MERRY WIDOW
NEW YORK PREMIERE: *August 4, 1943.* PRINCIPAL DANCERS: *Lubov Roudenko, Milada Mladova, Chris Volkoff, James Starbuck.*

WHAT'S UP?
NEW YORK PREMIERE: *November 11, 1943.* PRINCIPAL DANCERS: *Jimmy Savo, Phyllis Hill, Don Weissmuller.*

DREAM WITH MUSIC
NEW YORK PREMIERE: *May 18, 1944.* PRINCIPAL DANCER: *Zorina.*

SONG OF NORWAY
NEW YORK PREMIERE: *August 21, 1944.* DANCERS: *Alexandra Danilova, Frederic Franklin, and others from the Ballet Russe de Monte Carlo.*

MR. STRAUSS GOES TO BOSTON
NEW YORK PREMIERE: *September 6, 1945.* PRINCIPAL DANCERS: *Harold Lang, Babs Heath, Margit Dekova.*

THE CHOCOLATE SOLDIER
NEW YORK PREMIERE: *March 12, 1947.* PRINCIPAL DANCERS: *Mary Ellen Moylan, Francisco Moncion.*

WHERE'S CHARLEY?
NEW YORK PREMIERE: *October 11, 1948.* PRINCIPAL DANCER: *Ray Bolger.*

COURTIN' TIME
NEW YORK PREMIERE: *June 13, 1951.* PRINCIPAL DANCERS: *Gloria Patrice, Peter Conroy.*

Motion Pictures with Choreography by Balanchine

DARK RED ROSES *(1929)*
DANCERS: *Lydia Lopokova, George Balanchine, Anton Dolin.*

THE GOLDWYN FOLLIES *(United Artists, 1938)*
DANCERS: *Zorina and the American Ballet.*

ON YOUR TOES *(Warner Bros., 1939)*
PRINCIPAL DANCERS: *Zorina, Lew Christensen, André Eglevsky.*

I WAS AN ADVENTURESS *(20th Century-Fox, 1940)*
DANCERS: *Zorina, Lew Christensen.*

STAR-SPANGLED RHYTHM *(Paramount, 1942)*
DANCER: *Zorina.*

PHOTO CREDITS

Photographers or sources of photographs used in this book are listed below in alphabetical order.

Courtesy, Karin von Aroldingen, 60.

Courtesy, George Balanchine, 24, 27, 30, 33, 41, 50, 52, 63.

Courtesy, Anatole Chujoy, 155.

Coburn, courtesy, The Museum of Modern Art/Film Stills Archive, 7.

Courtesy, Dance Collection, New York Public Library, 72, 122, 131, 143, 176, 200, 204.

Courtesy, Anton Dolin, 118.

Courtesy, Felia Doubrovska, 107, 109.

Fred Fehl, 248, 253, 283.

Carolyn George, 254, 328, 350, 355, 363, 374, 378, 383, 397.

Collection GV, 193.

Courtesy, Hachette, 82, 138.

Boris Kochno, courtesy, Ballet Society, 74, 86, 92.

Boris Kochno, courtesy, Hachette, 94.

Tanaquil Le Clercq, 170.

George Platt Lynes, courtesy, Dance Collection, New York Public Library, 146, 202, 206, 214, 223, 225, 241 (left).

George Platt Lynes, courtesy, Lew Christensen, 172.

Maharadze, courtesy, Dance Collection, New York Public Library, 174.

Courtesy, The Museum of Modern Art/Film Stills Archive, 191.

C. Newell, courtesy, Lew Christensen, 161.

Courtesy, Eugenie Ouroussow, 229.

Walter E. Owen, 241 (right), 242.

Irving Penn. Photograph for Vogue, Copyright ©1948, by The Conde Nast Publications Inc., 238.

Sasha, courtesy, Dance Collection, New York Public Library, 96, 114.

Sasha, courtesy, BBC Hulton Picture Library, 89, 102 (lower).

Courtesy, Sovfoto, 287.

Bert Stern, 285.

Martha Swope, 2, 5, 9, 12, 17, 19, 21, 22, 103, 158, 210, 211, 245, 250, 264-272, 290, 293, 294, 299, 300, 302, 305, 312, 318, 319, 320, 322, 327, 335, 337, 342, 346, 348, 380, 385.

Richard Tucker, courtesy, Dance Collection, New York Public Library, 102 (upper).

United Press International Photo, 182.

Vaganova Choreographic Institute, 36, 56.

Roger Wood, 111, 113, 199, 231.

428

INDEX

Page numbers in *italics* refer to illustrations.

Abbott, George, 177
Abdy, Lady, 76, 87
Adagio Lamentoso, 377, *378*
Adams, Diana, viii, 7, *9*, *199*, 228, 259, 269, 282, *283*, 292
Adventure in Ballet, 218
Afternoon of a Faun, 240, 355
Age of Anxiety, 234
Agon, viii, *9*, 16, 209, 247, 255, *264-71*, 273-74, 275, 280, 281, 306, 326, 349, 358
Aida, 168
Allegro Brillante, 247
Alma Mater, 160, 161-62, *161*
Alonso, Alicia, 218
Amberg, George, 201
American Ballet Company, 164-75, 183, 332
   at the Metropolitan Opera, 165-75
   dissolution of, 175
   first season of, 160-62
   Latin American tour of, 197-98, 208
American Ballet Theatre, 335, 353, 354, 361-62, 376, 394
   See also Ballet Theatre
American Dancer, 132
American Guild of Musical Artists, 304, 376
American in Paris, 187-89, 190, 192
Anchutina, Leda, 161, *174*
Andersen, Ib, 371, 373
Andreyanov, Samuel Constantinovitch, *36*, 39, 42, 44, 284
Andriessen, Juriaan, 230
Apollo (Apollon Musagète), 7-8, *96*, 98-104, *102-103*, 106, 110, 112, 115, 132, 150, 173, 209, 216, 259, 334, 358
   Bruhn's experience with, 365-67
   revisions of, 358-61
Ardolino, Emile, 349
Arensky, Anton S., *60*, 67
Argyle, Pearl, 142
Aroldingen, Karin von, *103*, 296, *318*, 329, 330, 337, *337*, 338, *342*, *348*, 373, 384, 395
   Balanchine's relationship with, 341-43, 392
Ashley, Merrill, 349, 371, 372
Ashton, Frederick, 234, 235, 249, 317
Astaire, Fred, 246, 388
Atkinson, Brooks, 181
Aubade, 129
Auden, W. H., 4-5, 204, 330
Auric, Georges, 137

Babel, Isaac, 34, 56
Babes in Arms, 177, 184
Bachiana, 307
Bach, Johann Sebastian, 258, 306-07
Baiser de la Fée, Le, 173, 216
Baker, Josephine, 178
Balanchine, George:
   ancestors of, 26
   awards presented to, 345, 356
   "baby ballerinas" and, 81-83, 136-37
   birth and childhood of, 25-34
   catalogue of works, 390-91
   choreographic influences on, 57-61
   choreographic process of, 4, 8-18
   classicism of, 57, 98, 99, 100, 197, 233, 234, 251-53
   clothing of, 5, 13, 133, 287
   contemporary-music ballets by, 253-55
   corps de ballet used by, 251-52, 296
   curtain calls of, 23, 282, 385
   dancers' performance techniques and, 18-20, 282-84, 368-69
   dancers' relationships with, 330-36, 365-69, 375-77
   dancing abilities of, 90-91
   death of, 394
   education of, 31, 34-35, 37-46, 48-51, 75
   eye problems of, 369, 382, 386
   fatalism of, 47, 128-29, 314, 321-24
   first American ballet by, 156-60
   first choreography by, 53-54
   first meeting with author, vii
   first review of ballet by, 54-55
   funeral and memorials of, 394-95, 396
   heart attack and angina suffered by, 351-52, 356-57, 361, 369-70, 382-83
   home life of, 242-44, 324-25
   humor of, 62-64, 79-80, 168, 182-83
   influence on New York City Ballet, 19-20, 260-61
   knee injury of, 91-93, 127, 306
   lavish spectacles as interest of, 32-34, 347-49, 388-89
   letter-writing avoided by, x, 164
   living quarters of, 164, 185, 242-43, 324-25
   "Malaross" as nickname of, 192
   migration to U.S., 132, 151, 152
   military career considered by, 32
   mime abilities of, 42, 298-299
   movie-ballet innovations of, 187, 190
   musical-comedy innovations of, 180-81, 184
   musicality of, 11-13, 15, 16, 80, 100,

429